FO **T**

FOOD FOR THOUGHT

The Debate over Eating **MEAT**

Edited by **STEVE F. SAPONTZIS**

 **Prometheus Books**

59 John Glenn Drive
Amherst, New York 14228-2197

Published 2004 by Prometheus Books

Inquiries should be addressed to
Prometheus Books
59 John Glenn Drive
Amherst, New York 14228–2197
VOICE: 716–691–0133, ext. 207
FAX: 716–564–2711
WWW.PROMETHEUSBOOKS.COM

08 07 06 05 04   5 4 3 2 1

Library of Congress Cataloging-in-Publication Data

Food for thought: the debate over eating meat / edited by Steve F. Sapontzis.
  p. cm.
Includes bibliographical references.
ISBN 1–59102–118–9
  1. Vegetarianism. I. Sapontzis, S. F. (Steve F.)

TX392.F63 2004
613.'62—dc22

                                                                    2003023665

Printed in the United States of America on acid-free paper

CONTENTS

SECTION THREE: THE RECENT PHILOSOPHICAL DEBATE OVER THE MORAL STATUS OF ANIMALS AND ITS IMPLICATIONS FOR OUR DIET

SECTION FOUR: TRADITIONAL AND CONTEMPORARY RELIGIOUS TEACHINGS ABOUT OUR RELATION TO ANIMALS

SECTION FIVE: THE FEMINIST DEBATE OVER THE RELATION BETWEEN THE TREATMENT OF ANIMALS AND OF WOMEN

SECTION SIX: THE ENVIRONMENTAL DEBATE OVER RESPECTING PREDATORY NATURE AND PROTECTING ANIMALS

SECTION SEVEN: WHICH IS MORE IMPORTANT, RESPECTING CULTURAL DIVERSITY OR PROTECTING ANIMALS?

EDITOR'S
INTRODUCTION

While introducing Sally to Jack, Charlie added, "Sally's a vege-tarian." Jack stared for a moment, not knowing how to respond. Finally he said, "Glad to meet you, Sally. I'm Presbyterian, myself." That's an old joke, but it correctly identifies that being a vegetarian both means different things to different people and is a mystery to others. I've heard people say such things as: "I guess I'm a partial vegetarian; I don't eat nearly as much red meat as I used to"; "I'm a veggie, too; I eat only invertebrates"; "She says she's a vegetarian, but she sure loves her clam chowder"; "Real vegetarians don't eat eggs or cheese"; "Vegetarianism—isn't that one of those Eastern cults?" "I was a vegetarian for a while, but I didn't lose any weight, so I moved on to Pridikin"; "Those animal rights crazies want to change us all into vegetarians; it's downright un-American!" Thus, the word "vegetarian" is used to refer both to something that admits of degrees and to a pure something that one either is or isn't, to something enshrined in religious tradition and to something that is a passing dietary fad, to something that has been the subject of sophisticated intellectual debate and something that has been the butt of complacent political jibes. Such diversity should at least forewarn us that the topic of this anthology is not a simple one. It is not complex in the way that chemistry and calculus are, which require skillful mathematical reasoning and the mastery of scientific language and equipment. Rather, meat eating versus vegetarianism is a topic that is complex in the way history and the law are. It is a topic that has grown haphazardly over much time with in-put from many different sources reflecting many different human concerns, psychological and social, ethical and factual, religious and political, even nutritional and metaphysical. While understanding this topic doesn't require the brilliance of an Einstein, it is best approached with the patience of Job.

What I'd like to accomplish in this introduction is to give you, the reader, information that will help you understand what the following essays are debating, what motivates this debate, and what its touchstone issues are. The purpose of such understanding is not just or even primarily to equip you to write an erudite paper on this subject (though that may be the immediate goal of those of you reading this book for a class). The "big picture" goal of expanding your understanding of this topic is to help you think more effectively about it, so that you can come to feel that wherever you come down on this issue, your position is not arbitrary, uninformed, thoughtless, insensitive, or otherwise intellectually deficient. And make no mistake, unlike abortion, gun control, capital punishment, and so many other of our most hotly debated issues, meat eating versus vegetarianism is an issue on which you cannot avoid taking a position, and soon. If you are not munching while reading this, you'll be eating something soon, and when you do, you'll be taking a position on this issue. Such a simple thing—biting into a burger, cutting a steak, popping a McNugget into your mouth—but, like the tip of the iceberg, so much lies beneath the obvious. The goal of these essays—as of so much philosophy—is that we become aware of these extended implications and consequences of our actions so that, at the very least, we know that we are not going about our lives in ignorance of what we're doing and so that, more hopefully, knowing what we're doing, we can do our best.

TERMINOLOGY

"Vegetarianism" is best defined in terms of what a person does *not* eat: a vegetarian is someone who does not eat the flesh of animals. "Meat" is the English word commonly used to refer to the flesh of animals, though sometimes it is used more restrictively, in opposition to "fish" and "fowl." Even those two terms contain surprises: Catholic dietary regulations have allowed sea turtles and frogs to count as "fish." All the authors in this anthology have spontaneously adopted the more encompassing usage of "meat," so in what follows fish and fowl should be understood to be *categories* of meat.

There are also categories of vegetarians and at least two different, common ways of distinguishing these categories. The first of these focuses on why people do not eat meat. Some people are vegetarians by necessity: they would eat meat if they had the opportunity to do so, but circumstances, most often poverty, prevent them from eating meat. There is no common label for such people, probably because the causes of their vegetarianism have generally not been part of the "to eat or not to eat meat" debate—debates being about matters of choice. The one notable exception here is the feminist discussion of meat eating. When meat is scarce, it is most likely—if not always—men who eat it and women who are *denied* it. "Nonvolitional vegetarians" has been suggested to refer to those who are vegetarians but not by choice.

Among those who choose, "health vegetarians" refers to those who avoid eating meat because they think such a diet is better for their health. This may be a strictly personal judgment; the individual finds that he feels better when he doesn't eat meat. Or it may be somewhat broader; the person may believe that it's healthier for all people like her—for example, people over sixty or people with a history of heart disease—to avoid eating meat. Or this may be a universal judgment; the person may believe that a diet without meat is the healthiest for all people.

The contrasting term is "ethical vegetarians," which refers to people who avoid eating meat because they believe eating meat is ethically objectionable. Although this cannot be a strictly personal judgment—since ethical issues by definition are broader than personal preferences—ethical vegetarians can believe that all people should avoid eating meat—called "universal ethical vegetarianism"—or that vegetarianism is ethically required only of members of their group. This more limited position occurs when the ethical reasons for avoiding meat include membership in a particular caste or adherence to a particular religion. The limited position also occurs when "necessity" figures into the ethical reasoning, as when people believe that eating meat is ethically acceptable only if it's necessary for survival. This may be not only a temporary condition—like the case of people trapped by a blizzard—but also a permanent one—like the case of peoples who live in climates where they cannot gather or grow sufficient vegetable food to survive. Thus, some ethical vegetarians—sometimes called "contextual vegetarians"—contend that although it is ethically incumbent on those of us living where we can readily live well without eating meat, vegetarianism is not ethically required of those who do not find themselves in such fortunate circumstances.

Though these are contrasting reasons for not eating meat, it's clear that someone can be both a health and an ethical vegetarian. Nor are the reasons for both positions entirely independent. For example, Kathryn P. George argues against universal ethical vegetarianism because of the health risks a vegetarian diet poses for women. Nonetheless, much of the debate over meat eating during the past several decades has proceeded as if a vegetarian diet can be a healthy one. The following essays by Collura, Barnard/Kieswer, and Dwyer/Loew here focus on relevant physiological and nutritional issues concerning meat eating, but the rest of the debate here focuses on ethical vegetarianism.

A second important distinction among those who avoid eating meat concerns whether they consume animal products, particularly eggs and dairy products. Some people who avoid eating meat also avoid eating animal products; such people are called "vegans." Vegetarians who eat both eggs and dairy products are "lacto-ovo vegetarians." A person can also be a "lacto vegetarian" if she eats dairy products but not eggs, or an "ovo vegetarian" if she practices the reverse. Honey is an animal product that could be an issue here, but although vegans don't eat honey, there is no common label for vegetarians who do eat honey. They could be called "apiary vegetarians," since beekeepers are apiarists.

A more pressing need for a label derives from recent discussions about the ability to feel pleasure and pain. Some people who have ethical objections to eating most meat products nonetheless believe eating animals that are incapable of feeling pleasure or pain, such as clams and other mollusks, is ethically acceptable. This is because they believe ethical issues always ultimately concern trying to maximize pleasure or minimize pain; consequently, consuming something that cannot feel pleasure or pain, be it mineral, vegetable, *or animal*, cannot in and of itself be an ethical issue. (I put that qualifier in, because there may be *other* ethical issues involved, as when you pick apples from your neighbor's tree without getting permission.) These vegetarians may even avoid eating eggs and dairy products because of the suffering commonly endured by animals in bringing those products to market. Thus, there can be ethical vegetarians, even vegans who eat clam chowder. (The vegans will use rice milk or soy milk instead of cream.) Though this sort of position is well-represented in the ethical debate over meat eating—which has recently focused on the suffering of animals on "factory farms"—a common label has not developed for these people. They generally refer to themselves just as vegetarians or vegans. Since the term "sentient" has come to be used in ethics to refer to beings capable of feeling pleasure or pain, "sentience vegetarians" might be an appropriate label for this group.

A similar complexity and lack of terminology exists among meat eaters. Some social critics, such as Scruton, and environmentalists, such as Ferré, who do not ethically object to eating meat, do object to factory farming. They are not vegetarians, since they eat meat that is raised on traditional, family farms or comes from hunting, and may even be moderate to severe critics of vegetarianism. Still, their ethical concerns with the suffering of animals, the decline of our culture, or the destruction of the environment renders their positions significantly different from those who have no ethical problem with meat eating. We might label these people "traditionalist meat eaters."

Thus, both objections to and defenses of meat eating differ both in kind and degree to the point where simply talking about meat eaters versus vegetarians is grossly oversimplifying the issues involved in and the positions taken in the contemporary debate over meat eating. It is unfortunate that our vocabulary has not yet sufficiently developed to provide common labels for the nuances of this debate, but it is important in understanding the essays in this anthology—and to developing your own thinking in this area—to keep these distinctions in mind.

ISSUES

Within the ethical debate over meat eating several touchstone, often discussed issues have emerged. I want to outline these here, not in any sort of attempt to resolve them but as a guide to understanding why the following essays focus on certain topics.

The first thing to note is a curiosity: although when we think about meat eating versus vegetarianism, what we focus on is what we put in our mouths, that's not what the ethical debate is about. Some religious teachings focus on what we eat: certain foods, like pork and shellfish, are condemned as "unclean," and adherents of the religion should avoid eating them. The focus is not on what happens to animals—or to people—in producing these foods but on what religious "law" teaches it is right and proper for us to eat. Even when, as with some Jewish rules about kosher meat, the religious teachings concern where the meat comes from and how it is prepared, these teachings do not focus on what animals and people have to endure in the production and preparation of meat but on what we should not put in our mouths, for example, blood or crawly creatures. Similarly, with health vegetarianism, the focus is on minimizing the amount of unhealthy substances we put in our bodies. It is claimed that a diet free of meat contains fewer of these substances and is, therefore, better for our health. It is what meat contains, not what animals or people go through to produce the meat, that is the issue. When the ethics of eating meat is debated, however, the focus is on what animals and people have to go through to produce meat, what would happen to them if meat eating were abandoned, how meat eating affects them indirectly through the environmental consequences of meat production and reinforcing social stereotypes, and so forth. The act of consuming meat is not the ethical issue.

The ethical debate over meat eating that has been so lively and extensive for the past quarter century, both among philosophers and the general public, was triggered by revelations of the suffering animals endure in the production of meat, particularly when modern, "intensive husbandry" techniques are employed. These techniques involve keeping animals closely confined so that their environment and diet may be carefully regulated to produce the maximum quality and quantity of meat for the minimum investment in food, shelter, land, and labor. These factory farms seem to produce significant psychological suffering for animals, since the close confinement frustrates many of their natural instincts and deprives them of such elementary pleasures as sitting in the sun and stretching their legs. Coping with these frustrations even leads to practices that seem to cause the animals physical pain: for example, slicing the beaks off chickens, so they can't peck each other, and cutting off the tails of pigs, so they won't chew on each other. (See the essays by Rachels, Singer, and Gruzalski for brief descriptions of factory farming and the books by Singer [1990], Harrison, Mason and Singer, and Eisnitz, listed in Further Reading, for extensive discussion of these issues.)

Pain, be it psychological or physical, is a red flag for ethical concern. We condemn cruelty, particularly sadism, where someone enjoys inflicting pain on others, and we are troubled by suffering that seems unnecessary to accomplish some greater good. The latter is the basis for the famous "problem of evil" in theology: If God is so good and powerful, why is there so much suffering in the world? Minimizing pain and maximizing pleasure have even been offered by philosophers, particularly those called "utilitarians," as the fundamental concern of ethical theory and practice. So, revelations of the pain inflicted on animals to produce meat have not only an immediate emotional pull on most of us, they also tie into basic, uncontroversial ethical principles and practices.

Nonetheless, factory farming has not been resoundingly condemned and abandoned as vegetarianism becomes the dominant diet of Western culture. This is doubtless due in large part to our unwillingness to admit that something we have done day-in and day-out throughout our lives is ethically wrong and that we should forego a pleasure we partake in several times a day. But besides these psychological obstacles to ethical reform, though probably inspired by them, the revelations of animal suffering have been countered by a variety of responses questioning their ethical significance:

> Do animals really suffer in the production of meat? Are we just anthropomorphizing farm animals, that is, imagining that they feel as we would in similar circumstances? Is the suffering endured by animals perhaps really much less than it at first sight appears to be, since they are much less sensitive to issues of freedom than we are, don't have anything else to compare their lives to, lack our emotional attachments to parents, children, and other family members, or are just tougher than we are, so aren't bothered by living in conditions that would hurt or depress us?
>
> What about the pleasure produced by eating meat, might not that outweigh the pain involved? Wouldn't there be many fewer animals

alive, and people, too, if we didn't eat meat? Doesn't the pleasure enjoyed by these greater populations justify the pain needed to produce them? Wouldn't the ethical directive to maximize pleasure over pain point us toward reforming some of our animal husbandry practices rather than abandoning meat eating altogether?

Isn't factory farming what's really ethically objectionable, not only because it causes animals to suffer, but also because it adversely impacts the environment and our culture in many ways and ties into standard vices such as greed, insensitivity, indifference, self-indulgence, and willful ignorance about the wider consequences of our actions? Isn't the moral of these revelations about factory farming that we should return to more traditional forms of raising and hunting meat, not that we should abandon meat eating altogether?

These are all real questions, not rhetorical ones. They are not immediately, obviously adequate defenses of meat eating but issues debated in the following essays and for you to think about. Indeed, this debate over the pains and pleasures involved in producing and consuming meat has become so complex and the calculations so difficult, that many people, including philosophers and theologians, have come to feel that the ethical rightness or wrongness of eating meat must be based on other, clearer factors. Despite what utilitarians have recommended, ethical traditions have included and continue to include goods, guidelines, and goals whose purpose is not obviously to maximize pleasure over pain. These other ethical values can even be used to evaluate pleasures and pains, as when we negatively value some pleasures as depraved and positively value certain pains as character builders. Similarly, if we were considering a practice in which billions of people were imprisoned and slaughtered, we wouldn't readily accept assurances that in spite of appearances to the contrary, this practice actually leads to maximizing pleasure as an adequate ethical defense of that practice. Many people would even condemn offering such assurances as grossly insensitive to ethical values. There are values involved here, they would insist, that are so important that even if such a practiced maximized pleasure, it would still have to be ethically condemned because it violated those values.

This reaction opens the door to a variety of questions about how the welfare of animals and the taking of animal lives fit into our ethical principles and concerns:

Do animals have rights, perhaps even a natural right to life? Or can only people have rights, perhaps because rights are the products of social and legal agreements in which only those who agree to respect the rights of others are entitled to have their rights respected by those others? Do animals, then, have ethical significance only through their relation to people, for example, as being other people's property, or as a resource for a community of people to enjoy, or as tools for developing and reinforcing such human virtues as responsibility and compassion?

If human rights are not merely social conventions, how do we justify extending them to all people but to no animals? Since some animals are as intelligent or sociable or virtuous as some people, aren't they as entitled to rights to life, liberty, and the pursuit of happiness as those people? If we don't begin with a prejudice in favor of our own kind, how can we justify extending such basic rights to all but only humans? What makes a human life valuable *in itself*, so that it is wrong to painlessly kill a person, and why are animal lives not valuable *in themselves*, so that it is not wrong to painlessly kill them?

What about religious traditions? Do they teach that we humans have a God-given right to sacrifice animals for our benefit or that we have a special responsibility to care for God's creation? In order to reach "the better world" portrayed in religious teachings, do we need to change our traditional attitudes toward and use of animals?

A major and controversial ethical outlook to emerge during the past quarter century is "feminist ethics." Are the subjugation of women and the exploitation of animals intrinsically related? Does eliminating the former, by rejecting patriarchal social orders and hierarchical worldviews, entail eliminating the latter also? Or is ethical vegetarianism an idea that is insensitive to the special needs and roles of women? How would replacing rule-based ethics with a feminist "ethic of caring" impact what we should eat?

In addition to the active debate over "animal rights," the past quarter century has witnessed an equally active debate about "environmental ethics." What are the implications of such ideas as "biotic communities," "holistic relations," and "environmentally based values" for our conception of our place in the world and of how we should treat other animals? If our sacrificing of animals for our benefit has traditionally been justified by believing that we are "better" than they are, a "superior" kind of being, does accepting biological evolution require rethinking how we should treat *other* animals? On the other hand, if the natural order is based on one life form feeding off another, does not respecting nature and affirming life point us in the direction of accepting our historic place as meat eaters in the food chain?

Again, these are all open questions, questions that are debated in the following essays, questions that you need to think about yourselves as you read these essays and come to a decision about what you'll be eating after you read them. However, just listing these questions should indicate that the ethical debate over meat eating is in no way an isolated matter. Working your way through this issue at least opens the door to, if not requires, thinking critically about religious teachings you may have received, your beliefs about what makes life valuable, whether contemporary culture is progressive or destructive, feminism and environmentalism, and philosophical theories about the nature, origins, and fundamental principles of ethics in general. Although we can, and did, define vegetarianism simply in terms of avoiding eating meat, reaching a *decision* about whether or not to eat meat, based on our ethical beliefs and feelings, is not a simple matter but one of those defining questions in our lives. How we come down on this issue expresses where we stand on the position of human beings in the world, our relation as a species to other species and to nature in general, and our cultural ideals for making the world a better place.

The Essays

I do not want to manipulate your reading of the following essays, nor provide a *Cliff's Notes* sort of alternative to reading them. However, I do want to conclude this introduction by giving you an idea of what to expect from them.

The first two essays are more survey than advocacy. Daniel Dombrowski provides a compact history of how the ethical debate over vegetarianism has developed over some three millennia of Western culture. What he advocates is not what we should eat but that we should be aware of this long history in making our decision. Randall Collura surveys our knowledge of pre-history to answer the question of whether we are "physiologically determined" to a specific diet. He concludes that our ancestors have bequeathed us considerable dietary latitude. The next two essays discuss health and nutrition. Neal Barnard and Kristine Kieswer extol the health benefits of vegetarianism and answer common health questions about a meatless diet. Johanna T. Dwyer and Franklin M. Loew discuss the health risks for "vulnerable groups," such as women and children, of diets devoid of animal products and how those risks may be overcome.

In the section on the recent philosophical debate, all the authors are advocates. As noted above, one of the major divisions among moral philosophers is between those who emphasize basing our ethical decisions on maximizing pleasure or minimizing pain and those who believe that questions of right are fundamental, be they natural rights or rights deriving from something like a social contract. Both these positions are represented on both sides of the meat eating versus vegetarianism debate, and all four of the possible permutations are ably argued in this section.

James Rachels develops a "we should not inflict pain unnecessarily" argument for vegetarianism, discussing both how it is accepted by a wide variety of people and how contemporary studies of animal psychology and cognition impact the ethical questions about eating meat. Roger Scruton counters by emphasizing the mental, emotional, and spiritual differences between humans and animals, arguing that although we have moral obligations to care for animals, eating meat in a rich context of social relations and respectful attitudes is morally justified. Evelyn Pluhar defends vegetarianism on the grounds that logical consistency requires us to extend to animals the right to life we recognize for all humans. Peter Singer develops the classical utilitarian argument for vegetarianism: producing meat, particularly on factory farms, creates a tremendous excess of pain over pleasure, just the opposite of the moral good. R. G. Frey, also a utilitarian, counters that given the great demand for meat, those moved by ethics to become vegetarians do not actually improve the lot of animals. Bart Gruzalski echoes Singer's position and provides answers to objections to it, including the one raised by Frey. Stephen R. L. Clark locates the debate over vegetarianism within the context of the virtues prized as ideals for us to work toward in fully developing our humanity. Virtue, rather than general welfare or rights, was the basis for classical moral philosophy, as developed by such thinkers as Plato and Aristotle, and has lately again become an alternative approach to ethics that many philosophers find attractive. Finally, Carl Cohen feels that the right to life, like all other moral rights, can belong only to human beings; it is a logical blunder, he insists, to talk of moral rights belonging to animals, since they cannot understand and act on moral principles.

The section on religious teachings concerning meat eating contains both survey and advocacy. Mainstream Judaism, Christianity, and Islam have not condemned meat eating, though in all three cases there have been enduring minority vegetarian traditions. Roberta Kalechofsky discusses both the justification of meat eating and the bases for vegetarianism in Judaism. Richard Foltz does the same for Islam. Both of them emphasize that despite the mainstream teachings of these religions, there are significant grounds for vegetarianism to be found in the sacred writings of both religions. Tom Regan argues that the Garden of Eden story establishes vegetarianism as the ideal diet for Christians. Andrew Linzey argues that although the Bible condones meat eating, the lives of animals belong to God, not humans, and this places moral restrictions on meat eating. John Berkman describes how Catholic tradition relates abstaining from eating meat to the spiritual practice of fasting and the vice of gluttony. James Gaffney discusses diverse beliefs from early India through later Hinduism, Buddhism, Jainism, and Chinese religion to "the many-sided vegetarianism" of Gandhi. Finally, Rod Preece critically discusses Native American practices and religious teachings concerning hunting, meat eating, and the bond between humans and animals.

In the section on the relation between meat eating and feminism, advocacy resumes center stage. Carol J. Adams describes the interlacing of meat eating with male dominance and racism, providing motivation for opponents of patriarchy and hierarchical social orders to adopt a vegetarian diet. In response, Kathryn Paxton George contends that arguments for universal vegetarianism are insensitive to the differences in male and female nutritional needs, and therefore represent a continuing male bias in moral philosophy. Deane Curtin's response to such bias is to reject the pursuit of universal rules and to advocate "contextual moral vegetarianism," wherein diet is a situated response to contemporary realities. Finally, Lori Gruen contends that because animals are "beings with whom we can empathize, they can no longer be seen merely as food."

The essays in the next section of this book are by environmentalists, and both develop opposing positions and attempt to bridge the gap between them. Though he definitely condemns factory farming, Ned Hettinger is worried that much "animal liberation" philosophy is "life-denying" and involves a rejection of the natural order, which is based upon predation. Jennifer Everett argues that respecting nature does not require indifference to suffering; our compassionate feelings are as natural as our predatory inclinations. Frederick Ferré develops another middle environmental position emphasizing that even if our moral obligations to animals do not require vegetarianism, they do require that we raise and slaughter animals in ways that are respectful of their interests. Marti Kheel combines the holistic community approach of environmentalism with the caring ethic of feminism to offer an ecofeminist "invitation" to vegetarianism.

The last two essays here concern the question of ethical relativism: is the case for ethical vegetarianism just an expression of the preferences of some members of affluent societies, preferences that not only impose no obligation on peoples of other cultures but that are also insensitive to cultural and situational differences? Val Plumwood vigorously criticizes universal ethical vegetarianism, developing her own context-sensitive, semi-vegetarian position, which she calls "Ecological Animalism." Gary L. Comstock carefully analyzes real and imagined cases of subsistence hunting and concludes that interfering with cultural traditions in order to protect animals can frequently be justified. This is similar to our belief that we should oppose slavery and anti-Semitism, even where they are well-established traditions in other cultures.

So, there you have it, a rich banquet of food for thought. Dare I say it? *Bon appétit!*

Section One

A CONTROVERSY WITH A LONG PAST

1 | A VERY BRIEF HISTORY OF PHILOSOPHICAL VEGETARIANISM AND ITS INFLUENCE

Daniel Dombrowski

THE ANCIENT, MEDIEVAL, AND MODERN PERIODS

The idea that it is morally wrong to eat animals held sway for about one thousand years among some of the most prominent ancient Greek and Roman philosophers, including Pythagoras, Empedocles, Theophrastus, Ovid, Plutarch, Plotinus (who both refused to eat meat and shunned medical help that relied on the suffering of animals), Porphyry (who wrote a book-length defense of philosophical vegetarianism), and, perhaps, Plato. It is one of the best-kept secrets in the history of ideas that Plato's Republic was to have been a vegetarian city (see, e.g., *Republic* 372). The vegetarians from this period (600 BCE until 300 CE) had several reasons for their eating practices, including, on the one hand, a mythic belief in transmigration of souls, such that animals were past or future human beings, hence to eat them was something like murder, and, on the other hand, the more plausible and modern-sounding view that animals can suffer, hence to inflict suffering and death on them unnecessarily or gratuitously is an example of cruelty (the argument from sentiency).

Of course these ancient philosophical vegetarians did not convince everyone of the soundness of their belief in the moral status of animals, and, as a result, they received criticism from certain philosophers, such as

Aristotle and the Stoics. These thinkers thought that human rationality placed members of our species morally above nonhuman animals. Although Aristotle and the Stoics did not deny that human beings were animals, they, along with many other ancient philosophers, were anthropocentrists: they believed that human beings were central and that any value animals had was the instrumental value they provided for the flourishing of human beings.[1]

The ambivalence toward animals in the ancient period is found in the medieval period as well, although it must be admitted that anthropocentrists clearly had the upper hand in this latter period. Medieval thinkers' attitudes toward animals were largely informed by the Jewish and Christian scriptures (and, in Islamic thinkers, by the Koran). On the one hand, the biblical view is that human beings, but not animals, are created in the image of God (e.g., Genesis 1:24–28), hence they deserve respect that animals do not deserve. This tendency has heavily influenced the way most Jews, Christians, and Muslims have viewed animals, leading to the dominant view in these religions that lasts until the present that eating animals is morally permissible. The two most influential thinkers of the medieval period, St. Augustine in the fifth century and St. Thomas Aquinas in the thirteenth century, exemplify this view.

There is a minority view, however, that suggests that the vegetarianism in the Garden of Eden story in Genesis indicates what *should be* the case regarding human relations with animals. In effect, meat eating is a divine concession to human sinfulness after the fall. Some scholars see vegetarian tendencies in the Jewish scriptures (e.g., the prophet Isaiah condemned animal sacrifices), in Jesus' belief that God cares even for the fall of a sparrow (Matthew 10:28), in a prayer by St. Basil, and in St. Francis of Assisi's famous sense of kinship with animals: we are all creatures of an omnibenevolent God, he thought. (Although some—e.g., Peter Singer—point out that Francis's universal love fails to distinguish between the moral status of a rock and that of a bird, thereby diminishing the latter.) On this minority view, anthropocentrism is not as appropriate for religious believers as theocentrism (the belief that God is the center of the universe).[2]

In short, premodern thinkers offer many insights regarding the moral status of animals and regarding the appropriateness of a vegetarian diet. But it must be admitted that at the start of the modern world in the West anthropocentrism was firmly in place due to the views both of prominent ancient Greek thinkers that human rationality gave human beings a moral status that allowed them to use animals for human purposes and of influential medieval thinkers that human beings' superiority to animals, due to humans being made in the image of God, entailed not a caring stewardship of animals but sheer domination over them.

Before moving to the modern world, a few words about vegetarianism and Eastern religions are in order. Many people assume that there is a far more exalted view of animals found in Asian religions than in Judaism, Christianity, and Islam. But this is a difficult case to make. It must be granted that Hinduism (more than Judaism, Christianity, or Islam) encourages us to see human affinity to animals, but in Hinduism vegetarianism is: (a) a duty only for members of the upper caste and (b) not due primarily to a concern for animals themselves, but to a concern for the spiritual improvement or liberation (*moksa*) of these upper-caste human beings. The famous "pro-life" Jain sect within Hinduism is not an exception in this regard. Further, Hindu concern for animals is often connected to a belief in transmigration, as it was for Pythagoras in the ancient Greek period in the West.

Likewise, in Buddhism monks are often expected to be vegetarian (as are many Catholic monks) for the purpose of spiritual purification, but this monastic asceticism has had very little impact on the dietary practices of the general population, as anyone who has traveled to traditionally Buddhist countries knows. Similar ambivalence toward animals can be found in Confucianism and other Asian religions. Nonetheless, just as religious believers in the West are often encouraged to exert care for God's creation, so also adherents to Hinduism, and to religions like Buddhism that have derived from Hinduism, are often encouraged to practice *ahimsa* (nonviolence) with respect to animals.[3]

It should not be assumed that with the rise of the modern world in the West that the moral status of animals improved and that vegetarianism was more widely practiced. In some ways the plight of animals got worse. In the ancient and medieval worlds, at least, each animal was viewed as possessing a soul (*psyche* in Greek, *anima* in Latin), albeit a nonrational soul. Animals were clearly seen as besouled, sentient beings; that is, they could feel pleasure and especially pain. But the rise of modern science called this assumption into question. Renaissance humanism was, in fact, a type of *human*ism that revived the ancient Greek dictum of the sophists that "Man is the measure of all things" and that prepared the way for the first truly great modern philosopher and one of the first great figures in the rise of modern science in the seventeenth century: René Descartes.

Descartes is famous (or infamous) for a defense of dualism, wherein human beings are made up of two sorts of stuff: immaterial souls or minds, on the one hand, and material bodies, on the other. Animals are denied souls or minds, on his view, and as a result they are seen by him as strictly material bodies that operate with machinelike regularity (animal mechanism). This view was conducive to literal vivisection, the practice of cutting open animals for experimental purposes while they were still alive and without anesthesia. On the Cartesian view, the resulting screams of animals would be compared to the sounds of metal parts that are scraped against each other without lubricant between them. Many philosophical vegetarians consider Descartes's view of animals as the absolute nadir in that animals are not only denied rationality (as in Aristotle and the Stoics) and theological status by not being made in the image of God (as in most medieval thinkers), they are even denied sentiency when they are seen as mechanisms or as increments of capital in the burgeoning world of modern science and market capitalism.[4]

Although most modern philosophers were not as extreme in their view of animals as was Descartes, his anthropocentrism is typical. For example, Immanuel Kant's view of animals in the eighteenth century is that we have moral duties *regarding* animals, but not *to* them. This is a view that relies on the similar stances of the ancient Greek Stoic philosophers and of St. Thomas Aquinas. For example, we ought not to abuse our neighbor's dog because to do so would be to show disrespect to the neighbor. Or again, we ought not to be cruel to animals because to do so would be to make us more likely to be cruel to fellow human beings. In other words, we may have *indirect* duties regarding animals, but no *direct* duties to them. However, the fact that we *can* be cruel to animals (contra Descartes), but not to trees or stones, seems to involve a distinction that enhances the moral status of animals beyond the thinglike status given to them by Kant.[5]

Three tendencies in modern philosophy (from the seventeenth until the nineteenth centuries), however, are conducive to moral concern for animals and thus to vegetarianism. One is a certain skepticism regarding extravagant claims made on behalf of human rationality. If it is the possession of rationality that gives human beings the moral prerogative to use animals for human purposes, then skepticism regarding the extent of human rationality, which results in much more continuity between human beings and animals, brings that prerogative into question. The eighteenth-century Scottish philosopher David Hume was such a skeptic. He also argued that human beings are moral agents not so much by virtue of their rationality as by virtue of their passions (e.g., sympathy, grief, etc.), which they share with nonhuman animals.[6]

A second, and more influential, development in modern philosophy that was conducive to concern about animals was the emancipatory spirit of the enlightenment. This spirit had implications not only for the liberation of women, blacks, and other human beings, but also for the liberation of animals. The utilitarian philosophers Jeremy Bentham and John Stuart Mill in the nineteenth century harnessed this emancipatory spirit in terms of a utilitarian calculus of interests, wherein the goal of ethics was to produce the greatest good for the greatest number of sentient beings, including animals. As Bentham famously put the point, "the question is not, Can they *reason*? Nor, Can they *talk*? But, Can they *suffer*?" Indeed animals *can* suffer, according to the utilitarians. So, since our moral judgments should focus on the goal of maximizing pleasure and minimizing pain for the greatest number in society, we must take an inventory of all those who are capable of pleasure and pain. And since animals have that capacity, their well-being must be included in our moral deliberations. Presumably plants and extremely simple (e.g., single-celled) animals would not be included because they do not possess central nervous systems, which make the experience of pain or suffering possible.[7]

And third, in the mid-nineteenth century, Charles Darwin made it clear not only that human beings are animals (which biologists from the time of Aristotle had known), but also that human beings are descended from animals. The traditional view that all and only human beings have inherent worth, with animals merely a means to a human end, began to break up before Darwin, but he completed the job by decisively showing that human beings are not set apart from other animals, but are part of the same natural order and indeed are kin to animals. Further, Darwin made it clear that one is not committing the pathetic fallacy (the Greek *pathos* refers to a misfortune) by attributing feelings like anxiety, grief, dejection, despair, fear, and suffering to animals; Darwin detected each of these in animals.[8]

HISTORICAL THINKING

Historians of philosophy are inevitably asked the question, Why study thinkers who lived hundreds or even thousands of years ago, very often in far-off places? An adequate response to this question would have to include a heavy dose of skepticism regarding the supposed originality of contemporary philosophers. That is, it should be emphasized that contemporary debate regarding philosophical vegetarianism involves, whether explicitly or implicitly, *historical* thinking. Our attitudes toward the possible rights of animals have not been formed from scratch, but have been profoundly shaped by the historical figures briefly mentioned above.

Consider, for example, the two most important figures in the contemporary rebirth of philosophical vegetarianism: Peter Singer and Tom Regan. (The thousand-year history of philosophical vegetarianism in the ancient world is evidence that Singer's and Regan's efforts indeed constitute a rebirth of philosophical vegetarianism, rather than its creation out of absolutely nothing.) Put simply, Singer is a utilitarian in the tradition of Bentham and Mill. Singer's accomplishment within this tradition is to take Bentham's and Mill's considered attitude toward the suffering of animals, a consideration necessitated by the utilitarian calculus of pleasure and pain, and to apply it to largely unconsidered daily practices like eating meat and wearing leather, and to largely unconsidered laboratory practices that affect daily living, as in the testing of cosmetics and pharmaceuticals.[9]

Further, Regan, despite the fact that he is a staunch defender of animal rights and of philosophical vegetarianism, is at base a Kantian. Kant himself is famous for the distinction between things, which can be used as mere means for the purposes or ends of others, and persons, who are dignified subjects worthy of moral respect. In a word, persons are ends in themselves rather than mere means to some other ends. Regan buys into this Kantian distinction, but, unlike Kant, he places animals into the ends-in-themselves category. This is because, on Regan's view, animals are subjects of their own lives with inherent value, not merely instrumental value for the sake of human beings.[10]

The internecine debate between Singer and Regan is thus part of the larger historical debate between utilitarians and Kantians, respectively. Under certain circumstances, Singer thinks, animals may be used for human purposes if they are killed as painlessly as possible and if they are replaced with new animals who take their places. If the greatest good for the greatest number is produced by the use of animals, then such use is morally permitted on Singer's utilitarian version of animal "rights" (the scare quotes are crucial here). Regan, by way of contrast, defends a much stronger (Kantian) version of animal rights. On Regan's view, and on Evelyn Pluhar's similar view, our calculations regarding the ways we treat animals ought to be constrained by duties we have toward them in light of these strong (inalienable?) rights. Hence, Regan's view is not utilitarian, but deontological (from the Greek word for duty, *deontos*).[11]

The skepticism noted above on the part of Hume and others (e.g., Michel de Montaigne—whose favorite author was the ancient Greek vegetarian, Plutarch—and Voltaire) regarding the claim of human superiority to animals, due to human rationality, also has echoes in contemporary philosophy.[12] For example, although Steve Sapontzis does not very often explicitly refer to Hume's skepticism, Sapontzis nonetheless shows that such skepticism has more serious implications than Hume realized for our eating habits and for other ways in which we interact with animals. Hume's skepticism regarding exaggerated claims made in favor of human rationality, claims that have implications for how we should view animals, were held in check, it seems, by his conventionalism and by his own exaggerated confidence in human (largely meat eating) culture. But Sapontzis keeps alive the Humean belief that we tend to both overestimate our own rationality and underestimate the practical reason of animals.[13]

James Rachels is a contemporary defender of animal rights who has tried to explicate the historical significance of Darwin for moral philosophy. Many philosophers, he thinks, have kept alive a pre-Darwin version of anthropocentrism, as if Darwin had never lived. The most significant implication of Darwin's thought for moral philosophy, Rachels thinks, an implication that Darwin himself was aware of only dimly, is that species membership is not a *morally* relevant category. Rational beings—of whatever species, whether human or nonhuman—should be considered as moral equals. Likewise, nonrational yet sentient beings—of whatever species, whether nonhuman or human—should also be considered as moral equals. That is, "speciesism" is analogous to racism and sexism in that all three depend on the use of irrelevant or arbitrary characteristics of a being when making moral decisions: whether race or sex or species membership.[14]

I have alleged that debates regarding the moral status of animals involve, whether explicitly or implicitly, *historical thinking* in that philosophical originality tends to consist in novel ways of appropriating or combining or criticizing attitudes and arguments inherited from the past. Thus far I have illustrated this thesis through examples of contemporary historical thinking in defense of animals that is reliant on the relatively recent past, from the enlightenment to the present: Singer's utilitarianism, Regan's Kantianism, Sapontzis's skepticism, and Rachels's Darwinism.

Several examples from the anti–animal rights camp could also be cited to illustrate the thesis regarding the unavoidability of historical thinking. Robert Nozick, for example, defends Kantianism for people and utilitarianism for animals. However, what he means by "utilitarianism for animals" is closer to R. G. Frey's view of utilitarianism than it is to Singer's view in that Nozick and Frey think that by minimizing pain in the slaughterhouse and laboratory, contemporary meat eating and scientific experiment practices can continue largely unabated.[15] And Peter Carruthers quite incredibly keeps alive Descartes's view that animals are either incapable of pain or at least are incapable of pain consciously perceived; as a result, on Carruthers's view, animals are not appropriate objects of moral concern.[16] Further, many contemporary religious believers in the Abrahamic religions (Judaism, Christianity, and Islam) echo the view of St. Thomas Aquinas and others that, because only human beings are made in the image of God, and hence are participants in a divine community of love, animals are gifts to *us* from God for *our* use.[17]

It should be noted that not all of the parties in the current debate regarding the rights of animals are influenced primarily by thinkers from the past few centuries, or even from the medieval period. Stephen R. L. Clark, for example, has a detailed view of the moral status of animals and a defense of philosophical vegetarianism that relies heavily on the ancient Greek thinkers mentioned above: Pythagoras, Plato, Plutarch, Plotinus, Porphyry, and, in a peculiar way, Aristotle. It is true that the main difference between the ancient defense of animals and more recent defenses of them is that ancient vegetarians (along with vegetarians in Eastern religions and the minority of vegetarians in the Abrahamic religions) tend to emphasize the effect that cruelty to animals has on *us*. That is, it is obviously wrong to inflict gratuitous suffering on others; to do so indicates a character flaw in us that is at odds with the life of virtue. Aristotle's pupil Theophrastus made precisely this point by arguing that Aristotle should have defended this view if he wished to be consistent in his pursuit of virtue as a moderate path between (overly self-indulgent as well as self-denying) extremes. Contemporary philosophical vegetarians, by way of partial contrast, tend to emphasize the rights of animals themselves, rather than the virtues or vices of humans who eat (or who refuse to eat) them.[18]

However, we should not make too much of this contrast. There has recently been a rebirth of virtue ethics that has led philosophers to reconsider not only the decision-making procedures to be used in ethics and the moral status of the beings affected by our decisions, but also the character traits (virtues and vices) of the persons making the decisions. Conversely, in the ancient world philosophical vegetarians were not solely concerned with the state of soul of the philosopher, but also with the moral status of animals themselves. Several ancient philosophers have given evidence that they supported what is today called the argument from sentiency: because it is morally wrong to inflict unnecessary or gratuitous suffering and/or death on a being who is sentient, it is wrong for us to inflict such suffering and/or death on animals when a healthy (indeed, they thought, health*ier*) life is possible on a vegetarian basis.

In fact, some ancient philosophical vegetarians defended not only the argument from sentiency, but also the more complicated argument from marginal cases. This argument (hereafter: AMC) centers on the idea that if we make rationality or sophisticated language-use the criterion for direct moral status, as was common not only in the ancient world but in our world as well, then the marginal cases of humanity (severely retarded human beings, infants, those who are senile, etc.) are not worthy of moral respect. This would be a disastrous result! But if we "lower" the criterion for moral status to, say, sentiency (so as to protect all of the marginal cases of humanity), in order to be consistent we should protect sentient animals as well. It is for this reason that Rachels refers to AMC not as the argument from marginal cases, but as the argument for moral consistency. Consider the version of AMC defended by Porphyry in the third century CE:

> To compare plants, however, with animals is doing violence to the order of things. For the latter are naturally sensitive (*aisthanesthai*), and adapted to feel pain, to be terrified and hurt (*kai algein kai phobeisthai kai blaptesthai*); on which account also they may be injured (*adikeisthai*). But the former are entirely destitute of sensation, and in consequence of this, nothing foreign, or evil (*kakon*), or hurtful (*blabe*), or injurious (*adikia*), can befall them. For sensation is the principle of all alliance (*kai gar oikeioseos pases kai allotrioseos arche to aisthanesthai*). . . . And is it not absurd (*alogon*), since we see that many of our own species (*anthropon*) live

from sense alone (*aisthesei monon*), but do not possess intellect (*noun*) and reason (*logon*) . . . but that no justice is shown from us to the ox that ploughs, the dog that is fed with us, and the animals that nourish us with their milk, and adorn our bodies with their wool? Is not such an opinion most irrational and absurd?[19]

Indeed.

Almost all of the major parties in recent debates regarding philosophical vegetarianism have developed positions either for or against this ancient argument. To take one example among many, Stephen R. L. Clark defends the argument, but he dislikes the label "marginal cases." Clark thinks, due to his commitment to preserve the best in the Judeo-Christian tradition, that nonrational yet sentient human beings do not have a marginal moral status, but rather deserve full-fledged moral concern from us, as do animals. That is, Clark is opposed to the social contract tradition that goes back through Thomas Hobbes in the seventeenth century to the ancient Stoics: morality does not exist primarily to serve the purposes of self-seeking, rational adults who consider themselves "normal." Rather, it exists to protect the defenseless.[20]

Several thinkers in the anti–animal rights camp, however, see things differently. The contractualist view that morality primarily involves rational contractors who can use language in a sophisticated way is very much at work in Carruthers's stance, along with the stances of Michael Leahy and Carl Cohen.[21] A related approach is taken by cultural relativists and multiculturalists and cultural traditionalists who argue that attitudes toward animals that are historically embedded in a particular culture are largely immune to criticism from those who are outside the culture. As the ancient historian Herodotus realized, however, this stance might permit not only human beings eating nonhuman animals, but human beings eating other human beings as well.[22]

Finally, some ecoholists are opposed to animal rights because they think that our primary moral concern should be the health of ecosystems or of the earth's biosphere rather than the health of individual human beings or nonhuman animals, the latter of which can be hunted/farmed and eaten. The view that the parts are for the whole is as old as Plato's *Republic*, although the contemporary version of this view found in ecoholism is somewhat novel. As Aldo Leopold famously put the point, "A thing is right when it tends to preserve the integrity, stability, and beauty of the biotic community." The sharp differences in the animal rights debate are apparent when we notice Tom Regan's label for this position: environmental fascism.[23]

CONCLUSION

From the above it should be clear both that the moral status of animals has posed a problem for philosophers for quite some time and that they have been quite ambivalent on this topic. Contemporary philosophical vegetarians can perhaps receive solace from the late-nineteenth-century American philosopher Josiah Royce, when he said the following in a context far removed from the moral status of animals:

> Whenever I have most carefully revised my moral standards, I am always able to see . . . that at best I have been finding out, in some new light, the true meaning that was latent in old traditions. . . . Revision does not mean mere destruction.[24]

Perhaps the tradition of philosophical vegetarianism going back to Pythagoras and traveling through many in the Platonic tradition will one day win out over its dialectical opponent, which traces its meat-eating lineage back to Aristotle and the Stoics.

A final note. Perhaps it is surprising that the Platonic tradition in philosophy has been more favorable to animals than the Aristotelian tradition of empiricism. One might suspect that empiricists would have paid more careful attention to the sufferings of animals than those who supposedly had their heads full of mathematical and other abstractions. But it is the modern industrial complex, with its perversion of empiricism, that ravages the earth and the animals on it at a rate that is unparalleled in human history. It is precisely a Platonic spirit of (at least temporary) detachment from popular culture that may be necessary in order to notice what should, it seems, be obvious: that it cannot be true that it is morally permissible to be the cause of avoidable ill or gratuitous suffering to sentient animals.[25]

NOTES

1. On ancient vegetarianism and ancient critics of vegetarianism, see Daniel Dombrowski, *The Philosophy of Vegetarianism* (Amherst: University of Massachusetts Press, 1984); and Richard Sorabji, *Animal Minds and Human Morals* (Ithaca, NY: Cornell University Press, 1993). The best primary source is Porphyry, *On Abstinence from Killing Animals*, trans. Gillian Clark (Ithaca, NY: Cornell University Press, 2000); Porphyry summarizes the work of many other ancient thinkers. Finally, see Aristotle's "Politics," in *The Basic Works of Aristotle* (New York: Random House, 1941), 1:3.

2. See Louis Berman, *Vegetarianism and the Jewish Tradition* (New York: Ktav, 1982); Hannah Kasher, "Animals as Moral Patients in Maimonides' Teachings," *American Catholic Philosophical Quarterly* 76 (2002): 145–63; Judith Barad, *Aquinas*

on the Nature and Treatment of Animals (Lanham, MD: Rowman and Littlefield, 2001); and Andrew Linzey, *Animal Theology* (Champaign: University of Illinois Press, 1995). For a primary source regarding the dominant medieval view regarding animals, see St. Thomas Aquinas, *Summa Theologiae*, Blackfriars ed. (New York: McGraw-Hill, 1972), IIaIIae, question 64, articles 1 and 3.

3. A good place to start regarding the status of animals in the great world religions are the essays in Tom Regan, ed., *Animal Sacrifices* (Philadelphia: Temple University Press, 1986), particularly the essays by Basant Lal on Hinduism, Christopher Chapple on Buddhism, and Rodney Taylor on Confucianism.

4. On Descartes's view of animals see Tom Regan, *The Case for Animal Rights* (Berkeley: University of California Press, 1983), pp. 1–33. Also see John Cottingham, " 'A Brute to the Brutes?': Descartes' Treatment of Animals," *Philosophy* 53 (1978): 551–59.

5. See Immanuel Kant, *Lectures on Ethics*, trans. Louis Infield (New York: Harper and Row, 1963), pp. 239–40. Also see two articles by A. Broadie and Elizabeth Pybus, "Kant's Treatment of Animals," *Philosophy* 49 (1974): 375–84; and "Kant and the Mistreatment of Animals," *Philosophy* 53 (1978): 560–61.

6. See Michael Seidler, "Hume and the Animals," *Southern Journal of Philosophy* 15 (1977): 361–72.

7. On Jeremy Bentham, see Tom Regan and Peter Singer, eds., *Animal Rights and Human Obligations*, 2nd ed. (Englewood Cliffs, NJ: Prentice-Hall, 1989), pp. 25–26. On John Stuart Mill, see Owen Goldin and Patricia Kilroe, eds., *Human Life and the Natural World* (Peterborough, ON: Broadview Press, 1997), pp. 187–200. These two anthologies are good places to find relevant selections on the moral status of animals not only from Bentham and Mill, but also from many other major figures in the history of philosophy and the history of religion: the Bible, Plato, Aristotle, Cicero, Porphyry, St. Augustine, St. Thomas Aquinas, St. Francis of Assisi, René Descartes, Baruch Spinoza, John Locke, Voltaire, Immanuel Kant, Jean-Jacques Rousseau, Charles Darwin, Ralph Waldo Emerson, Albert Schweitzer, and others.

8. See Charles Darwin, *The Expression of the Emotions in Man and Animals* (New York: Appleton, 1898).

9. See Peter Singer's now classic study, *Animal Liberation*, new rev. ed. (New York: Avon Books, 1990); see especially Singer's chapter titled "Man's Dominion: A Short History of Speciesism."

10. See Regan's magnum opus, *The Case for Animal Rights.*

11. See Peter Singer's *Practical Ethics* (Cambridge: Cambridge University Press, 1979) on the replaceability argument. Also see a criticism of this argument in Daniel Dombrowski, "The Replaceability Argument," *Process Studies* 30 (2001): 22–35. Finally, see Tom Regan, "Utilitarianism, Vegetarianism, and Animal Rights," *Philosophy and Public Affairs* 9 (1980): 305–24; and Evelyn Pluhar, *Beyond Prejudice: The Moral Significance of Human and Nonhuman Animals* (Durham, NC: Duke University Press, 1995).

12. See Michel de Montaigne, "Apology for Raimond de Sebonde," in *The Essays* (Chicago: Encyclopedia Britannica, 1952). Also see Voltaire, "Animals," in *Voltaire's Philosophical Dictionary* (New York: Knopf, 1924); Voltaire is responding to Descartes.

13. See Steve Sapontzis, *Morals, Reason, and Animals* (Philadelphia: Temple University Press, 1987), especially pp. 28, 147.

14. See James Rachels, *Created from Animals: The Moral Implications of Darwinism* (Oxford: Oxford University Press, 1990).

15. See Robert Nozick, "About Mammals and People," *New York Times Book Review*, November 27, 1983; also see Nozick's *Anarchy, State, and Utopia* (New York: Basic Books, 1974). Finally, see R. G. Frey, *Interests and Rights* (Oxford: Clarendon Press, 1980).

16. See Peter Carruthers, *The Animals Issue* (Cambridge: Cambridge University Press, 1992); also see Peter Harrison, "Theodicy and Animal Pain," *Philosophy* 64 (1989): 79–92.

17. See, e.g., James Reichmann, *Evolution, Animal "Rights," and the Environment* (Washington, DC: Catholic University of America Press, 2000).

18. On Theophrastus see Porphyry, *On Abstinence from Killing Animals*. Also see Stephen R. L. Clark, *The Moral Status of Animals* (Oxford: Clarendon Press, 1977); and *Animals and Their Moral Standing* (London: Routledge, 1997).

19. See Porphyry, *On Abstinence from Killing Animals*, III:19. I have relied here on the older translation of this work by Thomas Taylor in Porphyry, *On Abstinence from Animal Food* (London: Centaur Press, 1965). For the Greek edition see J. Bouffartigue and M. Patillon, *Porphyre de l'abstinence* (Paris: Les Belles Lettres, 1977), 3 vols., with French and Greek on facing pages. Also see Stephen Newmyer, "Plutarch on the Moral Grounds for Vegetarianism," *Classical Outlook* 72 (1995): 41–43; Randolph Feezell and William Stephens, "The Argument from Marginal Cases: Is Speciesism Defensible?" *Contemporary Philosophy* 16 (1994): 7–16; and the magisterial book by Johannes Haussleiter, *Der Vegetarismus in der antike* (Berlin: Topelmann, 1935).

20. See Stephen R. L. Clark, "Utility, Rights, and the Domestic Virtues," *Between the Species* 4 (1988): 235–46.

21. See Michael Leahy, *Against Liberation* (London: Routledge, 1991). Also see Carl Cohen, "Do Animals Have Rights?" *Ethics and Behavior* 7 (1977): 91–102.

22. On cultural relativism see James Rachels, *The Elements of Moral Philosophy* (Boston: McGraw-Hill, 1999), pp. 20–36. For a more sympathetic account of cultural traditions concerning animals, see Roger Scruton, "From a View to a Death: Culture, Nature, and the Huntsman's Art," *Environmental Values* 6 (1997): 471–81.

23. See Aldo Leopold, *A Sand County Almanac* (New York: Oxford University Press, 1969), pp. 224–25. For a more recent defense of Leopold's view see J. Baird Callicott, *In Defense of the Land Ethic* (Albany: State University of New York Press, 1989). On Regan's contrast between the rights view and the ecoholist view see *The Case for Animal Rights*, pp. 362, 396.

24. Josiah Royce, *The Philosophy of Loyalty* (New York: Macmillan, 1908), p. 11.

25. See Stephen R. L. Clark, "Ancient Philosophy," in *The Oxford Illustrated History of Ancient Philosophy*, ed. Anthony Kenny (Oxford: Oxford University Press, 2001), pp. 25, 380.

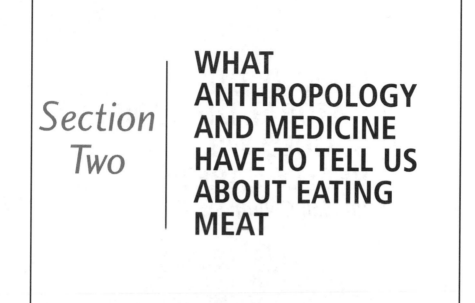

Section Two

WHAT ANTHROPOLOGY AND MEDICINE HAVE TO TELL US ABOUT EATING MEAT

2 | WHAT IS OUR NATURAL DIET, AND SHOULD WE REALLY CARE?

Randall Collura

What is our natural diet? This question has been a central issue in the vegetarian movement for 150 years or more. Vegetarian authors have explored the question through comparative anatomy and physiology of varying sophistication. The conclusion has usually been that humans are best suited to a vegetarian diet, which shouldn't come as a great surprise. The evidence presented, however, has never been definitive, and I don't believe it ever will be. Implicit in the question is the belief that our natural diet would certainly be the best diet for us. Natural equals best—or does it? Perhaps our myths have clouded our thinking. Even if we could determine our true natural diet, would we be able to find the foods that comprised it? We wouldn't find them in our local supermarket; we have changed our foods as dramatically as we have changed our eating habits. Should we even be asking this question in the first place? Or should we be asking instead what the best diet would be for us today, with our current lifestyle and food choices, and forget about a mythical (natural) perfect lost diet? Let's explore the issue.

The Garden of Eden is a powerful and pervasive myth, at least in Western cultures. Allusions to this myth are everywhere. Snakes, apples, fig leaves, and the concept of a lost carefree paradise or "golden age" are so much a part of our collective consciousness that they are taken for granted.

The idea is extended to our evolutionary history as well. We lived in a forest paradise until something (climate change?) forced us to move to the harsh savannah to fend for ourselves and in the process lost our innocence. Perhaps this myth resonates so universally because, in part, the story mirrors our own development as individuals. We are provided for as we grow up in a safe home where we are looked over by powerful beings who have our interest at heart. We are eventually expected to leave that nice home and fend for ourselves (and this is wrapped up with our loss of innocence). Even our scientific tale of the evolution of life on earth is informed by and told as a creation myth, as the narrative always leads to and ends with the evolution of us.[1] This mythology leaves us open to calls for a "return to nature," to reclaim "ancient wisdom" and to live a more pristine life. The following quote is from a book published in 1896 that advocates a raw, mostly fruit and nut diet; the author was Adolf Just, a German naturopath:

> In paradise man lived originally free from sin and disease, in perpetual joy and unclouded happiness. But man lost paradise—was driven from it. The ancient myths, especially the myths concerning paradise, which we find among all civilized peoples, embody the profoundest truths regarding the original state of man and the primitive history of mankind.[2]

How does the Garden of Eden myth square with reality? Not very well. The last 150 years or so have brought a revolution in the scientific understanding of our closest ape relatives and our true evolutionary history. Until the 1970s our place within the primates was a bit uncertain, although we have always been thought of as closely allied with the great apes. Since that time our close relationship with the chimpanzees has been demonstrated without any doubt. It is very likely that the ancestors of modern humans were living (and probably looking) much like today's chimpanzees only six million years ago. As we continue to carefully study our great ape cousins, the "jungle paradise" we inhabited long ago begins to look a little harsher and less friendly. In modern ape habitat, fruit is abundant at some times but quite scarce at others. The fruits that are available would not appeal to our domesticated tastes as they are much less sweet and have a lot more fiber than those found in supermarket bins. Common chimpanzees make war on neighboring groups, killing males and often injuring females. Apes carry parasites, suffer from broken bones, and die of diseases that also affect humans. Aggression and infanticide are unpleasant realities of many primate societies. By just about any measure we are much better off or have the potential to be much better off than our ancestors and close relatives. Myth, however, is often more powerful than truth—or perhaps just more appealing to believe. The first thing we need to do in order to look at this issue clearly is to abandon the Garden of Eden mythology.

How have vegetarian authors looked at our diet in the past? Pick up a book on vegetarianism from the 1880s or the 1980s and you are likely to find a chapter on our natural diet. In fact, there will probably not be much difference among such chapters written a hundred years apart. The logic is simple: by comparing our anatomy and physiology with that of other animals we should be able to determine the diet to which we are most suited. I've heard the same arguments made in an evolutionary or biblical context. Call it "physical dietary determinism." The focus is usually on tooth shape and size, length and complexity of the digestive tract plus some other features. Are we more like the carnivores or the herbivores? What about omnivores? Humans are classifiers—we like to put things into categories—but how rigid are these designations? In the natural world there are no iron-clad divisions such as "the carnivores." It's not that there aren't natural groups formed by lines of descent, but these groups aren't necessarily homogeneous. Furthermore, animals change what they eat over time. They must. Because all mammals are derived from a common ancestor, dietary changes must have occurred at many points in mammalian evolution, including along the branch leading to humans.

It's clear that we aren't specialized carnivores like cats, narrowly adapted to a flesh diet. Few would argue that we are, however. It's clear that we aren't specialized herbivores like the artiodactyl ruminants (i.e., cows), either. They have evolved a digestive system that, with the help of cellulose-digesting microbes in a special foregut, can process roughage that most other mammals can't. Interestingly, a group of Old World monkeys (and one New World bird) developed a similar system independently. Other mammals, including some primates, digest some roughage in the hindgut. The human hindgut doesn't seem to be enlarged for this purpose, however. In fact our digestive system doesn't seem very specialized at all. Our teeth aren't much help either. One thing that defines humans and our hominid ancestors (species that evolved since our split with the chimpanzees) is reduced canines. A quick look at the great apes (chimpanzees, gorillas, and orangutans) shows pretty large canines, yet they are supposed to be our vegetarian cousins. It turns out that these teeth are used in intraspecies competition: males vying for and sometimes fighting over access to females. If males don't fight over females (i.e., if they form pair bonds) large canines may be unnecessary. Our teeth may have more to say about our social system than our diet. The bottom line is that nothing about our anatomy or physiology dictates a vegetarian diet (or precludes one either). So much for physical dietary determinism.

What about the diets of our close living relatives? Studies of great ape eating habits have clearly shown that our closest nonhuman relatives subsist primarily on plant foods. But are they really vegetarian? It's important to keep in mind that vegetarianism is a human concept. Other animals may have plant-based diets, but they aren't vegetarian in the sense of intentionally avoiding foods of animal origin. For instance, most primates will consume insects when they are available. Chimpanzees love termites and make specialized tools to catch them. Ants and grubs are ape favorites as well. Common chimpanzees will hunt and eat mammals also, although this is rarer. Pygmy chimpanzees (or bonobos) don't hunt as much but still occasionally eat flesh. This species, which is just as closely related to humans as common chimpanzees, are also generally less aggressive. Both kinds of chimpanzees prefer ripe fruit when it's available. In general, our closest relatives have diets that are mainly plant-based but none of them vegetarian in our sense of the word.

What about food in human evolution? Since we have learned more about our evolutionary history, modern authors advocating various ways of eating have expanded dietary comparisons to include species and diets from our past. Throughout almost all of the last six million years, our ancestors existed as small nomadic groups living by hunting and gathering. The amount of meat and other animal foods probably rose gradually to become a significant portion of at least some of our ancestors' diets. How significant is an open question, and opinions may say more about the current thinking about human evolution than they do about any real scientific estimate. Does that pile of bones with stone-tool marks on them correspond to one meal or a complete lifestyle? How could we tell if hunting was something that was done three times a week or three times a year? Gathering and eating a piece of fruit or digging up a tuber don't leave traces in the fossil record.

Reconstructing past diets is no easy task. In fact, it's not that easy to determine what people are eating *today*, either in contemporary hunter-gatherer (H/G) societies or our own. Diets often change on a seasonal basis and to get a full picture, surveys need to be taken throughout the year. Diets may even change from year to year depending upon rainfall, availability of game and other factors. One recent analysis of worldwide contemporary H/G diets found a relatively high proportion of these groups rely upon animal foods for more than half of their energy requirements, regardless of latitude. However, the archaeological record clearly shows dramatic shifts in the mental and technological capabilities of our ancestors after about fifty thousand years ago. How would the reduced hunting capabilities of archaic *Homo sapiens*, or *Homo erectus*, have altered the ratio of hunted versus gathered foods? If we were able to go back in time and sample human societies scattered throughout the globe thirty thousand years ago or ninety thousand years ago—looking at what they ate and how they lived and died—I'm sure we would find an enormous amount of variability.

Dietary changes that occurred throughout most of human evolution were gradual, although certainly not insignificant. The changes that occurred with the invention of agriculture, however, both in terms of diet and lifestyle, were rapid and dramatic shifts from anything that had existed previously. In one sense, our diets probably became more plant based and less reliant on wild-animal foods (as they had been millions of years prior). However, the grains that became the staples of our Neolithic (New Stone Age: after about ten thousand years ago) diets were foods introduced only shortly before their domestication. Shifts in activity levels, mobility, and population density were also very dramatic changes from the lifestyle of the small bands of nomadic hunter-gatherers that spread throughout the world in the Paleolithic (Old Stone Age: prior to ten thousand years ago).

The last few hundred years have brought even more dramatic changes to the diets and lifestyles of Westernized societies. Mechanized agriculture and other aspects of industrialization have further reduced the average daily energy expenditures (exercise). Global networks of trade ensure that plants and animals domesticated in one part of the world are raised in similar climates all over the planet. New World domesticates such as maize and potatoes are now grown in Africa and Europe, while Asian domesticates such as rice are grown in the New World. Many of these changes are beneficial; however, some have reduced dietary quality dramatically. Refinements in milling techniques that efficiently separate out the bran and germ from wheat result in a flour that has a longer shelf life but is far less nutritious. The production of refined sugar from cane and beets has also dramatically altered the relationship between nutrients and calories. It is now possible to consume a diet adequate in total calories yet almost completely devoid of any other nutrients. Another dramatic change in Western diets is the inclusion of larger and larger amounts of meat from domesticated animals, which tends to be higher in fat than meat from wild game.

So, how far back should we go to find our "natural diet"? One hundred years, five hundred years, twenty thousand years, more? "Paleodiet" advocates[3] (paleodiets include only foods available before agriculture) would say that modern humans have the genetic constitution of our Paleolithic ancestors but diets and lifestyles that are very different from what they had. The "diseases of civilization"—which include atherosclerosis, hypertension, diabetes, cancer, osteoporosis, hearing loss, dental caries, alcohol-related diseases, and obesity—are the result of the discordance between our ancient genetic makeup and our modern lifestyles and diets—according to these advocates. This presumes we haven't adapted to these new lifestyles and diets. But how long does it take to adapt to a new diet? The emerging consensus regarding genetic evolution is of great variability in the rates of change. Our genes are a patchwork of remarkable stability and amazingly rapid change, depending upon the selective pressures on individual genes. While it is true that we share a large percentage of our genetic makeup with our ancestors, other primate species, and indeed with all other animals, this in no way negates the importance of the genes that do differ. The genetic differences between chimpanzees and ourselves are quite small yet the manifestations of those differences are quite dramatic. In addition, changes in diet seem to be capable of inducing rapid evolutionary change due to the central importance of diet in species survival. One example is the retention of lactase expression (the ability to digest milk sugar or lactose) in adults whose ancestors have utilized animal milk as a food source. Recent genetic changes have only begun to be investigated, and there may be many genetic adaptations to dietary changes that have occurred in the last ten thousand years.

It is far less likely that the changes in diet and lifestyle that have occurred since the Industrial Revolution have had a significant impact on our genetic makeup. Interestingly, paleodiet advocates stress the recent origin (within the last hundred years or so as a major health problem) for the major diseases that mark Western civilization; however, agriculture is many thousands of years old. If Neolithic foods were to blame for these diseases, we would have a multithousand-year history of them. Why have paleodiet-promoting authors suggested a return to a more-than-ten-thousand-year-old diet as a prescription for diseases that have become a major problem only since the Industrial Revolution? There are no convincing reasons to start eating like a "caveman."

Perhaps then, instead of a Paleolithic prescription for the diseases of modern civilization, we need a Neolithic prescription. Unlike questions regarding the ratio of plant and animal foods in the diets of our distant ancestors, it's an easy task to pick out the changes that occurred so recently that there is a written record. A Neolithic diet would be based on whole grains with a much greater proportion of unrefined foods and far less meat and sugar. (The macrobiotic diet as well as a whole food vegetarian diet could be considered Neolithic diets.) Lifestyle changes would include greater amounts of exercise—although not to the level of contemporary hunter-gatherers. I'm not suggesting that all aspects of Neolithic life should be replicated. However, there are many aspects of industrial ecology that should be called into question. The widespread use of pesticides, herbicides, preservatives, and other chemicals in our food supply may have long-term consequences that are unappreciated and understudied. Many of these substances have uncontested benefits, but without a true understanding of the costs, proper decisions regarding their use can never be made.

Another popular dietary movement that looks backward in its search for a better diet is raw foodism.[4] Advocates of raw food diets are fond of saying (with derision) that modern humans are the only animals that cook food. How long humans have been cooking food is currently an active question in anthropology. It is safe to say that at some point in human evolution we started cooking foods and prior to that our diets were all raw. This change may have been as far back as the origin of *Homo erectus* (1.8 million years ago) or as late as the origin of modern *Homo sapiens* (forty thousand to one hundred thousand years ago). In any case, there is no evidence that starting to eat cooked foods had any detrimental effects on us—quite the contrary, by all unbiased accounts humans are doing quite well in comparison to our raw-eating ape relatives. The current raw food movement is an offshoot of the vegetarian movement, and eating raw is sometimes considered the "next dietary level." Where exactly this progression might lead isn't really clear—"breathatarianism" perhaps? In any case, it might be instructive to look at a central theme of the raw movement: food enzymes.

The food enzyme concept can be summarized as follows: Living cells contain enzymes that mediate all activities within the cell. Foods that are raw, including those that have been warmed but not above a certain critical temperature (this temperature varies from author to author), retain their enzymes intact. These active enzymes, obtained from raw foods, are an essential component of our diet. By consuming foods that contain active enzymes, we conserve our own supply of enzymes that can then be utilized for important cellular functions rather than digestion. Food enzymes may also be absorbed, redistributed, and used throughout the body. There is an almost mystical importance and quality ascribed to enzymes. They are said to contain the "life force," and this is destroyed by cooking (i.e., by heat). This is why raw food diets are also called "living food" diets. Unfortunately, there is *no* merit to this concept and, as any thoughtful high school biology student could show, no way that active enzymes in food could be an essential dietary component.

The food-enzyme concept starts with an important observation about the biochemistry of living cells: the central role of enzymes in mediating biochemical reactions. So far, so good; but one crucial fact about enzymes is glossed over in this argument: enzymes are *very* specific. There are many thousands of different enzymes in a typical cell, each mediating a specific biochemical reaction. Enzymes are proteins, often working in concert with metal ions and cofactors. Proteins are made of long chains of about twenty different amino acids that are arranged in a specific order. This order is dictated by the DNA sequence that codes for the protein. The activity of specific enzymes is regulated by the production of the protein when required and the complex interplay of enzymes that regulate the activities of other enzymes. The important fact is that enzymes are not interchangeable. Specifically, enzymes from food, no matter how active, would be useless to us as enzymes because they were produced to mediate the activities of the cells in the plant (or animal) that became our food. Enzymes required to produce a wheat grass sprout are quite different from those needed to make red blood cells.

In any case, enzymes and other structural proteins don't make it through our digestive system intact. The whole purpose of the digestive system is to break down macromolecules to their components for absorption. Proteins are broken down into amino acids, starches to sugars, and lipids to fatty acids. These components are then transported to our cells to become the building blocks for the proteins (including enzymes), carbohydrates, and lipids we require in our cells. This is very basic biology. Furthermore, there is nothing mystical about enzymes. Some operate at high temperatures (like those in organisms living near deep ocean vents) and others preferentially at low temperatures. Some at high pH, some at low pH. Some are very unstable and will break down quickly, while others (such as lysozyme) can be boiled in acid and then function quite well (in fact, this is how researchers purify lysozyme). These differences in function are the result of specific evolutionary pressures over long periods of time. Enough about enzymes.

To be perfectly clear, there is nothing wrong with raw foods. Fresh fruits and vegetables are excellent sources of many nutrients, and even the most conservative nutrition guidelines promote their consumption. On the other hand, cooking shouldn't be considered a sin. Cooking destroys some nutrients but makes others more available. It also makes a wide range of foods edible that are almost useless as food otherwise. Humans have done quite well eating a diet of mixed raw and cooked foods.

So why are people drawn to extreme diets such as raw food or paleodiets? Part of it is the "return to Eden" mentality outlined above—simple solutions for complex problems. Testimonials are another powerful factor in convincing people to change their diets. They often involve dramatic cures from serious, life-threatening diseases. If people say that they were near death and a certain diet cured them, others take notice. In this way, these diets take on an almost religious character and followers have a similar kind of faith and fervor. Testimonials are not scientific evidence, however, and people promoting completely different diets will often present testimonials that are virtually interchangeable (perhaps any change from a diet of cola and junk food is a potentially good change). If one half of one percent of the people who try a particular diet have a marked improvement in health and the remainder show no change (or do poorly), that's not really such a great endorsement (and the improvements might have occurred by chance). However, if five thousand people try that diet there will still potentially be twenty-five impressive-sounding testimonials out there. For many on extreme diets, food becomes an obsession. One author coined a term for obsession in the quest for a perfectly healthy diet: "orthorexia nervosa."[5] This is not to suggest that eating healthy is a disorder, but that some people in an effort to get a perfectly pure and health-promoting diet might stray onto the path toward an eating disorder. No diet will allow you to live forever—our ape cousins certainly don't. For all our dietary impurity, we outlive chimpanzees by decades on average.

What does this all mean for vegetarians and vegans? Are these diets natural? I would argue that humans don't really have a natural diet. We evolved eating a wide variety of diets containing both plant and animal foods. We could spend time and energy trying to figure out what these were, but this would still only tell us where we have been—not where we are. We really don't know how healthy our ancestors were or how long they lived, anyway. We can be certain that they survived, of course; otherwise, we would not be here. However, as modern humans in Western industrial societies (or any contemporary society), we want to know what foods and lifestyle choices will provide the best chance of a long and healthy life right here and right now.

There is a lot of scientific evidence to show that vegetarian and vegan diets are potentially as healthy as or healthier than mixed diets. There is no reason for ethical vegetarians or vegans to sacrifice their ethics and alter their eating habits so their diets are more "natural." Indeed, one could argue that no diet consisting of today's foods is really natural—and that's not necessarily a bad thing. Over the last ten thousand years we have not only changed what foods we eat; we have also changed the foods themselves. Someone from the Paleolithic wouldn't recognize most of the fruits and vegetables in our supermarkets. Artificial selection (people choosing only certain seeds, usually from the best plants, to be sown the following year) has produced foods lower in fiber, sweeter, and larger than their natural relatives. They have also been selected to contain lower amounts of compounds, such as tannins, alkaloids, and oxalates, that plants produce to thwart herbivores. Remember, it's only in the Garden of Eden myth that plants are created for our benefit. In the real world, plants don't usually "want" to be eaten and have evolved all sorts of defenses. Our current quality and selection of foods (I'm referring to whole, unprocessed foods) may not really be "natural," but it's probably better than at any point in the past.

However, it is important that vegans and vegetarians not ignore potential problems with certain vitamins and other nutrients under the false assumption that their diets are "natural" and therefore perfect—a common notion in my experience. In the same vein, though from the opposite direction, it's curious how the traditional dietetic community will harp on the lack of vitamin B_{12} in a vegan diet—implying that without supplements it is inherently deficient and restrictive—while ignoring the many vitamin and mineral supplements added to common foods (iodine in salt, B vitamins in grain products, vitamin D in milk, calcium in many foods, etc.). Do these important additions make "standard" mixed diets inherently deficient and restrictive? Deficiencies of certain nutrients may have been a common feature of existence throughout human evolution, or they might be the result of very recent changes in food processing technologies and lifestyle or both. In any case, vegetarian and vegan diets shouldn't be singled out as special in this regard, nor should vegetarians and vegans be complacent.

Dietary arrogance and ancient mythology have no place in modern food policy and nutrition. Neither do pressures from specific food producers and industries. We need to be looking, in an unbiased fashion, at what dietary regimes will promote long and healthy lives for people living with current food and lifestyle choices. Much nutritional research seeks answers that are far too narrow to address this larger question and/or is funded by entities that seek a particular answer. Broader inquiries that do seek to address the wider relationships among longevity, disease, and diet may provide some answers, and this is certainly a better way to proceed.[6] No diet will ever provide the potentially endless and 100 percent disease-free life of mythology. However, vegetarian and vegan diets can provide a lifetime of healthy nutrition.

NOTES

1. See Deaniel Quinn, *Ishmael*, reissue ed. (New York: Bantam Books, 1995).

2. Adolf Just, *Return to Nature*, 4th ed., 1896 (English translation published by trans. B. Lust, New York: Volunteer Press, 1904).

3. See, for example, S. Boyd Eaton, *The Paleolithic Prescription* (New York: Harper Collins, 1988).

4. See, for example, Stephen Arlin et al., *Nature's First Law: The Raw-Food Diet*, 2nd ed. (San Diego: Maul Brothers Publishing, 1997).

5. See Steven Bratman, MD, *Health Food Junkies: Overcoming the Obession with Healthful Eating* (New York: Bantam Doubleday Dell, 2000).

6. See, for example, the China-Oxford-Cornell study, www.nutrition.cornell.edu/ChinaProject/.

3 | VEGETARIANISM
The Healthy Alternative
Neal Barnard and Kristine Kieswer

In the last century, and especially in recent decades, researchers have zeroed in on dozens of newly discovered—or newly appreciated—plant nutrients that the human body requires for health and longevity. From Harvard University came word that foods rich in lycopene, the red color in tomatoes and watermelon, could cut prostate cancer risk. Tufts University scientists linked vitamin C with a reduction in cataract risk. Studies from Yale University found that a whole range of plant nutrients, including beta-carotene, folate, and fiber, appear protective against gastric and esophageal cancers. Lutein and zeaxanthin from green leafy vegetables fight macular degeneration, the leading cause of blindness in older people. There seems to be almost no limit to the gold mine of beneficial nutrients in plants.

On the flip side, no single food has been more hotly debated than meat—not just in regard to its nutritional makeup (heavy in fat and cholesterol), but in regard to whether we need it at all. Many people eat meat simply for taste or convenience, some for the sake of habit, and many out of family tradition. Advertisers certainly do a good job of talking it up. But science tells a whole different story.

EPIDEMIOLOGY: HUMAN STUDIES
GIVE MEAT A FAILING GRADE

Physicians practicing today have unparalleled access to human studies on nutrition and disease. As populations have changed their diets due to cultural changes or relocating to new homelands, they have provided enormous amounts of epidemiological information about who gets sick and who stays well. In Asia, a traditional diet using rice and vegetables as staples has served the population well, leading to lower rates of serious illness. By contrast, in North America, where diets are based on meat and dairy products—and where no fewer than *one million* chickens are consumed *every hour*—heart disease, stroke, diabetes, and cancer are rampant.

Few people disagree that it's a good idea to have smaller meat portions, snack on apples or carrots, eat more broccoli, and opt for a veggie burger over a beef patty. The question is, should we dump meat altogether? Major epidemiological studies indicate the answer is yes, and the elimination of meat from the diet is indeed one of the most powerful determinants of human health. Early clues came from 1950s observations of vegetarian California Seventh-Day Adventists, showing their cancer mortality rates were 50 to 70 percent of the general population for most cancer sites that are unrelated to smoking and drinking.[1] International studies from Norway, Japan, and the Netherlands found similar patterns. A 1994 study of six thousand British vegetarians followed for twelve years reported a cancer mortality rate that was 40 percent of the general population rate and 60 percent of that of a comparison group of meat eating controls, even after adjusting for smoking, body mass index, and social class. A second large British study found that cancer rates in vegetarian women were 76 percent those of population rates, and an eleven-year German study produced similar findings. Researchers hypothesize that this protection comes from the exclusion of meat and also from the inclusion of a variety of plant foods with cancer-preventive nutrients.

Two large human studies have brought important new evidence on the comparison of diets of plant versus animal origin. The China-Cornell-Oxford study is a collaborative effort of Cornell University, the Chinese Academy of Preventive Medicine, and Oxford University. China Study I, now regarded as the most comprehensive study of diet, lifestyle, and disease ever completed, prompted lead researcher T. Colin Campbell, Ph.D., to conclude that "Americans will not reduce their rate of cancers, cardiovascular disease, and other chronic, degenerative diseases until they shift their diets away from animal-based foods to plant-based foods." China Study II, which gathered new data from mainland China and sixteen counties in Taiwan, goes further, suggesting that "even small increases in the consumption of animal-based foods were associated with increased disease risk." The studies also found that increased levels of animal-based proteins, including protein from dairy products, almost certainly contribute to significant bone loss. Vegetable-based diets, on the other hand, clearly protected against osteoporosis.

Meanwhile, the U.S. government's long-running Framingham Heart Study has underscored what excessive fat and cholesterol can bring. In this Massachusetts-based study, most participants consumed a typical Western diet. Not surprisingly, the most common cause of death in Framingham is cardiovascular disease. However, those with a cholesterol level near 150 were practically heart-attack proof. And, clearly, the easiest way to get to a healthy, low cholesterol level is to avoid the products—meats, dairy, and eggs especially—that are packed with cholesterol and saturated fat. Dietary cholesterol, as we know, is derived solely from meat and other animal products. Dean Ornish, MD, and Caldwell Esselstyn, MD, independently showed the power of omitting meat from the diet entirely. The results of their studies were revolutionary for preventive medicine, its practitioners, and patients everywhere.

As reported in *Lancet*, Dr. Ornish's 1990 Lifestyle Heart Trial started twenty-eight patients with heart disease on a 10 percent fat vegetarian diet, moderate exercise, stress management training, and smoking cessation. A control group received standard care. Without the use of lipid-lowering drugs, 82 percent of the vegetarians experienced a *reversal* of their coronary artery disease.[2] Standard-care patients generally deteriorated. While the lifestyle plan was initially regarded as "radical," it is now recognized as the state of the art in cardiac care.

Dr. Esselstyn, head of the Section of Thyroid and Parathyroid Surgery at the Cleveland Clinic, and associate professor in the Department of Surgery at the Ohio State University School of Medicine, conducted a twelve-year study of patients with severe heart disease, using a vegetarian diet and drug regimen. Within five years, angiographic tests revealed a reversal of heart disease in most patients.[3]

A meat-free diet can play a role in preventing other catastrophic illnesses as well. With 65 percent of Americans now overweight or obese, cases of type 2 diabetes are climbing fast. A study by the Physicians Committee for Responsible Medicine and Georgetown University tested a vegetarian diet on patients with the disease. Two-thirds of participants lowered or completely eliminated their need for oral diabetes medications. On average, members of the vegetarian group lost sixteen pounds in twelve weeks, despite having no restrictions on calorie intake.[4] All dishes were made from grains, vegetables, beans, and fruit. Previous studies found similar results when the diet was paired with exercise; however, this study demonstrated that diet alone could profoundly improve outcomes for people with diabetes. Reducing the occurrence or severity of diabetes can in turn help patients avoid heart attacks, kidney disease, blindness, and limb amputations.

In 1999, the *Quarterly Journal of Medicine* reviewed a large pool of scientific data on vegetarian diets, concluding that they could indeed play a significant role in weight loss, cholesterol, glucose, and insulin regulation, the prevention of heart disease, ocular macular degeneration, stroke, diverticulosis, gallstones, colon cancer, and breast cancer.

FREQUENTLY ASKED QUESTIONS

What Are Healthy Sources of Protein?

Protein is used for building, maintaining, and repairing body tissues. Protein building blocks, called amino acids, can be synthesized by the body in various forms. However, nine essential amino acids cannot be manufactured by the body and must be obtained from the diet. A variety of grains, legumes, and vegetables easily provides all nine.

Eating a traditional Western diet, the average American consumes about double the protein her or his body needs. Excess protein can contribute to osteoporosis and loss of kidney function. In addition, if our main sources of protein tend to be animal products, we end up with too much fat and saturated fat. Most people are surprised to learn that protein needs are actually much less than what they have been consuming. The Recommended Dietary Allowance (RDA) for protein for the average, sedentary adult is only 0.8 grams per kilogram of body weight. To calculate individual needs, the following equation can be used: body weight (in pounds) x 0.36 = recommended protein intake. This formula is designed to overestimate protein needs. Most people do well with less protein, and there is no need to have more.

Can a Meat Diet Cause Iron Overload?

The body needs a certain amount of iron for healthy blood cells, but beyond this rather small amount, iron becomes a dangerous substance, acting as a catalyst for the formation of free radicals. Because of this, higher amounts of iron in the blood mean higher cancer risk and other problems.

Once iron is absorbed by the digestive tract, the body stores it. Most of us accumulate much more iron than we need. In spite of what iron supplement manufacturers would have us believe, iron *overload* is much more common in America than iron deficiency. The reason is the daily diet of red meats, which contributes much more iron than many people can safely handle over the long run. A diet of grains, vegetables, fruits, and beans provides adequate iron, without the risk of excess.

How Can Vegetarians Get Enough Vitamin B_{12}?

Produced by bacteria and other one-celled organisms in the small intestines of animals, vitamin B_{12} made by humans is not well absorbed and retained. Found mainly in animal products, small amounts may be found in plant products due to bacterial contamination. However, these plant and fermented foods, such as spirulina, sea vegetables, tempeh, and miso, do not provide an active and reliable source, so vitamin B_{12} must be obtained elsewhere in the diet.

For individuals following a diet free of all animal products, vitamin B_{12} needs can easily be met by consuming a variety of vegan foods such as fortified breakfast cereals, fortified soymilk, and fortified meat analogues. Nutritional yeast, such as Red Star Vegetarian Support Formula, is also a dependable source. It is best to check the Nutrition Facts label or the ingredient list to ensure it has the active form of vitamin B_{12}, called cobalamin or cyanocobalamin. Nearly all common multivitamins, from Flintstones to One-A-Day to Stress Tabs, also contain B_{12}.

Where Are Essential Fatty Acids Found?

Linoleic acid and linolenic acid are basic fats used to build specialized fats called omega-6 and omega-3 fatty acids. Both are important in the normal functioning of all tissues of the body. Deficiencies are responsible for a host of symptoms and disorders including abnormalities in the liver and kidney, changes in the blood, reduced growth rates, decreased immune function, and skin changes, including dryness and scaliness. When taken in adequate amounts, essential fatty acids help prevent atherosclerosis and reduce the incidence of heart disease and stroke. They also help with ulcerative colitis, menstrual pain, and joint pain.

While supplements and added oils are not typically necessary in the vegetarian diet, good sources of omega-3 fats should be included daily. Alpha-linolenic acid, a common omega-3 fatty acid, is found in many vegetables, beans, whole grains, nuts, and seeds. While these foods are generally very low in fat, the traces of fat they do have tend to be proportionately high in alpha-linolenic acid. More concentrated sources can be found in flaxseeds and flaxseed oil, soy products, walnuts, and wheat germ. Linoleic acid is very common, occurring in many vegetable oils. Some people use a special omega-6 fatty acid, called gamma-linolenic acid, for therapeutic purposes. It can be found in more rare oils, including black currant, borage, evening primrose, and hemp oils.

Fish oils have been popularized as an aid against everything from heart problems to arthritis. The bad news about fish oils is that the omega-3s they contain are highly unstable molecules that tend to decompose and, in the process, unleash dangerous free radicals. Research has shown that omega-3s are found in a more stable form in vegetables and beans. Fish products are also often contaminated with residues of pesticides and industrial chemicals.

In promoting cardiovascular health, ensuring the proper growth and development of a child, or relieving pain, a vegetarian diet rich in vegetables and legumes can supply adequate intake of essential fatty acids. Adding flaxseed oil to salads or ground flaxseeds to breakfast cereals are simple ways to incorporate extra omega-3 fatty acids into the diet for those who wish to do so.

Do Healthy Carbohydrates Facilitate Weight Loss?

The old myth was that pasta, bread, potatoes, and rice are fattening. Not true. In fact, carbohydrate-rich foods are perfect for permanent weight control. Carbohydrates contain fewer than half the calories of fat, which means that replacing fatty foods with complex carbohydrates automatically cuts calories. Populations that consume carbohydrate-rich diets—Asians and vegetarians, for example—are the thinnest people on the planet.

But, calories are only part of the story. If you were to overdo it with carbohydrates—eating a bit more than you need—your body treats these extra calories differently than fat calories. The secret is in the storage. It is very inefficient for the body to store the energy of carbohydrates as body fat—converting carbohydrate to fat burns 23 percent of the calories of the carbohydrate—but dietary fat is converted easily into body fat. Only 3 percent of the calories in fat are burned in the process of conversion and storage. It is the *type* of foods people choose, and not so much the *amount*, that affects body fat the most.

How Does a Vegan Diet Protect the Bones?

Because osteoporosis is widespread in North America, affecting up to 44 million people, a lot of focus has been placed on calcium, the mineral that makes up much of our bone structure. Compared to other countries, however, America and other affluent nations consume a great deal of calcium through dairy products such as milk, cheese, yogurt, and ice cream. Still, brittle bones plague many older adults. We take calcium in, but it doesn't stay put. That's because diets high in protein, particularly animal protein, can cause calcium to be lost from the body. Experiments have shown that when volunteers eat meat, calcium shows up in their urine. However, when plant protein replaces meat protein, subjects are able to maintain good calcium stores with an intake of just 450 milligrams per day—less than half of the recommended daily intake of 1,000 to 1,300 milligrams currently set for Americans. The World Health Organization recommends about 500 milligrams of calcium per day, and this can easily be found in green leafy vegetables and beans.

What about the Special Needs of Pregnant and Nursing Women?

In 1990, the Institute of Medicine of the National Academy of Sciences set guidelines for weight gain during pregnancy from fifteen to forty-five pounds, depending on height and build. This range reduces the risk for premature birth, poor fetal growth, the need for cesarean delivery, and postpartum weight retention. Beginning in the second month of pregnancy, about 250 to 300 additional calories are required each day, which can come from a cup of baked beans, a cup and a half of brown rice, *or* three servings of fruits and vegetables—in other words, much less food than many imagine. The Vegetarian Nutrition Dietetic Practice Group of the American Dietetic Association created a simple meal-planning guide for pregnant women in 1996, which sets forth simple and inexpensive ideas for consuming extra calories:

The body's requirement for vitamin B_{12} is only slightly increased during pregnancy (2.2 mcg vs. 2.0 mcg) and is easily obtained from prenatal vitamins. Vitamin B_{12} is also found in fortified soymilks and cereals.

In 1987, a study of 1,700 pregnancies in vegan women showed that complications were very rare. Although preeclampsia, a condition of increasing blood pressure, is common among omnivores, the study of vegan women showed only one case of preeclampsia in twenty years, and just one in a hundred babies had to be delivered by cesarean section.[5]

The ideal food for a newborn baby is mother's milk. It provides essential nutrients, prevents illness, and is easily digested. Unfortunately, along with healthy nutrients that come from the mother's diet, come contaminants as well. Luckily, mothers who adhere to the New Four Food Groups of grains, vegetables, beans, and fruit will maintain a diet low in fat, rich in vitamins and minerals, and far lower in chemical residues, compared to diets containing meats or dairy products. Fish is particularly high in pollutants such as mercury, PCBs, and other pesticides that can pass through breast milk to nursing babies.

What about the Special Needs of Growing Children?

Most pediatricians recommend introducing solid foods between four and six months of age. Wheat is more frequently allergenic to babies and should not be introduced before the sixth or seventh month, or even after the first birthday. At the start, cereals can be thinned with breast milk, soy formula, or water. One by one, healthy fruits and vegetables can be introduced as long as they are bite-sized, mashed, or thoroughly cooked.

Eating habits learned in childhood often stay with us throughout life. Population studies show that countries in which meat, egg, and dairy consumption is low enjoy a correspondingly low incidence of heart disease, high blood pressure, and many kinds of cancer. Unfortunately, in North America and Europe, it is clear that acclimating young children to fried, heavily processed, salty, and fatty foods can set the stage for poor health in adulthood. In addition to laying the groundwork for chronic disease, meats and eggs often harbor bacteria such as E. coli, campylobacter, or salmonella, which can cause serious—sometimes deadly—infections.

EMERGING DISCOVERIES

In addition to providing protection from obesity, heart disease, stroke, cancers, hypertension, type 2 diabetes, and osteoporosis, a plant-based diet has caught the interest of researchers in other areas of medicine.

Diet may help prevent multiple sclerosis (MS), an autoimmune disease causing loss of nerve function. It has long been clear that low-fat diets slow the progression of the illness. And at the twelfth Meeting of the European Neurological Society, scientists announced that eating smoked sausages in childhood may increase the risk of developing MS. Previous studies suggested that the nitrates used in meat preparation, along with the chemicals in smoke, could contribute to other autoimmune problems, and these studies have associated a fatty diet with MS.

In 2001, Swedish researchers discovered that a gluten-free, vegan diet relieved symptoms of rheumatoid arthritis. Another study tested a mostly raw, vegan diet in fibromyalgia patients with the majority finding significant improvement after several months.

Avoiding certain foods appears to make endometriosis less likely. Foods tainted with certain industrial chemicals appear to encourage the implantation of cells in the abdomen. Polychlorinated biphenyls tend to accumulate in animal fat, and the major route of human exposure is through food, particularly fish. They also show up in meats and dairy products. University of Texas researchers found that Americans are exposed to twenty-two times the suggested maximum limit of dioxin, a common organochlorine contaminant. Blood samples taken from vegans showed they have less dioxin in their bodies than average Americans.

As reported in *Obstetrics and Gynecology* in 2001, women following a low-fat, vegetarian diet experienced significant reductions in menstrual pain and PMS symptoms. The research was conducted by the Physicians Committee for Responsible Medicine in conjunction with the Department of Obstetrics and Gynecology at Georgetown University Medical Center.

Avoiding animal protein helps preserve the calcium in your bones. As reported in the *American Journal of Kidney Diseases* in 2002, a study that required healthy adults to follow a high-protein, carbohydrate-restricted diet for two weeks found that participants lost 55 percent more calcium and experienced a marked acid load on the kidneys, increasing their risk for developing kidney stones.

Vegetarian foods help people avoid food-borne illnesses. A 2001 study in the *New England Journal of Medicine* found that 20 percent of ground chicken, beef, pork, and turkey samples taken from supermarket coolers were contaminated with salmonella, 84 percent of which was resistant to antibiotics. The routine use of antibiotics in farmed animals has made treatment of such illnesses difficult as consumers become more and more resistant to drugs they regularly ingest from animal products.

Vegan diets may reduce the risk of brain disorders that cause dementia. This possibility was first raised with the emergence of bovine spongiform encephalopathy (BSE or "mad cow disease"), a fatal central nervous system disease first identified in the United Kingdom in 1986. Affected cows show increased apprehension, poor coordination, difficulties in walking, and weight loss. Scientists put the blame for BSE on the practice of feeding cattle the remains of sheep infected with scrapie, a disease with many similarities to BSE and whose name comes from the fact that affected animals develop a persistent itch that causes them to scrape off their wool or hair. Prions that cause BSE are believed to be the culprits in variant cases of Creutzfeldt-Jakob disease (CJD), the most common transmissible encephalopathy in humans. First identified in the 1920s, the disease can take as long as thirty years to manifest, but it proceeds quickly once symptoms start. In weeks to months, affected individuals lose mental faculties and muscle coordination, pass into a coma, and die.

However, more common dementing illnesses may relate to diet as well. A recent report from the *Archives of Neurology* found that saturated and hydrogenated fats in the diet appear to increase the risk for developing Alzheimer's disease. Researchers at the Rush Institute for Healthy Aging in Illinois found that fatty diets were a major predictor of who would develop dementia over the next four years. Those in the upper fifth of saturated fat intake had 2.2 times the risk of succumbing to the disease. Saturated fats are common in dairy products, meat, and tropical oils.[6]

Evidence continues to grow for the value of meatless diets in pregnancy and childhood. University of Southhampton researchers found that mothers who ate a meat diet with few carbohydrates during pregnancy bore children with an increased risk for high blood pressure as adults.

A Vegetarian Diet: Benefits for the Rich, Benefits for the Poor

As we turn our attention to global health problems, the value of a vegan diet becomes even clearer. To feed the poor, it is clear that programs relying on animal agriculture are a recipe for long-term environmental and financial disaster because meat production is a terribly inefficient use of grain. Just 2 percent of the corn produced in the United States is eaten by humans; 77 percent goes to feed livestock. While 4 million acres of U.S. farmland are used to grow vegetables, a whopping 56 million acres produce hay for livestock. A 2000 report from the United Nations Commission on Nutrition Challenges of the 21st Century warned that unless major changes are made, 1 billion children will become disabled over the next twenty years from inadequate caloric intake. The first step, according to the experts, is to encourage human consumption of grains, fruits, and vegetables. Add to the equation the cost of ravaged landscapes, polluted waterways, antibiotic resistance, and a whole range of other environmental effects not yet fully understood by scientists, and the disadvantages of animal agriculture become quite evident.

Some may ask whether a plant-based diet provides sufficient nutrition for growth and development, in light of the sometimes inadequate diets of developing countries. However, evidence suggests that plant-based diets are actually ideal, and that improved childhood health depends on many other factors, particularly good hygiene and adequate medical care. Between 1950 and 1980, childhood growth rates and adult stature in China increased steadily as the consumption of a diet extremely low in animal-based foods remained constant. Controlling parasitic diseases and supplying adequate calories—not adding meat to the diet—were leading factors in resolving the country's most pressing public health threats.

Today, however, fast-food restaurants and Western eating habits have invaded much of the rest of the world. In some parts of China, the population is now consuming a diet that is close to 35 percent fat, up from 10 percent just twenty years ago. Cornell researchers estimate that the medical cost to China, should dietary patterns continue to mimic those of North America, will soon reach $300 billion to $600 billion per year.

Notes

1. R. L. Phillips, "Role of Life-Style and Dietary Habits in Risk of Cancer among Seventh-Day Adventists," *Cancer Research* 35 (1975): 3513–522.

2. D. Ornish et al., "Can Lifestyle Changes Reverse Coronary Heart Disease? *Lancet* 336 (1990): 129–33.

3. C. B. Esselstyn Jr., "Updating a 12-Year Experience with Arrest and Reversal Therapy for Coronary Heart Disease (An Overdue Requiem for Palliative Cardiology)," *American Journal of Cardiology* 84 (1999): 339–41.

4. A. S. Nicholson et al., "Toward Improved Management of NIDDM: A Randomized, Controlled, Pilot Intervention Using a Lowfat, Vegetarian Diet," *Preventive Medicine* 29 (1999): 87–91.

5. J. P. Carter, T. Furman, H. R. Hutcheson, "Preeclampsia and Reproductive Performance in a Community of Vegans," *Southern Medical Journal* 19 (1987): 692–97.

6. M. C. Morris et al., "Dietary Fats and the Risk of Incident Alzheimer's Disease," *Archives of Neurology* 60 (2003): 194–200.

4

NUTRITIONAL RISKS OF VEGAN DIETS

*Johanna T. Dwyer and
Franklin M. Loew*

INTRODUCTION

This essay addresses the potential health risks of vegan diets specifically for women and children. The evidence suggests that the health benefits of vegan diets can be preserved, and the risks avoided, by careful dietary planning. In theory, both vegan and omnivorous dietary patterns can be healthy, but in practice both may be suboptimal.

DEFINITIONS

Vegan vegetarians are those who eat no animal foods at all. Near-vegans are those who eat so little that the effects on nutrient intake from food alone are similar. . . . Not all vegan diets are equivalent from the nutritional standpoint, since eaters vary in their other dietary proscriptions and prescriptions. Vegans also have varied non-food-related behaviors that affect health. Vegan diets are associated with "vegan lifestyles": those who avoid

This essay is an abridged version of "Nutritional Risks of Vegan Diets to Women and Children: Are They Preventable?" published in *Journal of Agricultural and Environmental Ethics* 7, no. 1 (1994): 87–109.

eating animal foods also tend to share other food avoidances and other lifestyle practices, sometimes including an avoidance of conventional health and medical services. Alternative diet use often occurs among those with unconventional views in other respects, so this is not a phenomenon unique to vegans. These other characteristics that vary between vegans and others can also influence health and nutritional status, and must be accounted for in attributing cause and effect to diet alone. Attitudes toward health care may affect whether conventional therapeutic measures will be accepted for preventing or treating malnutrition. Further, some vegans avoid animal foods because of religious or ethical beliefs rather than for health reasons. For them, the effects of veganism on their health are less important than other very deeply held beliefs.

CAVEATS

Vegan diets differ from each other (as well as from omnivorous diets) in the amounts and types of nutrients and other biologically active substances (cholesterol, fiber, etc.) that they furnish. For example, raw foods, fruitarian diets, and vegan diets based on cereal staples all differ. The potential health benefits of vegan diets are reviewed at length elsewhere.[1] While the risks of deficiency disease appear to be greater on certain vegan diets, the risks of diseases of excess appear to be greater on certain omnivorous diets.

This essay is restricted to examining evidence of the effects of vegan diets in the United States.

METHODOLOGICAL ISSUES

Methodological issues present formidable barriers to quantifying the risks and benefits of vegan diets. The first problem, discussed above, is that vegan diets are heterogeneous. Results from those following one diet cannot be translated automatically to those on other regimens.

Experimental designs are *difficult* to implement in studying vegan diets. . . . In the absence of more definitive evidence, we must use the few extant studies based on an entire birth cohort of macrobiotic infants whose diets were near-vegan, and the many studies based on case reports or small-scale (and not necessarily representative) surveys, to assess risks and benefits in light of current knowledge in the nutritional sciences.[2] All of these approaches have their inadequacies. More time needs to be spent on definitive studies and less on rhetoric to determine the risks involved in eating vegan diets, especially for the most nutritionally vulnerable groups.

Are Some Individuals at Higher Risk on Vegan Diets?

Nutritionists often refer to certain groups in the population, such as pregnant and lactating women, infants, growing children (including adolescents), and the elderly, as being nutritionally vulnerable. One reason some members of these groups are more nutritionally vulnerable is their increased need for protective nutrients. In addition, the elderly have lower calorie intakes and their intakes of protective nutrients also tend to be lower. At the same time, their nutritional needs may increase because the prevalence of chronic disease rises with age. Thus, all of these groups have higher nutrient needs as expressed in nutrient density (in other words, they need more nutrients per kilocalorie of food taken in).

When individuals are economically deprived as well, they, too, are referred to as a vulnerable group. Few studies focus directly on "poor" vegans living in Western countries. Existing studies are mostly samples of convenience and not population based. In one study that did have a sampling frame, vegetarians tended to be less affluent than nonvegetarians. Representative samples of the population are available in only a few studies. Regardless of their actual income, however, the reasons vegetarians give for their eating pattern are almost never purely economic. Therefore, while it is possible that monetary barriers to obtaining medical care or other needed services may sometimes be present, they are unlikely. Finally, risks of malnutrition increase further for those who have difficulty choosing adequate food due to factors such as infirmity (as among the frail elderly) or physical dependence upon others (as with infants, the aged, and many women).

The concept of these groups' nutritional vulnerability has a firm scientific basis and is demonstrable with controlled observations and experiments. The magnitude of their risks is more difficult to estimate from the existing scientific literature. A single dramatic effect, either positive or negative, is more likely to get published than a series in which no diet-related effects were found. For many conditions, such as low birth weight, which are influenced by nutritional factors, there are so many other factors involved that effects are difficult to discern.

Some examples follow of groups that are likely to be at special risk if they consume vegan diets, according to studies in the existing literature. The risks depend on the type of vegan diet, period in the life cycle, presence of disease, use of vitamin and mineral supplements, and on other habits and characteristics of the eaters. The risks of a vegan diet to these various female groups are significantly greater than the risks to healthy adult males.

Pregnancy

A recent report of the Committee on Maternal Nutrition of the Food and Nutrition Board, National Academy of Sciences provides a comprehensive report on nutritional status in pregnancy, and specifically addresses vegetarianism.[3] Vegan women can meet increased needs for most nutrients during pregnancy by diet alone. However, iron needs rise so much after the second trimester that supplements are usually needed, since plant sources of iron are less bioavailable than heme iron (i.e., a smaller proportion is absorbed in the gut). Low-dose iron supplements (30 mg ferrous iron daily) help to maintain maternal blood hemoglobin levels at 10.5 g/dL in the second and 11 g/dL in the third trimester. Iron supplements also assure maintenance of maternal iron stores during pregnancy and maximize fetal iron stores. These are less well absorbed than heme iron but if taken in sufficient quantity provide ample amounts of iron. Therefore the Committee recommended supplements of 30 mg ferrous iron daily for all women in the second and third trimesters, regardless of their diets. It recommended 300 g of folic acid per day (now increased since the 1992 U.S. Public Health Service Advisory for Women of Reproductive Age to 400 hg per day). Higher doses of iron should be avoided since zinc intakes tend to be low in vegan vegetarians, and high doses of iron may depress serum zinc levels.

Although reasonable amounts of trace elements like iron and zinc can be provided by vegetarian and vegan diets, flesh foods provide larger, more easily absorbed amounts of them and thus either they or iron supplements are advantageous in pregnancy. For example, low zinc intakes (of 7.5 mg/day) were reported in a series of Hindu vegetarian pregnant women.[4] If the pregnant woman's intake of calcium was less than 600 mg daily, and the individual was under twenty-five years of age, the committee recommended a 600-mg calcium supplement for all pregnant women. The belief that those who do not use milk and milk products have few or no calcium needs is not correct.

Deficiencies in vitamin D were found in over two-thirds of the pregnant vegetarian Indian and Pakistani women dwelling in the United Kingdom in one study.[5] A supplement of 10 gg (400 IU) per day of vitamin D was suggested for vegans or for others whose blood levels are low due to avoidance of meat, milk, eggs, and fish.

Vegans are also advised to take supplements of 2 micrograms of vitamin B_{12} daily when pregnant. The rationale for this recommendation is that while vegetarian diets that include eggs, milk, or cheese provide enough vitamin B_{12} for pregnancy needs, occasional B_{12} deficiency has been observed in adult vegans who have avoided eggs and milk for many years. Those with abnormal gastrointestinal function such as atrophic gastritis or bacterial overgrowth of the small intestine are especially at risk. Occasionally their infants have also been found to be B_{12} deficient.

Lactation

The nutritional aspects of lactation have also recently been authoritatively reviewed.[6] The experts on the National Academy of Sciences committee recommended exclusive breast-feeding for all healthy-term infants until at least four to six months of age, and longer if complemented by appropriate introduction of other foods. Vegetarian mothers in the United States are more likely to breast-feed, and to do so for longer (often into the second year of life), than their omnivorous counterparts. Therefore the amount and quality of human milk is particularly critical for the nutritional health of the breast-fed infant of vegan parents.

Vegan diets eaten by the mother during lactation alter milk composition in many ways, including fatty acid composition and levels of some amino acids, such as 1-taurine and 1-carnitine. However, the most important alterations from the standpoint of infant health are in vitamin D and vitamin B_{12} levels.

The milk of both vegetarians and nonvegetarians is low in vitamin D, providing less than 200 International Units (IU) per liter, whereas the RDA for a six-month-old infant is 400 IU (or 10 wg), and breast milk output rarely is even a liter per day. The milk of vegan women who consume no vitamin D–fortified foods or vitamin supplements, or who live in colder parts of the country, is likely to be especially low in the vitamin. The low amount of vitamin D in milk is usually not critical in the first few months of life, because fetal stores suffice, but later on, biochemical signs and clinical evidence of rickets may become evident. When breast-feeding is continued into the second year of life and no supplementary source of vitamin D is fed, rickets (disordered bone growth) due to it has been reported among both vegetarians and nonvegetarians. For all infants, vitamin D supplementation of 300 IU from birth to six months and 400 IU (10 wg) thereafter is suggested. Vitamin D–fortified soy milk formulas provide such amounts if commercial formulas are fed. The NAS committee concluded that while human milk is ordinarily a complete source of nutrients for the young, exclusively breast-fed infant, older infants (even if breast-fed) may be at risk of vitamin D deficiency regardless of maternal diet if the infant and mother are not exposed regularly to sunlight, or if the mother's intake of vitamin D is low. To avoid vitamin D deficiency in the mother, especially when exposure to ultraviolet light is low, a 10-wg supplement of vitamin D was suggested. To avoid it in infants, a vitamin D supplement is also helpful.

Vitamin B_{12} is found only in animal foods, and for this reason, vegans are likely to have low stores. Vitamin B_{12} concentrations in breast milk depend on both maternal body stores and B_{12} intakes. Maternal stores of B_{12}, and consequently their breast milk, are likely to be deficient in vegans, especially those who have consumed unsupplemented vegan diets for most of their lives. The committee concluded that breast-fed infants are susceptible to deficiency of vitamin B_{12} if the mother eats little or no animal food. The deficiency is usually not apparent until later infancy, and may be present in the infant even when the mother is asymptomatic. To decrease risks of deficiency, the committee recommended intakes of 2.6 micrograms a day of vitamin B_{12} from a supplement or from yeast grown on B_{12}-enriched media. Other vitamin B_{12}-fortified or enriched foods may also be used. Vitamin B_{12} is not available to humans from spirulina or from seaweeds. In seaweed, the vitamin's presence depends on the variable presence of phytoplankton trapped within it and not in the plant itself.

Although the risk of hemorrhagic disease in infants is low, all infants are at some risk unless they are supplemented with a single dose of vitamin K at birth. If mothers refuse such treatment they put their infants at risk.

Iron status is usually adequate in term infants until four to six months of life because fetal hemoglobin suffices. If the infant is premature and iron stores are low at birth, iron deficiency may develop sooner. Iron status usually becomes a problem among exclusively breast-fed infants and in infants who are not given iron-fortified formula or iron supplements after six months of age. Normal iron status is usually maintained among full-term infants up to that point, because liver stores of iron and fetal hemoglobin suffices.

In the few studies of breast-feeding vegetarians, vitamin A intakes appear to be satisfactory. Other nutrients rarely appear to be a problem. Vegans who cannot breast-feed their infants and wish to feed them vegan diets should use commercial formulas made from soy isolate, which contain methionine, calcium, zinc, iron, riboflavin, vitamin B_{12}, vitamin D, and other nutrients in amounts sufficient to meet all nutritional needs of infants. Homemade or unfortified soy milk is not a good alternative for young infants because it lacks added calcium, iron, and vitamins B_{12} and D. Also, it may not be heated sufficiently, and thus the antitrypsin factor (which is present in soybeans and acts as an inhibitor of one of the gut enzymes) may still be activated. Soy milk should be reserved for later in childhood, and care should be taken to use a fortified product.

Vegan and other women who avoid milk, cheese, and other calcium-rich milk products were encouraged by the committee to increase their intakes of other culturally appropriate dietary calcium sources, and, if intakes of these were insufficient, calcium supplements were suggested (600 mg elemental calcium daily, taken at meals). Vegan diets are not necessarily low in protein or in phosphorus. Also, other inhibitors as well as enhancers of calcium bioavailability may be present, so it cannot automatically be inferred that vegans have lower calcium levels. If intakes of both calcium and vitamin D are low, the mother may develop secondary hyperparathyroidism in order to maintain normal serum calcium levels, depleting bone calcium stores.

Childhood

One of us has elsewhere reviewed the nutritional implications of vegetarianism for children.[7] Vegan diets fed to infants today range from inadequate to healthful. Vegan and other diets that are healthful for adults may be inadequate for the special needs of infants. Infants who are born premature, small for dates, who are ill in the perinatal period, or who suffer from other disadvantages need particular diets tailored to meet their special and often higher nutrient needs. Additional supplementation of iron, calcium, vitamin D, and other nutrients may also be required.

The greatest challenge to the parents of vegan infants comes in the weaning period. After four to six months of age, some source of energy other than breast milk must be provided because milk production is inadequate to sustain the infant's calorie needs for rapid growth. Current recommendations from expert groups are to feed commercial soy or cow milk formulas throughout the first year of life. Cow milk and soy milk are low in iron to begin with, so if they are fed, iron intakes tend to be low, and occult gastrointestinal bleeding may occur if products are not extensively heated. Also, homemade soy milk and some commercial products are not fortified with vitamins D, B_{12}, or calcium. Finally, soy products, including soy milk, can be allergenic.

Weaning foods must provide sufficient protein, vitamins, iron, and other minerals to meet the normal nutritional needs of infants. Otherwise nutrient supplements of nutrients in short supply must also be provided. Solids are introduced when the child is developmentally ready. If cereal-based weaning foods or paps that are relatively high in water and bulk (but low in energy) are used, they must be fed in large amounts to meet the growing infant's energy needs. Vegan infants may not be able to obtain enough of this high-bulk food to meet their energy needs after weaning from the breast. Frequent feedings and concentrated calorie sources can increase caloric density.

Other Times of Life

Few studies exist on the diets or growth of vegan adolescents. More work needs to be done to determine their nutritional status, since the pubertal growth spurt is a time of increased needs.

Similarly, relatively little work is being done on elderly persons who are vegans. This is another group that deserves attention, since the prevalence of chronic degenerative diseases increases with aging. Some, such as coronary artery disease and high blood pressure, may be beneficially affected by vegan diets. However, other chronic diseases may be negatively influenced by aging associated changes. For example, atrophic gastritis increases, possibly compromising the absorption of vitamin B_{12}, iron, and other nutrients. Recent studies from China among middle-aged and elderly women who (although not vegetarians or vegans) had very low intakes of calcium from all sources, indicate that there is an association between intake levels in youth and bone density later in life. Also the metabolism of vitamin D may alter with age. If needs for extrinsic sources of this nutrient are not met, dietary deficiencies may result.

Other Issues

Iron Deficiency Anemia

Risks of iron deficiency anemia are probably greater for vegan women than others. During pregnancy, iron supplements are recommended for all women, including vegan women, since it is extremely difficult to obtain enough iron to meet maternal and fetal needs from food sources alone (see discussion on pregnancy, above). Also, the bioavailability of non-heme iron in plant foods is lower than that of the heme iron found in animal foods. Other inhibiting substances, such as phytates, phosphates, bran, polyphenols, fiber, and tannins, may also be higher in plant-based diets, and these have greater effects in retarding non-heme than heme iron absorption. While vegan diets are usually richer in ascorbic acid, this single iron absorption enhancer may not be sufficient to overcome the many inhibitory factors; hence the rationale for assigning an increased risk. Various groups of vegans must be assessed separately. Those who consume iron-fortified foods or other sources of iron may be in good nutritional status (as are vegan infants fed commercial iron-fortified soy formula), while others may have major deficiencies and clinically apparent iron deficiency anemia.

Concerns about iron deficiency in infancy and childhood are of special importance because of several recent studies suggesting that there are associations between iron deficiency in infancy and changes in behavioral development.[8] For this reason the American Academy of Pediatrics suggests for all infants (including vegan infants): breast milk for five to six months and 1 mg/kg iron thereafter for exclusively breast-fed infants, iron-fortified formulas (1 mg/L) for non-breast-fed infants for the first twelve months of life; avoidance of whole cow milk in the first year of life (extensive heat processing as in formula or evaporated milk prevents occult gastrointestinal bleeding, whereas pasteurization alone does not) and introduction of iron-rich cereal when solids are fed. When infants are weaned to table foods, the bioavailability of iron on vegan diets must be assessed, taking into account both promoters and inhibitors of iron absorption.

Risks of Vitamin D Deficiency

If regular exposure to sunlight is recommended for both omnivorous and vegan individuals, is the nutrition literature misrepresenting the facts when it states possible risks of vitamin D deficiency appear greater for vegans? Regular sunlight exposure is recommended but only in moderation in view of the dangers of melanoma. Also, health authorities now recommend use of sunscreens, which screen out the ultraviolet rays of the wavelength necessary to convert the provitamin to vitamin D in the skin. The evidence indicates that in fact risks of vitamin D deficiency are greater for vegans. The major source of vitamin D in American diets is fortified cow milk or milk products and, to a lesser extent, other animal foods. Vegans receive very little vitamin D unless they use vitamin D–fortified soy milk or formula, or large amounts of fortified breakfast cereals. Second, at certain times of life, and in certain climates, the ultraviolet rays of the sun are not sufficient to convert all of the provitamin D in the skin into vitamin D that can be used in human tissues. Vegans do not always use nor do they always provide their infants with vitamin D supplements or foods that are fortified with vitamin D, such as commercial soy formula. For this reason there is good evidence that risk of vitamin D deficiency is greater for vegans. Also, there are a number of clinical case reports among vegetarians and vegans, but virtually none among omnivores confirming this impression.

Calcium Deficiency

As to the issue of calcium deficiency, there is no clear evidence about whether risks of osteoporosis are more or less for vegans. Some aspects of the lifestyles of many vegans (not necessarily dietary) probably favor bone health, such as physical activity, nonsmoking, possibly caffeine disuse, and the like. Other aspects, such as low vitamin D and calcium intakes, probably increase risks of calcium deficiency, failure to achieve peak bone mass, and possibly later osteoporosis. Dietary protein intakes of vegans are not necessarily lower than those of omnivores. In any event it is well established that high protein intakes promote calcium excretion, but high phosphorus intakes often work in the opposite direction, so that it is difficult to predict absolute effects in mixed diets without direct experiments.

The presence of phytates and other inhibitors of calcium absorption on diets high in plant foods may further increase risks. However, compensatory mechanisms may be operating, and direct observational studies are needed. Vegan diets are not necessarily lower in protein than other diets, so altered calcium excretion due to lower protein intakes cannot be assumed. There is every reason to assume that the Recommended Dietary Allowances for calcium apply to vegans as a group. The benefits may be long term. According to the recent report of one expert group:

> The most promising nutritional approach to reduce the risk of osteoporosis in later life is to ensure a calcium intake that allows the development of each individual's genetically programmed peak bone mass during the formative years. The importance of meeting recommended allowances at all ages is stressed, but with special attention to intakes through childhood to age 25 years.[9]

CONCLUSION

Eating patterns and other health-related practices are in a state of flux, and data on the health impacts of these alterations must be constantly monitored, updated, and evaluated. We need more and better studies on the nutrition of vegans, vegetarians, and omnivores to better to define those at risk and those not so.

We conclude that all known nutritional risks of vegan diets can be avoided by appropriate dietary planning that results in intakes of nutrients from foods (or, in some instances from supplements) that meet levels suggested in the Recommended Dietary Allowances. The health benefits that may accrue from appropriately planned vegan diets or from omnivorous diets planned to meet recommendations of the Committee on Diet and Health, and the Recommended Dietary Allowances are important and can be achieved by all Americans. We agree with the American Dietetic Association that "vegetarian diets are healthful and nutritionally adequate when appropriately planned."[10] Vegan diets unplanned in the light of newer knowledge of nutrition sciences and selected by nutritionally ill-informed individuals pose particular risks of deficiency, particularly to women and children. This is especially true if access to and use of preventive and curative health services are poor.[11]

NOTES

1. See P. Johnston, ed., *Proceedings of the Second International Vegetarian Congress*, published as a supplement to the *American Journal of Clinical Nutrition* (1994).

2. See J. T. Dwyer, "The Vegetarian Infant," *Infant Nutrition Update* 3 (1993): 1–3.

3. See *Alternative Dietary Practices and Nutritional Abuses in Pregnancy: Proceedings of a Workshop*, report of the Committee on Nutrition of the Mother and Preschool Child, Food and Nutrition Board Commission on Life Sciences of the National Research Council (Washington, DC: National Academy Press, 1982).

4. See Campbell Brown et al., "Zinc and Copper in Asian Pregnancies: Is There Evidence for a Nutritional Deficiency?" *British Journal of Obstetrics and Gynaecology* 92 (1985): 875–85.

5. See J. D. Maxwell et al., "Vitamin D Supplements Enhance Weight Gain and Nutritional Status in Pregnant Asians" *British Journal of Obstetrics and Gynaecology* 88 (1981): 987–91.

6. See the report of the Institute of Medicine, Subcommittee on Nutrition During Lactation, "Nutrition during Lactation" (Washington, DC: National Academy Press, 1991).

7. See J. T. Dwyer, "Nutritional Implications of Vegetarianism for Children," in *Textbook of Pediatric Nutrition*, ed. R. M. Suskind and L. Lewinter-Suskind, 2nd ed. (New York: Raven Press, 1993), pp. 181–89, and "Vegetarianism in Children," in *Handbook of Pediatric Nutrition*, ed. P. M. Queen (Gaithersburg, MD: Aspen Publishers, 1993), pp. 171–86.

8. See F. A. Oski, "Iron Deficiency in Infancy and Childhood," *New England Journal of Medicine* 329 (1993): 190–93.

9. See the *Recommended Dietary Allowances, 10th Edition*, prepared by the Subcommittee on the 10th Edition of the RDA, Food and Nutrition Board (Washington, DC: National Academy Press, 1989).

10. "Position of the American Dietetic Association on Vegetarian Diets," *Journal of the American Dietetic Association* 11 (1994): 1317–19.

11. For extensive references to the relevant scientific literature, see the original, unabridged version of this essay. The latest edition of the *Dietary Reference Intakes* is available from the National Academy Press, Washington, DC.

Section Three

THE RECENT PHILOSOPHICAL DEBATE OVER THE MORAL STATUS OF ANIMALS AND ITS IMPLICATIONS FOR OUR DIET

5

THE BASIC ARGUMENT FOR VEGETARIANISM

James Rachels

I

In 1973 Peter Singer, who was then a young, little-known philosopher from Australia, published an article called "Animal Liberation" in the *New York Review of Books*.[1] The title suggested that there was a parallel between our treatment of animals and the unjust treatment of blacks and women. At first, it was hard to take the comparison seriously. Many proponents of "black liberation" and "women's liberation," as those movements were then known, found the comparison insulting, and most philosophers thought the topic was hardly worth discussing. But Singer kept at it, writing more articles and a now-famous book. It is now commonly said that the modern animal-rights movement grew out of those works. Thanks to Singer, many people, including me, became convinced that a fundamental change in our attitude toward animals was necessary. The indispensable first step was becoming a vegetarian.

The argument that persuaded me to become a vegetarian was so simple that it needs only a little elaboration. It begins with the principle that it is wrong to cause pain unless there is a good enough reason. The qualification is important, because causing pain is not always wrong. My dentist causes me pain, but there's a good reason for it, and besides, I consent. My children's doctor caused them pain when he gave them their shots, and they did not consent, but that was all right, too. However, as the principle says, causing pain is acceptable only when there is a good enough reason for it. Justification is required.

The second step in the argument is to notice that in the modern meat-production business, animals are made to suffer terribly. There is a reason for this suffering, too. We eat the meat, and it helps to nourish us. But there is a catch: we could just as easily nourish ourselves in other ways. Vegetarian meals are also good. Nonetheless, most people prefer a diet that includes meat because they like the way it tastes. The question, then, is whether our enjoyment of the way meat tastes is a good enough reason to justify the amount of suffering that the animals are made to endure. It seems obvious that it is not. Therefore, we should stop eating the products of this business. We should be vegetarians instead.

I will call this the basic argument. It has a limited application. It says nothing about animals raised on old-fashioned family farms or animals killed in hunter-gatherer societies. It addresses only the situation of people like us, in modern industrial countries. But it does point out, in a simple and compelling way, why those of us in the industrial countries should not support the meat-production business as it now exists.

When I emphasize the argument's simplicity, I mean that it does not depend on any controversial claims about health or on any religiously tinged notions of the value of life. Nor does it invoke any disputable ideas about "rights." Further claims of these kinds might strengthen the case for vegetarianism, but the basic argument does not depend on them. Nor does it rest on any contentious philosophical theory about the nature of morality. Philosophers sometimes misunderstand this when they think it is a merely utilitarian argument and that it can be refuted by refuting utilitarianism. But the basic argument is not tied to any particular theory about the nature of ethics. Instead, it appeals to a simple principle that every decent person already accepts, regardless of his or her stand on other issues. The most striking thing about the argument is that it derives such a remarkable conclusion from such a sober, conservative starting point.

The basic argument, then, is common ground for people of various moral and political persuasions. Matthew Scully is in most respects the antithesis of Peter Singer. Scully, a former speechwriter for various Republicans including President George W. Bush, recently surprised his conservative friends by writing a book, *Dominion: The Power of Man, the Suffering of Animals, and the Call to Mercy,*[2] in which he detailed the cruelties of the modern factory farm—cruelties that are, in his words, "hard to contemplate."[3] Scully reports:

> Four companies now produce 81 percent of cows brought to market, 73 percent of sheep, half our chickens, and some 60 percent of hogs. From

these latter, the 355,000 pigs slaughtered every day in America, even the smallest of mercies have been withdrawn. In 1967 there were more than a million hog farms in the country; today there are about 114,000, all of them producing more, more, more to meet market demand. About 80 million of the 95 million hogs slaughtered each year in America, according to the National Pork Producers Council, are intensively reared in mass-confinement farms, never once in their time on earth feeling soil or sunshine. Genetically engineered by machines, inseminated by machines, monitored, herded, electrocuted, stabbed, cleaned, cut, and packaged by machines—themselves treated as machines "from birth to bacon"—these creatures, when eaten, have hardly ever been touched by human hands.[4]

Scully visited some of these automated pig farms in North Carolina, and his report is chilling. Sows have been engineered to weigh five hundred pounds each. Pigs are crowded twenty each in pens only seven-and-a-half feet square. The close confinement creates problems in managing the animals. Pigs are intelligent and social animals who normally build nests and keep them clean. They will not urinate or defecate in their nests, as they must do in the pens. They form bonds with other animals. They want to suck and chew, but in the pens, being deprived of a normal environment in which they can do these things, they begin to chew on the tails of the animals in front of them. In such close quarters, the victims cannot escape. The chewing causes infection, and sick pigs are no good. The solution is "tail docking," a procedure recommended by the U.S. Food and Drug Administration, in which the pigs' tails are snipped (without anesthetic) by pliers. The point is to make the tails more sensitive to pain, so that the animals will make a greater effort to avoid their neighbors' attacks. Surveying the whole setup, the operator of one such "farm" observes: "It's science driven. We're not raising pets."[5]

When critics of the meat-production industry report such facts, their accounts are often dismissed as "emotional appeals." But that is a mistake. It may be true that such descriptions engage our emotions. However, emotionalism is not the point. The point is to fill in the details of the basic argument. The basic argument says that causing pain is not justified unless there is a sufficiently good reason for it. In order to apply this principle to the case of factory farming, we need to know how much pain is involved. If only a little pain were being caused, a fairly insubstantial reason (such as our gustatory pleasure) might be sufficient. But if there is extensive suffering, that reason is not enough. Thus, these facts are a vital part of the argument, and it is necessary to keep them in mind when considering whether the argument is sound. For those of us who have no firsthand knowledge of the subject, reports by such relatively impartial observers as Matthew Scully are indispensable.

Another report recently appeared in the *New York Times Magazine*.[6] The author, Michael Pollan, went to a great deal of trouble to find out what happens to cattle who are raised and slaughtered for beef. "Forgetting, or willed ignorance, is the preferred strategy of many beef-eaters,"[7] he says, but Pollan wanted to see for himself the conditions in which the animals live and die. So he bought a steer—"No. 534"—at the Blair Brothers Ranch in South Dakota, and followed its progress to the slaughterhouse. No. 534 spent the first six months of his life in pastures alongside his mother. Then, having been weaned and castrated, he was shipped to Poky Feeders, a feedlot operation in Garden City, Kansas.

"A cattle feedlot," says Pollan, "is a kind of city, populated by as many as 100,000 animals. It is very much a premodern city, however—crowded, filthy and stinking, with open sewers, unpaved roads and choking air."[8] Fecal dust floats in the air, causing irritation to the eyes and lungs. Searching for No. 534, Pollan found his animal standing in a "deep pile of manure."[9] Dried manure caked on the animals is a problem later, in the slaughterhouse, where steps must be taken to ensure that the meat does not become contaminated. In the feedlot itself, disease would kill the animals were it not for massive doses of antibiotics.

At the Blair Brothers Ranch, No. 534 ate grass and was given corn and alfalfa hay to fatten him up. In his last six weeks at the ranch, he put on 148 pounds. After being shipped to Poky Feeders, he would never eat grass again. His diet would be mostly corn and protein supplement, "a sticky brown goop consisting of molasses and urea."[10] Corn is cheap, and it produces "marbled" beef, although it is not what the animals naturally desire. In a grisly sort of forced cannibalism, the animals are also fed rendered cow parts. The animals could not live on this diet for long—it would "blow out their livers," said one of the feedlot operators. But they are slaughtered before this can happen. The diet is effective, however: the animals weigh more than 1,200 pounds when taken to the slaughterhouse.

No. 534 was slaughtered at the National Beef Plant in Liberal, Kansas, a hundred miles down the road from Poky Feeders. This is where Pollan's personal observations come to a stop. He was not allowed to watch the stunning, bleeding, and evisceration process; nor was he permitted to take pictures or talk to the employees.

Opposing cruelty should not be seen as a specifically liberal or conservative cause. Scully, the conservative Republican, emphasizes that one should oppose it "even if one does not accept [the animal rights advocates'] whole vision of the world." He makes a point of distancing himself from Peter Singer, who champions various left-wing causes. Singer is wrong about the other issues, says Scully, but he is right about the animals.[11]

II

The basic argument seems to me obviously correct. But its very obviousness suggests a problem: if it is so simple and obvious, why doesn't everyone accept it? Why doesn't everyone who has this argument explained to them become a vegetarian? Of course, many people do, but most do not. Part of the explanation may be that it is natural for people to resist arguments that require them to do things they don't want to do. If you want to go on eating meat, you may pay no attention to arguments that say otherwise. Moreover, people generally do not respond to ethical appeals unless they see others around them also responding. If all your friends are eating meat, you are unlikely to be moved by a mere argument. It is like an appeal for money to provide vaccinations for third-world children. The argument that the vaccinations are more important than your going to a movie may be irrefutable, considered just as an argument. But when no one around you is contributing, and your friends are all going to the movie, you are likely to ignore the charitable appeal and spend the money on popcorn instead. It is easy to put the children out of mind.

All this may be true. But there is a more pressing problem about the basic argument—at least, a more pressing problem for me, as a philosopher. Many of my professional colleagues are unmoved by this argument, and I am not sure why. Those who study ethics, especially from a nonreligious point of view, often find the argument compelling. But others do not. This is puzzling because professional philosophers—those who teach in colleges and universities—study arguments dispassionately, and while they often disagree, they disagree about arguments only when the issues are tricky or obscure. But there is nothing tricky or obscure about the basic argument. Thus I would expect that, on so simple a matter, there would be widespread agreement. Instead, many philosophers shrug the argument off.

The same is true of other academics who study cognitive science, psychology, and biology. They are at least as smart as I am, if not smarter, and they are morally decent people. Yet, while I think the basic argument is compelling, many of them do not. It is not that they think the argument makes a good point, even though they are unwilling to act on it. Rather, they find the argument itself unconvincing. How can this be?

Sometimes philosophers explain that the argument is unconvincing because it contains a logical gap. We are all opposed to cruelty, they say, but it does not follow that we must become vegetarians. It only follows that we should favor less cruel methods of meat production. This objection is so feeble that it is hard to believe it explains resistance to the basic argument. It is true enough that, if you are opposed to cruelty, you should prefer that the meat-production business be made less brutal. But it is also true that, it you are opposed to cruelty, you have reason not to participate in social practices that are brutal as they stand. As it stands, meat producers and consumers cooperate to maintain the unnecessary system of pig farms, feedlots, and slaughterhouses. Anyone who finds this system objectionable has reason not to help keep it going. The point would be quickly conceded if the victims were people. If a product—curtains, let's say—were being produced by a process that involved torturing humans, no one would dream of saying: "Of course I oppose using those methods, but that's no reason not to buy the product. After all, the curtains are very nice."

Many in the animal-rights movement believe that scientists are blinded by the need to justify their own practices. The scientists are personally committed to animal experimentation. Their careers, or the careers of their colleagues, are based on it, and they would have to stop this research if they conceded that animals have moral claims on us. Naturally they do not want to do this. Thus they are so biased in favor of current practices that they cannot see the evil in them. This explains why they cannot see the truth even in something so simple as the basic argument.

Perhaps there is something to this, but I do not want to pursue it. On the whole it is a condescending explanation that insults the scientists, cuts off communication with them, and prevents us from learning what they have to teach us. It should be noted, however, that the basic argument about vegetarianism is independent of any arguments about animal experimentation. Indeed, the case against meat eating is much stronger than the case against the use of animals in research. The researchers can at least point out that, in many instances, their work has a serious purpose that can benefit humankind. Nothing comparable can be said in defense of meat eating. Thus, even if some research using animals was justified, meat eating would still be wrong.

I believe a better explanation is in terms of the overall difference between how scientists and animal-rights advocates think about the nature of nonhumans. Defenders of animal rights tend to see the differences between humans and nonhumans as slight. They frequently emphasize how much the animals are like us, in order to argue that our ethical responsibilities to the animals are similar to our responsibilities to one another. Animals are pictured as intelligent and sociable creatures who love their children, who experience fear and delight, who sulk, play, mourn their dead, and much more. So how can it be denied that they have rights, just as we do? I have argued in this way myself, more than once.

Many scientists, however, see this as naive. They believe the differences between humans and other animals are vast—so vast, in fact, that putting humans in a separate moral category is entirely justified. Moreover, they feel they have some authority on this score. After all, the scientific study of animals is their professional concern. In light of this, how should we expect them to react when they are confronted by belligerent amateurs who insist they know better? It is only natural that the scientists should disregard the amateurs' arguments.

A case in point is the anthropologist Jonathan Marks, who teaches at the University of North Carolina at Charlotte. In 1993, Peter Singer and Paola Cavalieri, an Italian writer on animal issues, initiated a campaign known as "the Great Ape Project," an effort to secure basic rights for our closest relatives, the chimpanzees, gorillas, and orangutans.[12] The rights being demanded were life, liberty, and freedom from torture. Marks was invited to participate in a debate about these demands, and he recorded his thoughts in an engaging book, *What It Means to Be 98% Chimpanzee*.[13] "Since their brains are closely related to our brains," Marks says, "it should come as no surprise that the apes can approach humans in their cognitive functions."[14] Despite this, "Apes are often objectified by callous and cynical entrepreneurs, who neither regard them nor treat them as the sentient, emotionally complex creatures they are."[15] Marks does not think this is acceptable. "Apes deserve protection," he says, "even rights."[16]

Reading these words, one would expect Marks to be an ally of Singer and Cavalieri. But he is not. The Great Ape Project, he thinks, is completely wrongheaded. Why? Marks's attempt at philosophical argument is unimpressive—he says the critical issues are that chimps, gorillas, and orangutans aren't human, and that in any case we are politically powerless to guarantee such rights even for humans. Of course, these arguments get us nowhere. Everyone knows the animals aren't human; the point is that they are sufficiently like humans to deserve the same basic protections. And the fact that we cannot ensure rights for humans does not mean that we should stop thinking humans ought to have them.

The underlying reason for Marks's scorn of the animal-rights ideology becomes clear when he turns to the scientific study of animal behavior. The similarities between humans and other great apes, he intimates, is only superficial: "Where clever, controlled experimentation has been possible, it has tended strongly to show that in specific ways, ape minds work quite differently from human minds."[17] For support, he cites the work of the psychologist Daniel J. Povinelli, who argues that chimpanzees' conceptions of physical interactions (as, for example, when a hook is used to manipulate an object) are very different from human understanding.[18] Marks does not say how this fits with his earlier assertion that "Apes deserve protection, even rights," but clearly, in his view, the latter thought trumps the former.

We find this pattern repeated again and again: The scientists concede that the animal rights advocates have a bit of a point, but then the scientists want to talk about the facts. They think we do not know nearly enough about the details of how animal minds work to justify any firm moral conclusions. Moreover, such knowledge as we do have suggests caution: the animals are more different from us than it seems. The advocates of animal rights, on the other hand, think the facts are well enough established that we can proceed without further ado to the ethical conclusions. Anyone who suggests otherwise is viewed as dragging their feet, perhaps to avoid the unpleasant truth about the injustice of our behavior toward the animals.

III

What are we to make of all this? One obvious idea is that we should take seriously what the scientists tell us about what animals are like and adjust our moral conceptions accordingly. This would be an ongoing project. It would take volumes even to begin, by considering what is currently known. But those volumes would be out of date by the time they were completed, because new discoveries are being made all the time.

However, where the basic argument is concerned, the only relevant part of this project would be what science can tell us about the capacity of animals to experience pain. Jeremy Bentham famously said, "The question is not, Can they *reason*? nor Can they *talk*? but *Can they suffer?*"[19] To this we might add that, contrary to Jonathan Marks, it is irrelevant whether chimps have a different understanding of physical interactions. It is irrelevant, that is, if we are considering whether it is acceptable to treat them in ways that cause them pain.

This point is easily misunderstood, so it is worth elaborating just a bit. Of course, the facts about an individual are important in determining how that individual should be treated. (This is true of humans as well as nonhumans.) How an animal should be treated depends on what the animal is like—its nature, its abilities, and its needs. Different creatures have different characteristics, and these must be taken into account when we frame our ethical conceptions. The scientific study of animals gives us the factual information we need. But not every fact about an individual is relevant to every form of treatment. *What facts are relevant* depends on *what sorts of treatment* we are considering. To take a simple example, whether an animal can read is relevant if we are considering whether to admit him to university classes. But the ability to read is irrelevant in deciding whether it is wrong to operate on the animal without anesthesia. Thus, if we are considering whether it is wrong to treat pigs and cattle in the ways we have described, the critical issue is not whether their minds work in various sophisticated ways. The critical issue is, as Bentham said, whether they can suffer.

What does science tell us about this? The mechanisms that enable us to feel pain are not fully understood, but we do know a good bit about them. In humans, nocioceptors—neurons specialized for sensing noxious stimuli—are connected to a central nervous system, and the resulting signals are processed in the brain. Until recently it was believed that the brain's work was divided into two distinct parts: a sensory system operating in the somatosensory cortex, resulting in our conscious experiences of pain, and an affective-motivational system associated with the frontal lobes, responsible for our behavioral reactions. Now, however, this picture has been called into question, and it may be that the best we can say is that the brain's system for processing the information from the nociceptors seems to be spread over multiple regions. At any rate, the human nocioceptive system also includes endogenous opiods, or endorphins, which provide the brain with its natural pain-killing ability.

The question of which other animals feel pain is a real and important issue, not to be settled by appeals to "common sense." Only a completed scientific understanding of pain, which we do not yet have, could tell us all that we need to know. In the meantime, however, we do have a rough idea of what to look for. If we want to know whether it is reasonable to believe that a particular kind of animal is capable of feeling pain, we may ask: Are there nocioceptors present? Are they connected to a central nervous system? What happens in that nervous system to the signals from the nocioceptors? And are there endogenous opiods? In our present state of understanding, this sort of information, together with the obvious behavioral signs of distress, is the best evidence we can have that an animal is capable of feeling pain.

Relying on such evidence, some writers, such as Gary Varner, have tentatively suggested that the line between animals that feel pain and those who do not is (approximately) the line between vertebrates and invertebrates.[20] However, research constantly moves forward, and the tendency of research is to extend the number of animals that might be able to suffer, not decrease it. Nocioception appears to be one of the most primitive animal systems. Nocioceptors have now been identified in a remarkable number of species, including leeches and snails.

The presence of a perceptual system does not, however, settle the question of whether the organism has conscious experiences connected with its operation. We know, for example, that humans have perceptual systems that do not involve conscious experience. Recent research has shown that the human vomeronasal system, which works through receptors in the nose, responds to pheromones and affects behavior even though the person is unaware of it. (It was long believed that this system was vestigial in humans, but it turns out that it is still working.) The receptors for "vomerolfaction" are in the nostrils, alongside the receptors for the sense of smell; yet the operation of one is accompanied by conscious experience, while the operation of the other is not.[21] We do not know why this is so. But this suggests at least the possibility that in some species there may be nocioceptive systems that do not involve conscious experiences. In that case, those animals might not actually feel pain, even though various indications are present. Is this true of leeches and snails? of snakes? of hummingbirds? We may have strong hunches, but we don't really know.

Clearly, then, we still have a great deal to learn about the phenomenon of pain in the animal world, and the scientists who work in this area are right to caution us against quick-and-easy opinions. The ongoing study of animal pain is a fascinating subject in itself, and it has enormous importance for ethics. But should this make us less confident of the basic argument? If the issue were our treatment of snails and leeches, perhaps it should. But pigs and cattle are another matter. There is every reason to believe they feel pain—the facts about their nervous systems, their brains, their behavior, and their evolutionary kinship to human beings, all point to the same conclusion as common sense: our treatment of them on factory farms and in the slaughterhouses is one of the world's great causes of misery. If further investigation were to prove otherwise, it would be one of the most astonishing discoveries in the history of science.

Strict vegetarians may want more than the basic argument can provide, because the basic argument does not support sweeping prohibitions. If opposition to cruelty is our motive, we will have to consider the things we eat one at a time. Of course we should not eat beef and pork produced in the ways I have described, and we ought also to avoid factory-farm poultry, eggs, and milk. But free-range eggs and humanely produced milk are all right. Eating shrimp may also turn out to be acceptable. Moreover, from this point of view, not all vegetarian issues are equally pressing: eating fish may be questionable, but it is not nearly as bad as eating beef. This means that becoming a vegetarian need not be regarded as an all-or-nothing proposition. From a practical standpoint, it makes sense to focus first on the things that cause the most misery. As Matthew Scully says, whatever one's "whole vision of the world" may be, the pig farms, feedlots, and slaughterhouses are unacceptable.[22]

NOTES

1. Peter Singer, "Animal Liberation," *New York Review of Books*, April 5, 1973.

2. Matthew Scully, *Dominion: The Power of Man, the Suffering of Animals, and the Call to Mercy* (New York: St. Martin's Press, 2002).

3. Ibid., p. x.

4. Ibid., p. 29.

5. Ibid., p. 279.

6. Michael Pollan, "This Steer's Life," *New York Times Magazine*, March 31, 2002, pp. 44–51, 68, 71–72, 76–77.

7. Ibid., p. 48.

8. Ibid., p. 50.

9. Ibid., p. 68.

10. Ibid., p. 50.

11. Scully, *Dominion*, pp. 326–38.

12. Peter Singer and Paola Cavalieri, *The Great Ape Project: Equality and Beyond* (London: Fourth Estate, 1993).

13. Jonathan Marks, *What It Means to Be 98% Chimpanzee: Apes, People, and Their Genes* (Berkeley: University of California Press, 2002).

14. Ibid., p. 189.

15. Ibid., p. 185.

16. Ibid., p. 188.

17. Ibid., p. 195.

18. Daniel J. Povinelli, *Folk Physics for Apes: The Chimpanzee's Theory of How the World Works* (Oxford: Oxford University Press, 2000).

19. Jeremy Bentham, *The Principles of Morals and Legislation* (New York: Hafner, 1948; originally published in 1789), p. 311.

20. Gary Varner, *In Nature's Interests? Interests, Animals Rights, and Environmental Ethics* (New York: Oxford University Press, 1998).

21. L. Monti-Bloch, C. Jennings-White, and D. L. Berliner, "The Human Vomeronasal Organ: A Review," *Annals of the New York Academy of Sciences* 855 (1998): 373–89.

22. I have learned a great deal from Colin Allen's essay, "Animal Pain," as yet unpublished. It is the best discussion of the question of animal pain known to me.

6 | THE CONSCIENTIOUS CARNIVORE
Roger Scruton

The question whether it is right to eat the flesh of other animals is as old as civilization. Traditional societies have often assigned a religious significance to eating, regarding food as a potential source of spiritual pollution, which cannot be ingested unless purified by ritual and permitted by the gods. Qualms about meat eating have therefore often been soothed by God's dietary commands. By distinguishing the permitted from the forbidden species, God cancels our anxiety, and the fact that it has so often needed God to step in with a solution is a sign that there really is a problem. What problem, exactly? Answers to this question tend to be either absurd, like the theory of transmigration of souls, or circular, like the invocation of God's will. Nevertheless, the problem persists, and seems to have lost none of its force with the decline of organized religion. Indeed, even in people who define themselves as atheists, vegetarianism may retain the character of an absolute imperative, a prophylactic against pollution that has all the marks of pious observance.

I am not suggesting that vegetarianism is simply a religion subsitute: it has a substantial following in traditional religious communities, too. Thus, on June 25 of this year [2002] Bishop Timothy Dolan remarked that his first priority as the tenth Archbishop of Milwaukee would be to talk with those "meat-and-potato Catholics" who are "the strength of any diocese."

The Catholic Theological Society of America promptly called an emergency meeting, adopted a resolution condemning Dolan's "insensitivity to our animal companions," and asserted that vegetarianism is "the more excellent way of Christian nutrition."[1]

It is important to study such religious responses, since they remind us that, in discussing the rights and wrongs of meat eating, we encounter the deep divide between us and other species twice over. First, there is the fact that, unlike the other animals (or at least, those of them that we eat), we are moral beings who order our lives according to concepts of right and wrong, virtue and vice, freedom and accountability. And then there is the related fact that eating, for us, is not what it is for the other animals. A person's encounter with food may be an occasion of festivity and celebration; it may also be deeply unsettling, compromising, and humiliating. It can even be (for the Christian) a petition for divine forgiveness and an avenue to redemption. Eating has in every traditional society been regarded as a social, often a religious, act, embellished by ritual and enjoyed as a primary celebration of membership.

Indeed, the difference between humans and other animals is never more vividly to be witnessed than in their contrasting attitudes to food. Animals feed, while people eat. This distinction (between *fressen* and *essen*) is one on which Leon Kass has meditated at length in his eloquent book, *The Hungry Soul*.[2] Kass draws on Aristotle's account of practical reason, on sociology in the phenomenological tradition and on ancient and biblical literature to explore the difference between eating and feeding. And he concludes that rational beings defy their own nature if they regard food purely as fuel for the body, and not also as a moral and spiritual challenge. Rational beings are nourished on conversation, taste, manners, and hospitality, and to divorce food from these practices is to deprive it of its true significance.

The special relation of people to their food finds emblematic expression in the face. Human beings have neither claws nor fangs. They do not eat by pressing their mouth to their food, but by raising their food to their mouth, which is the organ of speech and therefore of reason. The mouth is the center of the face, and it is in the face that the human person is most immediately encountered in the form of looks and glances, smiles, grimaces, and words. People therefore place their food into their mouths with special care, usually by means of an instrument that creates a distance between the food and the face, so that the glance, the smile, and the self remain visible while eating.

Rational beings rejoice less in filling themselves than in the sight of food, table, and guests dressed for a ceremonial offering. Their meals are also sacrifices, and anthropologists have occasionally argued that the origin of our carnivorous ways lies in the burnt offerings of ancient ritual. Only rational beings make gifts, and it is the giving of food, usually as the central episode in a ceremony, that is the core of hospitality, and therefore of those actions through which we lay claim to our home and at the same time mutely apologize for owning it. (Cat lovers may dispute that sentence, believing that their favorites bring gifts of mouse, frog, and lizard into the house. But those would be gifts only if the cat, in surrendering them, simultaneously affirms and relinquishes a right of ownership. That is not something that can be accomplished by a creature that lacks the concept of a right.)

In the fast-food culture food is not given but taken, which is one reason why, in such a culture, nobody is properly "at home." The solitary stuffing of burgers, pizzas, and "TV dinners"; the disappearance of family meals and domestic cooking; the loss of table manners—all these tend to obscure the distinction between eating and feeding. And for many people vegetarianism is a roundabout way of restoring that distinction. Vegetables are gifts of the earth: by eating them we reestablish contact with our roots. They offer a way of once again incorporating food into the moral life, hedging it in with moral scruples, and revitalizing the precious sense of shame.

We are unique among the animals, or nearly so, in our omnivorousness. Our eating is motivated occasionally by need, but also by a love of superfluity that causes us to rearrange our world and to engage in ceaseless experiment. At the same time we bind ourselves in laws—such as the dietary laws of Leviticus—which reinforce the idea of food as a spiritual commodity. And again, vegetarianism can be seen as an attempt to recuperate this idea by reintroducing a conception of dietary sin. Omnivorousness, in the human species, is the result of reason; so, too, is the refusal to be omnivorous.

I don't think there can be any vindication of meat eating that does not engage with the religious feelings that prompt our dietary habits, and which also forbid them. Although I do not think that there is a compelling moral argument against meat eating, I do believe that the onus lies on the carnivore to show that there is a way of incorporating meat into a life that respects the moral and spiritual realities, and which does not shame the human race, as it is shamed by the solitary "caveman" gluttony of the burger-stuffer.

But first, it is necessary to address the moral question that vegetarians characteristically put before us—the question whether it is right to kill non-human animals for their meat, or right to kill them at all. To answer this question we must avail ourselves of an account—however provisional—of the relation between ourselves and other animals, along with a theory of moral judgment. It is a prevailing fault among both the defenders and the attackers of "animal rights" that they do neither of those things, but concentrate instead on analogies, borderline cases, and moral puzzles, often in the context of some argumentum ad hominem that begs the most important questions. So I shall begin by summarizing a position for which I have argued more fully in *Animal Rights and Wrongs* and which, though incomplete and controversial, at least has the merit that I sincerely believe it.[3]

The mental life of humans exists at another level from that of the other species with which we have daily dealings. Like dogs and cats, we are conscious. Like them, we feel sensations, emotions, and desires. Like them, we have beliefs and a changing store of information. But, unlike them, we have a consciousness of self and of the distinction between self and other. We have a conception of the past and the future as well as the present; of the possible and the impossible as well as the actual. We act and think in terms of a distinction between the world as it is, and the world as it seems, and in everything we distinguish our own interests and desires from those of other people and other animals.

We humans make free choices based on the conscious evaluation of alternatives. We assess and criticize one another's actions. We exert over our lives a sovereignty that we require others to respect, and which we must respect in turn. We are accountable for our actions and try to resolve our conflicts by agreement rather than by force. In short, we are moral beings. That is why the concept of a right is useful to us. A right is a veto in the hands of the one who possesses it, and we assign rights in order to protect the sovereignty of the individual.[4] Until this protection is offered, the individual cannot be sure that negotiation is the wisest social strategy. Hence rights are a fundamental instrument in the attempt to establish government by consent: where rights are not respected, consent cannot be assumed.

Dogs, cats, and horses are not moral beings, and to treat them as though they were is not just senseless; it is also cruel. It means making demands on them that they cannot possibly understand. Cats would have to respect the right to life and dogs the right to privacy. And both would have to be called to account for their actions and punished for their faults.

Defenders of animal rights point to infants and imbeciles as proof that there can be rights without duties. But the example proves the opposite. Infants and imbeciles have an imperfect understanding of duty, hence they are accorded only very basic rights or even (in the case of some unborn infants) no rights at all. And we ascribe rights to infants and imbeciles because they belong to the same kind as you and me: the kind that, in normal conditions, grows into a full-fledged member of the moral community. Dogs and cats cannot form part of such a community: they are not the kind of thing that can settle disputes by dialogue, that can exert sovereignty over its life and respect the sovereignty of others, that can respond to the call of duty or take responsibility in a matter of trust. They are entirely nonjudgmental, which is why they make such agreeable pets. Even the worst of us can win the heart of a dog.

Although animals have no rights, it does not follow that we can treat them as we wish. Needless to say, the question of the grounds of moral judgment is one of the deepest and darkest in philosophy. Hence the understandable tendency, among the defenders of animal liberation, to avoid it—or, if not to avoid it, to adopt some kind of Benthamite utilitarianism that bypasses all the difficult metaphysical and epistemological questions that are raised by ordinary moral argument. If we rephrase morality as a cost-benefit balance sheet, we can easily conclude that animals are part of the equation. But we are forced also to conclude that the rights of human beings are negotiable interests, and their duties provisional rules of thumb. Both those results are inherently paradoxical and lie at the heart of the devastating, and in my view unanswerable, objections that philosophers have made to the utilitarian conception of morality. Moral judgment should not be seen as a kind of economic reasoning, but as setting the limit to economic reasoning. Morality tells us where calculation stops. Those who demote human rights to negotiable interests have no difficulty in believing in animal rights, but only because what they call a right is no more than a defeasible claim.

The calculus of rights and duties stems from our nature as moral beings, and from the need to set the ground rules for a negotiated life among strangers. It tells us that rights are to be respected, and duties obeyed. It confers equality of moral status on all participants to the moral dialogue, and imposes on us an obligation to justify our conduct in the face of adverse criticism. It brings with it a battery of concepts that entirely transform the worldview and emotions of those who possess them: concepts like justice, desert, and punishment, which lie at the heart of our interpersonal responses. But, however important this calculus may be, as a source of moral feeling, it is not the only source and would be impotent without the motives upon which it draws.

The first of these motives, and the largest source of our moral duties toward animals, is sympathy. While animals have "sympathetic responses," in the sense of responses that are caused by the emotions of those in their nearest vicinity, they do not have sympathy. For sympathy is based on a conception of self and other, and of the distinction between them. It is a disposition to take the feelings of another into account, and erupts in charitable gestures designed to alleviate the other's suffering and promote the other's happiness. It is not sympathy that binds the beehive or maintains the herd, but the force of species life, which is opaque to us, even if we believe that we can explain it.

Readers will be familiar with sociobiological theories of animal "altruism," including the "inclusive fitness" theory, which explains the apparent altruism of animals in terms of the "goals" of their "selfish" genes. Whatever we think of this kind of theory, it is not a theory of sympathy, but at best an explanation of gregarious behavior in kinship groups. And I doubt that any philosophical reader of Mary Midgley's or David Stove's work would be disposed to believe it, let alone to confuse animal altruism with the kind of self-abnegating sympathy that enables human beings to lay down their lives for strangers.[5]

There are two other sources of moral judgment, besides those already mentioned. The first is our attitude to virtue and vice. We are drawn to the traits of character that uphold the moral community, and repelled by those that undermine it. We have a vivid conception of the likable, lovable, or admirable person, and of the nasty or contemptible person whom we should rather avoid. Those conceptions are by no means arbitrary, but grow from the very same social and rational responses that feed our judgments of human actions. Although our conceptions of virtue and vice are malleable, and change with changing social circumstances, they have an immovable core that derives from the experience of society itself.

Finally there is the source of moral feeling that is most often neglected in the literature, but that in many ways bears most nearly on our relations with the animal kingdom. I use the term "piety" to refer to this source, meaning not the adherence to this or that religious doctrine, but the underlying recognition of our fragility and dependence, and the attitude of respect toward the world and the creatures that live in it, upon which religions draw for much of their inspiration. This, I believe, is what the Romans meant by *pietas*, and it is the attitude that so many people—from environmental groups to landscape painters, from conservationists to animal welfare activists—are attempting to recapture, in a world where the results of human presumption are so horribly apparent. Even in an age that does not recognize it under its traditional name, piety is ever-present, a necessary motive in the living and a guarantee offered to those unborn. I suspect that the deepest motive for vegetarianism is the sense of the impious nature of much that we do by way of supplying, fulfilling, and displaying our appetite for the flesh of other species.

If animals had rights then there would be absolute limits to the things that we could do to them. We could not, for example, kill them, breed them for our purposes, train them without their consent, or take them into captivity. We certainly could not raise them for food, still less raise them in the kind of conditions that have become normal in the industrialized world. But the moral problem arises precisely because animals do not have rights, so that the principles that impede our invasions of other people do not serve to protect them. How therefore should animals be treated?

The only simple answer is: it depends. Once we discard the notion that animals have rights, the moral emphasis shifts to human duties. As in the case of people, our duties toward animals arise from the relationships that bind us, and the responsibilities that those relationships imply. Animals bred or kept for our uses are not honorary members of the moral community—as pets or "companion animals" are. Nevertheless the use that we make of them imposes a reciprocal duty of care. If these animals were moral beings then we could not, morally speaking, make use of them as we do—just as we cannot enslave human beings or breed them for food. And if the life of an animal bred for food were simply one long torment, the only relief from which is the final slaughter, we should certainly conclude the practice to be immoral. Utilitarians might disagree—since a utilitarian can justify any amount of suffering, provided the greater happiness is achieved by it. But that is one of the things that is wrong with utilitarianism. Moreover, until we have specified duties, moral judgment cannot begin, and duties cannot be assigned by the Greatest Happiness Principle. Their ground lies in the past, not the future, and they cannot be overridden merely because some good can be achieved by disobeying them.

To criticize battery pig farming as violating a duty of care is surely right and proper. But the argument does nothing to condemn other livestock practices. There is surely scope, here, for some comparative judgments. Consider the traditional English beef farmer, who fattens his calves for thirty months, keeping them on open pasture in the summer, and in warm roomy barns in the winter, feeding them on grass, silage, beans, and maize, attending to them in all their ailments, and sending them for slaughter, when the time comes, to the nearby slaughterhouse, where they are instantly dispatched with a humane killer. Surely, such a farmer treats his cattle as well as cattle can be treated. Of course, he never asked them whether they wanted to live in his fields, or gave them the choice of lifestyle during their time there. But that is because he knows—from instinct rather than from any philosophical theory—that cattle cannot make such choices, and do not exist at the level of consciousness for which freedom and the lack of it are genuine realities.

Animals raised for meat are, for the most part, gregarious, gentle, and dependent. They are unhappy in isolation, and emotionally dependent on the proximity of their kind. In the winter they must be sheltered; in the summer, if they are lucky, they are out to grass, or (in the case of the pig and the chicken) free to roam in a place where they can hunt for scraps of food. Human standards of hygiene are alien to their nature, and their affections, unlike ours, are general and transferable, without tragic overtones. Such animals, tended in the traditional way, by a farmer who houses them together in the winter, and allows them to roam in the summer, are as happy as their nature allows. Assuming that their needs are satisfied, only two questions arise in the farmer's mind: when and how they should be killed—for that they must be killed is evident, this being the reason why they live. Death is not merely a moral question. There is an economic aspect that no farmer—and no consumer—can afford to ignore. And I suspect that those who believe that it is immoral to raise animals for meat have in mind the moment of death, and the economic calculation that prompts us to cut short a life in its prime.[6]

Human beings are conscious of their lives as their own; they have ambitions, hopes, and aspirations; they are fatally attached to others, who cannot be replaced in their affections but whose presence they feel as a need. Hence there is a real distinction, for a human being, between timely and untimely death. To be "cut short" before one's time is a waste—even a tragedy. We lament the death of children and young people not merely because we lament the death of anyone, but because we believe that human beings are fulfilled by their achievements and not merely by their comforts.

No such thoughts apply to domestic cattle. To be killed at thirty months is not intrinsically more tragic than to be killed at forty, fifty, or sixty. And if the meat is at its best after thirty months, and if every month thereafter represents an economic loss, who will blame the farmer for choosing so early a death? In so doing he merely reflects the choice of the consumer, upon whose desires the whole trade in meat, and therefore the very existence of his animals, depends.

But what about the manner of death? That it should be quick is not in dispute. Nevertheless, there is a distinction between sudden death and death preceded by terror, and to the conscientious farmer, who has looked after animals from day to day, living with them and providing for their needs, this terror is not merely unwelcome but a betrayal of trust and a dagger of accusation. Livestock farmers therefore prefer to see their animals dispatched suddenly and humanely in the place where they have lived, by skilled slaughterers who know how to kill an animal without awakening it from its soporific routine. Failing that, they will look for a nearby abattoir, where the animals can be taken without the discomfort of a long journey, and without being handed over to some nameless and unanswerable death machine.

Health and safety regulations are destroying those old and humane practices. Animals are now driven for many miles, to be herded into the death machine by people who have never cared for them, who have no regard for their sufferings, and who see them as no more than living meat on its way to the supermarket. This is the kind of thing at which humane people should protest. However, the mere suggestion that there might be a risk to themselves is enough to silence their feeble consciences, to cancel those flutters of grief over doe-eyed calves and panicking porkers, and to whitewash all negative emotions as the bloodless and cellophaned product is taken down from the shelf. What is at risk here, however, is not the consumer—who was never really in jeopardy from the traditional livestock farmer—but the relation between the farmer and his animals. A crucial episode in the care of the herd has been taken from the farmer's hands. Domestic animals have been moved one step further down the ladder from companions to things.

And this, surely, is the moral crux. Livestock farming is not merely an industry—it is a relation, in which man and animal are bound together to their mutual profit, and in which a human duty of care is nourished by an animal's mute recognition of dependency. This alone explains why people will continue in this time-consuming, exhausting, and ill-paid occupation, resisting the attempts by bureaucrats and agribusinesses to drive them to extinction. Anybody who cares for animals ought to see this kind of husbandry as a complex moral good, to be defended on the one hand against those who would forbid the eating of meat altogether, and on the other hand against those carnivores who prefer the unseen suffering of the battery farm and the factory abattoir to the merest suggestion of a personal risk.

The life of the cattle farmer is not an easy life, nor is the relation between man and animal always as harmonious as it appears in the thousand children's books devoted to life on the farm. Nevertheless, as with all forms of husbandry, cattle farming should be seen in its full context—and that means as a feature of the total ecology of the countryside. Traditional livestock farming involves the maintenance of pastureland, properly enclosed with walls or hedges. Wildlife habitats spring up as the near-automatic by-products of the boundaries and shady places required by cattle. This kind of farming has shaped the English landscape, ensuring that it retains its dual character as producer of human food and complex wildlife habitat, with a beauty that is inextricably connected to its multifarious life. In this way, what is, from the point of view of agribusiness, an extremely wasteful use of land, becomes, from the point of view of the rest of us—both human and animal—one of the kindest uses of land yet devised.

I have abbreviated the story. But it could be expanded into a full vindication of livestock farming, as conferring benefits on all those, the animals included, who are part of it. When animals raised for their meat are properly looked after, when all duties of care are fulfilled, and when the demands of sympathy and piety are respected, the practice cannot be criticized except from a premise—the premise of animal rights—which I believe to be incoherent. So where is the moral fault?

This question returns me to the remarks from which I began. The real force of the vegetarian argument stems, I believe, from a revulsion at the eating of meat, and at the meat eating character. And it is entirely true that the indifference of modern carnivores to the methods used to reduce the cost of their habit is a morally repulsive characteristic against which it is wholly natural to rebel. The repulsiveness is enhanced by the solipsistic fast-food culture, and by the removal of food from its central place in domestic life and in the winning of friends. From Homer to Zola meat has been described as the focus of hospitality, the primordial gift to the stranger, the eruption into the world of human conflict of the divine spirit of peace. Take all that away, reduce meat to an object of solitary greed like chocolate, and the question naturally arises: why should life be sacrificed, just for this?

As I indicated, this question has a religious dimension. From the point of view of morality, it has a clear and rational answer: namely, that the life that is sacrificed would not exist, but for the sacrifice. A great number of animals owe their lives to our intention to eat them. If we value animal life, therefore, we should endorse our carnivorous habits, provided it really is life, and not living death, on which those habits feed. From the point of view of religion, however, the question presents a challenge. It is asking the burger-stuffer to come clean; to show just why it is that his greed should be indulged in this way, and just where he fits into the scheme of things, that he can presume to kill again and again for the sake of a solitary pleasure that creates and sustains no moral ties. To such a question it is always possible to respond with a shrug of the shoulders. But it is a real question, one of many that people now ask, as the old forms of piety dwindle. Piety is the remedy for religious guilt, and to this emotion we are all witting or unwitting heirs. And I suspect that people become vegetarians for precisely that reason: that by doing so they overcome the residue of guilt that attaches to every form of hubris, and in particular to the hubris of human freedom.

I believe, however, that there is another remedy, and one more in keeping with the Judeo-Christian tradition. It is, in effect, the remedy suggested by Kass: not to abandon our meat eating habits, but to remoralize them, by incorporating them into loving human relations, and using them in the true Homeric manner, as instruments of hospitality, conviviality, and peace. That was the remedy practiced by our parents, with their traditional "Sunday roast" coming always at midday, after they had given thanks. (That is the real meaning of Bishop Dolan's wholly innocent reference to "meat-and-potato Catholics"—in other words, Catholics with a genuine home life.) The lifestyle associated with the Sunday roast involves sacrifices that those brought up on fast food are largely incapable of making—meal times, manners, dinner-table conversation, and the art of cookery itself. But all those things form part of a complex human good, and I cannot help thinking that, when added to the ecological benefits of small-scale livestock farming, they secure for us an honorable place in the scheme of things, and neutralize more effectively than the vegetarian alternative, our inherited burden of guilt.

NOTES

1. See Richard John Neuhaus, "Seeking a Better Way," *First Things* 126 (October 2002): 100.

2. Leon Kass, *The Hungry Soul: Eating and the Perfection of Our Nature* (Chicago: University of Chicago Press, 1999).

3. Roger Scruton, *Animal Rights and Wrongs,* 3d ed. (London: Metro Books and Demos, 2000 [now available from Continuum]).

4. See Loren Lomasky, *Persons, Rights, and the Moral Community* (Oxford: Oxford University Press, 1987).

5. See Mary Midgley, "Gene Juggling," *Philosophy* 54, no. 210 (1979): 439–58, and David Stove, "'He ain't heavy; he's my brother': Altruism and Shared Genes," in his *Darwinian Fairy-Tales* (Bowling Green, OH: Avebury Books, 1996).

6. In the recent debate in Britain over hunting with hounds, one of the most curious arguments used by those opposed to the practice is that hounds become useless for hunting in their fifth or sixth year, when they are habitually shot, even though—had they been kept as pets—they might have enjoyed four or more years of life thereafter.

7 THE RIGHT NOT TO BE EATEN

Evelyn B. Pluhar

"**I** do not care what happens to a cow!" Why on earth, wondered the exasperated writer whose letter to the editor in *Vegetarian Times* caught my eye several years ago, should the magazine "waste" so much ink on factory farm abuses?[1] Surely, he testily observed, the only legitimate reason for becoming a vegetarian is concern for one's health. Concern for the cows, pigs, chickens, turkeys, ducks, and other creatures whose flesh humans prize, is, according to that particular vegetarian, plainly misplaced. There are sound *human-centered* reasons for considering a vegetarian diet: why also promote vegetarianism for the sake of "food animals"?

Vegetarianism does indeed promote human interests, from the perspective of the individual and of the human population as a whole. Mainstream nutritionists affirm that appropriately planned vegetarian diets, from lacto-ovo to vegan diets, are beneficial for health and longevity and appropriate for all stages of life, including pregnancy and breast-feeding.[2] The overall ecological benefits of vegetarianism are also well documented, as are its implications for the alleviation of world hunger and starvation. A typical U.S. omnivore needs 3.5 acres of cropland per year to sustain himself or herself. An ovo-lacto vegetarian needs 1/2 an acre, while a vegan needs 1/6 of an acre. The land needed to feed one average omnivore would feed twenty-one vegans.[3] There is an urgent need for more food as our population climbs upward from the 6 billion mark. Every five to ten days, hunger kills as many people as the atomic bomb dropped on Hiroshima.[4] Although political factors certainly play a role in this tragedy, current total food production is also inadequate. It is no simple matter to increase food production levels: genetically engineered high-yield crops, for example, are too expensive for most of the world's subsistence farmers to afford and contribute to the loss of genetic diversity, a loss that imperils future food production. Theoretically, of course, such problems could be solved. We humans could greatly reduce our total numbers on the earth (through birth control rather than starvation and epidemics, one hopes) and we could literally eat less high on the hog, greatly decreasing the strain on water and soil. Very moderate meat consumption, given a considerably lower human population, would be compatible with health and ecological sustainability. Until we are blessed with such a prospect, vegetarianism is in the interests of humans, with two exceptions: the ones who live in areas where complete vegetarianism is not a feasible option and the ones who profit financially from the food production industry (more discussion of these exceptions is to come).

Let us return to the letter writer's challenge. Why should we consider any interests other than human interests? What about the nonhumans whom so many members of our species relish? I will argue that we have the strongest of reasons to weigh their interests along with our own: respect for the basic moral rights possessed by all beings who can care about what experiences befall them. After making the case for broad-based ethical vegetarianism, I will address objections from prominent animal rights critics.

WHY WE SHOULD CARE ABOUT WHAT HAPPENS TO A COW (AND OUR OTHER COUSINS)

A moral right is a justified claim against moral agents by or on behalf of a morally significant being. As far as we can tell, humans are the only beings on this planet who are moral agents (i.e., capable of understanding and acting upon moral principles). Rights claims, then, are addressed to us: we are obligated to treat and to refrain from treating morally significant beings in certain ways. If nonhumans have moral rights, it follows that they are morally significant beings; however, it does not follow that they would have the same rights as any given human being. *Nonbasic moral rights,* such as the right to an education and to fairness in the workplace, are held only by those beings with the capacity to exercise those rights. Individual humans may and do have widely different nonbasic rights. If any nonhumans have moral rights, the same would hold for them, in relation to each other as well as to human beings. Thus, beings who are equally morally significant (e.g., a small child and a typical adult) may not have the same non-basic moral rights. They do share the same *basic rights*, however, such as a right to life and a right not to be tortured. Any such rights, of course, are prima facie (i.e., not absolute). Moral agents can justifiably kill or hurt morally significant beings in self-defense and possibly other circumstances as well (e.g., if it is the "moral patient's" rational wish and in her or his best interests). The question then is: do any nonhuman animals have a prima facie right to life and a prima facie right not to suffer at human hands? If so, vegetarianism would be an ethical obligation for every moral agent in a position to practice it.

Tom Regan, the founder of the contemporary philosophical animal rights movement, has argued extensively and strongly for the rights position.[5] His critics, including some within the movement itself, have expressed reservations about the ultimate justification of the case he has made. It is beyond the scope of this paper to address those criticisms.[6] Instead, I offer an alternative justification for the rights view. The argument that follows takes its inspiration from Alan Gewirth,[7] though it goes considerably beyond the scope of his initial argument, and he would not agree with that argument's extension to nonhuman animals.

The rights argument pertains to any being who is capable of acting to achieve goals; that is, to any agent. As an agent, one has basic interests in and desires for life, health, and general well-being. Because one wants and needs these things, one also thinks that others should at the very least not interfere with one's attempts to get them; that is, one holds that others must not interfere. This is tantamount to one's claiming the right to non-interference in these regards. What justifies one's insistence is the fact that, as an agent, one cannot live and thrive unless these desires can be fulfilled. But if this is what justifies one's insistence, then consistency requires one to respect others' pursuit of their goals, for they, too, cannot otherwise live and thrive! Thus, the argument goes, all agents should be accorded basic moral rights. Any agent who is mentally advanced enough to claim rights and then realize their universality perforce becomes a *moral* agent, however immorally he or she might go on to behave. Psychological and ethological research supports the contention that numerous humans *and* nonhumans are agents, even though they are not all capable of the abstract conceptual thought required for actually claiming rights and becoming moral agents. Now, what about humans and nonhumans who have desires and needs as agents do but are unable to fulfill their desires on their own? Individuals who are too young or too physically or mentally impaired to be agents still have desires and needs that they want to have satisfied (e.g., for food, water, warmth, shelter, and love). The fact that they cannot achieve these goals on their own does not mean that they have no rights; it means that they need more assistance than noninterference. Babies, children, many accident victims, and the severely mentally disabled are sentient (they have the capacity to have experiences, including pain experiences), but they are not agents. So are some very young and relatively simple nonhuman animals. If reflective agents must, to be consistent, accord rights to others who have desires they want to have fulfilled, all sentient nonagents who have desires should likewise have rights accorded to them. All, from the reflective agent to the tiny baby, are able to care about what happens to them in the next moment.[8] It follows that, other things being equal, moral agents should not regard any of them as entrées or side dishes.

WHAT COULD BE WRONG WITH THE HUMANE RAISING AND SLAUGHTER OF "FOOD *ANIMALS*"?

Ethical vegetarianism based on the rights view sketched above is incompatible with the view that there can be nothing objectionable about humane meat production. One can rejoice in any significant reduction of cruelty to sentient beings, but simply eliminating that cruelty is not sufficient. Suppose that the leading factory-farming nation in the world, the United States, were to follow the current path of the European Union (EU) and phase out the most distressing practices. The EU has agreed to the complete banning of veal crates by 2007 and battery hen cages by 2012; the tethering and lengthy crating of pregnant sows is to be phased out by 2013.[9] Were we to follow their lead, in time all our cattle would graze, our pigs would be untethered, and their shelters would contain straw and adequate space. Chickens would be released from their cramped cages into roomy shelters with roosts, and allowed to enjoy the life a chicken has evolved to enjoy. Slaughter would inflict minimal terror and pain. Unquestionably, the animals raised and killed for their body parts would have better lives and deaths than is their lot now, but it does not follow that turning them into main courses would then be morally justified. After all, few of us would endorse treating members of our own species in such "humane" ways. All of us, regardless of our intelligence levels, are capable of caring about what is happening to us. We struggle against slaughter; we do not consent to being made "sacrificial animals." Small children protest against attack, even if they cannot use words. So do the fish drowning in air and the chicken being garroted. Even if we are killed unknowingly and painlessly in our sleep, we have lost what life would have otherwise brought to us. Arguments one often hears when nonhumans are under discussion—"But they wouldn't have existed if we hadn't bred them for this purpose"; "their lives in the wild would be far more dangerous and unpleasant"—lose appeal if we apply them to human flesh farms or to Swiftian[10] solutions to the problems of the homeless. Even the kindliest of keepers and butchers would have much to answer for if human rump roasts were featured menu items. Care for some yummy milk-fed biped, anyone?

If humans deserve to be treated respectfully regardless of their intellectual prowess, so do many nonhumans, regardless of how tasty they may be to us. Moral agents are obligated to be consistent and fair in their actions. (Small children, mentally limited humans, dogs, cats, tigers, and so on, are by contrast not morally responsible for what they do.) When we vividly reflect on the matter, emotions are in tune with obligations. If we try to imagine what it is like to be a sacrificial animal (including a sacrificial human animal), we are far less inclined to create one, particularly when we are motivated merely by a matter of taste. Any beings who are capable of caring about what happens to them, who can prefer one outcome to another, have lives that are not morally reducible to others' pleasure. We can care about them because *they* can care: they have a stake in what each future moment brings, just as we do. You do not have to be proficient at calculus or poetry to have a life that matters to *you*.

CAN AN ETHICAL VEGETARIAN CONSUME EGGS AND DAIRY PRODUCTS?

The rights position I have argued for does not rule out all farming involving nonhuman animals. There can be no moral objection to mutually beneficial, ecologically responsible human-nonhuman relationships. Milk and eggs can be exchanged for shelter, food, and care. I know a number of people living on "no kill" farms who treat their chickens, cows, and goats with respect and warmth. These farms bear no resemblance to large, "efficient" operations where nonhumans are regarded as living milk faucets or egg factories. Such farms are not utterly unlike some third-world agricultural units in largely lacto-vegetarian countries like India. Dairy products or eggs are generally not necessary for human health, but in some areas where other food sources are unavailable they may be a vital part of the diet. In other areas such products are desired but not needed. Chickens and cows would not be wronged by respectful farming,[11] though care must be taken not to overtax planetary resources. By the same token, these animals would not be wronged if their bodies were to be eaten after they had died natural deaths. The same holds, need I add, for dead humans! In practice, though, I suspect that, barring an emergency, few of us could stomach eating the bodies of individuals whom we have cared for or perceived as highly morally significant. I could no more barbecue Lancelot the pig (my "adoptee" on a no-kill farm) than I could roast my dear dead Granny. (Perhaps this is a cultural bias. I can imagine funeral rituals in which eating the bodies of the dead—human or otherwise!—would be a loving and respectful act. It might not be a very healthy practice, however!)

CAN NONHUMAN ANIMALS REALLY CARE ABOUT WHAT HAPPENS TO THEM?

Defenders of the meat production industry, as well as those vegetarians whose diets are motivated solely by concerns for their own health, have several objections to rights-based ethical vegetarianism. First, many of them claim that we have no evidence that so-called food animals are capable of caring about what befalls them. They accuse vegetarians like myself of anthropomorphism when we attribute preferences to nonhumans. Some of them go so far as to say that nonhumans are not even *conscious* (i.e., that they lack sentience), thus following in the intellectual footsteps of René Descartes.[12] Others deny that nonhumans can be *self*-conscious, claiming that the capacity to care about yourself presupposes some kind of awareness of self. I have elaborately refuted the equally elaborate neo-Cartesian arguments of the first camp elsewhere, so I will not repeat those fatal objections here.[13] Philosophers and scientists who deny that nonhumans can be *self*-conscious hold that the intellectual sophistication allegedly required for such a capacity is beyond nonhumans' ken. Of course, sophisticated mental operations would also be beyond the ken of quite a few humans. Nonetheless, preverbal children and mentally limited but sentient humans, despite their intellectual "shortcomings," give every indication of caring about what happens to them—as do cows, chickens, dogs, fish, etc. If one insists on such a high standard for self-consciousness, then the claim that preferences would be impossible without self-consciousness is extremely implausible.

Alternatively, if one holds that a less sophisticated sense of self would be sufficient for having preferences, there is every reason to believe that many nonhumans *and* mentally undeveloped or limited humans do have such a sense. They give no indication of confusing themselves with other objects or humans: they appear to know quite well that *they* are hungry or in pain. Moreover, *learning*, as opposed to mechanically responding to a stimulus, seems to require some sense of self, some central core to which memories and motivations can be referred. Few people seriously deny that nonhuman animals and very young humans can learn.[14] Now, one cannot learn from disconnected sensations: these must be unified into experiences—coherent units—that one can remember and anticipate. Bernard Rollin has argued that having experiences, as opposed to being buffeted by an onslaught of discrete sensations, is conditional upon one's synthesis of sensory input, and that this synthesis is in turn conditional upon awareness of oneself, however primitive that awareness might be:

> What this means is that in order for a being to have unified experience of objects in relations, it must be the same consciousness which experiences the beginning of an event as the end, or the top of an object and its bottom. In other words, if it were not the same you that viewed the top of a tall building as the bottom and the middle, there could be no experience of "the tall building." But this same point must hold true for animals too; they must be able to realize that an event is happening to them in order to learn from it.[15]

Anyone who denies that nonhumans can be conscious or self-conscious has some serious explaining to do. On their view, how are we to construe complex, flexible, apparently creative behavior by nonhumans? To date, they have offered no plausible explanations of this behavior.[16] We are no more justified in claiming that a veal calf cannot mind what is happening to him in his two-foot-wide crate than we would be in holding that a child kept chained in a closet is too mentally undeveloped to be bothered by her imprisonment.

WHAT ABOUT INVERTEBRATES?

In all fairness, however, it must be acknowledged that some nonhuman animals may well lack the neurophysiological complexity necessary for sentience. Is a scallop capable of feeling pain? What about its fellow mollusks: oysters, clams, and mussels? If they are sentient, then this is very far from obvious. On the other hand, octopuses, who are also mollusks, at least appear to be sentient. Perhaps they are lifted into the sentience sphere by their much greater physical complexity. Then again, might their simpler cousins have primitive ways of registering pleasant and unpleasant sensations? It is true that our understanding of pain and pleasure mechanisms is based on neurophysiological structures in vertebrates; nevertheless, in some *in*vertebrates, analgesia and anesthesia control what looks like pain behavior. Moreover, earthworms produce endorphins, the hormone associated with pleasure and pain regulation in humans.[17] In view of these facts, along with our considerable remaining ignorance about these difficult matters, we are morally safer if we treat such beings as sentient. Most of us can have healthful diets without resorting to meals of mollusks or other invertebrates; if it is possible that they are sentient, why take the chance of causing additional pain and death? They stand to lose a great deal more than we would gain. Humans who are not so lucky as we are, who live in areas where food supplies are limited, are in a different position. If invertebrates are available, these humans may have to eat them to avoid malnutrition.[18]

Now consider another question that is at least as hard to answer as the question of sentience. We think it is wrong to simply use other individuals, human or nonhuman, when those individuals are capable of caring about their own lives. Suppose we set aside the issue of whether invertebrates are capable of feeling anything: let us give them the benefit of the doubt, as I suggested above. Are we genuinely entitled to make the additional assumption that they can *care* about what is happening to them? Beings who can be aware of tissue damage but cannot be bothered by that damage, now or in the future, are not obviously wronged by being torn apart; if they are incapable of ever caring about living or not living, they are not obviously wronged by death. Can we know that these simpler animals are the sorts of beings who are capable of being wronged?

A few things can be said here. Many invertebrates, as well as vertebrates, *behave* as if they prefer not to have tissue damage or to lose their lives, though we cannot be sure that they have such preferences. They undeniably lack the neurological structures required for the affective behavior displayed by humans, structures we share with other mammals and partially share with all other vertebrates. Nonetheless, those invertebrates may have analogous structures. Evolutionary theory suggests that the existence of such structures would have considerable survival value. Beings motivated to stay alive are well served when they recoil from situations that we find painful; struggling to escape a killer also has obvious advantages. Once again, in view of the high stakes involved, we are morally justified in extending the benefit of the doubt to those invertebrates.

The Unfounded Charge of Misanthropy

Let us now consider the objection that the detractors of ethical vegetarianism and "animal rights" views in general raise most often. One sees it in the popular press and in the works of very well credentialed scientists and philosophers. Those detractors charge that people who refuse to use products resulting from the exploitation of nonhuman animals suffer from a lack of proportion: the legitimate interests of human beings who produce, market, and enjoy such products are being subordinated to a misplaced concern for nonhumans. In the critics' view, we ought to "put people first": if we do not, we must clearly value nonhumans more highly than humans. In short, ethical vegetarians are dismissed as misguided misanthropes.

A good example of this objection is provided by philosopher Peter Carruthers, one of those neo-Cartesians who denies that nonhuman animals are even conscious. Carruthers has argued that *even if nonhumans are capable of suffering,* it is nonetheless morally objectionable to go against the interests of humans who gain from activities that cause pain to nonhumans. He defends factory farming and the testing of cosmetics on sentient beings, even if the products—chicken McNuggets or a new brand of mascara—satisfy relatively trivial preferences. After all, he points out, humans make their livings and generate profits from such industries: these legitimate interests should not be harmed.[19] He attacks not only "animal liberation" efforts but also any concern for "animal welfare," on the grounds that even moderate concern (e.g., working for the humane slaughter of all "food animals") is "an irrelevance to be opposed rather than encouraged."[20] Throughout his book, *The Animals Issue*, Carruthers dismisses people who persist in having such concerns as "animal lovers." As we all know, this phrase as commonly used has at best a patronizing ring. One cannot help being reminded of other "_____-lover" epithets, also employed to sneer at alleged sentimental foolishness.

Those of us who think that nonhumans should not suffer and die to satisfy people's hankering for Big Macs or new shades of eye shadow respond that our point is not that nonhumans should be valued above humans. Vital interests in well-being and life, we say, should trump trivial interests, regardless of the species on either side of an issue. Salaries and profits do not sanctify enterprises that cause enormous suffering: we certainly do not excuse child pornographers who use and abuse live models by pointing out that these entrepreneurs have a legitimate interest in making money! Simple justice requires that we take the children's interests into account. Why, then, should we not take the interests of factory-farmed animals into account? (I do not suggest that people in the factory-farm business have the evil motives of child pornographers. Nor need these businesspeople suffer unduly if animal interests are finally taken seriously by consumers. Any changes away from intensive animal food production would be driven by choice and by market, and thus likely to be gradual. Everyone involved in the industry would face no more dislocation than anyone else involved in demand-driven business.) How is such a demand for fairness misanthropic? At this point, ethical vegetarians go on the offensive.

The Countercharge of Speciesism

The misanthropy charge is based on bigotry. If we have good reason to believe that nonhumans care about what happens to them, just as a small child, a mentally limited human, and a normal adult human care about what happens to them, what could warrant our dismissing their interests? Make no mistake about it: no one whose interests were taken seriously would be confined to a veal crate or a battery hen cage. Our willingness to ignore or trivialize the misery of nonhumans for the sake of gratifying our own less vital cravings is no more defensible than is bigotry aimed at other hapless humans. "Speciesism," to use the famous term coined by Richard Ryder and popularized by Peter Singer, is just as unjustified as racism, sexism, heterosexism, and all their odiferous cousins. Singer explicitly fastens on the comparison:

> Racists violate the principle of equality by giving greater weight to the interests of members of their own race when there is a clash between their interests and the interests of those of another race. Sexists violate the principle of equality by favoring the interests of their own sex. Similarly, speciesists allow the interests of their own species to override the greater interests of members of other species. The pattern is identical in each case.[21]

It is no accident that Singer chose the phrase "animal liberation" to describe the movement he first endorsed in the 1970s, in the days when "women's liberation" and "black liberation" were rallying cries. Since then, Carol Adams has argued that we have more than a parallel here: she sees a direct link between sexual and racial violence and the butchering of non-human animals.[22] The blind arrogance that results in *all* of this carnage against our fellow planet-dwellers is at issue. Far from being misanthropic, ethical vegetarians hold that "animal liberation" *is* "human liberation."

The Misanthropy Charge Revisited: Does Animal Liberation Trivialize Human Liberation?

Opponents of ethical vegetarianism pour scorn on all such comparisons. Philosophers Leslie Francis and Richard Norman were among the first to charge that talk of "speciesism" and "animal liberation" is highly insulting to racial minorities and victims of sexual discrimination. They believe that argumentation such as this "trivializes" the "real" movements for dignity and rights:

> Liberation movements have a character and a degree of moral importance which cannot be possessed by a movement to prevent cruelty to animals.[23]

Political philosopher Carl Cohen agrees with their assessment, emphatically rejecting the argument that speciesism is no more justified than racism and sexism:

> This argument is worse than unsound; it is atrocious. It draws an offensive moral conclusion [i.e., that speciesism is as objectionable as racism and sexism] from a deliberately devised verbal parallelism that is utterly specious.[24]

Why "utterly specious?" Cohen explains that bigotry directed at humans is morally objectionable because it finds differences where there are no *morally relevant* differences. Humans have basic moral rights arising from their status as moral agents (i.e., as individuals capable of understanding and acting upon moral precepts). Nonhumans, however, are not moral agents, so they plainly lack moral standing. (Francis and Norman make the same presumption, although they prefer to emphasize the rich mutual relationships that moral agents can engage in as members of a moral community. They hold that the interests of beings with whom it is not possible to have such communication cannot be as morally significant as the interests of moral agents.)

Anyone who does not already agree with the view that rights are restricted to moral agents will find no argument whatsoever in the remainder of Cohen's article to convince them of the "atrocious" error of their ways. The only support he offers for his position is the contention that other famous philosophers—Saints Augustine and Aquinas, Hegel, F. H. Bradley, H. A. Pritchard, and Kant—also believed it to be true.[25] This appeal to authority is not compelling, since the views of the above philosophers, eminent as they are, are far from sacrosanct. The moral agency view of rights is presupposed by them rather than defended.

Peter Carruthers also takes Cohen's view. Let us now return to him for a defense of both it and his contention that even trivial human interests trump vital nonhuman interests. He rejects ethical theories that would accord moral significance to nonhumans and opts instead for a version of the moral theory of "contractualism." According to that version, moral significance is restricted to highly autonomous moral agents who establish moral rules by mutual consent. As far as we know, no nonhuman animals would qualify for such exalted status. (Neither, obviously, would a great number of humans. Carruthers attempts to show that in a morally acceptable society, very young and mentally limited humans would nevertheless not be treated as other animals are now treated, even though those humans would have no inherent moral standing. However, Carruthers is quite unsuccessful in trying to avoid the unpalatable implications for the treatment of these vulnerable humans.)[26] Thus, it would follow from Carruthers' contractualism that, as he puts it, since nonhuman animals have "no moral standing . . . [t]here is therefore nothing *to* be weighed against the claims of a human being."[27]

Now, why should we accept Carruthers's contractualism? He tells us why: contractualism, unlike Peter Singer's "equal consideration of interests" view, coheres with our allegedly "deeply imbedded" and "common sense" belief that "[it is] intuitively abhorrent that the lives or sufferings of animals should be weighed against the lives or sufferings of human beings."[28] Contractualism is deemed to be "the most acceptable moral theory," then, primarily because it implies that this supposed belief is correct. Nonhuman animal interests are of no importance in comparison to human interests because, he goes on to say, this follows from contractualism, "the most acceptable framework for a moral theory."[29] So, we are to accept the position that nonhuman animal interests do not count in comparison to human interests because it follows from "the most acceptable moral theory," and we are to find that theory the most morally acceptable because it coheres with the position that nonhuman animal interests do not count in comparison to human interests! As Steve Sapontzis has observed, we have here an example of "one of the tidiest circular arguments in the history of philosophy."[30]

Carruthers and Cohen are not alone in failing to establish the moral agency view of moral significance. But as of yet, no one has *shown* that this is the source of moral significance.[31] It is easy to see why only moral agents can be held morally accountable for their actions, since they, by definition, are the only beings who can comprehend and apply moral principles. Clearly, however, it does not follow from this that moral agents are the only morally significant beings. Being able to *recognize* moral significance is sufficient but not obviously necessary for *having* moral significance. Moreover, this view, if consistently followed, would morally disenfranchise legions of humans who cannot achieve moral agency.[32] Nothing would rule out their being vivisected or served as appetizers along with the bacon bits and goose liver. So much for speciesism!

A Personal Conclusion

A 1993 report broadcast by National Public Radio's "Morning Edition" gives us an arresting example of the blindness of speciesism.[33] In the small town of Olney, Texas, some hunters meet every year to participate in "The One-Armed Dove Hunt." People with missing hands or arms promote "amputee pride" by competing to shoot the largest number of mourning doves. Most competitors have lost their limbs in combat or by accident. Deprived of their (fleshly) arms by violence as many of them have been, these hunters seek to promote their self-esteem by blasting small birds to smithereens. (There is also a skeet-shooting contest, but it draws considerably less interest.) These events are followed by a massive barbecue for two hundred featuring yet more dismembered bodies. One of the participants opined that no one who had not been hurt as he had been could really understand what it's like: "There ain't nobody who's got two arms that, you know, can say, 'I know how you feel.' They don't know how you feel."[34] It very evidently has never occurred to this hunter to wonder about how a "winged" dove must feel. I am struck by another remark made by an amputee hunter: "Only time you want to cry is when you lose somebody, a good dog or a good wife, or one of your children. That's the only time a man should cry."[35] When sorrow is restricted to the loss of a loved one, including the occasional bird dog, emotional amputeeism flourishes. Alas, there is a lot to cry about in this story.

I hasten to add that I feel no scorn for the hunters of Olney. For most of my life, I was just as selective in my moral concern. I cannot remember a time when I did not share my life with a dog or a cat, loving each one of them dearly, but I gave little heed to other animals. My father, one of the most wonderful, compassionate men I have ever known, was an enthusiastic bird hunter and fisherman. Our home in Appalachian Kentucky was decorated with stuffed animal bodies, all of which I took for granted. Our bellies were filled with all manner of nonhuman animal parts, and we loved it: As a child, I even ate brains and tongue, knowing full well what they were—without a pang. My attitudes were thoroughly inconsistent. For example, I refused to hunt, but I ate the results; I recoiled from fishing after my one "success" at age six—I still remember how the hook pierced the worm (thank goodness, my grandmother did it for me) and how the small fish struggled—but I ate fish for years, including that pathetic victim of my youthful efforts, "Evelyn's fish." I ate chicken too, even though I once saw my grandmother wring the neck off her old layer for Sunday dinner. Somehow I was able to disassociate the living, suffering animal from the table centerpiece and the living-room wall. If anyone had tried to barbecue my beagles, though, I am sure I would have been guilty of attempted murder!

It took me years to realize that my attitudes were contradictory and my participation in nonhuman suffering and death indefensible. Philosophical reflection played an important part in this: I learned enormously much from the early supporters of moral significance for nonhuman animals, especially Tom Regan and Peter Singer. I learned a great deal from their critics, too. I honestly could not find any way to justify the continued exploitation of sentient beings. If it was wrong to discriminate on the basis of race, gender, sexual orientation, and age, as clearly it was, then there could also be no way to justify discrimination merely on the basis of species. The most important factor in my change of heart and mind, however, was my willingness, however reluctant and horrified, to imagine what it must be like to be skewered, shot, crammed in a cage with six other hens, imprisoned in a two-foot-wide crate in the dark for all of my short life, burned, shocked, force-fed, and hung by my feet fully conscious until the mechanical knife slit my throat. Once I saw the victims of these practices as living, suffering centers of consciousness, I realized that making meals of them, regardless of how "humane" our methods are, is morally unacceptable.

Once more of us humans perceive the supermarket meat section as their morgue; veal parmesan as tortured calf parmesan; Thanksgiving turkeys as decapitated, eviscerated bodies; and "baked funeral meats" as themselves in need of a funeral, we will be a lesser blight on the denizens of our planet. We might also find it a little easier to look at ourselves in the mirror.

NOTES

1. Richard McGinnis, "Letter to the Editor," *Vegetarian Times* (August 1993): 8.

2. American Dietetic Association (ADA), "Vegetarian Diets: Position of the ADA," *Journal of the American Dietetic Association* 97, no. 11 (1997): 1317–21. See also American Dietetic Association and Dieticians of Canada (ADA and DC), *Manual of Clinical Dietetics*, 6th ed. (Chicago, IL: American Dietetic Association, 2000). Kathryn P. George has argued otherwise in several articles and a recent book, *Animal, Vegetable, or Woman? A Feminist Critique of Ethical Vegetarianism* (New York: State University of New York Press, 2000). Her empirical claims and arguments have been refuted by several philosophers and not a few feminists, including myself. See, e.g., Evelyn Pluhar, "Vegetarianism, Morality, and Science Revisited," *Journal of Agricultural and Environmental Ethics* 7, no. 1 (1994): 77–82; Greta Gaard and Lori Gruen, "Comment on George's 'Should Feminists Be Vegetarians?'" *Signs: Journal of Women in Culture and Society* 21, no. 1 (1995): 230–41; and David Boonin, review of *Animal, Vegetable, or Woman?* by Kathryn P. George, *Environmental Ethics* 24, no. 4 (2002): 429–32.

3. Gary Francione, *Introduction to Animal Rights: Your Child or the Dog?* (Philadelphia: Temple University Press, 2000), p. 15. See also John Robbins, *The Food Revolution: How Your Diet Can Help Save Your Life and the World* (Berkeley, CA: Conari Press, 2001).

4. G. T. Miller, *Living in the Environment: Principles, Connections, and Solutions,* 8th ed. (Belmont, CA: Wadsworth, 1994), p. 367.

5. Tom Regan, *The Case for Animal Rights* (Berkeley: University of California Press, 1983).

6. See Evelyn Pluhar, *Beyond Prejudice: The Moral Significance of Human and Nonhuman Animals* (Durham, NC: Duke University Press, 1995), pp. 231 ff. for a full discussion of my own and others' questions about Regan's arguments.

7. Alan Gewirth, *Reason and Morality* (Chicago, IL: University of Chicago Press, 1978).

8. For a full discussion and elaborate defense of this line of argument, see Pluhar, *Beyond Prejudice,* chap 5.

9. Peter Stevenson, "Fighting Factory Farming: The European Experience," *Farm Sanctuary News* (Winter 2000): 1–5. The United Kingdom and Sweden have already abolished some of these practices.

10. See Jonathan Swift's brilliantly savage satire, "A Modest Proposal for Preventing the Children of Poor People from Being a Burthen to their Parents or Country, and for Making Them Beneficial to the Publick," reprinted in *Animal Rights*

and Human Obligations, ed. Tom Regan and Peter Singer (Englewood Cliffs, NJ: Prentice Hall, 1976), pp. 234–37.

11. Gary Varner has argued that, given the standards of Western "efficiency," it is not possible to provide milk (and eggs) for large-scale commercial consumption without causing extra deaths to the nonhumans. However, he holds that it might be possible to avoid such killing if small-scale sustainable agriculture is practiced. See his "What's Wrong with Animal Byproducts?" *Journal of Agricultural and Environmental Ethics* 7, no. 1 (1994): 7–17.

12. See Peter Carruthers, "Brute Experience," *Journal of Philosophy* 86 (1989): 258–69, and Peter Harrison, "Theodicy and Animal Pain," *Philosophy* 64, no. 247 (1989): 79–92.

13. See Pluhar, *Beyond Prejudice*, pp. 12–46.

14. For scientific evidence of nonhuman animal learning, see, e.g., Donald Griffin, *Animal Minds* (Chicago, IL: University of Chicago Press, 1992). Stephen Clark's *The Nature of the Beast* (Oxford: Oxford University Press, 1982) is also very illuminating on this topic.

15. Bernard Rollin, *The Unheeded Cry: Animal Consciousness, Animal Pain, and Science* (Oxford: Oxford University Press, 1989), p. 140. (For more discussion of Rollin's and others' arguments concerning self-consciousness, see Pluhar, *Beyond Prejudice*, chap. 1.)

16. See Rollin, *The Unheeded Cry*, for a carefully documented account of behaviorists' failure to provide any reasonable explanation of nonhuman (or human!) animal behavior.

17. Ibid., p. 154.

18. For extended discussion of conflicts between the lives of humans and other animals, and how such conflicts might be resolved ethically, see Pluhar, *Beyond Prejudice*, chap. 5. For a related discussion, see Paul Taylor, *Respect for Nature* (Princeton, NJ: Princeton University Press, 1986), chap. 6.

19. Peter Carruthers, *The Animals Issue* (Cambridge: Cambridge University Press, 1992), pp. 160, 166.

20. Ibid., p. 168.

21. Peter Singer, *Animal Liberation*, 2nd ed. (New York: Random House, 1990), p. 9.

22. Carol J. Adams, *The Sexual Politics of Meat* (New York: Continuum, 1990).

23. Leslie Francis and Richard Norman, "Some Animals Are More Equal Than Others," *Philosophy* 53 (1978): 527. Unlike Carruthers, however, the authors oppose cruelties inflicted by factory farming, although they deny that nonhumans can have a right to life (also on p. 527).

24. Carl Cohen, "The Case for the Use of Animals in Biomedical Research," *New England Journal of Medicine* 315, no. 14 (October 2, 1986): 867.

25. Ibid., pp. 865–66.

26. See Carruthers, *The Animals Issue*, pp. 114–21, 163–65. (See Pluhar, *Beyond Prejudice*, chap. 2, for the refutation.)

27. Ibid., pp. 156–57.

28. Ibid., p. 195.

29. Ibid., p. 196.

30. Steve Sapontzis, review of *The Animals Issue,* by Peter Carruthers, *Canadian Philosophical Review* 13, no. 4 (1993): 140–42.

31. See, for example, Regan, *The Case for Animal Rights*, chap. 5, for detailed examinations and refutations of the claims and arguments made by highly restrictive rights theorists. See also Pluhar, *Beyond Prejudice*, chaps. 2, 5.

32. Various attempts have been made to argue that so-called marginal humans should or would still be protected: e.g., on grounds of benevolence, fairness, potential, kinship, emotions. Not one of these attempts succeeds. See Pluhar, *Beyond Prejudice*, chap. 3.

33. "Olney, Texas Hosts One-Armed Dove Hunters," reported on *Morning Edition*, National Public Radio, September 28, 1993. My account is based on the transcript of that morning's program, pp. 14–16.

34. Ibid., p. 15.

35. Ibid., p. 16.

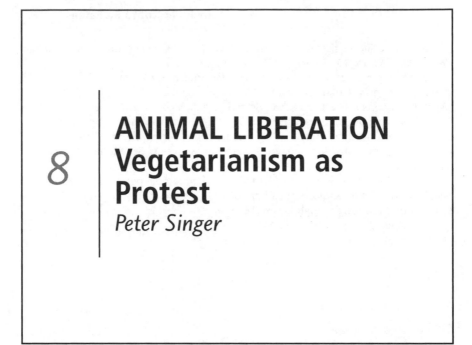

ANIMAL LIBERATION
Vegetarianism as Protest

Peter Singer

ALL ANIMALS ARE EQUAL

Jeremy Bentham, the founder of the reforming utilitarian school of moral philosophy, incorporated the essential basis of moral equality into his system of ethics by means of the formula: "Each to count for one and none for more than one." In other words, the interests of every being affected by an action are to be taken into account and given the same weight as the like interests of any other being. A later utilitarian, Henry Sidgwick, put the point in this way: "The good of any one individual is of no more importance, from the point of view (if I may say so) of the Universe, than the good of any other." More recently the leading figures in contemporary moral philosophy have shown a great deal of agreement in specifying as a fundamental presupposition of their moral theories some similar requirement that works to give everyone's interests equal consideration—although these writers generally cannot agree on how this requirement is best formulated.[1]

It is an implication of this principle of equality that our concern for

This essay is drawn from chaps. 1, 3, and 4 of Singer's *Animal Liberation*, 2d ed. (New York: New York Review of Books, 1990).

others and our readiness to consider their interests ought not to depend on what they are like or on what abilities they may possess. Precisely what our concern or consideration requires us to do may vary according to the characteristics of those affected by what we do: concern for the well-being of children growing up in America would require that we teach them to read; concern for the well-being of pigs may require no more than that we leave them with other pigs in a place where there is adequate food and room to run freely. But the basic element—the taking into account of the interests of the being, whatever those interests may be—must, according to the principle of equality, be extended to all beings, black or white, masculine or feminine, human or nonhuman.

Thomas Jefferson, who was responsible for writing the principle of the equality of men into the American Declaration of Independence, saw this point. It led him to oppose slavery even though he was unable to free himself fully from his slaveholding background. He wrote in a letter to the author of a book that emphasized the notable intellectual achievements of Negroes in order to refute the then common view that they had limited intellectual capacities:

> Be assured that no person living wishes more sincerely than I do, to see a complete refutation of the doubts I myself have entertained and expressed on the grade of understanding allotted to them by nature, and to find that they are on a par with ourselves . . . but whatever be their degree of talent it is no measure of their rights. Because Sir Isaac Newton was superior to others in understanding, he was not therefore lord of the property or persons of others.[2]

Similarly, when in the 1850s the call for women's rights was raised in the United States, a remarkable black feminist named Sojourner Truth made the same point in more robust terms at a feminist convention:

> They talk about this thing in the head; what do they call it? ["Intellect," whispered someone nearby.] That's it. What's that got to do with women's rights or Negroes' rights? If my cup won't hold but a pint and yours holds a quart, wouldn't you be mean not to let me have my little half-measure full?[3]

It is on this basis that the case against racism and the case against sexism must both ultimately rest; and it is in accordance with this principle that the attitude that we may call "speciesism," by analogy with racism, must also be condemned. Speciesism—the word is not an attractive one, but I can think of no better term—is a prejudice or attitude of bias in favor of the interests of members of one's own species and against those of members of other species. It should be obvious that the fundamental objections to racism and sexism made by Thomas Jefferson and Sojourner Truth apply equally to speciesism. If possessing a higher degree of intelligence does not entitle one human to use another for his or her own ends, how can it entitle humans to exploit nonhumans for the same purpose?[4]

Many philosophers and other writers have proposed the principle of equal consideration of interests, in some form or other, as a basic moral principle; but not many of them have recognized that this principle applies to members of other species as well as to our own. Jeremy Bentham was one of the few who did realize this. In a forward-looking passage written at a time when black slaves had been freed by the French but in the British dominions were still being treated in the way we now treat animals, Bentham wrote:

> The day may come when the rest of the animal creation may acquire those rights which never could have been withholden from them but by the hand of tyranny. The French have already discovered that the blackness of the skin is no reason why a human being should be abandoned without redress to the caprice of a tormentor. It may one day come to be recognized that the number of the legs, the villosity of the skin, or the termination of the os sacrum are reasons equally insufficient for abandoning a sensitive being to the same fate. What else is it that should trace the insuperable line? Is it the faculty of reason, or perhaps the faculty of discourse? But a full-grown horse or dog is beyond comparison a more rational, as well as a more conversable animal, than an infant of a day or a week or even a month, old. But suppose they were otherwise, what would it avail? The question is not, Can they reason? nor Can they talk? but, Can they suffer?[5]

In this passage Bentham points to the capacity for suffering as the vital characteristic that gives a being the right to equal consideration. The capacity for suffering—or more strictly, for suffering and/or enjoyment or happiness—is not just another characteristic like the capacity for language or higher mathematics. Bentham is not saying that those who try to mark "the insuperable line" that determines whether the interests of a being should be considered happen to have chosen the wrong characteristic. By saying that we must consider the interests of all beings with the capacity for suffering or enjoyment Bentham does not arbitrarily exclude from consideration any interests at all—as those who draw the line with reference to the possession of reason or language do. The capacity for suffering and enjoyment is a prerequisite for having interests at all, a condition that must be satisfied before we can speak of interests in a meaningful way. It would be nonsense to say that it was not in the interests of a stone to be kicked along the road by a schoolboy. A stone does not have interests because it cannot suffer. Nothing that we can do to it could possibly make any difference to its welfare. The capacity for suffering and enjoyment is, however, not only necessary, but also sufficient for us to say that a being has interests—at an absolute minimum, an interest in not suffering. A mouse, for example, does have an interest in not being kicked along the road, because it will suffer if it is.

If a being suffers there can be no moral justification for refusing to take that suffering into consideration. No matter what the nature of the being, the principle of equality requires that its suffering be counted equally with the like suffering—insofar as rough comparisons can be made—of any other being. If a being is not capable of suffering, or of experiencing enjoyment or happiness, there is nothing to be taken into account. So the limit of sentience (using the term as a convenient if not strictly accurate shorthand for the capacity to suffer and/or experience enjoyment) is the only defensible boundary of concern for the interests of others. To mark this boundary by some other characteristic like intelligence or rationality would be to mark it in an arbitrary manner. Why not choose some other characteristic, like skin color?

Racists violate the principle of equality by giving greater weight to the interests of members of their own race when there is a clash between their interests and the interests of those of another race. Sexists violate the principle of equality by favoring the interests of their own sex. Similarly, speciesists allow the interests of their own species to override the greater interests of members of other species. The pattern is identical in each case.

Down on the Factory Farm

For most human beings, especially those in modern urban and suburban communities, the most direct form of contact with nonhuman animals is at mealtime: we eat them. This simple fact is the key to our attitudes to other animals, and also the key to what each one of us can do about changing these attitudes. The use and abuse of animals raised for food far exceeds, in sheer numbers of animals affected, any other kind of mistreatment. Over 100 million cows, pigs, and sheep are raised and slaughtered in the United States alone each year; and for poultry the figure is a staggering 5 billion. (That means that about eight thousand birds—mostly chickens—will have been slaughtered in the time it takes you to read this page.) It is here, on our dinner table and in our neighborhood supermarket or butcher's shop, that we are brought into direct touch with the most extensive exploitation of other species that has ever existed.

In general, we are ignorant of the abuse of living creatures that lies behind the food we eat. Buying food in a store or restaurant is the culmination of a long process, of which all but the end product is delicately screened from our eyes. We buy our meat and poultry in neat plastic pack-ages. . . . Very few farms were ever as idyllic as the traditional image would have us believe. Yet we still think of a farm as a pleasant place, far removed from our own industrial, profit-conscious city life. . . . These comfortable assumptions bear little relation to the realities of modern farming. For a start, farming is no longer controlled by simple country folk. During the last fifty years, large corporations and assembly-line methods of produc-tion have turned agriculture into agribusiness.

The first animal to be removed from the relatively natural conditions of the traditional farm was the chicken. Human beings use chickens in two ways: for their flesh and for their eggs. There are now standard mass-pro-duction techniques for obtaining both of these products.

Promoters of agribusiness consider the rise of the chicken industry to be one of the great success stories of farming. At the end of World War II chicken for the table was still relatively rare. It came mainly from small independent farmers or from the unwanted males produced by egg-laying flocks. Today in the United States, 102 million broilers—as table chickens are called—are slaughtered each week after being reared in highly auto-mated factory-like plants that belong to the large corporations that control production. Eight of these corporations account for over 50 percent of the 5.3 billion birds killed annually in the United States.[6]

The essential step in turning chickens from farmyard birds into manu-factured items was confining them indoors. A producer of broilers gets a load of ten thousand, fifty thousand, or more day-old chicks from the hatcheries, and puts them into a long, windowless shed, usually on the floor, although some producers use tiers of cages in order to get more birds into the same size shed. Inside the shed, every aspect of the birds' environ-ment is controlled to make them grow faster on less feed. Food and water are fed automatically from hoppers suspended from the roof. The lighting is adjusted according to advice from agricultural researchers: for instance, there may be bright light twenty-four hours a day for the first week or two, to encourage the chicks to gain weight quickly; then the lights may be dimmed slightly and made to go off and on every two hours, in the belief that the chickens are readier to eat after a period of sleep; finally there comes a point, around six weeks of age, when the birds have grown so much that they are becoming crowded, and the lights will then be made very dim at all times. The point of this dim lighting is to reduce the aggres-sion caused by crowding.

Broiler chickens are killed when they are seven weeks old (the natural lifespan of a chicken is about seven years). At the end of this brief period, the birds weigh between four and five pounds; yet they still may have as little as half a square foot of space per chicken—or less than the area of a sheet of standard typing paper. (In metric terms, this is 450 square centimeters for a hen weighing more than two kilos.) Under these conditions, when there is normal lighting, the stress of crowding and the absence of natural outlets for the birds' energies lead to outbreaks of fighting, with birds pecking at each other's feathers and sometimes killing and eating one another. Very dim lighting has been found to reduce such behavior and so the birds are likely to live out their last weeks in near-darkness.

Of all the animals commonly eaten in the Western world, the pig is without doubt the most intelligent. The natural intelligence of a pig is comparable and perhaps even superior to that of a dog; it is possible to rear pigs as companions to human beings and train them to respond to simple commands much as a dog would. When George Orwell put the pigs in charge in *Animal Farm*, his choice was defensible on scientific as well as literary grounds.

The high intelligence of pigs must be borne in mind when we consider whether the conditions in which they are reared are satisfactory. While any sentient being, intelligent or not, should be given equal consideration, animals of different capacities have different requirements. Common to all is a need for physical comfort. We have seen that this elementary requirement is denied to hens; and, as we shall see, it is denied to pigs as well. In addition to physical comfort, a hen requires the structured social setting of a normal flock; she may also miss the warmth and reassuring clucks of the mother hen immediately after hatching; and research has provided evidence that even a chicken can suffer from simple boredom.[7] To whatever extent this is true of chickens, it is certainly true, and to a greater extent, of pigs. Researchers at Edinburgh University have studied commercial pigs released into a seminatural enclosure, and have found that they have consistent patterns of behavior: they form stable social groups, they build communal nests, they use dunging areas well away from the nest, and they are active, spending much of the day rooting around the edge of the woodlands. When sows are ready to give birth, they leave the communal nest and build their own nest, finding a suitable site, scraping a hole, and lining it with grass and twigs. There they give birth and live for about nine days, until they and their piglets rejoin the group.[8] As we shall see, factory farming makes it impossible for the pigs to follow these instinctive behavior patterns.

Pigs in modern factory farms have nothing to do but eat, sleep, stand up, and lie down. Usually they have no straw or other bedding material, because this complicates the task of cleaning. Pigs kept in this way can hardly fail to put on weight, but they will be bored and unhappy. Occasionally farmers notice that their pigs like stimulation. One British farmer wrote to *Farmer's Weekly* describing how he had housed pigs in a derelict farmhouse and found that they played all around the building, chasing each other up and down the stairs. He concluded: "Our stock need variety of surroundings. . . . Gadgets of different make, shape and size should be provided. . . . Like human beings, they dislike monotony and boredom."[9]

This common-sense observation has now been backed up by scientific studies. French research has shown that when deprived or frustrated pigs are provided with leather strips or chains to pull, they have reduced levels of corticosteroids (a hormone associated with stress) in their blood.[10] British research has shown that pigs kept in a barren environment are so bored that if they are given both food and an earth-filled trough, they will root around in the earth before eating.[11]

When kept in barren, overcrowded conditions pigs are prone to "vice," as hens are. Instead of feather-pecking and cannibalism, pigs take to biting each other's tails. This leads to fighting in the pig pen and reduces gains in weight. Since pigs do not have beaks, farmers cannot debeak them to prevent this, but they have found another way of eliminating the symptoms without altering the conditions that cause the trouble: they cut off the pigs' tails.

According to the U.S. Department of Agriculture: "Tail docking has become a common practice to prevent tail biting of pigs in confinement. It should be done by all producers of feeder pigs. Cut tails 1/4 to 1/2 inch from the body with side-cutting pliers or another blunt instrument. The crushing action helps to stop bleeding. Some producers use a chicken debeaker for docking; this also cauterizes the cut surface."[12] This is a disgraceful recommendation. Here are the candid views of a pig producer on tail docking: "They hate it! The pigs just hate it! And I suppose we could probably do without tail-docking if we gave them more room, because they don't get so crazy and mean when they have more space. With enough room, they're actually quite nice animals. But we can't afford it. These buildings cost a lot."[13]

BECOMING A VEGETARIAN

Now that we have understood the nature of speciesism and seen the consequences it has for nonhuman animals, it is time to ask: What can we do about it? There is one thing we can do that is of supreme importance; it underpins, makes consistent, and gives meaning to all our other activities on behalf of animals. This one thing is that we take responsibility for our own lives, and make them as free of cruelty as we can. The first step is that we cease to eat animals. Many people who are opposed to cruelty to animals draw the line at becoming a vegetarian. It was of such people that Oliver Goldsmith, the eighteenth-century humanitarian essayist, wrote: "They pity, and they eat the objects of their compassion."[14]

As a matter of strict logic, perhaps, there is no contradiction in taking an interest in animals on both compassionate and gastronomic grounds. If one is opposed to inflicting suffering on animals, but not to the painless killing of animals, one could consistently eat animals who had lived free of all suffering and been instantly, painlessly slaughtered. Yet practically and psychologically it is impossible to be consistent in one's concern for non-human animals while continuing to dine on them. If we are prepared to take the life of another being merely in order to satisfy our taste for a particular type of food, then that being is no more than a means to our end. In time we will come to regard pigs, cattle, and chickens as things for us to use, no matter how strong our compassion may be; and when we find that to continue to obtain supplies of the bodies of these animals at a price we are able to pay it is necessary to change their living conditions a little, we will be unlikely to regard these changes too critically. The factory farm is nothing more than the application of technology to the idea that animals are means to our ends. Our eating habits are dear to us and not easily altered. We have a strong interest in convincing ourselves that our concern for other animals does not require us to stop eating them. No one in the habit of eating an animal can be completely without bias in judging whether the conditions in which that animal is reared cause suffering.

It is not practically possible to rear animals for food on a large scale without inflicting considerable suffering. Even if intensive methods are not used, traditional farming involves castration, separation of mother and young, breaking up social groups, branding, transportation to the slaughterhouse, and finally slaughter itself. It is difficult to imagine how animals could be reared for food without these forms of suffering. Possibly it could be done on a small scale, but we could never feed today's huge urban populations with meat raised in this manner. If it could be done at all, the animal flesh thus produced would be vastly more expensive than animal flesh is today—and rearing animals is already an expensive and inefficient way of producing protein. The flesh of animals reared and killed with equal consideration for the welfare of animals while they were alive would be a delicacy available only to the rich.

All this is, in any case, quite irrelevant to the immediate question of the ethics of our daily diet. Whatever the theoretical possibilities of rearing animals without suffering may be, the fact is that the meat available from butchers and supermarkets comes from animals who were not treated with any real consideration at all while being reared. So we must ask ourselves, not: Is it ever right to eat meat? but: Is it right to eat this meat? Here I think that those who are opposed to the needless killing of animals and those who oppose only the infliction of suffering must join together and give the same, negative answer.

Becoming a vegetarian is not merely a symbolic gesture. Nor is it an attempt to isolate oneself from the ugly realities of the world, to keep oneself pure and so without responsibility for the cruelty and carnage all around. Becoming a vegetarian is a highly practical and effective step one can take toward ending both the killing of nonhuman animals and the infliction of suffering upon them. Assume, for the moment, that it is only the suffering that we disapprove of, not the killing. How can we stop the use of the intensive methods of animal rearing just described?

So long as people are prepared to buy the products of intensive farming, the usual forms of protest and political action will never bring about a major reform. . . . This is not to say that the normal channels of protest and political action are useless and should be abandoned. On the contrary, they are a necessary part of the overall struggle for effective change in the treatment of animals. . . . The people who profit by exploiting large numbers of animals do not need our approval. They need our money. The purchase of the corpses of the animals they rear is the main support the factory farmers ask from the public (the other, in many countries, is big government subsidies). They will use intensive methods as long as they can sell what they produce by these methods; they will have the resources needed to fight reform politically; and they will be able to defend themselves against criticism with the reply that they are only providing the public with what it wants.

Hence the need for each one of us to stop buying the products of modern animal farming—even if we are not convinced that it would be wrong to eat animals who have lived pleasantly and died painlessly. Vegetarianism is a form of boycott. For most vegetarians the boycott is a permanent one, since once they have broken away from flesh-eating habits they can no longer approve of slaughtering animals in order to satisfy the trivial desires of their palates. But the moral obligation to boycott the meat available in butcher shops and supermarkets today is just as inescapable for those who disapprove only of inflicting suffering, and not of killing. Until we boycott meat, and all other products of animal factories, we are, each one of us, contributing to the continued existence, prosperity, and growth of factory farming and all the other cruel practices used in rearing animals for food.

NOTES

1. For Bentham's moral philosophy, see his *Introduction to the Principles of Morals and Legislation,* and for Sidgwick's see *The Methods of Ethics,* 1907 (the passage is quoted from the 7th ed., reprint, London: Macmillan, 1963), p. 382. As of leading contemporary moral philosophers who incorporate a requirement of equal consideration of interests, see R. M. Hare, *Freedom and Reason* (New York: Oxford University Press, 1963), and John Rawls, *A Theory of Justice* (Cambridge: Harvard

University Press, Belknap Press, 1972). For a brief account of the essential agreement on this issue between these and other positions, see R. M. Hare, "Rules of War and Moral Reasoning," *Philosophy and Public Affairs* 1, no. 2 (1972).

2. Letter to Henry Gregoire, February 25, 1809.

3. Reminiscences by Francis D. Gage, from Susan B. Anthony, *The History of Woman Suffrage*, vol. 1; the passage is to be found in the extract in *Voices From Women's Liberation*, ed. Leslie Tanner (New York: Signet, 1970).

4. I owe the term "speciesism" to Richard Ryder. It now appears in *The Oxford English Dictionary*, 2nd ed. (Oxford: Clarendon Press, 1989).

5. Bentham, *Introduction to the Principles of Morals and Legislation*, chap. 17.

6. *Broiler Industry* 178 (December 1987): 22.

7. Ian Duncan, "Can the Psychologist Measure Stress?" *New Scientist*, October 18, 1973.

8. R. Dunbar, "Farming Fit for Animals," *New Scientist*, March 29, 1984, pp. 12–15; D. Wood-Gush, "The Attainment of Humane Housing for Farm Livestock," in *Advances in Animal Welfare Science*, ed. M. Fox and L. Mickley (Washington, DC: Humane Society of the United States, 1985).

9. *Farmer's Weekly*, November 7, 1961, quoted by Ruth Harrison, *Animal Machines* (London: Vincent Stuart, 1967), p. 97.

10. R. Dantzer and P. Mormede, "Stress in Farm Animals: A Need for Reevaluation," *Journal of Animal Science* 57 (1983): 6–18.

11. D. Wood-Gush and R. Beilharz, "The Enrichment of a Bare Environment for Animals in Confined Conditions," *Applied Animal Ethology* 20 (1983): 209–17.

12. U.S. Department of Agriculture, *Fact Sheet: Swine Management*, AFS-3-8-12, Department of Agriculture, Office of Government and Public Affairs, Washington, DC.

13. F. Butler, quoted in John Robbins, *Diet for a New America* (Walpole, NH: Stillpoint, 1987), p. 90.

14. Oliver Goldsmith, *The Citizen of the World*, in *Collected Works*, ed. A. Friedman (Oxford: Clarendon Press, 1966), 2:60. Apparently Goldsmith himself fell into this category, however, since according to Howard Williams in *The Ethics of Diet* (abridged edition, Manchester and London, 1907, p. 149), Goldsmith's sensibility was stronger than his self-control.

9 | UTILITARIANISM AND MORAL VEGETARIANISM AGAIN
Protest or Effectiveness?
R. G. Frey

Twenty years ago, I published *Rights, Killing, and Suffering: Moral Vegetarianism and Applied Ethics*.[1] In it, I argued that the three main moral arguments on behalf of vegetarianism—that raising and killing animals for food violated one or more of their moral rights, that killing animals for food destroyed lives of value, that raising (and killing) animals for food in commercial societies inflicts pain on animals—did not work.

Moreover, I suggested that vegetarianism was not required on moral grounds of one who held a moral theory like the one I held, namely, some form of utilitarianism, and that it certainly was not required of a utilitarian on the ground that it was the "most effective" step one could take to reduce animal pain and suffering in the rearing (and killing) of animals for food. Indeed, I argued that one's act of abstaining from meat would not be causally efficacious at all in reducing animal pain, and I went into at some length reasons why I thought an emphasis on contributory causation, thresholds, and the like, all of which looked like they were involved in establishing some causal connection between one's abstention and reduction in animal suffering, did not establish that the actual consequences of one's act of abstention included any reduction in suffering at all.

I went on independently of this causal argument to suggest that an actual utilitarian calculation of the consequences of getting rid of meat, in the face of the entrenched role that meat plays in our lives, seemed very unlikely to me to indicate that utilitarians could think that moral vegetarianism was an effective step at all, let alone the "most effective" step one could take, to do something about animal suffering. Instead, I urged a direct engagement with the rearing (and killing) practices that most disturbed one and with the attempt to get farmers and members of the agribusiness lobby to deal with those very practices. For, as I tried to indicate, large-scale commercial farming struck me as here to stay, in a large, commercial meat industry, and we would do better directly to come to grips with the practices, such as the raising of veal calves, that spurred controversy over pain and suffering (at that time). I indicated that, in Britain, where I was living then, developments were under way to address some of the concerns over rearing practices that were the object of anger and protest, developments that, since I left in 1987, have since come to pass there.

As I now look back on this work, I still think that the three main arguments for moral vegetarianism do not work; I remain some form of utilitarian; I still think that the utilitarian argument in favor of moral vegetarianism does not work, not even, as I will indicate below, if one tries to move from actual to expected consequences in viewing the results of one's act of abstaining from meat; and I now know much more vividly, as I will also indicate, that large-scale commercial farming is here to stay. I still do not think, then, that a utilitarian has to be a vegetarian on moral grounds and that vegetarianism is an effective step to deal with the painful rearing practices that characterize commercial farming.

Commercial farming has exploded both in the number of animals farmed and in the profits that it reaps. When I argued about the causal effects of one's act of abstaining from meat, in a setting in which there was a large commercial market in meat (and fish) and where there were more than enough meat eaters in the market, and entering the market, to ensure that one's act had no actual effect on the market, I knew people in the meat industry in Britain who gave me figures about the rise in meat production there and in Europe. I knew that, for example, cattle and chicken production was booming and that the demand for product was such that demand would not merely ensure the survival of large-scale commercial farming in order to meet it but would also propel commercial farming methods and their employment forward. But, in truth, I had no idea just how many animals would come to be farmed, no idea as to the growth in numbers that lay just around the corner. I realized that barely viable societies, as they prospered, were likely to turn to meat consumption, despite the fact that more people could be fed with a grain economy, and I realized from British and European data that more prosperous economies were expanding meat production even as health worries about the overconsumption of meat gained credence. But I really had no idea as to the sheer growth in numbers of animals farmed that lay ahead.

How many actual animals, then, were being commercially farmed in the world each year? I remember distinctly in 1983 talking to an agricultural economist in London about this, and I remember as well telling someone—I think my eventual colleague Stephen Clark—that I was afraid that no one would believe the figure (about twelve billion) that we had worked out. To be sure, we lacked hard data on some places and indeed any data at all on meat-producing countries like Argentina, Brazil, and China; yet, even without these countries, or a host of others, we reached a figure of twelve billion. I worried that, if I used this figure, which seemed so enormous, that I would be accused of distorting the number of animals actually commercially farmed, in order to make it appear that the causal effect of one's act of abstaining from meat was bound to be imperceptible or exceedingly slight in a market so vast. I sometimes mentioned in talks that I had information about the actual number of animals being commercially farmed in the world, but I knew this number was rough at best. Projections based on it were likely to be rough as well, so when I indicated that I thought it overwhelmingly likely that commercial farming would boom and the meat industry not only would not be brought to its knees by people becoming moral vegetarians but would not even feel the effect, either in its profits or its rearing methods, of their becoming abstainers, I took these projections to be something around the figure of fifteen billion animals a year.

On this, it turns out, I was massively wrong. In fact, I think the figure is more like twenty to twenty-five billion today, with around eleven billion of that supplied alone by the United States and around nine billion of that supplied by Europe, Scandinavia, and Asia, I still have no data for Argentina, Brazil, or China, except gross economic terms of export and (projected, yearly) internal consumption. In fact, then, commercial farming has indeed boomed, and the number of animals now being so farmed is beyond anything that was true in 1983.

I think it is worth pausing over this increase in animals. I do not know how many people in the period since 1983 have become vegetarians on the moral grounds canvassed or, indeed, how many people have actually engaged these moral arguments in the consideration of what to eat; since much of the technical work on the arguments has been done by philosophers, and not all that many people read philosophical material, I assume the number is not all that great. But allow it to be many; the plain fact is that, at a time when the number of moral vegetarians is conceded to have risen by some percentage, the number of animals commercially farmed has risen by a staggering number. At a time when the very act of becoming a vegetarian was being touted as the "most effective" step one could take to do something about painful rearing practices, and as more people were taking that step, the number of animals being so reared has skyrocketed to a figure today that is simply gigantic. Even when we add together all those acts of abstention, the number of animals commercially farmed has exploded in the face of the very steps that were supposed causally to eliminate, or at least negatively affect, that farming and its practices. The entire argument, in short, has been overtaken by the sheer magnitude of increase in the number of animals farmed.

Suppose we focus upon the effects of one's individual act of becoming a vegetarian; the size of the market, the number of people in the market and the number of people coming into the market reduce the effects of one's act(s) of abstention to virtually nothing, even without going into all the technical talk of contributory causation, thresholds, and the production of threshold effects. One person's act is simply not going to have an effect on this market. But neither is this market going to be sensitive to the acts of more abstainers, either, if the number of people entering the market more than makes up for the number who go out of it.

Neither can abstainers claim that they at least have saved all those animals that would have been produced, if all the abstainers had stayed in the market and continued to eat meat; for absent some special consideration that might indicate otherwise, we do not have any reason to believe a market this large is sensitive to the eating habits of this group of moral vegetarians, not even if one makes that group to be, say, a million strong. For we have no reason, absent some special consideration, to think that a figure of one million is large enough in this market to lead to more animals being raised, since we have no reason absent some special consideration to think that a million raises demand in such a way that it is to be met only by a further increase in the number of animals bred. One is not entitled to this consideration by some assumption of charity, since in vast markets what might be called the "sensitivity to demand" occurs in a magnitude that lies far beyond what that demand might be in a small market, even when that demand needs further to be met. By this last qualification, I mean that a vast market may already have built into it capacity for excess demand compared to the past, at least if projections for the number of people coming into the market exceeds greatly projections for the number of people withdrawing from it, as is the case with the meat consumption market. Nor is there any way of estimating how many animals are saved from being reared, since we do not yet know that *any* animals are saved from being reared.

One can now see what might be one way of trying to work the causal argument in favor of moral vegetarianism. This is to switch from actual to expected consequences: one knows the actual consequences of one's act of abstention are likely to be imperceptible, but if one can make out that the expected consequences are large or significant, then one might want to hold that this gives one a ground for thinking that utilitarianism might require vegetarianism on the ground that vegetarianism is causally efficacious in dealing with painful rearing practices. One expects the consequences of one's act of abstention to be large or significant, even though one knows of acts of abstention in the past that their actual consequences have been imperceptible.

But to claim that these expected consequences would be large seems quite false: no one really believes that the expected consequences of anyone's act of abstaining, or of the acts of all those who abstain added together, is that the meat industry will be brought to its knees. One knows that billions of animals will be farmed, whatever I do, and one knows that in a period in which more people than ever before became moral vegetarians in the past the number of animals farmed rose massively. One cannot distort the magnitude of expected consequences in order to make it appear that they exceed the imperceptible character of actual consequences, viewed after the passage of time. What one thinks likely to happen has to reflect realistic assumptions both about the future and realistic assessments about the past, and a realistic assessment of the past forces one to conclude that in all those cases in the past where one thought expected consequences of abstaining from meat were large, in fact they turned out in actual consequences to be unbelievably small. (How, then, does one constantly "expect" large consequences in the future when one knows, when one has done so in the past, that all such expectations have in actual consequences been dashed?)

One could, however, claim that the expected consequences were not large but significant; that is, they occurred at some point or range or threshold at which further substantial threshold effects were produced. But one is not entitled to this assumption by way of charity; we need some reason to believe that such a threshold is being approached. What we know at the moment and what we know about the past help us in reaching this judgment, and what we know about the past is that, in all those cases where thresholds were thought to be approached and then exceeded, so that further substantial threshold effects were then to be in the offing, no such effects were actually ever produced. In all previous cases, if we thought expected consequences were at some significant point, it turned out that they were not, since at no point have any of our particular acts of abstaining in the past had any actual effect on the meat market. I cannot constantly claim that my act is at some threshold in expectation, only to find, in actual fact, that it was not, and then continue to project that further acts of mine are at the threshold of effect on the meat industry and its painful practices. Here, too, I cannot exaggerate expected consequences in order to deem them significant, and so beyond what I know the actual consequences of all my previous acts of abstention to have been.

So, I do not think this switch enables us to work the utilitarian argument about causal effect. It remains true, I think, that the causal effects of our acts of abstaining from meat are imperceptible, and even when we seek for the effects of all the acts of abstention by moral vegetarians added together, we do not yet have any idea of whether this addition results in the saving of any additional animals.

(A thought in passing: even if this addition did result in animals being saved, it is not clear to me that we have advanced the argument. For the promise held out in the early writing was that vegetarianism would produce a change in painful rearing practices, and all the additive point shows at best, were we to think it worked, is that some animals were not reared that would otherwise have been reared. This has not changed rearing practices in the slightest, and it was a mistake to have thought earlier that it might. For the painful practices to which one objected remain in place, and massively more animals are reared in them than earlier was true; to show that some animals were not born and so not reared under those practices is not to gain credit for having done anything about those practices. If animals that have not been born cannot be subjected to them, the animals born can, and this latter number is now massively beyond what was earlier true. Effecting those practices was what was promised those who became moral vegetarians.)

I have no objection to those who accept vegetarianism on some ground of protest at painful rearing practices. One could also put a sign against such practices on one's property, or take out an ad in the local paper against them, or work with meat producers to change them or, of course, do versions of all of these things. What was promised earlier, however, was not protest, but effectiveness, and this is what we do not have.

The sheer number of animals being commercially farmed has risen enormously, even as the number of moral vegetarians has also increased. This complicates the case for effectiveness because it reduces the plausibility of maintaining that one's acts of abstaining from meat have any effect on the meat industry at all. I underestimated the massive increase in the number of animals farmed. I estimated correctly the appeal the claim of effectiveness would have on people, who like to think, of course, that their efforts on behalf of moral causes have practical effect on those causes and their source of unhappiness in them. This is what cannot be demonstrated in the case of meat eating, so that we cannot employ an argument from causal efficacy in order to attract a utilitarian to the vegetarian cause.

Note

1. R. G. Frey, *Rights, Killing, and Suffering: Moral Vegetarianism and Applied Ethics* (Oxford: Blackwell, 1983).

WHY IT'S WRONG TO EAT ANIMALS RAISED AND SLAUGHTERED FOR FOOD

Bart Gruzalski

The ethical view that a person should live in such a way that she or he contributes as little as possible to the total amount of suffering in the world and as much as possible to the total of what is positive is called utilitarianism. In this essay I develop a classical utilitarian argument against eating animals raised and killed for food. After a brief description of some of the horrors of factory farming, I demonstrate the failure of five attempts to defend eating animals from a utilitarian perspective.

THE UTILITARIAN ARGUMENT AGAINST EATING ANIMALS RAISED AND SLAUGHTERED FOR FOOD

According to the classical utilitarianism of John Stuart Mill, actions are right insofar as they tend to produce the greatest happiness for the greatest number. For our purposes I will interpret this criterion as a principle regarding the positive and negative foreseeable consequences of individual actions.[1] When we apply this principle we must be responsive to the fact that most acts have several mutually exclusive foreseeable consequences that are of different values (e.g., rolling a die has six foreseeable consequences, and we may value some more than others), and we must take into account both the probability and the value of each of these foreseeable consequences in assessing an action. An action, on this account, is right if and only if it is the best bet a person can perform to avoid producing negative consequences and to bring about positive consequences. For example, even though the odds are very low that passing on a blind curve on a rural road will cause a horrific head-on collision, because the negative value of this highly improbable foreseeable consequence is so great, the overall assessment of the foreseeable consequences of passing on a blind curve is negative. Hence, performing this act would typically be wrong on our utilitarian principle. In applying this principle we use the standard conception of consequences: an event is a consequence of an action only if there is some other action the agent could have performed that would have prevented the occurrence of the event in question. For example, my glass being half full is a consequence of my holding it under the tap since, had I placed it on the counter instead, an alternative I could have performed, it would be empty.

From a utilitarian viewpoint it is wrong to eat animals raised and slaughtered for food because the process of raising and slaughtering animals causes tremendous suffering that would not occur were people vegetarians. To eat these animals is therefore wrong on utilitarian grounds unless there are positive foreseeable consequences that outweigh this animal suffering. There are positive consequences, the most obvious being that these animals become tasty morsels of meat. But it is doubtful that the enjoyment of those who are eating these animals can outweigh the sufferings of captivity and slaughter. Does a family at a Kentucky Fried Chicken experience such pleasure from eating chicken that this pleasure outweighs the frustration, pain, and terror that the chicken had to undergo in order to wind up on a coleslaw-garnished paper plate?

The plausibility of a utilitarian justification for eating meat is even weaker than the previous rhetorical question suggests. In order that eating meat be justified, the pain caused to animals by this practice must not only be *outweighed* by the omnivore's pleasure, but *there can be no alternative act that would foreseeably result in a better balance of pleasure over pain*. Since eating plants is one alternative, and since this alternative produces pleasures of taste, soundness of health, and no unnecessary suffering for animals, it follows that, if a person is trying not to contribute to unnecessary suffering in the world, then that person would not eat animals raised and slaughtered for food. This argument seems a no-brainer, but some philosophers have tried to refute it while adopting utilitarianism. After briefly reviewing some of what happens to animals in food production, I examine five attempts to provide a utilitarian defense of eating animals raised and slaughtered for food.

THE HORRORS OF FACTORY FARMING

Cruelty and brutality characterize factory farming: the overcrowding of factory-farm animals in stalls and cages; the frustrations of natural instincts to run, play, nuzzle, or just move about; the forced separation of offspring from mothers; the terrifying motorized transportation of animals from one location to another; and, finally, the unspeakable violence of assembly-line killings.

The producers of meat try to keep their treatment of animals out of the consumer's awareness. Consumers purchase meat so packaged and sanitized that they are never reminded of the terrors the animals had to experience. As long as the violence against animals is kept out of sight or abstracted into brief sentences, it is psychologically easy to claim that eating meat is morally permissible. Nevertheless, the sufferings and the terrors of these innocent beings are much too relevant to the moral life to be brushed aside. Consider what Richard Rhodes, who considered the killing of nonhuman animals "necessary," reports as he observed a slaughterhouse that was doing its job of slaughtering pigs "as humanely as possible." Rhodes writes:

> The pen narrows like a funnel; the drivers behind urge the pigs forward, until one at a time they climb onto the moving ramp. . . . Now they scream, never having been on such a ramp, smelling the smells [of death] ahead. I do not want to overdramatize because you have read all this before. But it was a frightening experience, seeing their fear.[2]

Nothing eliminates the reality of the violence that inflicts this horror on other sentient beings. Wayne Swanson and George Schultz, two advocates of the meat industry, write:

> No matter how much new technology is developed, and no matter how nicely meat is packaged, the central facts of the meat business cannot be changed. This is an industry built around noisy, foul-smelling animals whose fate is to have an eight-inch-long pin fired into their foreheads at point-blank range. Their blood and guts will spill forth on the killing floor, and their carcasses will be stripped and carved and chopped during a process that, although it is governed by "humane slaughter" laws, can be nothing other than gross and brutal.[3]

The words "gross and brutal" are not intended by their authors as anything but a realistic description by two advocates of the meat industry. Brutal violence is a necessary part of the process.

That cows, pigs, and chickens suffer frustration, fear, terror, and pain is inconvenient to the meat industry and even difficult on its labor force. Promoters of the industry encourage those who work in the industry to forget that these animals are sentient beings. J. Byrnes, writing for *Hog Farm Management*, offers the following advice:

> Forget the pig is an animal. Treat him just like a machine in a factory. Schedule treatments like you would lubrication. Breeding season like the first step in an assembly line. And marketing like the delivery of finished goods.[4]

If the workers can come to see animals as machines, and if the consumer can be kept from the realities of what is involved in producing the meat they purchase in cellophane-wrapped containers, then we have an instance of the kind of denial mechanism that helps characterize what Carol Adams calls institutional violence: "False naming ['meat' rather than 'animal'] and the structure of the absent referent [no animals on the plate, only food] create the permission for institutional violence. . . ."[5]

The meat industry relies on denial to support this institutional violence. Critics of meat production try to make people aware of the realities. James Mason and Peter Singer describe how living chickens are killed in accord with regulations: they are hooked onto conveyor belts that carry them, alive but upside down, into the killing room where their throats are slashed so they can bleed to death.[6] Gail Eisnitz documents the everyday treatment of cows and pigs that violates U.S. government regulations. Workers, who are supposed to stun pigs and cattle before they begin to kill and butcher them, often fail to do so. As a result, fully conscious animals are regularly stabbed, skinned (cows), or scalded (pigs) to death. In addition, to keep the assembly line moving quickly enough (so as not to be fired) workers hit cows with whips, chains, shovels, and boards, as well as beat hogs with lead pipes, sometimes beating them to death. All these actions occur daily in slaughterhouses under USDA oversight.[7]

DEFENSE ONE: EATING ANIMALS RAISED ON FAMILY FARMS

The first defense of eating animals we consider concedes that industrial farming is a horror. Instead, it argues for eating animals only if they have been raised on family farms. Michael Pollan claims that if we look at the carefully run family farm, "from the animal's point of view, the bargain with humanity has been a great success."[8] James Cargile has such a farm on which he raises pigs and gives them "everything a pig could want for a good life but a short one," claiming that their "short lives are better than no life at all."[9]

This family-farm defense of eating animals rests on an assortment of claims:

(1) The pleasures of the animals we raise would not occur if we did not raise them.
(2) The pleasures of these animals increase the total amount of happiness in the world.
(3) The burdens of these animals are outweighed by their pleasures.
(4) No alternative practice would increase the foreseeable amount of positive consequences in the world.

While (1) and (2) are true, (3) is problematic for a number of reasons. First, animals raised on family farms are violently and unexpectedly killed in the prime of their lives. For example, the lifespan of a pig is between ten and twenty years, yet pigs killed for food are often slaughtered at six months of age and almost always before two years of age. Broiler chickens, which are always female, are killed at about seven weeks, although the lifespan of a chicken is about seven years. What happens to the baby male chicks? Because males are considered less tasty, the baby male chicks are killed within days of hatching. Even worse for (3), family-farm animals are often killed in the horrific factory slaughterhouse. The cattle, pigs, and sheep on the family farm that Pollan believes offers a good bargain for animals are slaughtered in USDA-approved slaugherhouses.[10] Even if the short life of a social animal like the family-farm pig killed in a factory slaughterhouse were to have an overall positive value, this would be a very mixed positive at best. Furthermore, on those farms where farmers slaughter their own animals, these farmers likely find stunning devices too expensive and, in addition, may not have the daily practice of killing animals quickly. One would expect that the small farmer who clubs, slices, or shoots his animals might not infrequently confront an injured animal that is utterly terrified and even harder to kill. In these cases these very social animals, having lived with and come to trust their human companions, experience betrayal in the last moments of their lives at the hands of those they trusted. Finally, farmers restrict the natural activities of animals even on family farms. Cargile's pigs do not forage across the ridges and valleys of the Blue Ridge Mountains in packs of ten or twenty eating acorns. Cows are not allowed to raise their calves as long as they would in a natural setting. These observations show why (3) is somewhat suspect.

The decisive utilitarian claim of the family-farm defense of eating animals is (4): no alternative practice would increase the foreseeable amount of positive consequences in the world. The relevant alternative is vegetarianism. If we adopt the vegetarian alternative and stop raising marketable animals, we would need much less land to feed the same number of people, since plants yield about ten times as much protein per acre as meat. By not raising and not slaughtering animals for food, we would need to raise significantly less grain and so could allow over 80 percent of the resources currently used to feed livestock and poultry to be idle.[11] These resources—lands lying fallow, empty barns—which previously supported market-bound animals would now support other animals: chipmunks, mice, foxes, raccoons, deer, squirrels, and other unmarketable animals. Farmers shoot, poison, and trap some of these animals to protect both their market-bound animals and the feed for them, another negative consequence for animals caused by family farming. Farmers also radically decrease the numbers of unmarketable animals by destroying their habitat and restricting them from areas that would otherwise be part of their range. In contrast, the vegetarian alternative allows unmarketable animals to flourish in greater numbers. It will still be true that by being vegetarian we fail to support the lives and pleasures of *cows, chickens,* and *family-farm pigs,* but there is no reason to think that the pleasures of these animals are not on an even par with the pleasures of *squirrels, chipmunks, rabbits, prairie dogs, raccoons, foxes, mice, deer,* and *wild pigs.* This observation defeats the central idea behind the family-farm defense of eating farm animals: that the total amount of animal welfare is best increased if we raise animals for food. That claim is false. Animals overall would be better off if humans did not raise and slaughter some of them for food, even on family farms.

DEFENSE TWO: THE INSIGNIFICANCE OF ANIMAL PLEASURES AND PAINS

Although eating animals raised for food is not the best way to increase the amount of animal happiness in the world, a critic may argue that it is the best way to increase the amount of animal *and human* happiness. In developing the classical utilitarian position on the use of animals for food, I claimed that it is implausible to think that the suffering an animal experiences from confinement, transportation, and slaughter-related activities is outweighed by the pleasure of eating these animals. The meat eating utilitarian may object by claiming that I exaggerated the pertinent animal suffering. Once we correct this exaggeration, my critic argues, we have a plausible utilitarian defense of eating animals.

One source of this exaggeration, my critic may claim, is my implicit assumption that animal suffering and pleasure have the same intensity as human suffering and pleasure. Jan Narveson argues that human and animal pleasures and sufferings are not on a par. The argument has two steps. The first is that human beings have higher capacities. As Narveson writes, these capacities are grounded in our ability to be "acutely aware of the future stretching out before us, and of the past in the other direction."[12] Unlike lower animals, a human has a "capacity to have a conception of oneself, to formulate long-range plans, to appreciate general facts about one's environment and intelligently employ them in one's plans, and rationally to carry out or attempt to carry out one's plans."[13]

In light of these "higher capacities," Narveson proceeds to the second step of the argument:

> Isn't it reasonable to hold that the significance, and thus the quality, and so ultimately the utility, of the sufferings of beings with *sophisticated* capacities is different from that of the sufferings of lesser beings? Suppose one of the lower animals to be suffering quite intensely. Well, what counts as suffering of like degree in a *sophisticated* animal—one like, say, Beethoven or Kierkegaard, or you, gentle reader? If we are asked to compare the disutility of a pained cow with that of a pained human, or even a somewhat frustrated one, is it so absurd to think that the latter's is greater?[14]

Narveson's tentative conclusion is that the pleasures and pains of sophisticated beings are more valuable than those of less sophisticated beings. Hence, if farm animals are unsophisticated in the relevant sense, then the human pleasure of eating meat, being the pleasure of *sophisticated* beings, may outweigh the requisite suffering of unsophisticated farm animals.

This justification of eating meat also fails. The assumption that human beings are able to anticipate the future in ways that animals cannot does not show that we have a greater capacity for pleasure. One reason for doubt is that such abilities increase our capacity to *fail* to appreciate whatever is present to our senses. The Narveson who is eating filet mignon while anticipating an upcoming philosophical exchange or a Beethoven concert will, precisely because of this future-oriented mental activity, miss some or all of the potential pleasures of eating. But even if we assume that humans have some capacity to enjoy life more than animals, the capacity Narveson cites suggests that humans, because distracted by daydreams and future-oriented thoughts, may well enjoy life less, and in particular eating less, which is the critical experience on the human side of the controversy. On the animal side, Narveson's considerations do *not* support the claim that animal pains are dim. Ironically, they support the conclusion that the animal pains due to confinement, transportation, and slaughter are intensely and keenly felt, for there are no future-oriented distractions to mitigate the corresponding pain and fear.

Even if Narveson's account of pleasure and pain were not faulty, it would still fail to support a defense of eating meat. Any utilitarian justification of eating meat requires that the human pleasures compensating for the animal suffering cannot be caused equally well by an alternative. Given the plausible parity of the pleasures of vegetarian cuisine and meat-based cuisine, and given that the vegetarian alternative causes *less* animal pain, it follows that there is no utilitarian justification for eating meat even if animal pains were (as they are not) somehow less valuable.

DEFENSE THREE: ANIMALS DIE ANYWAY

Although the meat eater cannot justifiably downgrade the value of animal experiences, she may argue that there is a second reason to think that I have overestimated the animal suffering resulting from eating animals raised for food. Since animals die anyway, the argument goes, we cannot attribute the suffering associated with the death of an animal to the process of slaughtering animals for food. This reduction in the suffering attributable to animal husbandry leaves as relevant to the vegetarian debate only the sufferings of confinement, transportation, and diet. Since these are frustrations of animal preferences, we should look at the human preferences that are frustrated by giving up meat. One is the preference for the taste of meat. A second is a preference not to change a deeply ingrained habit. Since frustrating these preferences are costs meat eaters can avoid by continuing to eat meat, there is no significant difference between satisfying the relevant animal preferences versus satisfying the relevant human preferences. We therefore cannot condemn eating animals on utilitarian grounds, concludes the defender of eating meat, for both eating meat and its alternative lead to a similar amount of pleasure and frustration.

Let us begin our response with the preference not to change a deeply ingrained habit of meat eating. Frustrating this preference is a relatively short-term cost, whereas continuing to eat meat contributes to unnecessary animal suffering for the rest of the meat eater's life. Also, once the meat eater has become a vegetarian, her example will influence family and friends to consider vegetarianism as a possibility. Should she have children, they will have an ingrained habit of vegetarianism. On the positive side, the adventure of such a change of eating habits is, for many, an exciting and deeply satisfying culinary adventure. Part of the adventure is the discovery of new appetizing delights that feature vegetables as more than soggy garnishes. In addition, the vegetarian enjoys the satisfaction of knowing she is not contributing to the suffering of animals. Finally, by changing habits, she has adopted a healthier and more ecologically sound way of eating. All of these considerations undermine the claim that the preference not to change a deep meat eating habit can justify imposing continued suffering on animals.

That leaves the human preference for the taste of meat. It is useful to discuss this preference in the context of the sufferings imposed on animals prior to their slaughter. Here are a few examples of the suffering of animals from confinement: veal calves in small stalls unable to turn around and prevented from ingesting any nutritional iron; debeaked chickens imprisoned together for life in a crowded cage; smelly feedlots jammed with animals who lack shade from the summer sun. Even on family farms, as we saw in the discussion of "Defense One," farmers restrict the instinctive activities of animals. Although defenders of animal husbandry argue that the selective breeding of animals raised for food has changed some of the tendencies in their ancestor stock, it is reasonable to believe with the experts that "the natural, instinctive urges and behavioral patterns . . . appropriate to the high degree of social organization as found in the ancestral wild species . . . have been little, if at all, bred out in the process of domestication.[15]

When we take into account all of the restraints on animals raised for food, does the taste of meat outweigh them? One way to answer this question is to begin by asking whether the frustration experienced by a young boy forced to live and eat in his room for a month can be justified by the pleasure of his parents watching a couple of "adult" TV shows. If that comparison cannot clearly be made out in favor of the satisfaction of the parents' preference, and it cannot, it becomes implausible to think that satisfying the preference of eating meat outweighs the months of animal frustration caused by movement, diet, and socialization restrictions. Even worse for this defense, we are not weighing the frustrations of farm animals against the pleasures of eating meat but, instead, only against those pleasures *that cannot be gained by eating vegetarian meals.* Since much of the world's population finds that vegetarian meals can be delightfully tasty, there is good reason for thinking that the pleasures many people derive from eating meat can be completely replaced with pleasures from eating vegetables. Because the pleasures of a vegetarian cuisine are on a par with the pleasures of an omnivore's cuisine, the "outweighing" pleasures are so minimal that this defense of eating animals collapses.

Although the above considerations defeat this defense of eating animals, it is important to return to the central assumption of this defense: that we can set aside any consideration of the killing of animals for food since they die anyway. This assumption is false. Even in those slaughterhouses where animals are killed as painlessly as possible, the animals hear, see, and smell the slaughter and become terrified. Everything we have learned about animals suggests that in terms of experiencing terror, pain, grief, anxiety, and stress, these sentient beings are relevantly similar to humans. It is reasonable to believe that our knowledge of the quality of human dying will also inform us about the dying process of other animals. For humans, the most horrible deaths involve terror. Other factors that contribute to a difficult dying process are dying unexpectedly, dying from physical injury, and dying in unfamiliar surroundings. When none of these factors are present, the dying process is typically easier. From these minimal observations about human dying and the observation that food animals are typically slaughtered while terrified, in unfamiliar circumstances, and by means of an unexpected series of events (being fed one day, deprived of food the next, and then prodded up a ramp), we can draw some conclusions about the suffering of animals slaughtered for food. The first is that the experience of being slaughtered is no better for these animals than the worst deaths experienced in the wild and significantly worse than the deaths of animals that die from injury, disease, or old age in familiar and unterrifying surroundings. In addition, because the lifespan of an adult animal raised for food is much shorter than the lifespan of a similar adult animal in the wild, there will be more deaths per total adult population among farm animals than among wild animals of similar species. Hence, both in quantity and quality of deaths, slaughtering animals for food produces a great deal of death-related anguish and terror that would not occur but for humans eating these animals.

DEFENSE FOUR: SINCE A VEGETARIAN DIET KILLS SENTIENT BEINGS, WHY BOTHER?

The utilitarian arguments for vegetarianism mandate performing actions that, among the alternatives available to the person, are the best bets for causing the least amount of suffering and the most positive results. When we compare vegetarian and meat eating alternatives, utilitarianism seems to mandate the vegetarian alternative. But a defender of eating meat will remind us that the vegetarian alternative faces a problem analogous to the problem confronting the meat eater. Recall, she says, that the problem with eating farm animals is not in the eating, but rather in what is involved in producing meat as food: the frustration and pain caused by animal husbandry, followed by horrific assembly-line killings. The vegetarian, she continues, faces a similar problem. The problem is not in eating vegetables, but rather in the killing that is foreseeable in the production of vegetarian food.[16] In particular, to eat vegetables requires that someone raises, harvests, and brings vegetables to market. When people raise vegetables, especially on large farms, a number of sentient beings are killed in the process, including mice, voles, snakes, and small birds. Furthermore, getting vegetables to market requires using vehicles that also foreseeably kill sentient beings, including humans upon occasion. Hence, the production of vegetarian food, like the production of meat food, foreseeably causes the suffering and death of other sentient beings. Since the production of each causes animal suffering and death, it makes no difference whether we are vegetarians or omnivores. But since it does make a difference to those humans who are habituated to eating meat and who enjoy it, it follows, our defender of eating meat concludes, that it is permissible for the utilitarian to eat meat.

This argument overlooks a crucial difference in the amount of animal suffering and death caused by the vegetarian versus the amount caused by the meat eater. In the case of eating meat, the animals to be slaughtered are fed with corn, beans, and grain. Farmers produce this feed by plowing, tilling, harvesting, and then bringing it to market. These actions cause the deaths of sentient beings. Since it takes about sixteen times more grain to produce a pound of beef as it takes to produce a pound of grain for human consumption, it follows that the production of vegetarian food foreseeably causes fewer deaths than the production of feed for farm animals.[17] In addition, eating meat requires the killing of the animals being eaten. In short, many fewer sentient beings are killed by those who eat vegetables than by those who eat meat.

This answer to the defender of eating meat does not fully solve the difficulty. While it provides good utilitarian reasons for choosing a vegetarian diet over a diet including meat and so shows that eating animals raised and slaughtered for food is wrong, it does not show that a vegetarian diet is permissible from a utilitarian point of view. The reason is that there is a third alternative in addition to eating only vegetarian food or eating an omnivorous diet: not eating at all. Since not eating at all causes the death only of the sentient being who stops eating rather than the many who die in the production of vegetarian food, this raises the question of whether the utilitarian principle mandates starvation.

Ethics is intended as action-guiding within the framework of ongoing human life. It is therefore permissible to do what is necessary to stay alive. To act ethically we need to satisfy, on a continual basis, the basic needs of water, food, clothing, and shelter. The basic survival actions that satisfy these basic survival needs are therefore privileged from an ethical point of view, although they are still constrained within the overall utilitarian program. The utilitarian constraint mandates that a person may do a particular basic survival action only if there is no alternative basic survival action that would cause less suffering to sentient beings.

The fact that eating vegetarian food typically contributes to the foreseeable deaths of sentient beings does not show that the utilitarian is justified in eating meat. What it shows is that the simple utilitarian principle requires a very important and commonsense modification to permit humans to perform actions essential to human life. Without this modification, and assuming that the suffering and contentment of all sentient beings are roughly on a par, the utilitarian principle would prohibit eating either meat or vegetables. With this commonsense modification, it is permissible for human beings to perform the basic survival action of eating as long as the specific acts of eating cause as little suffering as possible to sentient beings when compared with alternative acts of eating.[18] Given that the production of vegetarian food causes the deaths of fewer sentient beings than the production of meat, the modified utilitarian principle condones vegetarianism and condemns eating animals raised and slaughtered for food.[19]

DEFENSE FIVE: THE INDIVIDUAL'S IMPOTENCY TO AFFECT ANIMAL SUFFERING

A final attempt to defend eating meat on utilitarian grounds rests on the claim that, for those of us who do not raise our own animals, there is little chance that any one of us will make a difference in the total amount of animal suffering by becoming vegetarian. Suppose, the argument goes, I buy meat from a retailer who is supplied by the meat industry. Because the meat suppliers are so large, if I stop eating meat, my action will have no effect on the number of animals raised. Hence, if I am trying to prevent unnecessary suffering, there is no animal suffering I prevent by becoming a vegetarian. But if I enjoy eating meat and am accustomed to doing so, and if becoming a vegetarian would cause me to suffer (if only for a short period), then I ought to continue to eat meat and not cause myself the unnecessary suffering of becoming a vegetarian, for there is no suffering I can prevent by becoming a vegetarian.

This argument is not sound. Recall that, in assessing what we should do, the utilitarian takes into account the probability and the value of each of the foreseeable consequences of her action and its alternatives to determine what is the best bet for bringing about positive consequences. In the case of purchasing meat, each individual act of *not* purchasing meat has a probability, however slight, of *reducing* animal suffering significantly.[20] Consider: if someone fails to purchase a chicken or other form of animal, there is a small probability that her act might well cause the butcher not to restock these animals as quickly. The butcher's not restocking as quickly has a foreseeable consequence, again with a small probability, of a distributor not restocking as quickly, which in turn has a foreseeable consequence of the slaughter of fewer animals, and so on, until eventually we come to the foreseeable consequence of fewer animals being raised for slaughter. These are among the foreseeable consequences of *not* purchasing meat. In contrast, purchasing meat, because of the causal chain of foreseeable consequences from butcher through slaughterhouse to farm, has a probability, again slight, of *increasing* animal suffering significantly. From the foreseeable consequence perspective, purchasing meat is like driving on the wrong side of the road on a blind curve "in the middle of nowhere": because each act has a very small chance of causing terrible consequences, the overall assessment of the foreseeable consequences of each shows that both are wrong from a utilitarian perspective. Being a vegetarian is a no-brainer if one is trying to bring about positive consequences and cause as little suffering as possible.

Conclusion

Utilitarianism provides a strong argument for not eating animals raised and slaughtered for food. We have looked at five utilitarian attempts to overcome this argument and to defend eating these animals. Each defense fails.

The arguments in this essay do not show that all meat eating is wrong. Nothing in this essay weighs against eating road kills, for example, and the arguments developed here do not explicitly criticize hunting and fishing, although several can be extended in this direction. What the arguments in the essay show is that if a person is trying to do what is the best bet of bringing about positive consequences and not contributing to the unnecessary suffering of sentient beings, that person will not eat animals that have been raised and slaughtered for food.[21]

Notes

1. For a precise statement of foreseeable consequence utilitarianism, and a defense of the foreseeable consequence approach, see my "Foreseeable Consequence Utilitarianism," *Australasian Journal of Philosophy* 59, no. 2 (June 1981): 163–76.

2. "Watching the Animals," *Harper's* (March 1979). Quoted in Peter Singer, *Animal Liberation* (New York: Random House, 1975), p. 157.

3. Harriet Schleifer, "Images of Death and Life: Food Animal Production and the Vegetarian Option," in *In Defense of Animals*, ed. Peter Singer (New York: Harper and Row, 1986), p. 72.

4. J. Byrnes, "Raising Pigs by the Calendar at Maplewood Farm," *Hog Farm Management* (September 1976): 30.

5. Carol J. Adams, "Feeding on Grace: Institutional Violence, Christianity, and Vegetarianism," in *Religious Vegetarianism: From Hesiod to the Dalai Lama*, ed. Kerry Walters and Lisa Portmess (Albany: State University of New York Press, 2001), p. 184.

6. James Mason and Peter Singer, *Animal Factories* (New York: Crown Publishers, 1980), pp. 65–66.

7. Gail Eisnitz, *Slaughterhouse* (Amherst, NY: Prometheus Books, 1997), pp. 17–108.

8. Michael Pollan, "The Unnatural Idea of Animal Rights," *New York Times Magazine*, November 10, 2002, p. 64.

9. James Cargile, "Comments on 'The Priority of Human Interests,'" in *Ethics and Animals*, ed. Harlan B. Miller and William H. Williams (Clifton, NJ: Humana Press, 1983), p. 249.

10. Pollan, "The Unnatural Idea of Animal Rights," p. 110.

11. John Robbins, *Diet for a New World* (New York: Avon Books, 1993), pp. 32–33.

12. Jan Narveson, "Animal Rights Revisited," in Miller and Williams, *Ethics and Animals*, p. 53.

13. Jan Narveson, "Animal Rights," *Canadian Journal of Philosophy* 7 (1977): 166.

14. Ibid., p. 168.

15. *Report of the Technical Committee to Enquire into the Welfare of Animals Kept under Intensive Livestock Husbandry Systems* (1965), cited as the *Brambell Report* in Singer, *Animal Liberation*, p. 135.

16. Mary Anne Warren, *Moral Status* (Oxford: Clarendon Press, 1997), pp. 78–84.

17. Robbins, *Diet for a New World*, p. 32.

18. This section articulates in utilitarian terms the view of Mahatma Gandhi on the ethical treatment of animals. See my *On Gandhi* (Belmont, CA: Wadsworth, 2002), chap. 4, "Nonviolence Toward Animals," pp. 27–32.

19. This section, a summary of an unpublished paper presented on several occasions, has benefited from comments (though not the agreement) of Henry West and Jeff McMahan.

20. For a recent account of why this approach solves the problem discussed in this section, see Gaverick Matheny, "Expected Utility, Contributory Causation, and Vegetarianism," *Journal of Applied Philosophy* 19, no. 3 (2002): 293–97.

21. This essay is a significant revision of my "The Case against Raising and Killing Animals for Food," in Miller and Williams, *Ethics and Animals*. I want to thank, again, Henry West for encouraging me to write that paper, and William DeAngelis, Michael Lipton, Stephen Nathanson, and Sharon Young for helpful comments. I am very grateful to Steve Sapontzis for comments on this revision. Finally, I am pleased to thank, again, Barbara Jones and Walter Knoppel for introducing me to vegetarianism in an intelligent, effective, and tasty manner.

11 | VEGETARIANISM AND THE ETHICS OF VIRTUE

Stephen R. L. Clark

PREFACE

In India "nonvegetarian films" are full of sex and violence, since "vegetarian" is the nearest that the English language gets to the ideal of purity that Hindu thought reveres. That ideal, of course, has never been proposed for everyone: not eating meat, like not having sex, is something that only the few can manage. The same was true in the Western vegetarian tradition: Porphyry's plea to his friend, that he not backslide, was partly founded on the importance to philosophers of a careful disengagement from corporeal desires:

> My discourse will not offer advice to every human way of life: not to those who engage in *banausic* [that is, manual] crafts, nor to athletes of the body, nor to soldiers, nor sailors, nor orators, nor to those who have chosen the life of public affairs, but to the person who has thought about who he is and whence he has come and where he should try to go, and who has principles about food, and about other proper behaviour, which are different from those in other ways of life.[1]

Porphyry also argued that nonhuman animals themselves deserved better than to be treated merely as means to human ends—but the ends he most objected to were ones that he thought corrupt. By not eating flesh the philosopher could keep his mind alert and hope for a better afterlife—though Porphyry himself did not employ the Pythagorean doctrine that we might find ourselves reincarnated in nonhuman form if we did not seize the chance of rising above the human.

The term "vegetarian" itself was coined in the 1840s from the Latin *vegetus* to mean "one who lives a healthy life" and to replace the older term "Pythagorean." The Vegetarian Society founded in the United Kingdom in 1847 at first prohibited alcohol and tobacco as well as meat.[2] Most modern Western vegetarians would probably prefer to emphasize some more altruistic motive: they refrain from flesh because they disapprove of the treatment of farm animals, or because they think that the meat industry wastes resources that should be better used for human benefit. Many would still argue—with good reason—that a vegetarian diet is usually *healthier* than the conventional Western diet, but this is rarely the central motivation for committed vegetarians.

Modern moralists have usually equated *moral* virtue with altruism: being good is a matter of doing *others* good (and what it is to do someone good is reckoned unproblematic). On these terms, the only *moral* argument for vegetarianism must be that the practice would be one that made for a better (pleasanter, healthier, more harmonious) world than the alternatives. And the arguments for choosing oneself to be vegetarian would be either that such a choice might bring that better world a little closer or that we ought to act as we would will *everyone* to act, even if in fact they don't. Bernard Shaw was mistaken if he seriously thought that any particular animal had a pleasanter or more fulfilled or longer life because he forswore flesh; at best, some animal that might have been bred to feed him never was (but more likely, just as many animals were bred and slaughtered). His dietary choices did no good to any actual animal. The altruistic argument may rest instead on the very long-term effects of individual choices: maybe we shall eventually achieve an agricultural economy that makes less use of animals, less intensively and less invasively. The problem with such long-term altruism is that the result is very uncertain. It is easy to *imagine* worlds and futures that appear to be better than this actual one—including worlds in which flesh foods are produced by biotechnological manipulations. It is very difficult to construct a strategy that leads to any of those worlds from here, and difficult to deny that we might actually *increase* the local sum of suffering by trying to alleviate the global sum.

The standard alternative to consequentialist analysis of moral action (as above) is to act upon those maxims that we can seriously will as universal law. Kant, notoriously, denied that we could have any duties toward nonhuman animals, following in this a long tradition of neglect. Because (it is said) nonhumans are not *rational*, we owe them no respect; because they can make no bargains, they deserve no credit. Porphyry followed Plutarch in denying both premises: nonhumans had a share in reason, even if it is less than ours,[3] and demonstrably have made bargains with us that we ought to keep.[4] Other humanists might also argue that we cannot take the vegetarian option as our maxim because we cannot will that *everyone* be vegetarian (since this would be to will the destruction of such creatures as cannot survive on such a diet).[5] It might on the other hand be argued that the vegetarian maxim *can* be universalized for some class (that is, all those who could survive on a less destructive diet should do so), whereas the standard nonvegetarian diet could not be willed as universal even for human beings without appalling environmental damage.

Such arguments can be revised continually. The practical moral for both consequentialists and deontologists must be to offer some ideal of character and action: to act consistently with some vision of a better world, whether or not the final calculation of expectable outcome, or the definitive judgment on what maxim can or cannot be universalized, has been achieved. Recent ethical theorists have preferred an Aristotelian account of right action: instead of thinking only of the possible *outcomes* of an act or strategy, or supposing that there is only one rational (and informative) rule of action, we are to think instead of what an admirable agent would find it natural to do. The right action under any circumstances is the one the virtuous agent would perform in seeking to do right—not as a means to some imagined outcome, but as the finest or most beautiful available option. It is sometimes easier to recognize an admirable agent than to work out what would serve any global aim: not knowing what will follow from what we do, nor how our successors will feel about the outcome, better (perhaps) to live in beauty here and now, without worrying too much about what is to come. Similarly, rules may be useful rules of thumb, but we cannot expect to have a definite and unambiguous rule to cover every circumstance. In either case, what matters is that the agent's *character* and *sense* be virtuous. And the agent is not less virtuous if she fails to achieve the global outcome she desires, nor even if the maxim of her action is not the only possibly universal one. By reemphasizing virtue modern moralists provide an entry to the older vegetarian tradition.

Purity, Virtue, and the Natural Life

Whatever the theoretical background, it is not unreasonable to acknowledge, admire, and seek to cultivate such virtues as courage, temperance, fairness, honesty, fidelity, and so on. Those virtues, or many of them, might also be invoked in condemnation of our current agricultural and other practices. Whatever "bargain of domestication" was once struck with poultry, sheep, and cattle has long been broken. To kill beyond necessity, for the sake of killing or for some marginal pleasure, is cruel or greedy.

> For any man who is just and good loves the brute creatures which serve him, and he takes care of them so that they have food and rest and the other things they need. He does not do this only for his own good but out of a principle of true justice; and if he is so cruel toward them that he requires work from them and nevertheless does not provide the necessary food, then he has surely broken the law which God inscribed in his heart. And if he kills any of his beasts only to satisfy his own pleasure, then he acts unjustly, and the same measure will be measured out to him.[6]

But even those moderns who prefer some version of virtue ethics over attempts to calculate the greater good (consequentialist ethics) or identify a maxim that can be universalized without contradiction (deontological ethics), may not much care for "purity." It is now a commonplace to argue that those who shrink from flesh foods or from the flesh are squeamishly or sanctimoniously contemptuous of corporeal existence and of those who have to dirty their hands with it. Brahminical culture may impose strict duties of purity on Brahmins—but at the expense of rendering untouchable all those who have to deal with excrement and dead bodies. To speak for purity is to seek to separate oneself from the common human condition, and so to establish some favored class of person. Porphyry drew on Hindu experience to answer the universalizing query, "If everyone imitates [the Brahmin or Samanaean] what will become of us?"

> Human affairs are not in chaos because of them, because not everyone has imitated them, and those that do so have brought order rather than chaos for their peoples. Nor did law compel them: the law allowed others to eat meat, but left these autonomous, respecting them as greater than itself; it made not them, but the others, subject to its justice as originators of wrong-doing. . . . There are many things that the law concedes to the common man but not to the philosopher, or even to the citizens of a well-run city. . . . The law has not forbidden people to spend their time in wine-bars, but nevertheless that is reprehensible in a decent man. Something similar, then, is evident in relation to diet: that which is conceded to ordinary people would not be conceded to the best. A man who engages in philosophy should prescribe for himself, as far as possible, the holy laws which have been determined by gods and by people who follow the gods. It is evident that the holy laws of peoples and cities impose purity on holy people and forbid them to eat animate food, and indeed prevent the masses from eating some kinds, whether from piety or because the food causes some harm. . . . The fully law-abiding and pious man should abstain from all [animate foods], for if in particular cases some people abstain in piety from some foods, the person who is pious in all cases will abstain from all.[7]

Egalitarians, it seems, can have no room for special rules of purity that only a few can live by. Correspondingly, virtues that only a few are likely to acquire cannot be virtues. Virginity, from being one of the highest terms of praise, is usually now regarded as a flaw to be remedied as soon as it is legally possible (though the dangers involved in the transition are partly recognized). Once a sexual practice is perceived to be one that many people will indulge or wish to indulge, it ceases—in the eyes of modern moralists—to be a vice. The only argument generally accepted against a common practice is that it is unhealthy: the same term might have been used a century ago to condemn impurity, but whereas our predecessors meant that only the spiritually sick would do such-and-such things, the modern moralist means only that the practices might lead to obvious disease. Similarly, nicotine and alcohol are no longer as desirable as once they were— but the reasons offered for forswearing them are usually related to the risks to health and safety that they pose, not that their use is symptomatic of a deeper sickness.

It is not only the modern egalitarian moralist that may distrust all talk of purity, cleanness, and spiritual health. Purity rules place limits on how we may live. If it would be wrong to eat pig flesh even to save one's life or the life of one's family, then the rule means more than life itself. To will that we should live purely even at the cost of dying may seem a paradigmatic contradiction: a maxim that cannot be willed at all. The apocryphal commander who declared that his forces had had to destroy the village in order to save it was hardly less coherent. Willing to abstain from sex, and from eating anything produced by sexual intercourse—as the Cathars did— can easily be represented as a will to destroy humanity. Obviously, it is not in fact impossible for humankind to survive a vegetarian diet (as it might not easily survive a total ban on intercourse), but the issue cannot so easily be laughed away. Is humankind or human life the natural, single, or superior end of moral action? And have we not been taught that laws are made for humankind, not human beings for law? Whatever interferes with a proper solidarity with human beings everywhere, it can be felt, is wrong. Purity rules—which might prevent someone eating forbidden foods or having improper relations even to save a life—are bound to be considered antilife.

Once again, there is no real present difficulty, for most of us, in abstinence from eating animals or even animal products. Nor are modern moralists entirely immune to feelings about purity or cleanliness: if it is an argument against abstinence from animal flesh that there might be occasions when we must eat this or die, it would equally be an argument against abstinence from eating people. Yet even those who argue that such a diet might sometimes be permissible or even obligatory will acknowledge that it would be right to feel polluted. Vegetarians may be similarly placed, acknowledging that there might be times when they would feed on flesh, or pardon those who did, and still insist that this would be unclean. Similarly, even those moralists who have rationalized many sexual practices that our predecessors thought defiling will have limits to their tolerance. Necrophiliacs, it could reasonably be argued, do no harm to their victims (who are dead), and any offense to living relatives could be ignored or mitigated. Are we to suppose that the only good reason for condemning necrophilia is the possibility of infection? Or shall we more honestly admit that the practice would be "unclean" even if it were antiseptic: an offense to an unarticulated image of what it is to be decently (which is, "cleanly") human?

So vegetarian purity rules are no more antilife than ordinarily liberal rules. On the one hand, very few of us will ever have to choose between our personal deaths and eating animals. On the other, it is part of the human condition that we must sometimes choose to die clean deaths or live polluted lives. The fact that even honest moralists may sometimes choose the latter—and perhaps seek justice, purification, absolution when they do—does not demonstrate that purity rules are void. According to Porphyry, "It would be terrible if, when the Syrians would not eat fish or the Hebrews pigs, and most of the Phoenicians and the Egyptians would not eat cows, and when many kings tried hard to make them change they would endure death rather than break the law, we should choose to break the laws of nature and the precepts of the gods for fear of people and what they might say."[8]

What is purity? Porphyry believed (drawing again on the Brahminical tradition): "holy men posited that purity is being unmixed with the opposite, whereas mixing is contamination. . . . Purity . . . is singling out and taking that which is natural and appropriate."[9] This was why, so Porphyry said, sex pollutes as well as eating meat, in that it involves a mixture of natures—or else, perhaps more plausibly, that it distracts the intellect.

> Why should we make the passions wither and ourselves die to them, why should we practice this every day, if it were possible (as some have argued) for us to be active in accordance with intellect while we are involved in moral concerns that are unsupervised by intellect? . . . If you can be concerned with the immaterial while eating gourmet food and drinking vintage wine, why not when having intercourse with a mistress?[10]

Porphyry intended that argument as a reductio, relying on a widespread recognition that sexual passion interfered with thought. If his opponents must concede that the philosopher should stay away from sex, why do they indulge in flesh foods for the sake of their taste or their effects (assumed to be sexually exciting)? Modern opponents are more likely to be amused by the suggestion that philosophers should be celibate, and distrustful of the suggestion that menstrual blood or seminal emission are unclean. We prefer, it may be, to dissolve boundaries rather than maintain them.

Opposition to the vegetarian option in Christian tradition has had one other root. The first objection (as above) was that vegetarians ("Pythagoreans") professed a code that—so it was thought—could not be popular: they drew, implicitly, a distinction between the common Christian and the Elect. Maybe there could be reason for some Christians to fast (as there might be reasons for some Christians to be celibate), but it could not be believed that celibate Christians occupied a higher plain than decently married Christians. The second objection (as above) was that the law was made for humankind, not humankind for the law—and correspondingly all precepts that seemed to demand we die rather than break them were suspect. Maybe there could be reasons for some Christians to die martyrs, but it would be wrong to seek out martyrdom. The third root lay in the sense that purity was exactly what the Christian doctrine had rejected: the whole distinction between clean and unclean had been stripped away because all flesh had been taken up into the Godhead. Gandhi attempted some such transvaluation even of excrement in his quest to redeem untouchables. Lepers, excrement, dead bodies, even animals sacrificed to idols[11] could no longer be thought unclean. The ordinary impulses of revulsion were, implicitly, renounced. If God Himself welcomed the corporeal into Himself, how should we exclude it?

All these Christian responses, of course, coexist with the very same attitudes that they reject, precisely because those attitudes are endemic. The radical rejection or transvaluation of purity rules is almost as unfamiliar and disturbing to the modern moralist as it would be in traditional society. The fact that we find other people's purity rules absurd or tragi-comic sometimes helps us forget that we have such rules ourselves—until a really radical challenge comes. *Our* rules, of course, are seen as rational, or rationalized as merely hygienic—which would make more sense if we showed much concern for *health* in general. It is not only Brahmins, nor only vegetarians or environmentalists, who fear "pollution" or wish to "clean up" their lives and habitats. Mainstream moralists and statesmen merely draw their lines in slightly different places. Boundaries are always troublesome, even for those who relish crossing them.

Philosophical Virtue

Ancient moralists—and not only those who lived a vegetarian or Pythagorean life—doubted that we could ever do anyone else good at all, since the only real good was virtue and no one can make another virtuous. Modern moralists assume that it is morally important to do others good (or at least to cause no harm to them), and may share a further assumption with less moralistic thinkers: doing good amounts to making people richer, healthier, or more popular. There is an ambiguity in the phrase "doing well": on the one hand, people are doing well if they earn more than the average, or have other things that wealth and health provide; on the other, they do well if they excel in some profession. Strictly, as Plato pointed out, these two things are distinct, but there is a widespread feeling that excellence must be rewarded economically. Professionals who find their income declining relative to other professions not only find it less easy to acquire the purchasable goods they want, but also conclude that their profession is less valued than it was, that excellence in it is no longer thought significant. Ancient moralists thought otherwise: purchasable goods were hardly goods at all (since none could guarantee a *finer* life), and the only excellence, in the end, worth valuing would be the virtue or virtues needed—precisely— to *live well* (that is, as Aristotle concluded, to *act* or *choose* well: to have the right priorities). Honor could be of value only if it were the recognition of real virtue. Wishing to have more possessions, by contrast, was the vice of *pleonexia*: a term now routinely—and misleadingly—translated as "wanting more than one ought."

The healthy *polis* described by Plato's Socrates in *The Republic* (which Glaucon calls "a city of pigs"') had a strictly vegetarian diet, until the desire for "tasty bits," for luxury, took hold. Greed for imported luxuries, territorial expansion, and a growing division between rich and poor were symptoms of an inflamed society, which must then—in Plato's imagination—be disciplined into a new sobriety. Plato elsewhere says there was a time when people thought it a great impiety to eat flesh, or pollute the altars of the gods with blood.[12] He was not the only philosopher to suppose so. Dicaearchus, it is said, blamed the collapse of the golden age on our progressive, carnivorous meddling with animals. In the age of Kronos, those of the golden race "slew no animal whatever."[13] Meat-eating features among the hill-shepherds who survived the flood, namely the Cyclopes[14] (the ogres of Greek fairy tale). But it is not *necessity* that constrains us now: "luxury, war, and injustice came in together with the slaughter of animals."[15]

The story of a golden age, when people still retained the natural virtues alongside their intelligence, is no more than a story—though one that still has power to move us. The truth is almost certainly that our first human ancestors, like chimpanzees, ate what meat they could. Unlike chimpanzees, they probably planned their hunts with empathetic knowledge of their prey. At any rate, most hunting societies have careful rituals to deflect the evil effects of killing by asking the prey's pardon or consent. Historical fantasy distinguishes the phases: in the first, and wholly blameless, era there were only bloodless sacrifices; in the second, we asked pardon, and sought to wash away the pollution of blood-guilt; in the third or modern age, we forgot the need for pardon, and reasoned away or rationalized our sense of being unclean. Only clean animals should be eaten, and only the butcher bore the stain of killing them—or perhaps his knife.[16]

The fantasy of a golden age may also be a fantasy of natural life: animals are innocent, as Plutarch argued in his *Gryllus* (drawing on an episode in Homer's *Odyssey*, when the witch Circe transforms Odysseus's crew into pigs). One of Circe's transmogrified victims, speaking—she says—for all, insists to Odysseus that he has no wish to become a human being again. Nonhumans, he says, are courageous, temperate, and prudent by nature, whereas people are only brave through fear, and afflicted with unnecessary lusts. "Bravery is an innate characteristic of beasts, while in human beings an independent spirit is actually contrary to nature."[17] It is people, and not pigs, who are the gluttons: "nothing that flies or swims or moves on land has escaped your so-called civilized and hospitable tables."[18]

The story is a fantasy: nonhuman animals, it is clear, do sometimes kill and feed beyond necessity and may display as many perversities as people do. That they can't help it may be no better an excuse than it is in the case of humans. Perversion or uncleanness may be as real among nonhumans as among us, and as much in need of purification. "And we, even if all wolves and vultures approve of meat eating, will not agree that what they say is just, so long as humans are naturally harmless and inclined to refrain from acquiring pleasures for themselves by harming victims."[19] If pollution is inevitable, some have supposed that there must be ways of clearing up the pollution that are correspondingly public and material—and philosophers like Heracleitus have mocked the claim. How could the blood of sacrifice cleanse the hands of blood? In adopting and adapting the language of purity and pollution to the needs of philosophical virtue, philosophers reckoned that true pollution was of the heart, and that it came through thinking (or from a failure to think straight). The issue for them was not merely what we did or did not do, but what our motives and attitudes might be. Shaw, on this account, was wrong to justify himself by the good he had notionally done to particular sheep or cattle, and optimistic even in supposing that his boycott of those goods would be a step on the way to a Brahminical reform. But he might well have been right to wish to dissociate himself from what would have been, for him, pollution. He could have had no *reason* to eat flesh except enjoyment of the kill or enjoyment of the tasty bits or wish, perhaps, for the nervous alertness that may come from a high-protein diet. All these, by the philosophers' argument, tend to divert us from our proper goal. The pollution lies in the perversion of our intellects. The cleansing of our intellects might also change our lives.

> Find me someone who is eager to live, so far as is possible, in accordance with intellect and to be undistracted by the passions which affect the

body, and let him demonstrate that meat eating is easier to provide than dishes of fruits and vegetables; that meat is cheaper to prepare than inanimate food for which chefs are not needed at all; that, compared with inanimate food, it is intrinsically pleasure-free and lighter on the digestion, and more quickly assimilated by the body than vegetables; that it is less provocative of desires and less conducive to obesity and robustness than a diet of inanimate food.[20]

Passing Beyond Purity

The Christian theme that I addressed before (that God's incarnation must cleanse corporeality of taint, and that there can no longer be a distinction between clean and unclean)[21] has been an argument against the vegetarian option. Vegetarians, it has been assumed, must be attempting to dissociate themselves from the corporeal, seeking to deny the Fall by acting as if we could sustain a purer way. Naturists have earned a similar condemnation: maybe we were once "naked and unashamed," but that age is gone with Kronos. So also pacifists, who seek to act by the rules of God's coming Kingdom before its time. In Plato's "age of Zeus" we all live under discipline, bound to commit injustices against each other, and to pay for them. Triptolemus, most ancient of Athenian legislators, laid down three laws (which were, it is said, still operative in Eleusis in the fourth century BCE): respect parents, honor the gods with crops, do not harm animals.[22] Maybe most animals (including human animals) are bound to disobey, and pay the penalty: those who have seen the truth (that we are kin) are equally bound to obey.

Greek and Hebrew appear to agree in this, though they tend to place the golden age, respectively, in time past and time to come. "I think that when friendship and perception of kinship ruled everything, no one killed any creature, because people thought the other animals were related to them."[23] God's oracle to Isaiah: "the wolf lives with the lamb, the panther lies down with the kid, calf and lion cub feed together with a little boy to lead them. The cow and the bear make friends, their young lie down together. The lion eats straw like the ox. The infant plays over the cobra's hole; into the viper's lair the young child puts his hand. They do no hurt, no harm, on all my holy mountain, for the country is filled with the knowledge of Yahweh as the waters swell the sea."[24] The covenant of peace lies on the far side of a transformation, for God "will create new heavens and a new earth, and the past will not be remembered, and will come no more to men's minds."[25] In that new world none will hurt or harm; here, it often seems, we—which is all of sentient creation—are condemned to hurt and harm each other. "You bring darkness on, night falls, all the forest animals come out: savage lions roaring for their prey, claiming their food from God."[26] In the new world, there will be no marriages, no temples, and no courts of law. There, we shall call no man "father." There, we shall be naked and unashamed. But it does not necessarily follow, so mainstream moralists have argued, that we should try to live by those laws here and now. Vegetarians, according to Karl Barth,[27] are trying, like conscientious naturists, to anticipate the Kingdom.

In this age only compulsion could make the wolf lie down with the kid. Better, we might suppose, to accept the laws of nature. Less mythologically, the mainstream may accept that animals in our care should be treated with respect, that they be spared some natural ills as the price for using them in the service of the bloated city. To demand more than that— that they be released from their captivity and granted legal defenses against oppression—is too romantic a thought to be serious. Jesus' parable of the wheat and tares makes a similar point: the tares cannot be eliminated without tearing up the wheat, and so must be left to grow together till the Day of Harvest.[28] Our involvement in the corporeal world, the world of competition and possessive lust, is permitted, even required of most of us. Even those, if there are any, who are excused that involvement have no higher moral or spiritual standing. The pollution incurred by corporeal involvement has been cleansed, or paid for, or carried forward through the cross of Christ. From all of which Christians since Augustine have concluded that the vegetarian option is at least not a Christian duty, and may even—if its motive is contempt for the corporeal—be forbidden.

Porphyry, like other Platonists and Pythagoreans, was persuaded that these arguments were excuses. The better path, he thought, required a disengagement. Philosophers should not endorse iniquity. Platonists and Pythagoreans, like Porphyry, agreed with Abrahamic theists that the corporeal world was not entirely lost: matter, or corporeality, was the principle of evil, but no actual corporeal thing was anything but beautiful. Matter as such is almost nothing: the mere possibility that things decay and are transformed. To be at all is to be beautiful, and there is nothing that is not an image of the divine. To be disengaged from the corporeal is not to despise corporeal things: on the contrary, it is by disengagement that we come to see their beauty. As Aristotle insisted, in even the smallest or basest entity there is something wonderful and beautiful.[29]

So the proper form of life is not one dedicated to the pursuit of pleasure, nor of status. Instead the ancient tradition presented a way of living and thinking that recognizes the value of all the creatures, human and otherwise, with whom we share the world. That state of being is valuable in itself, and is conceived as naked. "Let us go stripped, without tunics, to the stadium, to compete in the Olympics of the soul. Stripping off is the starting point, without which the contest will not happen."[30] Maybe our destination is not a stadium, but a shrine. Edward Herbert, Earl of Cherbury, in 1624 wrote:

> Those who would enter the shrine of truth must leave their trinkets, in other words their opinions, at the entrance, or as one might say in the cloakroom. They will find that everything is open or revealed to perception as long as they do not approach it with prejudice.[31]

This is not merely a piece of Cartesian rationalism or methodological skepticism. The prejudices of which we must strip ourselves are not only unfounded claims to knowledge, but the stereotypes and misplaced evaluations that bedevil us. The world of fame and fortune, of everyday concerns, is, so Marcus Aurelius had warned, "a dream and a delirium."[32] The world of our immediate perception and imagining is centered upon ourselves, and full of vermin, pests, and pets. In brief, we see things through the framework of our very own conception of what counts as clean or unclean. To be stripped naked is at once to be purified—and to abandon the categories of purity and pollution. "To the pure all things are pure" is the doctrine at the heart of Platonism, just as "to the pure all things are rather sordid" lies at the heart of the sort of miscalled Puritanism that has given purity a bad name.

The charge against vegetarians has been that they must despise the world, and wish to be detached from it. Mainstream moralists have argued, bizarrely, that it is because we *value* animals that we are entitled to enjoy imprisoning, maiming, killing, eating them. The converse claim is that it is vegetarians who have the chance of valuing what is: by stripping away the false perception that such creatures exist *for us*, we are enabled to see them in their beauty.

> Aristotle says that animals learn many things from each other and many things from humans; and everyone testifies that he spoke truly—every horse-breaker and groom and rider and charioteer, every huntsman and mahout and herdsman and all the trainers of wild animals and birds. A well-informed person concedes understanding to animals on this evidence; an ignorant person who has done no research about them is carried away, collaborating with his own aggression toward them. How, indeed, would he not abuse and misrepresent creatures he has chosen to carve up as if they were stone?[33]

To see them we must strip off our aggression. Conversely, by seeing them in their own beauty, we realize our own true, natural self: "the self of each of us is not anger or fear or desire, just as it is not bits of flesh or fluids either, but is that with which we reason and understand."[34]

It is in this context that the ancient notion that the natural life is to be preferred must be understood. The natural is not what ordinarily happens; in those terms, it would be natural for us to gobble up whatever we can manage. Plotinus (himself a committed vegetarian) acknowledged that "it is necessary that animals should eat each other; these eatings are transformations into each other of animals which could not stay as they were for ever, even if no-one killed them."[35] The corporeal world depends on these transformations (though they need not be as stressful as we make them), but *our* nature is to look elsewhere for inspiration.

The Stoic Epictetus, for once acknowledging that other creatures than the human have their needs and natures, imagines how a caged bird might speak: "My nature is to fly where I please, to live in the open air, to sing when I please. You rob me of all this and then ask what is wrong with me?"[36] Our nature likewise is not to bite, kick, imprison, or behead, but to do good, to work together, to pray for the success of others.[37] What is natural for us is our original nature, virtue stripped of prejudice, affectionate delight in being. This doctrine, of course, is located in a metaphysics strange to many moderns—but that is not my present concern. If we were not originally pure souls, then the ideal to which the ancients testified is not well described as our original or real nature, but it may remain our ideal. The Pythagorean Life that Porphyry extols to his backsliding friend depends on our seeing things straight, and helps to maintain that sight.

NOTES

1. Porphyry, *On Abstinence from Killing Animals*, trans. Gillian Clark (London: Duckworth, 2000), p. 40.

2. The prohibition was relaxed in 1877, resulting in a split between the Vegetarian and the London Food Reform Society, though the two societies merged again later.

3. Porphyry, *On Abstinence*, p. 85: "Even if we think more than they do, animals are not to be deprived of thinking, any more than partridges are to be deprived of flying because falcons fly more."

4. Ibid., p. 87: "Nature that created them has made them need humans and has also made humans need them, establishing an innate justice in them toward us and in us toward them."

5. I addressed the related issue of "the rights of wild things" in "The Rights of Wild Things," *Inquiry* 22 (1979): 171 ff., republished in *Animals and Their Moral Standing* (London: Routledge, 1997).

6. Anne Conway, *Principles of the Most Ancient and Modern Philosophy*, ed. A. P. Courdert and T. Corse (Cambridge: Cambridge University Press, 1996), p. 35 (the book was originally published, posthumously, in 1690.)

7. Porphyry, *On Abstinence*, p. 115; see also p. 37. What a Samanaean may have been, we do not clearly know: it may be that Porphyry was faintly aware of the heterodox Indian sects that came to be known as Buddhists or as Jains.

8. Porphyry, *On Abstinence*, p. 80.

9. Ibid., pp. 116, 190. Porphyry drew his knowledge of Hinduism from one Bardesanes of Babylon (154–222), a Christian who taught in Edessa, and met the Indian embassy to the Emperor Heliogabalus.

10. Porphyry, *On Abstinence*, p. 47.

11. See I Corinthians 8; compare Revelation 2:14.

12. Plato, *Laws* 6.782.

13. Porphyry, *On Abstinence*, p. 101. Dicaearchus was a late fourth-century pupil of Aristotle.

14. Plato, *Laws* 3.679; the Hebrew scriptures suggest that permission to eat flesh was only given after the Flood (Genesis 9). See further B. D. Shaw, "'Eaters of Flesh, Drinkers of Milk': The Ancient Mediterranean Ideology of the Pastoral Nomad," *Ancient Society* 13–14 (1982): 5–31.

15. Porphyry, *On Abstinence*, p. 101.

16. Ibid., p. 67. See also C. von Furer-Haimendorf, *Morals and Merit: A Study of Values and Social Controls in South Asian Societies* (London: Weidenfeld & Nicolson, 1967), p. 187, for similar rationalizations in the Buddhist tradition: "To kill a living creature is sin. . . . To kill yak and sheep is sin for the butchers, but not for those who eat the meat."

17. Plutarch, *Gryllus* 987f.

18. Ibid., 991d.

19. Porphyry, *On Abstinence*, p. 80: the sense of "naturally" I shall address below.

20. Ibid., p. 49. Note that "pleasure" in Porphyry's thought is a disruptive passion, and that "robustness" is not a virtue: "fat and sassy" is probably the phrase. See Gillian Clark, "Fattening the Soul: Christian Asceticism and Porphyry, *On Abstinence*," *Studia Patristica* 35 (2001): 41–51.

21. Acts of the Apostles 10:15.

22. Porphyry, *On Abstinence*, p. 118.

23. Ibid., p. 63. Porphyry may be transcribing Theophrastus, another pupil of Aristotle.

24. Isaiah 11:6ff.; see 65:17ff.

25. Isaiah 65:17; see Revelation 21:1.

26. Psalm 104:20ff.; see Job 38:39ff.

27. Karl Barth, *Church Dogmatics*, ed. G. W. Bromiley and T. F. Torrance (Edinburgh: T. & T. Clark, 1936), III, pt. 4, p. 350ff.

28. Matthew 13:24ff.

29. Aristotle, *De Partibus Animalium* 1.645a15f.

30. Porphyry, *On Abstinence*, p. 43.

31. Edward Herbert, *De Veritate*, trans. M. H. Carré (Bristol, UK: Arrowsmith, 1937), p. 72, after Philo *Legum Allegoriae* 2.56; Plotinus, *Enneads*, trans. A. H. Armstrong (London: Heinemann, 1978–88), I.6.7.

32. Marcus Aurelius, *Meditations* 2.17.1.

33. Porphyry, *On Abstinence*, p. 84; see also p. 92: "such behaviour strengthens that in us which is murderous and bestial and impassive to pity. But the Pythagoreans made kindness to beasts a training in humanity and pity."

34. Plutarch, *De Facie Lunae* 945a.

35. Plotinus, *Enneads*, III.2.15.

36. Epictetus, *Discourses* 4.1.24.

37. Ibid., 4.1.121.

12 A CRITIQUE OF THE ALLEGED MORAL BASIS OF VEGETARIANISM

Carl Cohen

There is no obligation to eat meat. But neither is there any obligation to refrain from doing so. The oft-alleged obligation to restrict oneself to a vegetarian diet is commonly grounded on the supposition that animals have moral rights. If they do have such rights then they surely have the right to live, and therefore (it is supposed) killing and devouring them must wrongfully violate their rights.[1] This argument is without merit because, in fact, animals do not have rights.

We care about animals, of course. Most of us care a great deal about them, and we very much want not to be thought uncaring. But there is widespread fear that one who denies that animals have rights is likely to be thought callous or even cruel; this results in a general reluctance to express a moral truth that everyone grasps intuitively: rights, which are central in the moral lives of humans, are not possessed by animals; animals do not have rights. *Why* they do not have them is explained below.

Before turning to that, however, I emphasize one consequence of this moral truth: We may conclude with confidence that opposition to the eating of meat is ungrounded insofar as that opposition is based upon

This essay is a revised version of "Why Animals Do Not Have Rights," in *The Animal Rights Debate*, ed. Carl Cohen and Tom Regan (Lanham, MD: Rowman and Littlefield Publishers, 2001), chap. 5.

claimed rights that are in fact illusory. Animals cannot be deprived of rights they do not have.

The reluctance to deny that animals have rights lies in a common confusion about the relation between our *obligations* to animals and the claim that they possess *rights*. Humans do have many obligations to animals, of course, as all decent persons will agree. Many go on to suppose that since such obligations are genuine, animals must have rights because if those rights were to be denied, the obligations owed to animals (not seriously in question) would need to be denied as well. This is a frequent and unfortunate mistake. Denying the reality of animal rights does *not* entail the denial of our obligations to animals. Most certainly it does not. I explain.

Reflect for a moment upon the obligations we humans owe to others. Some of these obligations may be traced to the fact that we are the targets of their rights. My obligation to repay the money I borrowed from you is the obverse of the right that you have to my payment of the debt. So, plainly, *some* of my obligations do arise from the rights of others against me. But that is by no means true of all obligations. A correct understanding of the true relation between rights and obligations is absolutely essential for sound moral judgments.

The common readiness to assent to the proposition that animals have rights is mainly a result of the hasty supposition that if we have obligations to them (which we surely do) they must have rights against us. But this is not so. Recognizing (correctly) that we are not morally free to do anything we please to animals, it is inferred (incorrectly) that they must therefore have "rights"— and that inference yields a defense of vegetarianism on moral grounds.

The premise that underlies such reasoning is the supposition of the *symmetrical reciprocity* of obligations and rights. It is a false premise, and its falsity is easy to discern. Between rights and obligations the relations are not symmetrical. Rights do entail obligations upon the targets of those rights, of course, as earlier noted. If you have a right to the return of money you lent me, I have the obligation to return that money, and so on. But we may not correctly infer from the fact that all rights impose obligations upon their targets that all obligations owed arise because one is the target of the rights of another.

A logical confusion underlies the mistake. From the true proposition that all dogs are mammals we certainly may not infer that all mammals are dogs. Universal affirmative propositions of the form "all dogs are mammals" or "all rights entail obligations," cannot be *converted simply* and retain their truth. *Some* mammals are dogs, yes, and *some* obligations do arise from rights. But it is a confusion of mind to conclude, from the fact that all dogs are mammals, that all mammals are dogs. It is no less a confusion of mind to conclude that because all rights entail obligations, all obligations are entailed by rights.

Very many of the moral obligations borne by each of us are owed to other persons or other beings who have no *rights* against us; reflection on everyday experience confirms this quickly. Our obligations arise from a great variety of circumstances and relations, of which being the target of another's right is but one. Illustrations of this rich and important variety are everywhere to be found; here are some:

a) Obligations arise from *commitments* freely made by a moral agent. As a college professor I promise my students explicitly that I will comment at length on the papers they submit, and from this express commitment obligations flow, of course. But my students understand that they have not the right to demand that I provide such comment.

b) Obligations arise from *the possession of authority.* Civil servants are obliged to be courteous to members of the public; presiding officers at a public forum ought to call upon representatives of different points of view in alternation; judges have the obligation to listen patiently to the arguments of parties disputing before them— but such obligations are not grounded in rights.

c) Obligations arise as a consequence of *special relations*: hosts have an obligation to be cordial to their guests, but guests may not demand cordiality as a right.

d) *Faithful service* may engender obligations: shepherds have obligations to their dogs, and cowboys to their horses, none of which flow from the *rights* of those dogs or those horses.

e) My son, eleven years old as I write this, may someday wish to study veterinary medicine as my father did. I will then have the obligation to help him as I can, and with pride I shall—but he has not the authority to demand such help as a matter of right. *Family connections* may give rise to obligations without concomitant rights.

f) My dog has no right to daily exercise and veterinary care, but I do have the obligation to provide these things for him. *Duties of care* freely taken on may bind one even though those to whom the care is given have not got a right to demand it. Recognizing that a beloved pet is suffering great pain, we may be obliged to put it out of its misery, but the tormented animal has no claim of right that that be done.

g) An act of *spontaneous kindness* done may leave us with the obligation to acknowledge and perhaps return that gift, but the benefactor to whom we are thus obliged has no claim of *right* against us.

And so on and on. The circumstances giving rise to obligations are so many and so varied that they cannot all be cataloged. It is nevertheless certain and plainly seen that it is *not only* from the rights of others that our obligations arise.

How then are rights and obligations related? When looked at from the viewpoint of one who holds a right and addresses the target of that right, they appear correlative. But they are plainly not correlative when looked at from the viewpoint of one who recognizes an obligation on himself, an obligation that does not stem from the rights of another. Your right to the money I owe you creates my obligation to pay it, of course. But many of my obligations to the needy, to my neighbors, to sentient creatures of every sort, have no foundation in their rights. The premise that rights and obligations are *reciprocals*, that *every* obligation flows from another's right, is utterly false. It is inconsistent with our intuitive understanding of the difference between what we believe we *ought* to do and what others can justly *demand* that we do.

This lack of symmetry is of enormous importance. It helps to explain how it can be true that, although animals do not have rights, it does not follow from this fact that one is free to treat them with callous disregard. It is silly to think of rats as the holders of moral rights, but it is by no means silly to recognize that rats can feel pain and that it is our obligation to refrain from torturing them because they are beings having that capacity. The obligation to act humanely *we owe to them* even though the concept of a right cannot possibly apply to them. We are obliged to apply to animals the moral principles that govern *us* regarding the gratuitous imposition of pain and suffering. We are the moral agents in this arena, not the rats. Act toward lesser creatures, as the saying goes, "not merely according to their deserts, but according to your dignities." We are restrained by moral principles in this way, but being so restrained does not suggest or suppose that the animals to whom we owe humane regard are the possessors of rights.

*   *   *

Animals cannot be the bearers of rights because the concept of right is *essentially human*; it is rooted in the human moral world and has force and applicability only within that world. Humans must deal with rats—all too frequently in some parts of the world—and must refrain from cruelty in dealing with them. But a rat can no more be said to have rights than a table can be said to have ambition, or a rock to exhibit remorse. To say of a pig or a fish that it has rights is to confuse categories, to apply to its world a moral category that can have content only in the human moral world.

Try this thought experiment: Imagine, on the Serengeti Plain in East Africa, a lioness hunting to feed her cubs. A baby zebra, momentarily left unattended by its mother, becomes her prey; the lioness snatches it, rips open its throat, tears out chunks of its flesh, and departs. The mother zebra is driven nearly out of her wits when at first she cannot locate her baby; finding its carcass at last, she will not leave its remains for days. The scene may cause you to shudder, but it is perfectly ordinary and common in the world of nature. If that baby zebra had any rights at all it certainly had the right to live; of all rights that is surely the most fundamental and the one presupposed by all others. So, if in that incident of natural predation, the prey has rights and the predator infringes those rights, we humans ought to intervene in defense of the zebra's rights, if doing so were within our power. But we do not intervene in such matters even when it is in our power; we do not dream of doing so. On the other hand, if we saw (or even suspected) that the lioness was about to attack an unprotected human baby playing at the edge of the forest, we would respond with alacrity, protecting the baby in every way within our power.

What accounts for the moral difference between those cases? Not convenience merely; protecting the baby may be dangerous, while intervening to save the baby zebra may be easy and safe. Humans are often in a position to intervene to avoid predatory killing, yet we deliberately refrain. Our responses to threatened humans differ fundamentally from our responses to threatened zebras. But why? No doubt we have greater empathy for the endangered human. But we also recognize, consciously or subconsciously, that between the moral status of the baby zebra and the moral status of the baby human there are profound differences. The human baby, we might say if later asked, has a right not to be eaten alive, and it has that right because it is a *human* being.

Do you believe the baby zebra has the *right* not to be slaughtered? Or that the lioness has the *right* to kill that baby zebra to feed her cubs? Perhaps you are inclined to say, when confronted by such natural rapacity (duplicated in various forms millions of times each day on planet earth) that *neither* is right or wrong, that neither zebra nor lioness has a right against the other. Then I am on your side. Rights are pivotal in the moral realm and must be taken seriously, yes; but zebras and lions and rats do not live in a moral realm; their lives are totally *a*moral. There *is* no morality for them; animals do no moral wrong, ever. In their world there are no wrongs and there are no rights.

One contemporary philosopher who has thought a good deal about animals puts this point in terms of the ability to formulate principles. Referring to animals as "moral patients" [that is, beings *upon* whom moral agents like ourselves may act], he writes:

> A moral patient [an animal] lacks the ability to formulate, let alone bring to bear, principles in deliberating about which one among a number of possible acts it would be right or proper to perform. Moral patients, in a word, cannot do what is right, nor can they do what is wrong. . . . [E]ven when a moral patient causes significant harm to another, the moral patient has not done what is wrong. Only moral agents can do what is wrong.

Just so. The concepts of wrong, and of right, are totally foreign to animals, not conceivably within their ken or applicable to them, as the author of that passage clearly sees. He is the noted advocate of animal rights, Tom Regan.[2]

Here is yet another thought experiment that illuminates our intuitive judgments about the moral status of animals: Imagine that, as you were driving to work the other day, a squirrel suddenly reversed its course and ran in front of your car. It being impossible for you to avoid hitting it, you clenched your teeth as you heard the telltale thump from beneath the automobile. Pained by the thought that the squirrel had been needlessly killed by your car, you silently express to yourself the hope that, if indeed it was killed, it was caused no great suffering; and you drive on. But now suppose that it was not a squirrel but a human toddler who ran into the path of your car and whom you hit through absolutely no fault of your own. Swerving in panic, we will suppose, you avoid a killing blow, but you cannot avoid hitting the child and it becomes plain that she has been badly injured by the impact. Anguish, fear, *horror* overwhelm you. Most assuredly you do not drive on, but stop in wretched torment, to do what can be done for the injured child. You rush it to medical care; its parents you contact at the earliest possible moment, imploring their understanding. Nothing you could possibly have done would have avoided the terrible accident, you explain—and yet you express tearfully your profound regret. At the first opportunity you arrange to visit the recuperating child; you bring it a present, wish it well; her injury and her recovery will be forever on your mind. And so on.

What accounts for the enormous difference between the response you make to the death of a squirrel, and to the injury of a human child, you being the cause of both, and in both cases entirely innocent of fault? Does that difference not spring from your intuitive grasp of the difference in the moral status of the two, your recognition that the one has rights, which you would not for all the world have deliberately infringed, while the other, although sentient and perhaps endearing, has no rights that you could possibly infringe?

Those who rely on animals for food, like medical investigators who use animals in research to advance human well-being, do not violate the rights of animals by their conduct because, to be blunt, animals have no rights. Rights do not apply to them.

Humans, on the other hand, certainly do have rights. How is this difference to be accounted for? Rabbits are mammals and we are mammals, both inhabiting a natural world. The reality of the moral rights that we possess (and that they do not possess) we do not doubt, and the importance of this great difference between them and us is equally certain. But we are unsure of the ground of these rights of ours. Where do they come from? We are a natural species too, a product of evolution as all animals are. How then can we be so very different from the zebras and the rats? Why are we not crudely primitive creatures, as they are, for whom the concept of moral right is a fiction?

Philosophers and theologians have long struggled, and struggle still, to explain the foundations of natural human rights. I do not propose to offer here the resolution of the deepest questions confronting human beings. But the sharp divide between the moral status of animals and that of humans we can say something more about.

It will be helpful to reflect upon the *kinds* of explanations of human rights that have been given by the greatest of moral philosophers. What has been generally held to account for the fact that humans, unlike animals, do have rights?

(1) Many have thought that the moral understanding of right and duty, by humans, is a *divine gift*, a grasp of the eternal law for which we have been peculiarly equipped by God. So thought St. Thomas of Aquinas, who argued tightly in defense of that view in the thirteenth century. All things, said he,

> are ruled and measured by the eternal law. . . . Now among all others, the rational creature is subject to divine providence in the most excellent way, in so far as it partakes of a share of providence. . . . Wherefore it has a share of the eternal reason, whereby it has a natural inclination to its proper act and end: and this participation of the eternal law in the rational creature is called the natural law. Hence the Psalmist after saying . . . "Many say, Who showeth us good things?" in answer to which question he says: "The light of Thy countenance, O Lord, is signed upon us.[3]

He thus implies that the light of natural reason, whereby we discern what is good and what is evil, which is the function of the natural law, is nothing else than an imprint on us of the divine light.[4] The power to grasp the binding power of moral law, and therefore the capacity to understand human rights, and to respect them, is on this account divinely endowed. No one has put this view more cogently than St. Thomas. The account he gave was not new in his day, nor has it lost its authority for many today.

Long before St. Thomas marshaled such arguments, other fathers of the Church, perhaps St. Augustine most profoundly, had pointed out that if God has made us in his own image, as we are taught, and therefore with a will that is truly free and "knowing good and evil,"[5] we, unlike all other creatures, must choose between good and evil, between right and wrong.[6]

(2) Philosophers have very commonly distrusted such theological reasoning. Many accounts of the moral dimension of human experience have been offered that do not rely upon inspired texts or supernatural gifts. Of the most influential philosophers, many have held that human morality is

grounded not in the divine but in the human moral community. "I am morally realized," wrote the great English idealist, F. H. Bradley, "not until my personal self has utterly ceased to be my exclusive self, is no more a will which is outside others' wills, but finds in the world of others nothing but self." What Bradley called "the organic moral community" is, he thought, the only context in which there can be right. "Realize yourself as the self-conscious member of an infinite whole, by realizing that whole in yourself."[7]

Before him, the great German idealist G. W. F. Hegel accounted for human rights as a consequence of the self-conscious participation of human beings in "an objective ethical order."[8] And there have been many other such accounts of rights, accounts that center upon human interrelations, upon a moral fabric within which human beings must always act, but within which animals never act and never can *possibly* act.

(3) Such reasoning is exceedingly abstract, and for that reason many find it unsatisfying. A better account of rights, an account more concrete and more true to their own experience, some think to be that given by ethical intuitionists and realists who rely upon the immediate moral experience of ordinary people. Human moral conduct must be governed, said the leading intuitionist H. A. Prichard, by the "underivative, intuitive cognition of the rightness of an action."[9] Would you know how we can be sure that humans have rights? Ask yourself how you know that you have rights. You have no doubt about it. There are some fundamental truths, on this view, for which no argument need be given. In that same spirit Sir David Ross explained our grasp of human rights as our recognition of moral "suitability": "fitness, in a certain specific and unanalyzable way, to a certain situation."[10] And that was the view of my teacher and my friend of happy memory, Professor C. D. Broad. Rights surely are possessed by humans, he thought, by humans but never by animals. The knowledge of right is immediately and certainly possessed.

(4) For those who seek a more naturalistic account of ethical concepts, there are, among others, the writings of Marx and his followers who explicitly repudiated all moral views claiming to have their foundation in some supernatural sphere. "The animal," Marx wrote, "is one with its life activity. It does not distinguish the activity from itself. It is its activity. But man makes his life activity itself an object of his will and consciousness. . . . His own life is an object for him. . . . Conscious life activity distinguishes man from the life activity of the animals."

Hence humans can concern themselves with human*kind*, and humans alone can understand their species; humans, unlike animals, make judgments that can be "universal and consequently free."[11] Moral judgments are typically universal in this sense. That is why, Lenin later wrote, "There is no such thing as morality taken outside of human society."[12] Every conception of moral right, on this view, is a reflection of the concrete conditions of life, but always the conditions of *human* life.

A more sophisticated ethical naturalism was presented by the American pragmatists John Dewey and George Herbert Mead, who shared the view that morality arises only in human community, but who emphasized the development of self within that community. We humans create our selves, selves that develop and become moral, Mead wrote, only through "the consciousness of other moral selves."[13]

Which among all these families of moral positions is most nearly true? Readers will decide for themselves. Differing ethical systems have been very briefly recapitulated here only to underscore the fact that, however much great thinkers have disagreed about fundamental principles, *the essentially human locus of the concept of right* has never been seriously doubted. Of the finest moral philosophers from antiquity to the present not one would deny—as the animal rights movement does seek now to deny—that there is a most profound difference between the moral stature of humans and that of animals, and that rights pertain only to the former.

*   *   *

The claim that there is no fundamental moral difference between animals and humans is the essential mark of what is loosely called the animal rights movement. "There is no rational basis," says Ingrid Newkirk, of People for the Ethical Treatment of Animals (PETA), "for saying that a human being has special rights." But in this she is profoundly mistaken; there *is* a rational basis for this distinction, a distinction of the deepest importance. The failure to grasp and respect that distinction leads some zealots to interfere with medical research, and others to insist that eating meat is a moral wrong. Reflect upon what it is that differentiates acts by humans from the acts of cows or rabbits. With Immanuel Kant we may say that critical reason reveals at the core of *human* action a uniquely moral will. There is, in humans, a unique capacity to formulate moral *principles* for the direction of our conduct, and we have a direct and immediate understanding of that capacity. Human beings can grasp the maxim of the principles we devise, and by applying those principles to ourselves as well as to others, we exhibit the autonomy of the human will. Humans, but never cows, confront choices that are purely moral. Humans, but certainly not pigs or chickens, lay down rules, moral imperatives, by which all moral agents are thought to be rightly governed, ourselves along with all others. Human beings are *self*-legislative, morally *auto*nomous.

To be a moral agent is to be able to grasp the generality of moral restrictions upon our will. Humans understand that there are some acts that may be in our interest and yet must not be willed because they are simply wrong. This capacity for moral judgment does not arise in the animal world; rats can neither exercise nor respond to moral claims. My dog knows that there are certain things he must not do, but he knows this only as the outcome of his learning about his interests, the pains he may suffer if he does what he's been taught is forbidden. He does not know, he *cannot* know (as Tom Regan agrees)[14] that any conduct is *wrong*. The proposition: "It would be highly advantageous to act in such-and-such a way, but I may not do so because it would be morally wrong" is one that no dog or bunny rabbit, however sweet and endearing, however loyal or loving or intelligent, can ever entertain, or intend, or begin to grasp. *Right is not in their world.* But right and wrong are the very stuff of human moral life, the ever-present awareness of human beings who *can* do wrong, and who by seeking (often but not always) to avoid wrong conduct prove themselves members of a moral community in which rights may be exercised and must be respected.

Every day humans confront actual or potential conflicts between what is in their own interest and what is just. We restrain ourselves (or at least we can do so) on purely moral grounds. In such a community the concept of a right makes very good sense, of course. Some riches that do not belong to us would please us, no doubt, but we *may* not take them; we refrain from stealing not only because we fear punishment if caught. Even if we knew that the detection of our wrongdoing were impossible, we understand that to deprive others of what is theirs by right is conduct forbidden *by our own moral rules.* We return lost property belonging to others even when keeping it might be much to our advantage; such return is the act that our moral principles call for. Only in a community of that kind, a community consti- tuted by beings capable of self-restricting moral judgments, can the concept of a *right* be intelligibly invoked.

Humans have such moral capacities. They are in this sense self-legisla- tive, members of moral communities governed by moral rules; humans possess rights and recognize the rights of others. Animals do not have such capacities. They cannot exhibit moral autonomy in this sense, cannot pos- sibly be members of a truly moral community. They may be the objects of our moral concern because they are sentient, of course, but they cannot possibly possess rights. People who eat animals do not violate the rights of those animals because, to be plain, they have none to violate.

I repeat one caveat for emphasis: It does not follow from the fact that animals have no rights that we are free to do anything we please to them. Most assuredly not. We do have obligations to animals, weighty obliga- tions—but those obligations do not, because they cannot, arise out of animal rights.

*   *   *

There is an objection sometimes raised to this view that deserves response and deserves also to be permanently put aside. It cannot be, the critic says, that having rights requires the ability to make moral claims, or to grasp and apply moral laws, because, if that were true, many human beings—the brain-damaged, the comatose, infants, and the senile—who plainly lack those capacities must be without rights. But that is absurd. This proves, the critic concludes, that rights do not depend on the presence of moral capacities.[15]

Objections of this kind arise from a misunderstanding of what it means to say that the moral world is a human world. Children, like elderly adults, have rights *because they are human*. Morality is an essential feature of human life; all humans are moral creatures, infants and the senile included. Rights are not doled out to this individual person or that one by somehow establishing the presence in them of some special capacity. This mistaken vision would result in the selective award of rights to some individuals but not others, and the cancellation of rights when capacities fail. On the contrary, rights are *universally* human, apply to humans generally. This criticism thus errs by treating the essentially moral feature of humanity as though it were a screen for sorting individual humans, which it most certainly is not. The capacity for moral judgment that distinguishes humans from animals is not a test to be administered to human beings one by one. Persons who, because of some disability, are unable to perform the full moral functions natural to human beings are not for that reason ejected from the human community. The critical distinction is one of kind. Humans are of such a kind that rights pertain to them *as humans*; humans live lives that will be, or have been, or remain *essentially* moral. It is silly to suppose that human rights might fluctuate with an individual's health, or dissipate with an individual's decline. The rights involved are human rights. On the other hand, animals are of such a kind that rights never pertain to them; what humans retain when disabled, rats never had.

The contrast between these two very different moral conditions is highlighted in the world of medical experimentation. Humans must *choose* to allow themselves to be the instruments of scientific research, and because humans have moral authority over their own bodies, we insist that humans may be the subject of scientific experiments only with their informed and freely given consent. Investigators who withhold information from potential subjects, or who deceive potential subjects, thereby making it impossible for them to give genuinely voluntary consent to what is done, will be condemned and punished, rightly. But this consent, which we think absolutely essential in the case of human subjects, is *impossible* for animals to give. The reason is not merely that we cannot communicate with them, or explain to them or inquire of them, but that the kind of moral choice involved in giving consent is totally out of the question for a chicken or a cow.

*   *   *

An objection of a different kind is raised by some advocates of animal rights. It goes like this:

> Animals have internal lives far more rich and complicated than most people realize; many animals are, as Tom Regan points out, "psychologically complex" beings. Therefore, the effort to distinguish the world of humans from the world of animals by pointing to some special capacity of humans cannot succeed. Although in lesser degree than humans, animals do have the capacities we commonly associate with humanity. Humans are rational, but animals can reason too; animals communicate with one another, not with languages like ours of course, but very effectively nonetheless. Animals, like humans, care passionately for their young; animals, like humans, exhibit desires and preferences. And so on and on. So there is no genuine moral distinction to be drawn.[16]

This objection has much popular appeal but it fails because it relies upon a mistaken assumption. *Cognitive* abilities, the ability to communicate or to reason, are simply not at issue. My dog certainly reasons, and he communicates rather well. Nor is it *affective* capacities that are at issue; many animals plainly exhibit fear, love, and anger, care for one another and for their offspring, and so on. Nor is it the exhibition of *preference*, or memory, or aversion that marks the critical divide; no one doubts that a squirrel may recall where it buried a nut, or that a dog would rather go on a walk than remain in the car. Remarkable behaviors are often exhibited by animals, as we all know. Conditioning, fear, instinct, and intelligence all contribute to individual success and to species survival.

Nor is the capacity to suffer sufficient to justify the claim that animals have rights. They surely can suffer; it is obvious that they feel pain. And because they are sentient in that way, they are properly a concern of morally sensitive humans; they are, we may say, morally "considerable." Of course. And that is why the moral principles that govern us oblige us to act thoughtfully, humanely, in our use of them.

But with all the varied capacities of animals granted, it remains absolutely impossible for them to act *morally*, to be members of a moral community. Emphasizing similarities between human families and those of monkeys, or between human communities and those of wolves, and the like, cannot ground the moral equality of species; it serves only to obscure what is truly critical. A being subject to genuinely moral judgment must be capable of grasping the *maxim* of an act, and capable, too, of grasping the *generality* of an ethical premise in a moral argument. Similarities between animal conduct and human conduct cannot refute, cannot even address, the profound moral differences between humans and the lower animals.

Because humans do have rights, and these rights can be violated by other humans, we all understand that humans can and sometimes do commit *crimes*. Whether a crime has been committed, however, depends utterly upon the actor's moral state of mind. If I take your coat from the closet honestly believing that it was mine, I do not steal it. A genuine crime is an act in which the guilty deed, the *actus reus*, is accompanied by a guilty state of mind, a mens rea. Humans can commit crimes not merely because we realize that we may be punished for acting thus-and-so, but because we recognize that there are duties that govern us; to speak of such recognition in the world of cows and horses is literally nonsensical. In primitive times cows and horses were sometimes punished at the bar of human justice. We chuckle now as we look back upon that practice, realizing that to accuse a cow of a crime marks the accuser as inane, confused about the applicability of moral concepts. Animals never can be criminals, obviously—not because they are always law-abiding, but because "law-abiding" has no sense in this context; moral appraisals do not intelligibly apply to them. And that is why it is not true, and never can be true, that animals have moral rights.

The fundamental mistake is one in which a concept (in this case, moral right) that makes very good sense in one context, is applied in another context in which it makes no sense at all. It may be helpful to reflect upon other spheres, very distant from morality, in which mistakes of the same general kind have been commonly made at great cost.

The world of metaphysical thinking is riddled with mistakes of that kind. In his *Critique of Pure Reason*, Immanuel Kant explains at length the metaphysical blunders into which we are led when we apply concepts fundamentally important in one sphere in another sphere in which those concepts can have no grip. In our human experience (for example), the concepts of time and space, the relations of cause and effect, of subject and attribute, and others, are fundamental and inescapable. But these are concepts arising only within the world of our human experience and are bound to it. When we forget that bond we may be misled into asking: "Was the world caused, or is it uncaused?" "Did the world have a beginning in time, or did it not?" Kant explains, in one of the most brilliant long passages in all philosophical literature, why it *makes no sense* to ask such questions.[17] "Causation" is a concept that applies to phenomena we humans encounter; it is a category of our experience and cannot apply to the world as a whole. "Time" is the sequential condition of our experience, the way we experience things, not a container within which the world could have begun. In his discussion of the *paralogisms* of pure reason, and following his analyses of the *antinomies* of pure reason, Kant patiently exhibits the many confusions arising from the *misapplication* of the categories of experience. Whatever our judgment of his conclusions about the limits of reason, his larger lesson in these passages is powerful and deep. The misapplication of concepts leads to fundamental mistakes, to nonsense.

So it is also when we mistakenly transfer the concept of a right from the human moral world where it is rightly applied to the status of humans, to the animal world where it has no possible applicability, and wrongly applied to the status of animals. To say that rats have rights is to apply to the world of rats a concept that makes very good sense when applied to humans, but makes no sense at all when applied to rats. That is why chickens, like rats and cows, *cannot* have rights. The claim that eating them deprives them of their rights, therefore, is nonsensical, and cannot be the ground of a moral defense of vegetarianism.

NOTES

1. Tom Regan, a leading proponent of the view that animals have rights, presents one version of this argument in "The Moral Basis of Vegetarianism," in *All That Dwell Therein: Animal Rights and Environmental Ethics* (Berkeley: University of California Press, 1982).

2. Tom Regan, *The Case for Animal Rights* (Berkeley: University of California Press, 1983), pp. 152–53.

3. The reference by St. Thomas is to Psalm 4, line 6.

4. St. Thomas Aquinas, *Summa Theologica*. First Part of the Second Part, Question 91, Second Article.

5. Genesis 3:22.

6. St. Augustine, *Confessions*, Book Seven, 397 CE.

7. Francis Herbert Bradley, "Why Should I Be Moral?" in *Ethical Studies* (Oxford: Clarendon Press, 1927).

8. Georg Wilhelm Friedrich Hegel, *Philosophy of Right*, 1821.

9. H. A. Prichard, "Does Moral Philosophy Rest on a Mistake?" in *Moral Obligation* (Oxford: Oxford University Press, 1949).

10. Sir David Ross, *The Foundations of Ethics* (Oxford: Clarendon Press, 1939), chap. 3.

11. Karl Marx, *Economic and Philosophical Manuscripts*, 1844.

12. V. I. Lenin, "The Tasks of the Youth Leagues," 1920, reprinted in *The Strategy and Tactics of World Communism*, supp. 1 (Washington, DC: U.S. Government Printing Office, 1948).

13. George Herbert Mead, "The Genesis of the Self and Social Control," in *Selected Writings*, ed. A. J. Reck (Indianapolis: Bobbs-Merrill, 1964).

14. Tom Regan, *The Case for Animal Rights*.

15. Tom Regan makes this objection explicitly in "The Moral Basis of Vegetarianism." Evelyn Pluhar develops the same argument in her contribution to this volume.

16. Objections of this kind are registered by Dale Jamieson, "Killing Persons and Other Beings," in *Ethics and Animals*, ed. H. B. Miller and W. H. Williams (Clifton, NJ: Humana Press, 1983), and by C. Hoff, "Immoral and Moral Uses of Animals," *New England Journal of Medicine* 302 (1980):115–18.

17. The analysis of these mistakes is given in what Kant calls the Transcendental Dialectic, which is the Second Division of the Second Part (Transcendental Logic) of the Transcendental Doctrine of Elements. The position Kant is defending is deep and difficult—but the general point he makes in the Transcendental Dialectic is readily accessible. Confusions and errors resulting from the misapplication of concepts in thinking about our *selves* he treats in a chapter called "The Paralogisms of Pure Reason"; confusions and errors resulting from the misapplication of concepts in thinking about *the world as a whole* he treats in a chapter called "The Antinomy of Pure Reason"; confusions and errors resulting from the misapplication of concepts in thinking about *God* he treats in a chapter called "The Ideal of Pure Reason." In all three spheres the categories (of which causation is only one example) that make sense only when applied to phenomena in our direct experience cannot be rationally employed. His analyses are penetrating and telling; the metaphysical blunders he exposes result in every case from the attempt to use categories having applicability in only one sphere in a very different sphere where they can have no applicability whatever.

Section Four

TRADITIONAL AND CONTEMPORARY RELIGIOUS TEACHINGS ABOUT OUR RELATION TO ANIMALS

13 | THE JEWISH DIET AND VEGETARIANISM
Roberta Kalechofsky

Genesis 1:28–30 and Genesis 9:1–4 are the two biblical passages that control the Jewish view of diet. The first passage, Genesis 1:28–30, is the commandment God gives to Adam and Eve to "eat seed, herb, and green things" or, in effect, to be vegetarians. The second passage describes a dramatic historical shift after the flood between human beings in relation to the natural world and their diet. In this passage, Noah has disembarked from the ark, builds a slaughter site, and begins to sacrifice animals, whereupon God gives humans permission to eat meat. The conflict between Genesis 1:28–30 and Genesis 9:1–4 is the conflict between a dietary commandment given in an idealized world and permission to eat meat given in the post-flood fallen world. Many religious and moral views concerning the Jewish diet flow from one or the other of these passages, and Jews regularly draw their arguments for or against vegetarianism based on these passages.

But these passages are not as simple as they seem to be on the surface. For example, in Genesis 1:28–30 there is an implication that the vegetarian diet is not only intended for humans but for animals as well, though we do not know of any era when there were no predatory animals in the world: that is, animals who eat other animals. Some predation, as far as we know, seems intrinsic to nature (though it is not as extensive as the "dog eat dog" view of the world would have us believe). There are Orthodox Jews who believe that if the Bible says that even the animals—lions and tigers—were vegetarian in the Garden of Eden, then it must have been so at one time. It is possible to speculate that great evolutionary changes transformed vegetarian animals into predatory ones, but there is no anthropological proof of this. Nevertheless, the prophet Isaiah drew his magnificent picture of peace, which depicts the lion and the lamb lying down together from Genesis 1:28–30, and the messianic tradition in Judaism is based on the faith that the Edenic world was vegetarian and that the messianic world will also be vegetarian.

Jewish mystical time is embraced by two vegetarian eras: one at the beginning of time and one at the end of time. This view has influenced endless Jewish mystics to be vegetarian. It was the commandment in Genesis 1:28–30 that influenced Rav Avraham Kuk, the first chief rabbi of mandatory Palestine in his belief that the Bible contains a promise of justice and well-being for the future animal world. (The first three chief rabbis of mandatory Palestine were vegetarian.) Kuk believed that this early diet was a harbinger of the future, that the permission to eat meat was only a temporary concession, because a God who is merciful to all creatures would not institute an everlasting law that permitted the killing of animals for food; eating meat, he believed, was God's concession to the depraved moral status of human beings. The permission to slaughter animals for food given to Noah, was a "transitional tax" or temporary dispensation until a "brighter era" would be reached when people would return to vegetarian diets. For Rav Kuk, the *Galut*—a Jewish word that means exile from God's presence—could be characterized by the carnivorous era between our ideal diet and the messianic age when our ideal diet would return. He wrote his views in an influential pamphlet, *A Vision of Vegetarianism and Peace*.

But it is the second passage, Genesis 9:1–4, which has governed most of Jewish history and the actual eating habits of the majority of Jews throughout their history. The conflict is between the ideal and actual reality. However, few Jews are cognizant of the fact that permission to eat meat was given with several penalties. It was hardly a free lunch. For one thing, human beings would now be separated from the animal world and indeed, from the rest of nature. The animals would flee human beings. More dire, human beings would now know war. Perhaps the implication here is that once having tasted blood, war becomes easier. The passage represents the Bible's view of the beginning of history, for the different peoples of the earth arise after the flood, divorced from nature and knowing war. The Jewish philosopher Martin Buber pointed out that the world in Eden was created with a blessing, but that history in the Noachic passage was created with a curse. So we would do well to consider the consequences of what the permission to eat meat means.

All the famous and complicated laws of the Jewish diet (*kashrut*) follow from this permission to eat meat. The permission was not unrestricted. It was given with the restriction, applicable to the whole human race, that no one was to eat a limb torn from a living animal or consume the animal's blood. Human beings were not to take their meat as the predatory animals do in the chase, the hunt, and the attack. The effect of this law (*"ever min hahai,"* Gen. 9:4) upon Jewish character was enormous. It is the source of the Jewish aversion to hunting, which continues to this day. Jews had permission to eat meat, but not to be predators. Isaiah called this commandment "the ancient covenant" and regarded violations of it with intense aversion (Isaiah 24:4–12).

The next law of *kashrut* limited the meat Jews ate to those animals who were vegetarian animals, which reveals the continuing aversion to the problem of predation in the world. Not only were Jews not to take their meat as predators, but they were not to eat predatory animals. Under Mosaic law, meat for the Jewish people was hereafter limited to the "clean" animals, or vegetarian ruminants. The animal to be eaten was to be chosen from the flock and sacrificed in recognition that its life belonged to God. Now, eating meat required an elaborate sacrificial system, with elaborate laws about sacrificing. It required a temple and a priestly class. After the fall of the temple, the institution of *shechitah* (ritual slaughter) evolved with further complications and laws. The rabbis felt that permission to eat meat was a concession to human weakness, and they continued to circumscribe its consumption with ever-increasing laws.

The Jewish diet is perhaps the most famous diet in the world because it is one of the best articulated, most complex, and most ancient diets. It has attracted the attention of food anthropologists such as Mary Douglas, who saw in the complex laws of *kashrut* a Jewish symbolism regarding the Jewish sense of order of the world and of creation. What the diet reflects is an abiding uneasiness with the problem of eating meat and with what Rabbi Arthur Green has called "the provegetarian bias in *Torah.*" We would do well to remember that these laws developed in an era when few Jews ate meat more than several times a year, and then mainly on festival occasions. Eating meat in the classical world, among Hebrews, Greeks, and Romans, was rare. In spite of the fact that the sacrificial laws bulk large in the Bible, there was only one temple in Jerusalem and few Jews had access to the temple in which to sacrifice an animal they could eat. Some social historians have speculated that Jews living outside of Judea from about the second century BCE to the second century CE in the Roman and Greek worlds—and that meant the majority of Jews during this period—may not have eaten meat at all except for the few times they went on pilgrimage to Jerusalem.

However, the diet of the rich Hebrew and the priestly class included meat several times a week, and this diet was supported by the sacrificial institution, which gained the wrath of the prophets who denounced the meat gluttony of the rich and of the temple priests. The diet of rich biblical Jews was different from the diet of the poor. Meat has always been associated with wealth and for this reason attracted the bitter criticism of the prophets who understood its divisive nature. Isaiah's disgust with the meat gluttony of the temple priests goes hand in hand with his criticism of the sacrificial system and his concern for the poor.

Nevertheless, for rich or poor, there never has been a commandment in Judaism to eat meat. "The provegetarian bias of *Torah*," spoken of by Rabbi Arthur Green can be traced in many biblical passages, such as Exodus 16:1 and Numbers 11:1–35, which contain the episode of the quail, or what we may call "the first recorded food riot in history." In this episode the Israelites become very contentious and begin to threaten Moses, saying that he should produce meat. God sends waves of quail, which seem to drop from the very skies. The Israelites are described as stuffing the quail into their mouths with such fury that the blood runs between their teeth. God punishes them with plague for their behavior, and the place where this happens is known as Kibroth hatavaah, or the Graves of the Lustful. It is from such accounts that rabbinic tradition has come to regard meat as "the food of lust," or of an ungainly appetite. The famous twelfth-century Rabbi Rashi commented on this episode that "it was right for God to punish the Hebrews for their demand for meat, for we can live without meat, but we cannot live without bread."

Talmudic statements point out the rabbis' disdain for eating meat: "Man shall not eat meat unless he has a special craving for it, and shall eat it only occasionally and sparingly"(Chulin 84a). "A man should not teach his son to eat meat" (Chulin 84a). The Talmud even made a special concession to replacing the shank bone on the seder plate during Passover with a beet, a potato, or a mushroom, and a statement in the Talmud acknowledges that "Bread, wine and oil are the pillars of nutrition." Though there is much discussion of meat, we know from sources outside the Bible, such as social anthropology, that, in fact, most Hebrews subsisted on a diet of "bread, wine and oil," supplemented with figs and fruit. A recent article in the *Jerusalem Report* described the eating habits of first-temple-period Israelites, who "breakfasted on bread dipped in olive oil, toasted wheat and figs; and in the evening ate legume broth, seasoned with Dead Sea Salt." John Cooper writes that "in ancient Israel the majority of the population lived on a diet of barley bread, vegetables and fruit, supplemented by milk products and honey, which was used as a universal sweetener."[1] Honey was from dates, and milk products were from sheep. This, incidentally, was the standard diet of Sumeria as well, one of the greatest empires during biblical times.

The general rabbinic judgment in the Talmud reflects an uneasy compromise with meat. It acknowledges the human lust for meat and the occasional need for it. "Human consumption of meat," Samuel Dresner writes in his study of the laws of *kashrut*, "which means the taking of an animal's life, has constantly posed a religious problem to Judaism, even when it has accepted the necessity of it."[2] The rabbis granted that meat had nutritional value, but the important issue was whether meat was necessary. Ice cream might be nutritional, but it is not a necessary nutritional food. Rashi's comment on the food riots in Exodus and Numbers is that "It was right for the Jews to cry for bread, but not for meat, for one can live without meat," reflects the distinction between necessary and unnecessary. Meat in the Bible is regarded as a food "of lust," not as necessary food. Discussions in the Talmud indicate that though the rabbis believed meat had nutritional value, they regarded it negatively, particularly after the temple fell and the sacrificial system, which, at least, restricted and lent dignity to the consumption of meat, came to an end.

Since eating meat was historically embedded in the sacrificial system from the time of Noah until after the temple fell in 70 CE, there was much discussion in the Talmud about what the status of meat should be after the fall of the temple. The association of eating meat with festivals bequeathed to the Jews the tradition that joyous occasions (*simchat yom tov*) should be celebrated with meat and wine, and this ancient practice bequeathed to many Jews down to our present era the feeling that holidays, *Shabbats*, weddings, *bar* and *bat mitzvahs* should be celebrated with great feasts that include meat. However, the association with meat was declared no longer to be in effect after the sacrifices ended. A talmudical text states: "In the days when the Temple was in existence, there was no rejoicing without meat . . . but now that there is no longer the Temple, there is no rejoicing without wine. . . ."[3] Jews are commanded to celebrate the holidays with wine and with joy, but there is no requirement to celebrate it with meat, and many Jews, particularly younger Jews who embrace vegetarianism, have discovered vegetarian food to be amply joyous for all festival occasions.

Since the blessings over food are required for the sanctification of eating, there is much discussion in Talmud Berakhot about foods, their values, and the requisite blessings to be associated with different foods. All things that are enjoyed require a blessing. For religious Jews to enjoy a pleasure without blessing the Creator is likened to theft. The model for the blessings is produce from the earth, and of these the perfect model are the seven foods of the land: wheat, barley, grapes, pomegranates, figs, olives, and honey. There are three different blessings for vegetables, for vegetables that grow above ground, for vegetables that grow below ground, and for cooked vegetables, but there is no special blessing for meat.

The rabbis agreed that the reason for the complexity of the laws of *kashrut* was to make the eating of meat difficult and to teach us refinement in our appetite and reverence for animal life. But the fact is that *kashrut* does not perform these functions for most modern Jews. The modern Western world, with its overabundance of meat eaten by urban people divorced from animal life, has severely changed the meaning of traditional *kashrut*. The Jewish appetite in reality was constrained by poverty and lack of meat, as were the appetites of other peoples. Abundant meat simply was not available, and when it became available in the last two centuries, Jews ate meat as much as everyone else in the West. Even though the laws of *kashrut* were by this time impossibly complex, they offered little restraint while they made the kitchen a prison for many observant Jewish house-wives. The disparity between historical aspiration and modern reality reached its breaking point in the twentieth century, and has made vegetarianism a very viable option for all kinds of Jews, Orthodox and non-Orthodox, who seek to revitalize the meaning of the Jewish dietary laws.

In the modern world human consumption of meat has increased a thousandfold, and respect for animal life has almost vanished. *Kashrut* has not achieved what the rabbis declared was its purpose: to limit our consumption of meat and to encourage compassion for animal life. "Reverence for Life . . . is the constant lesson of the laws of *Kashrut*."[4] but *kashrut*, as Dresner states, lacks "a satisfying modern formulation of its meaning and relevance."[5] Jewish vegetarianism restores *kashrut* to its original intentions and its original simplicity, where purpose and practice have a relationship and harmony that can easily be grasped. Jewish vegetarianism stems from the positive, life-affirming Jewish values to guard one's health, protect the environment, and revere life. The Union of American Hebrew Congregations' edition of *The Torah*, states the issue succinctly:

> In a larger sense we must rethink the whole question of eating, in view of our frequent statements that Judaism deals with every aspect of human life. Is it true that "a man is what he eats"? In what sense and in what degree? Some Jews of widely varied religious backgrounds have become vegetarians on principle. Perhaps it is time to examine the question: Is it right to kill any living thing for food?
>
> Moreover, the problem of food supply has become urgent and critical everywhere. Millions are always hungry, while others eat too much for their own good. . . . There are many religious aspects to the question of what we eat and how much and of what there is for others to eat.[6]

Vegetarian Judaism rests on five important Jewish mandates that are rooted in the Bible and that were expanded by talmudical and rabbinic commentary: *pikuach nefesh* (the commandment to guard your health and life); *tsa'ar ba'alei chaim* (avoid causing pain to any living creature); *bal tash-chit* (the commandment not to waste or destroy anything of value); *tzedakah* (to help the needy and work for a more just society); and *klal Israel* (to work for the welfare of the community). These mandates have been developed over millennia in the Talmud and in rabbinic commentary throughout the Middle Ages, and have guided the Jewish people throughout centuries. But knowledge and implementation of these mandates have declined since the advent of industrial society. Meat and our attitude toward food animals is at the heart of that decline. Nothing is so wasteful in nature as our present diet. It is a chief cause of environmental pollution. In countries where animals are "factory farmed," or raised with intensive rearing methods in feedlots, the antibiotics and chemicals used in the production of meat runs off into rivers and streams and pollutes them with dangerous chemicals. Excrement from livestock in general is 250,000 pounds per second, compared with 12,000 pounds per second for the human population. In the United States, where meat consumption is high, this animal excrement is a moving storehouse of toxic waste, pesticides, hormones, and antibiotics. Antibiotics fed to the animals do not go away. They are flushed into the ground, into our waters, and on to our vegetables and fruit. In 1988, the Environmental Protection Agency blamed agricultural runoff for the most extensive source of pollution. Additionally, the methane gases produced by cows contribute to about 15 percent of the greenhouse effect. A meat-based diet has corrosive effects on our health and, consequently, on our health-care system, which in turn seriously affects the economy of the poor and violates the mandate of *tzedakah* or charity. Meat today is not only unhealthy but also unethical because it involves huge wastes of other consumable goods such as grains, and ultimately impoverishes the poor. No other present dietary system responds to these five mandates so fully for Jews as ethical vegetarianism, which incorporates a Jewish spirituality. Rabbi Arthur Hertzberg declared in his "Jewish Declaration on Nature":

> Judaism as a religion offers the option of eating animal flesh, and most Jews do, but in our own century there has been a movement toward vegetarianism among very pious Jews. A whole galaxy of central rabbinic and spiritual teachers including several past and present Chief Rabbis of the Holy Land have been affirming vegetarianism as the ultimate meaning of Jewish moral teaching. They have been proclaiming the autonomy of all living creatures as the value which our religious tradition must now teach to all of its believers. Let this affirmation resound this day, and in days to come. Let it be heard by all our brethren, wherever they may be, as the commandment which we must strive to realize. This cannot be achieved in one generation, and it will not happen through pressure from within or without: Jews will move increasingly to vegetarianism out of their own

deepening knowledge of what their tradition commands as they understand it in this age.[7]

This "whole galaxy of central rabbinic and spiritual teachers" spans the spectrum of Reconstructionist, Orthodox, Conservative, and Reform Jews, as the anthology *Rabbis and Vegetarianism: An Evolving Tradition* indicates. The Reconstructionist rabbi Arthur Green has written:

> We Jews, who always looked upon killing for sport or pleasure as something alien and repulsive, should now, out of our own experience, be reaching the point where we find even the slaughter of animals for food morally beyond the range of the acceptable. If Jews have to be associated with killing at all in our time, let it be only for the defense of human life. Life has become too precious in this era for us to be involved in the shedding of blood, even that of animals when we can survive without it. This is not an ascetic choice, we should note, but rather a life-affirming one. A vegetarian Judaism would be more whole in its ability to embrace the presence of God in all of Creation.[8]

David Rosen, an Orthodox rabbi, has written:

> Indeed, Judaism as a way of life, seeks to inculcate in us a consciousness of the Divine Presence in the World and respect for life accordingly. The more we care for life, the closer we are in fact to God. Accordingly, an ethical vegetarian way of life expresses the most noble and sublime values and aspirations of Judaism itself, bringing us closer to its vision for society as a whole.[9]

The diet of biblical Jews was enshrined as the "seven sacred foods of the land of Israel": wheat, barley, grapes, figs, pomegranates, olives, honey (from dates). These are the foods promised to the Israelites when they enter Canaan in a magnificent passage in the Bible (Deuteronomy 8:8–9):

> For the Lord has brought us into a good Land
> A land with streams and springs and fountains,
> A land of wheat and barley, of vines, figs and pomegranates.
>   Of olive trees and honey

These foods have been enshrined in various Jewish rituals. During the biblical era, they were brought to Jerusalem during the spring holiday of Shavuot, or the holiday of First Fruit Offerings, to express thanksgiving. Many pilgrims made special baskets of these seven foods, and believed that those whose diet consists of them would enjoy good health and long life. We are in the process of rediscovering this wisdom.

Food is not an isolated phenomenon for Jewish people or for any people. It is deeply embedded in historical conditions and religious attitudes. It changes in response to social and historical forces. Food conveys symbols, it talks a language of history, of the senses, of etiquette, of class systems, of social relationships, of pleasure, of memories of holidays, and of special occasions. Vegetarianism gives Jews back their dietary history, unites them with God's intentions in the Garden of Eden, allows them to listen to the prophets in their criticism of meat gluttony and their concern for a just diet. It is as vegetarians, without need of a temple in which to sacrifice animals for food, that Jews may become a nation of priests, as Moses wished them to be, for they do not then need a special priest class to preside over the sacrifice of animals. It is as vegetarians that Jews can make every table in every home an altar to the blessing of earth's goodness, without harm to any creature.

NOTES

1. John Cooper, *Eat and Be Satisfied: A Social History of Jewish Food* (Northvale, NJ: Jason Aronson, 1993), p. 3.
2. Rabbi Samuel Dresner, *The Jewish Dietary Laws: Their Meaning for Our Time* (New York: Rabbinical Assembly of America, 1982), p. 24.
3. Pesachim 109a.
4. Dresner, p. 27
5. Ibid., p. 11.
6. W. Gunther Plaut, ed., *The Torah: A Modern Commentary* (New York: Union of American Hebrew Congregations, 1981) p. 813.
7. Address delivered at the twenty-fifth anniversary celebration for the World Wildlife Fund, Assisi, Italy, Fall 1986.
8. Roberta Kalechofsky, ed., *Rabbis and Vegetarianism: An Evolving Tradition* (Marblehead, MA: Micah Publications, 1995), p. 27.
9. Ibid., p. 55.

14 | CHRISTIANS ARE WHAT CHRISTIANS EAT
Tom Regan

In its simplest terms the animal rights position I uphold maintains that such diverse practices as the use of animals in science, sport, and recreational hunting, the trapping of fur-bearing animals for vanity products, and the practice of raising animals for human consumption are wrong because they systematically violate the rights of the animals involved. Morally, these practices ought to be abolished. This is the goal of the social struggle for animal rights. The goal of our individual struggle is to divest ourselves of our moral and economic ties to these injustices—for example, by not wearing the dead skins of animals and by not eating their decaying corpses.

Speciesists are people who think that humans and other animals should be treated differently because humans are humans and other animals are not. It would be wrong, they believe, to raise and slaughter humans for food but not wrong to do this to hogs and cows; wrong to create "models" of killer diseases in humans but not wrong to do the same thing to chimpanzees and rodents. The prejudicial character of this belief is evident after appeals to "intuition" have been unmasked and after first one, then another unsuccessful attempt to prove human superiority has

An earlier version of this essay was published in *Liberating Life: Approaches to Ecological Theology*, ed. Jay B. McDaniel (Maryknoll, NY: Orbis Press, 1990) and in Regan's *The Thee Generation* (Philadelphia: Temple University Press, 1991).

been defeated. Standard secular "proofs" fail miserably. Some (but not all) humans are rational. Some (but not all) humans are autonomous. Some (but not all) humans can use a language. Unless speciesists are prepared (which they are not) to consign humans who are deficient in these respects to the slaughterhouse or the research lab, they perforce must find some other characteristic possessed by all and only human beings.

CHRISTIANITY AND SPECIESISM

For those of us who cut our spiritual teeth on Christianity this challenge has a familiar response. Human beings—all of us—are said to be inherently more valuable than everything else because we are spiritually unique. This uniqueness stems from our having been created in the image of God. Thus, since all humans uniquely image God, we are able to cite a real (spiritual) difference between every member of our species and the millions of other species of creaturely life. And since this difference is a morally relevant one, Christian speciesists are able to defend their belief in human superiority. Or so it has been thought.

Now I am not ill-disposed to the idea that humans have a unique spiritual worth, nor am I ill-disposed to the idea that we possess it because we uniquely image God. However, the interpretation of these ideas I favor does not yield anything like the results favored by speciesism. This interpretation pictures humans as God's imaged presence in creation. By this I mean that we are expressly chosen by God to be God's vice-regent in the day-to-day affairs of the world; we are chosen by God, that is, to be as loving in our day-to-day dealings with the created order as God was in creating that order in the first place.

In this sense, therefore, there is a morally relevant difference between human beings and every other creaturely expression of God. Humans and humans alone are given the awesome freedom and responsibility to be God's representative within creation. And it is, therefore, only we humans who can be held morally blameworthy when we fail to do this, and morally praiseworthy when we succeed.

With this interpretation of our unique imaging of God we find a morally relevant difference others have sought. But, as should be evident, this difference by itself offers neither aid nor comfort to the speciesist. For to agree that only humans image God, in the sense that only humans have the moral responsibility to be loving toward God's creation, does not entail either that all and only humans have inherent worth or that all and only humans have superior inherent worth. It is perfectly consistent with our unique status as God's chosen representative within creation that other creatures have inherent worth equal to our own.

When viewed within a Christian perspective, is this possibility actually true? In particular, how does the Bible speak to this question? As very much a nonexpert in the area of biblical exegesis I am reluctant to give an answer. But like the proverbial fool who "rushes in" I shall make bold and hazard the opinion that there is no one, unambiguous, unwaivering biblical message. Many passages lend support to viewing all of nonhuman creation as having no or little value apart from human needs and interests, a reading that supports the tradition of Christian anthropocentrism. By contrast, other passages support views that are more or less nonanthropocentric. I do not profess to know how to prove that the anthropocentric reading is false or that a nonanthropocentric reading is true. Indeed, as I already have indicated, I do not believe the Bible offers just one answer to our question.

The upshot, then, is that we are left with the awesome responsibility of choosing between alternative biblical representations of the value of nonhuman creation, no one of which is clearly or incontrovertably the correct one. And this fact should, I believe, chasten us in our conviction that we have privileged access to the whole truth, and nothing but the truth. With minds so feeble, spirits so weak, and a biblical message so open to honest differences of interpretation between people of real faith and goodwill, all who take spiritual sustenance from the pages of the Bible ought to realize both the need for, and the call to practice, the virtue of tolerance.

Eden's Message

Having said this, I may now speak to my own reading of the biblical message and indicate why this message, as I understand it, not only fails to offer aid and comfort to speciesists, it actually presents a healthy spiritual antidote to this virulent moral prejudice.

I take the opening account of creation in Genesis seriously, but not, I hasten to add, literally. I take it seriously because I believe this is the point from which our spiritual understanding of God's plans in and hopes for creation must begin, and against which our well-considered judgments about the value of creation finally must be tested. It is therefore predictable that I find it significant that God is said to judge each part of creation "good" before humans came upon the scene and that humans were created by God (or came upon the scene) on the same day as the nonhuman animals to whom I have been referring—those whose limbs are severed, whose sensory organs are brutally removed, and whose brains are ground up for purposes of scientific research, for example. I read in this representation of the order of creation a prescient recognition of the vital kinship humans share with these other animals, a kinship I have elsewhere endeavored to explicate in terms of our shared biographical presence in the world, a view that, quite apart from anything the Bible teaches, is supported by both common sense and our best science.

What do I mean by "our shared biographical presence"? Let me illustrate my meaning by using the animals most of us know best, our favorite animal companions, cats and dogs. Like us, cats and dogs are in the world. Like us, they are aware of the world. Like us, what happens to them matters to them. There is a complicated psychological creature behind those eyes. Cats and dogs have a biography, not simply a biology. They are somebodies, not somethings.

The same is true of the other animals I have mentioned, animals we know less well, from cows and pigs to chimpanzees and seals, the other animal beings who were created (or came on the scene) on the same day as human beings. The chronological identity of the day of our creation is a metaphor for the psychological kinship we share with our biographical cousins.

But I find in the opening saga of creation an even deeper, more profound message regarding God's plans in and hopes for creation. For I find in this account the unmistakable message that God did not create nonhuman animals for our use—not in science, not for the purpose of vanity products, not for our entertainment, not for our sport or recreation, not even for our bodily sustenance. On the contrary, the nonhuman animals currently exploited in these ways were created to be just what they are: independently good expressions of the divine love that, in ways that are likely always to remain to some degree mysterious to us, was expressed in God's creative activity.

The issue of bodily sustenance is perhaps the most noteworthy of the practices I have mentioned since, while humans from "the beginning" were in need of food, there were no rodeos or circuses, no leghold traps or dynamite harpoons in the original creation. Had it been part of God's hopes in and plans for creation to have humans use nonhuman animals as food, it would have been open to God to let this be known. And yet what we find in the opening saga of creation is just the opposite. The "meat" we are given by God is not the flesh of animals, it is "all plants that bear seed everywhere on the earth, and every tree bearing fruit which yields seed: they shall be yours for food" (Gen. 1:29 [NEB]).

The message could not be any clearer. In the most perfect state of creation, humans are vegans (that is, not only is the flesh of animals excluded from the menu God provides for us, even animal products—milk and cheese, for example—are excluded). And so I believe that, if we look to the biblical account of "the beginning" as more than merely one among many considerations, but instead as an absolutely essential source of spiritual insight into God's hopes for and plans in creation, then, like it or not, we are obliged to find there a menu of divinely approved bodily sustenance that differs quite markedly from the steaks and chops, the roasts and stews most Christians are accustomed to devouring.

To a less than optimal or scholarly degree I am aware of some of the chapters and verses of the subsequent biblical record: the Fall, the expulsion from the Garden, the Flood. There is no debate about the details of this record I could win if paired against an even modestly astute and retentive young person preparing for first communion. I wear my biblical (and theological) ignorance on my sleeve. Nevertheless, I believe the essential moral and spiritual truth any open-minded, literate reader of the first chapter of Genesis must find is the one I already have mentioned, namely, that nonhuman animals were not placed within God's creation so that humans might roast, fry, stew, broil, bake, and barbeque their rotting remains.

In this reading of God's creative activity, therefore, I find a spiritual lesson that is unmistakably at odds with both the letter and the spirit of speciesism. This lesson, as I understand it, does not represent the non-human animals to whom I have been referring as having no or less inherent value than humans. On the contrary, by unmistakably excluding these animals from the menu of food freely available to us, as granted by God's beneficence, I infer that God asks us to recognize the independent value of these animals. They are not put here to be utilized by us. Rather, we are put here to protect them. In this respect the (supposed) Christian defense of speciesism emerges as part of the best offense of the animal rights position.

Some theologians have a different view. Eden never was, they say; the perfection of creation is something we are to work to bring about in the future, not something that was lost in the past. I do not know how to prove which vision of Eden, if either, is the true one. What I do know is that, in the present context, this question is entirely moot, since it is clear—clear beyond any doubt, as I read the Scriptures—that human beings simply do not eat nonhuman animals in that fullness of God's beneficence the image Eden represents. And this is true whether Eden once was (but was lost), or is yet to be (if we will but create it).

Two Objections, Two Replies

It remains true, nonetheless, that my attempt to explain and defend an egalitarian view of the inherent value of humans and other animals must face a number of important challenges. For reasons of length, if for no other, I cannot respond to all of them, not even all the most fundamental ones. The best I can do, before concluding, is describe and defuse two of the most common objections.

The first begins by observing that, within the traditions of Judaism and Christianity, every form of life, not simply humans and other animals, is to be viewed as expressive of God's love. Thus, to attempt to "elevate" the value of nonhuman animals, as I may be accused of doing, is possible only at the expense of "lowering" the value of everything else, which is unacceptable.

I think this objection misses the mark. There is nothing in the animal rights philosophy that either denies or diminishes the value of fruits, grains, nuts, and other forms of vegetative life, or that refuses to accept the possibility that these life forms and the rest of creation generally are so many ways in which God's loving presence is manifested. Nor is there anything in this philosophy that disparages the wise counsel to treat all of creation gently and appreciatively. It is an arrogant anthropocentrism, often aided and abetted in our history by a no less arrogant Christian theology, not the philosophy of animal rights, that has brought the earth to the brink of ecological disaster.

Still, this philosophy does find in humans and other animals, because of our shared biographical status in creation, a kind of value—inherent value—that other creatures do not possess, either not at all or less than we do. Is it possible to defend this view? I believe it is, both on the basis of a purely secular philosophy and by appeal to biblical authority. The secular defense I have offered elsewhere and will not repeat here.[1] As for the Christian defense, I shall merely reaffirm the vital importance of Genesis 1, which teaches, I believe, that vegetative life, not animal life, was meant to be used by us as food.

So much for the first challenge. The second one emanates from a quite different source and mounts a quite different objection. It begins by noting the large disparities that exist in the quality of life available to those who are affluent (the "haves") and those who are poor (the "have-nots"), especially those who live in third-world countries. "It is all well and good to preach the gospel of animal rights to those people who have the financial and other means to live it, if they choose to do so," this objection begins, "but please do spare us your self-righteous condemnation of the struggling—and often starving—masses of people in the world who really have no choice about what to eat or what to wear. To blame these people because they utilize animals is scandalous. It is to value animal life above human life. And this is misanthropy at its worst."

Now, this particular variation on the familiar theme of misanthropy (at least this is familiar to advocates of animal rights) has a point, up to a point. The point it has, is that it would be self-righteous to condemn the people in question for acting as they do, especially if we are acting worse than they are, as well we may. But, of course, nothing in what I have argued supports such a condemnation, and this for the simple reason that I have nowhere argued that people who eat animals, or who hunt and trap them, or who cut their heads off or burst their internal organs in pursuit of scientific knowledge, either are or must be evil people. The position I have set forth concerns the moral wrongness of what people do, not the comparative vileness of their character. In my view, it is entirely possible that good people sometimes do what is wrong, and evil people sometimes do what is right.

Indeed, not only is this possible, it frequently happens, and among those circumstances in which it does, some concern the actions performed by people in the third world. To make my meaning clearer, consider the following hypothetical example. Suppose we chance upon a tribe of hunter-gatherers who annually, on a date sacred to their tradition, sacrifice the most beautiful female child to the gods, in the hope that the tribe will prosper in the coming year. In my view this act of human sacrifice is wrong and ought to be stopped (which does not mean that we should invade with tanks and flamethrowers to stop it!). From this moral assessment of the wrongness of what these people do, however, it does not follow that we should condemn them as evil, vicious people. For it could be that they act from only the best intentions and with nothing but the best motives. Nevertheless, what these people do, in my view, is wrong.

What is true of the imaginary case of this tribe, is no less true of real-life cases where people in the third world raise and kill animals for food, cruelly subject other animals to forced labor, and so on. Anytime anyone reduces the inherent value of a nonhuman animal to that animal's utility value for human beings, what is done, in my view, is morally wrong. But it does not follow from this that we should make a negative judgment about the character of the human moral agents involved, especially if, as is true in the third world, there are mitigating circumstances. For it often happens that people who do what is morally wrong should be excused from moral blame and censure. A person who injures a family member, for example, in the mistaken belief that there is a burglar in the house, does what is wrong and yet may not be morally blameworthy. Similarly, those people in the third world who act in ways that are wrong according to the philosophy of animal rights, do what is wrong. But because of the harsh, uncompromising exigencies of their life, where it often literally is a matter of their life or their death that hangs in the balance, the people in the third world in my view should be excused from our harsh judgment of moral blame. The circumstances of their lives, one might say, are as mitigating as any circumstances can be.

In light of the preceding I hope it is clear why it would be a bad reading of the philosophy of animal rights to charge its proponents with a hearty appetite, if not for animal flesh, then at least for self-righteousness. When we understand the differences between morally assessing a person's act and morally assessing that person's character, and when we take cognizance of the appropriateness of reducing or eliminating moral blame in the face of mitigating circumstances, then the proponents of animal rights should be seen to be no more self-righteous than the proponents of any other philosophy.

CONCLUSION

Finally, then, in closing, I wish to make a few observations closer to home, so to speak. . . . In my view, we daily run the risk of succumbing to a detached hypocrisy. For the questions we must face concern not only the *idea* of the integrity of creation, they also ask how we *should live* if we are to express our thoughtful allegiance to this idea in our day-to-day life. This ancient question has no simple answer. There is much good that we would do, that we do not. And much evil that we would not do, that we find ourselves doing. The challenge to lead a good, respectful, loving life, just in our dealings with members of the human family, is onerous. How much more demanding will it be, then, if we widen the circle of the moral community to include the whole of creation.

How might we begin to meet this larger challenge? Doubtless there are many places to begin, some of which will be more accessible to some than to others. For my part, however, I cannot help believing that an appropriate place to begin is with the food on our plates. For here we are faced with a direct personal choice over which we exercise absolute sovereign authority. Such power is not always within our grasp. How little influence each of us really has when it comes to the practices of the World Bank, the agrarian land-reform movement, the cessation of armed conflict, crime, drug use, the scourge of famine. These large-scale evils stand beyond the reach of our small wills.

But not the food on our plates. Here we are at liberty to exercise absolute control. And here, then, it is only reasonable that we ask ourselves whether the choices we make about the food we eat have any bearing on our thoughtful attempt to honor the integrity of creation.

When we consider the biographical and, I dare say, the spiritual kinship we share with those billions of animals annually raised and slaughtered to be eaten; when, further, we inform ourselves of the truly wretched conditions in which most of these animals are raised, not to mention the deplorable methods by which they are transported and the gruesome, blood-soaked reality of the slaughterhouse; when we apprise ourselves of the massive destruction of the earth's ecology that, both directly and indirectly, is attributable to commercial animal agriculture; and when, finally, we take honest stock of our privileged position in the world, a position that will not permit us the excuse from moral blame shared by the desperately poor who, as we say, really have no choice; when we consider all these factors, then the case for abstaining from animal flesh has the overwhelming weight of both impartial reason and a spiritually infused compassion on its side.

True, to make this change will involve some sacrifices—in taste perhaps, in convenience certainly. And yet the whole fabric of Christian agape is woven from the threads of sacrificial acts. To abstain, on principle, from eating other animals, therefore, although it is not the end-all, can be the begin-all of our conscientious effort to journey back (or forward) to Eden, can be one way among others in which we reestablish or create that relationship to the earth which, if Genesis 1 is to be trusted, was part of God's original hopes for and plans in creation. It is the integrity of this creation we seek to understand and aspire to honor. In the choice of our food, I believe, we see, not through a glass darkly, but face to face, a small but not unimportant part of what must be done. For despite the prodigiousness of our ignorance, we do know this: Christians are what Christians eat.

NOTE

1. See my *The Case for Animal Rights* (Berkeley: University of California Press, 1983).

15 | THE THEOLOGICAL DEBATE ABOUT MEAT EATING
Andrew Linzey

Christians need to bring to the discussion about animal rights two theological insights. The first is that all human beings are sinners. "All have sinned and fall short of the glory of God," writes St. Paul.[1] None of us can be justified by our works in the sight of God. Our alienation from God and lostness in the world are the perennial themes of Christian preaching. Even the Son of man appears to accept his own part in the fallenness of the world. "Why do you call me good?" he asks. "No one is good except God alone."[2] This perspective, while recognizing real degrees of goodness and the possibility of human merit, accepts at the outset that there is no pure land. No human being can live free of evil. In consequence, self-righteousness is not only wrong, but also inappropriate. One of the main thrusts of the ethical teaching of Jesus seems directed against those who are cocksure of their own moral standing. Moral reformation, if it is to be pursued, must begin with ourselves. Such considerations mean simply that zealous campaigning, self-righteous postures, methods of intimidation—and especially violence—must be eschewed. To pursue even good ends by any means risks the increase of moral evil in the world.

This essay is a revised extract from Andrew Linzey, *Christianity and the Rights of Animals* (London: SPCK, 1987, and New York: Crossroad, 1989), pp. 101–104, 141–49. © Copyright 2003 by Andrew Linzey.

There is, of course, a dilemma here for all moral campaigners, whether for human or animal causes. To have moral insight at all frequently requires unusual emotions. Very few can conduct moral struggle without bitterness, acrimony, jealousy, or hatred. There is no easy way through all this. Perhaps all crusading causes necessarily involve conflict and with it the inevitable dangers of self-justification, exaggeration, and mistrust. J. S. Mill once wrote that "Every great movement must experience three stages: ridicule, discussion, adoption."[3] I wish I could persuade myself that it was all so straightforward. At the very least, animal campaigners would do well to endorse George Bernard Shaw's verdict that those who exploit animals are simply like the rest of us. "Custom will reconcile people to any atrocity; and fashion will drive them to acquire any custom." Again, "Far from enjoying it, they [in particular, people who experiment on animals] have simply overcome their natural repugnance and become indifferent to it, as men become indifferent enough to anything they do often enough."[4] At least, animal rightists should acknowledge our common guilt before God. A clean conscience is surely a figment of the imagination or, as Albert Schweitzer describes it, "an invention of the devil."[5]

The second insight is that with God all things are possible. Doubtless there is a fine line between endorsing every kind of human Utopianism on the one hand, and believing that with God's spirit all things can be made new, on the other. Moral visions, however, are characteristic of theology. In some sense all theology is visionary. As Isaiah found out, to have a vision of the holiness of God is to know oneself a sinner. "Woe is me!" he cries.

> I am lost
> for I am a man of unclean lips
> and I dwell among a people of unclean lips;
> yet with these eyes I have seen the King, the Lord of Hosts.[6]

At its best, the Christian tradition has articulated a vision that has sustained moral effort throughout centuries of history. Morality may depend upon theology in the way in which human will relies upon the imagination. If our moral theorizing is not to be reduced to utilitarian calculations and accommodating pragmatism, then we need some fundamental vision of how the world should be and how we are to play a part in achieving it. Of course there is some kind of balance to be struck here between, as Keith Ward calls it, "Scylla and Charybdis, between a loss of vision and idealism and an intolerant and repressive rule-worship."[7]

This needs to be held with the conviction that the Holy Spirit is ever before us, moving creation forward, however mysteriously, to the realization of God's hope for us and the created world. We can certainly betray God by fantasy and wishful thinking, but we can equally betray God by cutting our own moral notions to serve our own short-term interests. I like the line from Plato, who compares philosophers in a democratic state to those who "wrangle over notions of right in the minds of men who have never beheld Justice itself."[8]

If these insights are to be taken seriously then Christians need to commit themselves to the work of animal liberation with vision and humility.

First, vision. The goal is nothing less than the establishing of God's right in creation, and the liberation of nonhuman creation from the hand of tyranny. Isaiah again has just the right vision to feed our imagination and kindle our will:

> Then the wolf shall live with the sheep,
> and the leopard lie down with the kid;
> the calf and the young lion shall grow up together,
> and a little child shall lead them;
> the cow and the bear shall be friends,
> and their young shall lie down together.
> The lion shall eat straw like cattle;
> the infant shall play over the hole of the cobra,
> and the young child dance over the viper's nest.
> They shall not hurt or destroy all in my holy mountain;
> for as the waters fill the sea,
> so shall the land be filled with the knowledge of the Lord.[9]

This is surely a daunting prospect, describing as it does both cosmic redemption and universal peace. Cynics may deride the very possibility, but I do not think Christians are free to do so. It needs to be held together with the realization that God's hope for creation is not simply presented as a future state, but a realizable possibility through the Holy Spirit. The groaning and travailing of creation awaits the inspired children of God. In this way we can see that the God who demands is also the God who enables, or put more theologically, that what is given by God the Father is reconciled by God the Son and being redeemed by God the Spirit.

Second, humility. Christians do well to stop and pause before the mysterious workings of such a God. But having seen the vision, the task is to cooperate with its completion. Humanity is set within creation with the almost impossible commission to make peace, respect life, and affirm God as the center and goal of all existence. But because God's right will ultimately vanquish all wrong, humanity's almost impossible task is made possible by the very power that sustains humanity in existence. Therefore, all conscientious openness to the Spirit and every attempt, however trivial, to disengage ourselves from violence has spiritual meaning and purpose. No effort, however small, is lost within the divine economy.

But the question may be posed: How far do we take all this? The answer is obvious: As far as we are enabled by the Spirit. The creation waits—according to St. Paul—with eager longing for the revealing of the sons of God. And who are these? They are, simply put, Spirit-led individuals who will make possible a new order of existence; who will show by their life the possibility of newness of life. Quite practically the task required of us is to recognize God's own rights in creation, rights for animals to be themselves as God intends: to live; to be free; and to live without suffering, distress, and injury. Doubtless the vision cannot be realized at once. What God's time scale is we do not know. We can only trust and hope, taking one step at a time. I propose progressive disengagement from exploitation. Not all stages will be immediately possible. Some may appear more visionary than others; some more pragmatic than others. From where each of us stands, we see differently. What is overridingly important is that we all move as far as is possible. We have no alternative but to trust that the Spirit will do the rest.

The biblical tradition appears to give us two contrasting insights concerning the morality of eating meat. On one hand, humans as well as animals are commanded to be vegetarian. "I give you all plants that bear seed everywhere on earth, and every tree bearing fruit which yields seed: they shall be yours for food."[10] This command is reinforced by the messianic prophecies that specifically envisage a world at peace where "They shall not hurt, nor destroy in all my holy mountain."[11] On the other hand, after the Fall and the Flood God commands a new relationship whereby "Every creature that lives and moves shall be food for you; I give you them all, as once I gave you all green plants."[12] This "necessary evil," as it is described by Anthony Phillips,[13] has been justified throughout much of Christian history—we may suppose—because the Prince of Peace was himself not a thorough-going vegetarian. He possibly ate meat and almost certainly ate fish.

And yet, are these two traditions incompatible? The second command carried with it a puzzling condition—"But you must not eat the flesh with the life, which is the blood, still in it."[14] "The Hebrews recognized," comments Phillips, "that death occurred through loss of breath or blood, and since God was responsible for creation, both must belong to him."[15] Thus even within this permissive tradition, human beings are not given an entirely free hand. They do not have absolute rights over the lives of animals. Even the animal about to be eaten does not belong to its intending consumer. In this way the priestly tradition, while accepting the necessity of killing, refuses to accept that humans can appropriate the life of an animal. In short: according to the permissive tradition, the fact that humans kill is a necessary consequence of sin but the act of killing itself must not misappropriate the Creator's gift.

A Christian case for avoiding meat can therefore claim to have two justifications, even within the biblical tradition, which apparently condones meat eating. The first is that killing is a morally significant matter. While justifiable in principle, it can be practically justified only where there is real need for human nourishment. Christian vegetarians do not have to claim that it is always and absolutely wrong to kill in order to eat. It could well be that there were, or are, some situations in which meat eating was and is essential in order to survive. Geographical considerations alone make it difficult to envisage life in Palestine at the time of Christ without some primitive fishing industry. But the crucial point is that where we are *free to do otherwise* the killing of Spirit-filled individuals requires moral justification. It *may* be justifiable, but only when human nourishment clearly requires it, and even then it remains an inevitable consequence of sin. Karl Barth to his credit gives full weight to this point. What we do to animals in killing them is "very close to homicide"; that it can be justified is never "self-evident," and slaughter must never become a "normal element" in our thinking.[16]

The second point is that misappropriation occurs when humans do not recognize that the life of an animal belongs to God, not to them. Here it seems to me that Christian vegetarianism is well founded. For while it may have been possible in the past to rear animals with personal care and consideration for their well-being and to dispatch them with the humble and scrupulous recognition that their life should be taken only in times of necessity, such conditions are abnormal today. In the institutionalized and mass destruction of billions of farm animals every year, we see more clearly than anywhere else the predominant philosophy of animals as "things" in our regard. In increasingly secular societies, farm animals have become merely ends to human means.

Thus even within the permissive tradition that sometimes accepts the need to kill for food, there is still ample justification for vegetarianism, whether based on calculation of animal or human interests. Here are four currently canvassed arguments:

(i) *Humane slaughter is frequently a contradiction in terms.* It is ironical that the religious communities that keep literally to the biblical notion of draining blood prior to slaughter (without prior stunning) arguably practice what is now one of the most inhumane methods of slaughter. This at least is the view of the British Government's Farm Animal Welfare Council, which concluded that animals that have their throats cut while still conscious can suffer an agonizing period of fourteen to thirty-five seconds before complete unconsciousness.[17] Despite the thoroughness of the report, most of the Jewish and Muslim communities in Britain have resisted the practice of stunning prior to slaughter. Some Jews, to be fair, find *all* slaughter abhorrent and in obedience to what they regard as the primary biblical command have founded the International Jewish Vegetarian Society.[18] It would certainly not be possible to absolve Gentile methods of slaughter from inhumanity. The conveyor-belt method of destruction for poultry, where birds are stunned prior to throat-slitting, can cause prolonged suffering if the technology is faulty and even the captive-bolt system utilized for cattle and sheep crucially depends for its effectiveness upon the skill of the operator. Those who prefer to avoid condoning animal suffering would do well to live independently of the primary products of slaughter. It is said of St. Richard of Wyche that "when he saw poultry or young animals being conveyed to his kitchen [he never ate meat himself] he would say half-sadly, half-humorously, 'Poor, innocent little creatures: if you were reasoning beings and could speak you would curse us. For we are the cause of your death, and what have you done to deserve it?'"[19] The fact is that almost all slaughter is achieved at *some* cost in terms of animal suffering.

(ii) *Most meat is the product of intensive systems of farming.* While it is true that not all meat comes from intensively farmed animals, individuals who want to free themselves from all such systems would need to exclude many primary products from their diet, including pork, veal, and chicken. The only way of guaranteeing freedom from factory farmed produce is by not eating primary animal products and some by-products too. Karl Barth, it appears, endorsed vegetarianism as a "protest" against the excesses of farming.[20] Even if our concern is solely for the suffering that animals have to undergo in the process of farming, vegetarianism can be well justified as a practical gesture of conscientious objection.

(iii) *"Live more simply so that all of us may simply live."* This is the motto of the Lifestyle Movement, which suggests that individuals eat "less grain-fed meat, reduce their meat consumption, or become vegetarians." The welfare of animals is only part of the Lifestyle concern, which extends to "avoid[ing] wasteful use of resources and show[ing] care for the environment."[21] Personal asceticism is therefore recommended as a gesture toward a fairer, more caring world. The line from Edmund Burke is commended: "Nobody made a greater mistake than he who did nothing because he could only do a little."[22] Simplicity of diet has strong monastic support of course: "Except the sick who are very weak," maintains the Rule of St. Benedict, "let all abstain entirely from the flesh of four-footed animals."[23]

(iv) *"One man's meat is another man/woman/child's hunger."* The slogan is part of the "Enough" campaign, with its aim of reducing meat consumption. The campaign highlights the waste of resources involved in feeding grain to animals. "Every minute 18 children die from starvation, yet 40 percent of the world's grain is fed to animals for meat."[24] Vegetarianism for a trial period is advocated to "help the hungry, improve the environment" and "stop untold animal suffering."[25] Vegetarianism is also commended on health grounds, and it is true that research into the diet of vegans in particular showed some significant health advantages.[26]

Without wishing to disparage these arguments, it seems to me that the strongest argument for leaving flesh foods to one side is of a different sort. It begins by taking seriously the notion that the life of an animal does not belong to human beings but to God. What the biblical narratives are expressing is that nothing less than God's right is involved in the business of killing for food. While under situations of clear necessity, given the sinful world as it is, meat eating may sometimes be justified, it cannot be uniformly accepted as such. In other words, our mistake in interpreting Genesis has been to suppose that one exception can establish a permanent rule. Since God's world is a changing and dynamic creation, we have to be open to the possibility of moral change. This means quite simply that what was once thought to be right can subsequently be thought to be morally wrong and vice versa. What precisely may have been the moral freedom of our forebears is not easy to determine. In many instances we do not know enough about our past to make clear, unequivocal judgments. But one thing of which we can be relatively certain is that for most people living today in Western society, dependence upon primary animal products is not essential to fullness of life.

In 1926, Dean Inge, in an otherwise perceptive essay on the "Rights of Animals," argued that we could not give up flesh, because "we must eat something."[27] What Inge obviously did not appreciate, as many are only now beginning to grasp, is that we do not need to kill for food in order to eat well or to sustain healthy lives. Once this *has* been realized, it is difficult intellectually to find a route back. For if luxury rather than necessity can justify killing, where will it all end? "Honourable men may honourably disagree about some details of human treatment of the nonhuman," argues Stephen Clark, "but vegetarianism is now as necessary a pledge of moral devotion as was the refusal of emperor-worship in the early Church." Eating animals, says Clark, is "empty gluttony." "Those who still eat flesh when they could do otherwise have no claim to be serious moralists."[28] Clark's final comment goes further than I would want to go. Given the confusing interrelationship of light and darkness, blessing and curse, it is difficult to hold out for any truths so self-evident that people who fail to see them are somehow morally culpable. That said, Clark's conclusion has real force and its power has yet to be sufficiently appreciated by fellow Christians. Far from seeing the possibility of widespread vegetarianism as a threat to Old Testament norms, Christians should rather welcome the fact that the Spirit is enabling us to make decisions so that we may more properly conform to the original Genesis picture of living in peace with creation.

The Christian argument for vegetarianism then is simple: since animals belong to God, have value to God, and live for God, then their needless destruction is sinful. In short: animals have some right to their life, all circumstances being equal. That it has taken Christians so long to grasp this need not worry us. There were doubtless good reasons, partly theological, partly cultural, and partly economic, why Christians in the past have found vegetarianism unfeasible. We do well not to judge too hastily, if at all. We cannot relive others' lives, or think their thoughts, or enter their consciences. But what we can be sure about is that living without what Clark calls "avoidable ill"[29] has a strong moral claim upon us now.

Some will surely question the limits of the vegetarian world here envisaged. Will large-scale vegetarianism work in practice? Can animal farming really be turned to the growing of crops, grains, nuts, and lentils? Will a vegetarian world not mean fewer farm animals? These are questions to which we do not have sufficient answers. I confess that I am agnostic, surely legitimately, about the possibility of a world-transforming vegetarianism. But clairvoyance is not an essential prerequisite of the vegetarian option, and what the future may hold, and its consequences, cannot easily be determined from any perspective. What I think is important to hold on to is the notion that the God who provides moral opportunities is the same God who enables the world, slowly but surely, to respond to them. From a theological perspective no moral endeavor is wasted so long as it coheres with God's purpose for the cosmos.

Some vegetarians press their case to the exclusion of all by-products of the slaughterhouse, including not only dairy produce but also the wearing of leather shoes or woolen clothes. They argue that it is not sufficient to be a "vegetarian" in the least demanding sense (one who abstains from meat), or a lacto-vegetarian (one who abstains from fish, flesh, and fowl), but that one should become a vegan (one who abstains from all meat and dairy produce completely). Not without justification, they point to the exploitation of animals for the dairy, as well as the meat, industry. "The modern dairy cow leads a life of hell," according to the *New Scientist*. "Each year, hopefully, she produces a calf which means that for nine months of the year she is pregnant. And for nine months of the year she is milked twice a day. For six months she is both pregnant and lactating."[30] In addition, the separation of the calf from its mother within a period of days after its birth—a frequent practice—is a less than joyful experience. Indeed the British Government's Brambell Committee as early as 1965 reported that this practice "undoubtedly inflicts anguish on both," since cattle are "highly intelligent" and the "attachment between the calf and the mother is particularly strong."[31] Egg production, too, is not immune from criticism, since it invariably involves the slaughter of male birds and unproductive hens, which are deemed surplus to requirements.

Given present farming practice, the case against dairy produce appears strong. But unlike meat eating, the issue is surely less direct. It *can* be possible to produce milk from non-intensively farmed goats and cattle, and it *can* be possible to obtain eggs from free-range hens without slaughtering their male partners. But it is sadly a sign of how endemic our exploitation of animals has become that almost everywhere even that possibly legitimate use of animals has been turned into abuse.

How practicable is the vegan world, where only plant foods are grown and few animals are utilized directly in farming? "No one—whether nutritionist, physician, sociologist, or layman—can rebut the veganic argument in any important respect," argues Jon Wynne-Tyson. And yet, despite his eloquent advocacy of veganism, even he admits of limitations. "I am not yet a fully practicing vegan," he writes, "although I would like to be." The reason? "The pressures on most of us not to go the whole way are tremendous and, in many a family, sadly divisive."[32] The fact is that it is amazingly difficult to free ourselves completely from the by-products of slaughter and remain a member of ordinary society at least. A plausible case can be made for boycotting Australian wool in the light of the barbaric practices employed in the Australian wool industry,[33] but even if we decide to wear non-animal-derived shoes rather than leather ones, we still face the difficulty that many man-made substances are tested for their toxicity on animals. Even licking postage stamps may be problematic since most glues have their origin in the offal that results from the slaughterhouse. In short: although the "logic" of the vegan case may be "absolute," its practical ramifications are currently beyond at least some of us.

That does not mean, of course, that we should not go on *trying* to reduce our dependence upon all kinds of animal products. The production of animal-free cosmetics is a striking example of how individual initiative and business acumen can provide us with a most welcome choice. There are important signs that some business concerns are going out of their way to produce animal-free toiletries with "no animal products/testing" labels. In a whole host of ways active, conscientious consumers can make their wishes known and press for different kinds of products. All moves in this direction toward the nonutilization of animal products need to be strenuously supported by those concerned for animal rights.

But at the same time we need to dispel the myth of absolute consistency or "pure land" theology. "Western society is so bound up with the use and abuse of animals in so many fields of human endeavor," I have argued elsewhere, "that it is impossible for anyone to claim that they are not party, directly or indirectly, to this exploitation either through the products they buy, the food they eat, or the taxes they pay."[34] Vegans are right to prick the consciences of those who find some recourse to animal by-products inevitable, but they can mislead us if they claim some absolutely pure land that only they inhabit. Self-righteousness can be a killer not only of moral sense but also of moral encouragement.

We return in this way to our opening remarks concerning the need for humility as well as vision. What we need is *progressive* disengagement from injury to animals. The urgent and essential task is to invite, encourage, support, and welcome those who want to take some steps along the road to a more peaceful world with the nonhuman creation. We do not *all* have to agree upon the most vital steps, or indeed the most practical ones. What is important is that we all move some way on, if only by one step at a time, however falteringly. If someone is prepared to boycott factory-farmed foods, at least they have made a start. If that is all the humanity that person can muster, at least some creatures have been saved from suffering. If someone is prepared to give up only red meat, at least some animals will suffer and die less as a consequence. If someone is prepared to abandon just meat and fish, at least some other creatures have a chance of living in peace. The enemy of progress is the view that everything must be changed before some real gains can be secured. There can be areas of genuine disagreement even among those who are committed to a new world of animal rights. But what is essential for this new world to emerge is the sense that each of us can change our individual worlds, however slightly, to live more peaceably with our nonhuman neighbors.

"I could not but feel with a sympathy full of regret all the pain that I saw around me, not only that of men, but that of the whole creation," wrote Schweitzer in a telling passage in his autobiography. "From this community of suffering, I have never tried to withdraw myself." He concluded: "It seemed to me a matter of course that we should all take our share of the burden of suffering which lies upon the world."[35] The vision of Christlike lordship over the nonhuman is practically costly. Our moral choices inevitably entail sacrifice and pain. In this way we anticipate, if not actually realize, the future joy of all God's creatures.

NOTES

1. Romans 3:23 (RSV).
2. Mark 10:18 (NEB).
3. J. S. Mill, cited in Tom Regan, *The Case for Animal Rights* (Berkeley: University of California Press, 1983), preface page.
4. G. B. Shaw, "Killing for Sport" and "The Doctor's Dilemma," in *Prefaces* (London: Constable and Co., 1934), pp. 144, 258–59.
5. Albert Schweitzer, *Civilization and Ethics*, trans. C. T. Campion (London: Allen & Unwin, 1967), p. 221.

6. Isaiah 6:7 (NEB).

7. Keith Ward, "Changing Ethical Values: A Christian Assessment," *Today's Church and Today's World* (Lambeth Conference 1978 Preparatory Articles) (London: CIO Publishing, 1977), p. 74.

8. Plato, *The Republic*, trans. F. M. Cornford (Oxford: Oxford University Press, 1969), part VII, 518, p. 232.

9. Isaiah 11:6–9 (NEB).

10. Genesis 1:29 (NEB).

11. Isaiah 11:9 (NEB).

12. Genesis 9:3 (NEB).

13. Anthony Phillips, *Lower Than the Angels: Questions Raised by Genesis 1–11* (London: Bible Reading Fellowship, 1983), p. 48.

14. Genesis 9:4 (NEB).

15. Phillips, *Lower Than the Angels*.

16. Karl Barth, *Church Dogmatics, III/4, The Doctrine of Creation* ("The Command of God the Creator") (Edinburgh: T. & T. Clark, 1961), p. 354.

17. Farm Animal Welfare Council, *Report on the Welfare of Livestock When Slaughtered by Religious Methods* (London: HMSO, 1985), p. 19. The report recommended that "legislative provisions which permit slaughter without the stunning of animals (including poultry) by Jews and Muslims . . . be repealed within the next three years" (p. 25).

18. The London-based International Jewish Vegetarian Society is located at 853–855 Finchley Road, London NW11 8LX.

19. St. Richard, cited in Alban Butler, *Lives of the Saints*, rev. Herbert Thurston and Donald Attwater (New York: P. J. Kennedy & Sons, 1946) and in Ambrose Agius, *God's Animals* (London: Catholic Study Circle for Animal Welfare, 1970), p. 51.

20. Barth, *Church Dogmatics, III/4*, p. 355.

21. The Lifestyle Movement, *A Commitment to Personal Change* (booklet) (London: Lifestyle Movement, 1984), p. 2.

22. Edmund Burke, cited in *Live More Simply So That All of Us May Simply Live* (booklet) (London: Lifestyle Movement, 1984), p. 11.

23. *The Rule of St. Benedict*, trans. Justin McCann (London: Sheed and Ward, 1976), chap. 39, p. 46.

24. Enough Campaign, *One Man's Meat* . . . (London: Enough Campaign, 1986), p. 1.

25. Ibid.

26. See, for example, the pioneering work of Frey R. Ellis and V. M. E. Montegriffo, "The Health of Vegans," in Frank Wakes, ed., *Plant Foods for Human Nutrition* 2 (1971): 93–103.

27. W. R. Inge, "The Rights of Animals," in *Lay Thoughts of a Dean* (New York and London: Knickerbocker Press, 1926), p. 199.

28. Stephen R. L. Clark, *The Moral Status of Animals* (Oxford: Clarendon Press, 1977), p. 183.

29. Ibid., preface.

30. *New Scientist* (January 13, 1972), cited by Jon Wynne-Tyson, *Food for a Future: The Complete Case for Vegetarianism* (London: Centaur Press, 1979), p. 109.

31. Brambell Committee, *Report of the Committee to Enquire into Methods of Livestock Production* (London: HMSO 1965), also cited by Wynne-Tyson, *Food for a Future*, p. 108.

32. Wynne-Tyson, *Food for a Future*, p. 107.

33. See Christine Townend, *Pulling the Wool: A New Look at the Australian Wool Industry* (London: Hale and Iremonger, 1985), esp. pp. 65–75 for details of the gruesome practice of "mulesing."

34. Andrew Linzey, "The Place of Animals in Creation—A Christian View," in *Animal Sacrifices: Religious Perspectives on the Use of Animals in Science*, ed. Tom Regan (Philadelphia: Temple University Press, 1986), p. 140.

35. Albert Schweitzer, *My Life and Thought: An Autobiography*, trans. C. T. Campion (London: Allen & Unwin, 1933), pp. 279–80. Also cited and discussed in Andrew Linzey, "Moral Education and Reverence for Life," in *Humane Education—A Symposium*, ed. David Patterson (London: Humane Education Council, 1981), p. 124.

16 THE CONSUMPTION OF ANIMALS AND THE CATHOLIC TRADITION

John Berkman

Historically, most if not all Catholics have abstained from eating animal flesh as an expression of their faith. Although most have abstained only for certain periods of time, others have abstained permanently. While Catholics have abstained for a variety of reasons, this essay focuses on distinctively theological reasons why Catholics, especially in the early centuries of Catholicism, have chosen to abstain from animal flesh. On the one hand, this essay will show how such abstinence has been an aspect of the spiritual practice of fasting and a response to the capital vice of gluttony. On the other hand, it will also show how such abstinence has been predicated on Catholic doctrines concerning creation and nature, the Fall, and eschatology.

The history of Catholic thought on why a person should or should not consume animal flesh is complex, and yet no scholarly history of this subject is readily available. This may partially account for the fact that most general commentators on the ethics of eating animals treat the Catholic tradition on this question in a way that is simplistic at best, generally making no attempt to seriously analyze the depth or breadth of, for example, patristic teaching about abstaining from consuming animals as part of

Another version of this essay appeared in *Logos: A Journal of Catholic Thought and Culture* 7, no. 1 (2004): 174–90.

Christian *askesis* (i.e., training), or how such abstinence from animal flesh has been a central part of the Christian practice of fasting.

While relatively little serious, overarching analysis has been done with regard to the consumption of animals and the Catholic tradition, at least two things are clear. First, despite what some zealous advocates assert, there is no reason to believe that Catholic (or Orthodox or most Protestant) Christianity has ever been a strictly "vegetarian" faith.[1] On the other hand, contrary to what some recent advocates for animals are prone to proclaim, no even-handed assessment of the Catholic tradition as a whole can baldly assert that Catholicism has been averse to abstaining from animal flesh, nor that it has been inimical to concern for other animals.

It will be impossible to comprehensively address the tradition; thus my treatment of the question will be necessarily selective. Since I will focus on types of reasoning about abstaining from animal flesh, historical contextualization will be limited. Furthermore, it will not be possible to adequately address the large question that runs through the entire tradition as to whether the Catholic ethic is properly seen as perfectionistic (with allowances made for the weak), or should be seen as more modest, expecting obedience to fundamental moral principles, but considering the more rigorous aspects of the faith as counsels of perfection for those who enter "religious life."[2] Finally, limiting myself to relatively few sources in Scripture, patristic and medieval theologians, and current papal teaching, I am aware that questions can be raised as to what extent the tradition is adequately represented. In presenting the sources that I do, my modest goal is to show that, even in the few Catholic voices I present, the question of consuming animal flesh is significantly more complex and diverse than is typically recognized.

In this paper, I shall present three *kinds* of reasoning—medicinal, ascetical, and eschatological—for abstinence from animal flesh. These three kinds of reasoning are not independent, much less mutually exclusive. Although all three are interconnected and build upon one another, different authors and different periods in the tradition significantly diverge with regard to the emphasis placed on each of these kinds of reasoning.

Medicinal abstinence focuses on abstention from animal flesh for the sake of health. However, by "health" one should not think primarily of the contemporary understanding of physical health (e.g., lowering one's intake of cholesterol and saturated fats). For most of the Christian tradition, physical health cannot be neatly separated from spiritual health. Thus, when patristic authors advocate a simple, meatless diet in the interest of health, they foremost have in mind health as a kind of spiritual purity.

A diet free of animal flesh and other rich foods was generally thought to be a prerequisite for spiritual or philosophical (rather than athletic) ascetic practice.[3] Ironically (for my purposes), animal flesh was widely seen in the ancient world as medicinal for the physically sick or weak, but the patristic authors are not entirely agreed on its appropriateness even for such purposes. In counseling their fellow ascetics, St. Jerome and his friend Paula at times even seem to have discouraged the consumption of animals for the sick.[4] Their attitude, however, seems unusual. While early Christian monasticism generally disavows the consumption of animals, they seem to have made an exception for monks who were sick.[5] The general refusal of flesh foods gets embodied in the various rules for monastic orders. In the most famous of all the monastic rules—the sixth-century *Rule of St. Benedict*—monks are instructed that "[a]ll must refrain entirely from eating the flesh of quadrupeds, except for the sick who are really weak."[6] Benedict's rule is on the "liberal" end of such rules, limiting its scope only to four-legged animals.

Ascetical abstinence may be thought of as ethical abstinence in the etymological sense of ethics as matters to do with character. In her book on attitudes to food in late antiquity, Veronika Grimm argues that early Christians and their Jewish forebears had their eating (and sexual) practices regulated much more than those of the surrounding pagan culture.[7] However, the central concern for ancient Christian reflection on consuming animals—in contrast to contemporary reflection on, for example, the moral status of animals themselves—was how such consumption fits with the demands of Christian discipline or asceticism.[8] Like the Judaism out of which early Christianity emerges, early Christians are concerned with what constitutes appropriate dietary and sexual practices, both as aspects of perfecting their human nature and as obedience to the laws of God. The lack of attention to the status of animals is perhaps only part of the more general lack of emphasis on moral status. What is instead central for the early Christians is that all their practices are to be ordered to the love and service of God.

Questions regarding appropriate eating practices, including questions about consuming animal flesh, are found in the earliest Christian documents. In his epistles to the Christian communities in Corinth and Rome, St. Paul responds to such questions as how Christians are to celebrate the Eucharist[9] and whether Christians are to eat animal flesh that has been sacrificed to idols.[10] In the Corinthian community, there seems to have been a dispute between two factions (i.e., the "strong" and the "weak") over whether they should eat animal flesh or only vegetables. Although St. Paul is often interpreted as siding with the "strong" at Corinth but making concessions to the "weak" for the greater good of unity in the community, it has also been argued that St. Paul is entering a debate in which "religious" questions are inseparable from "social" questions of status, power, and privilege, and that the "weak" identify with the place and status of the poor, rejecting particular attitudes and practices of the dominant society.[11] In his letter to the Christian community at Rome, Paul appears at first to defend a laissez-faire approach to eating animal flesh (14:2–6) but winds up giving priority in practice to the argument of the weak (14:23–15:2).[12] Regardless of how, in the light of contemporary historical scholarship, one may think these passages are to be interpreted, influential exegetes such as Augustine and Aquinas (and hence much of the Christian tradition) have understood St. Paul to be denying in-principled objections to all consumption of animal flesh. However, ancient and medieval theologians (including Augustine and Aquinas) join the Church in commending fasting from animal flesh—at least during certain times or periods in the Christian year—as a universal part of the tradition.

From the beginnings of the Church, abstinence from animal flesh seems to be identified as part of the virtuous or ascetical life, largely as a key element in the Christian's response to the capital vice of gluttony. For gluttony—at least according to many of the church fathers—is *the* primal vice of the Christian faith.[13] Conversely, abstinence (e.g., fasting) is a virtue by which one overcomes the vice of gluttony.[14] Early Christian references to fasting typically refer not to periods of total abstinence from food, but to diets that restrict the amount of food eaten (certainly no more than necessary for nutrition) and to diets that avoid certain types of food (i.e., meat).[15]

Fasting, along with the Eucharist, are the most important food practices in the Catholic tradition.[16] In Scripture and Catholic tradition, fasting is often aligned with prayer and has a number of spiritual purposes. For Aquinas, fasting is a means not only of atoning for and preventing sins but also, more generally, of raising the mind to spiritual matters.[17] Whereas gluttony puts one to sleep, fasting draws one to prayer.

The consumption of animal flesh was closely aligned with gluttony (and hence inimical to the cultivation of the spiritual life) because, according to the dominant medical and dietary viewpoints of the ancient and medieval world, animal flesh was thought to be excessively nutritive, leading to an increase in all kinds of bodily secretions.[18] On the one hand, meat eating was seen to produce excessive phlegm, vomiting, and violent belching, as well as excess excrement, leading Chrysostom to proclaim: "The increase in luxury [in eating] is nothing other than the increase in excrement."[19] On the other hand, meat eating was also thought to produce excessive semen, and so restricting animal flesh was seen as a means of controlling lust.[20] Hence, abstaining from animal flesh as an aspect of abstinence was viewed as a means of controlling the two major sins of the flesh, gluttony and lust.

Eschatological abstinence is an element of a broader perspective on the Christian life, which seeks to embody a particular vision of the world, a world that existed prior to the Fall and a world that will be restored in the *eschaton*. For church fathers such as Chrysostom, Jerome, and Cassian, one's diet is particularly relevant to the goal of embodying the Edenic state, since they consider the original sin of Adam and Eve to be gluttony. Thus, dietary renunciation is seen to be a means of redressing this situation and returning to an Edenic state. Furthermore, Basil of Caesaria and Jerome note that fasting from flesh foods is an image of life as it was in the Garden of Eden, since in Paradise there was no sacrifice of animals or eating of animal flesh. While neither Basil nor Jerome rules out any consumption of animal flesh as inherently and necessarily sinful, Jerome notes that the allowance of flesh eating is only after the flood and due to "the hardness of human hearts."[21]

References by Chrysostom, Basil, and Jerome to the ascetic hearkening after the Edenic state is a pursuit of what the Catholic tradition refers to as the state of "original justice."[22] In this prelapsarian world, humans live in friendship with God and in harmony with the other animals. One sign of this harmony is that both humans and animals do not eat animal flesh.[23] After the Fall, the state of original justice and peace is gone; the world has become fundamentally disordered. The sin of humans leads not only to their fall but to the fall of all of creation.[24] Humans are no longer at peace with God, with each other, with other animals, or with the rest of creation. The alienation between humans and animals is exemplified by the fact that humans now eat them (Genesis 9:3).[25]

If a theological account of the world ends with the doctrines of creation and fall, then the world of predation is an existence to which humans and other animals have been abandoned. However, this is not where the Christian theological narrative ends. The world has been and is being redeemed in Christ. Far from being merely a part of the creative work of God, the work of redemption is the greater and more splendid work. This is because "[t]he first creation finds its meaning and its summit in the new creation in Christ, the splendor of which surpasses that of the first creation."[26] Christians live in a world where the Kingdom of God (or "new creation") has both come (i.e., a "realized" eschatology) and yet is not consummated (i.e., a "not yet" eschatology). St. Paul provides a vision of a redeemed creation, one where all forms of alienation brought about by the Fall are overcome:

> For creation awaits with eager expectation the revelation of the children of God; for creation was made subject to futility, not of its own accord but because of the one who subjected it, in hope that creation itself would be set free from slavery to corruption and share in the glorious freedom of the children of God. We know that all creation is groaning in labor pains even until now; and not only that, but we ourselves, who have the first fruits of the Spirit, we also groan within ourselves as we wait for adoption, the redemption of our bodies. (Romans 8:19–23)

When Catholics pray the Lord's Prayer, they pray that God's peaceable kingdom may come more fully in the world.

Thus, while human eating of animals (and other effects of the Fall) is a *description* of eating practices in a postlapsarian world (i.e., the way things *are*), it is not at all clear that it should be seen as a *prescription* for human eating practices (i.e., *not* the way things *ought* to be or ideally are).[27] The renunciation of animal flesh of many of the early Christian ascetics is a vision, not only back to the Edenic state but also forward to the eschatological Kingdom of God. As part of a broader program of renunciation, the fasting ascetic can be seen as doing at least two things: identifying with humanity as it was created in the *imago Dei*, and with the humanity that will once again fully possess that image, and make recompense for the failure of Adam and Eve to live up to their original fast (i.e., from the forbidden fruit in the garden). Observing monks and women ascetics who fast from consuming animals, Chrysostom compares them to Adam and Eve before the Fall, seeing them as having already partially recaptured the Edenic state.[28]

For many of the patristic authors, a recreation of the Edenic state involves not only abstaining from eating animals but also, as Basil notes, abstaining from sacrificing animals.[29] This brings us to the other most important eating practice in Christianity. The Eucharist is the remembrance of the sacrificial death of Jesus, a remembrance of thanksgiving in which believers share in Christ's body (I Corinthians 10–11). Through this practice Christians are incorporated into Christ's body, Christ's body being understood both individually and corporately. In the light of this, it is not surprising that some opponents accused the early Christians of cannibalism. Although there was significant diversity of food elements in early Christian Eucharists and/or *agape* meals, there is no evidence that animal flesh was ever a part of these celebrations of thanksgiving. What significance, if any, should be made of this?

In his extensive study of all the food elements that appear in early Christian ritual meals, Andrew McGowan notes that while bread and wine seem to have been the dominant elements from the beginning, the occasional choice of other elements is not insignificant. The appearance of oils, vegetables, and salt seem to be a means of emphasizing the rejection of meat, and its association with bloody sacrifice. Similarly, the appearance of milk (and/or cheese), honey, and olives in some celebrations can be seen as celebratory elements of a restored paradisiacal state, also distinguished from a society built on bloodshed.[30]

However, while eschatological abstinence is an encouragement or counsel to abstinence from animal flesh, it is not a command. Thus, for example, while St. Basil suggests that those who desire "to live their lives in imitation of the life of paradise" will want to exclude the consumption of animals from the diet, he explicitly does not forbid the consumption of animals, even for monks. Why is this? "Because God has permitted it after the Fall."[31] This distinction between abstention from animals as part of an ascetic discipline versus a juridical requirement is embodied in the fourth-century canons of the Council of Gangra, which sharply criticize the perceived arrogance of some of those who abstain and accuse those who consume animal flesh as being "without hope" (outside of the saved).

Here controversy over pushing the requirements of abstention from animal flesh shows the historically recurring tensions between ascetic (or perfectionist) Catholicism and that which the Church considers to be appropriately binding on all Christians at all times. It is a debate over the moral priority of what God originally intended for the world and what God intends for fallen humanity. These differences and tensions are of no small matter within the history of Catholicism, not only between ecclesiastical authorities (who may be seen to be guarding the moral probity of laypersons) and religious communities but also between and among religious communities themselves. The question of general abstinence from animal flesh is thus one of many questions the resolution of which depends upon to what extent one has a realized (as opposed to a "not yet") eschatology, the extent to which one believes that one can embody the coming Kingdom of God in one's present life.

In one of his writings on Christian hope, Pope John Paul II addresses the question of the extent to which we can have a "realized" eschatology. He notes that in much of the tradition, the teaching of a "realized" eschatology was only "faintly present." However, contrary to this traditional view, he argues that

> the truth which the gospel teaches about God requires a certain change in focus with regard to eschatology. First of all, eschatology is not what will take place in the future, something happening only after earthly life is finished. *Eschatology has already begun with the coming of Christ.* The ultimate eschatological event was His redemptive Death and His Resurrection. This is the beginning of "a new heaven and a new earth. (cf. Revelation 21:1)[32]

In this work and his encyclical *Evangelium vitae*, John Paul II is calling Catholics to have a more realized eschatology, a greater sense that no matter how small or "symbolic" one's steps may be, they contribute to the Gospel of life, which "is growing and producing abundant fruit."[33]

In the light of the above analysis of three reasons why Catholics have traditionally abstained from eating animals, what can we summarize? Although Catholicism has never been a "vegetarian" religion, it has always concerned itself with appropriate eating practices, especially the significance of abstaining from animal flesh. Furthermore, Catholic theology is certainly compatible with—and arguably encouraging of—a diet that perpetually abstains from animal flesh. The medicinal, ascetical, and eschatological forms of reasoning about abstaining from animal flesh move Catholics toward living excellently, through disciplined training of our bodies, the practice of virtue, and harmony—to the extent possible—with an eschatological vision of our God's world.

Although there is much to be gained from a historical perspective of Christian abstinence from animal flesh, it does not address some of the distinctly contemporary problems faced in late-modern capitalist societies at the beginning of the twenty-first century. For example, the twentieth century brought techniques of multiplying and sanitizing slaughter, in a way that typically bureaucratizes and regularizes cruel treatment of animals, and further alienates humans from this other part of the created order. It is a longstanding belief in the Catholic tradition that the virtues that Christians show or fail to show in relation to animals and the rest of creation influence one's ability to be virtuous in relation to other human beings.

But important as "instrumentalist" reasons may be for recognizing and advocating concern for all of God's creatures, they are not the last word. The Catholic tradition recognizes that other creatures have their own intrinsic worth that is not to be subsumed entirely to human desires and perfection. God's concern for other animals is not only instrumental to the welfare of human beings. God gives life to all creatures, and thus "life, especially human life, belongs only to God."[34] All creatures are created to celebrate God who gives life in a manner fitting to the form of life they have been apportioned by God.[35] While not the central theme of Pope John Paul II's *Evangelium vitae*, the intrinsic goodness of nonhuman life also is clearly affirmed.[36] In order to better acknowledge the God-given intrinsic worth of animals, Catholics do well to better recognize that ultimately animals exist neither for their own sake nor for the sake of human beings but for the glory of God. This "truth of creation" is affirmed eschatologically because we humans share with other animals a common destiny of transformation and glorification in God.[37]

NOTES

1. In fact, it is difficult even to understand to what extent Catholicism is vegetarian, since "vegetarian" is a nineteenth-century term, and it is difficult to read such a contemporary notion into Catholicism's two-thousand-year tradition.

2. Recent Catholic moral theology has witnessed a renewed interest in approaches to morality that make questions of character and the self methodologically prior to questions of moral norms. For most of the last four centuries, moral theology has been preoccupied with moral norms, with determining which acts

should be "obligatory," "permitted," "necessary," and/or "justified." One of the difficulties facing a moral methodology that presumes the priority of moral norms is that it has a difficult time articulating the nature of the appropriate concern for non-human animals and the environment more generally. For further analysis of methodological options for Catholic moral theology, see John Berkman, "How Important Is the Doctrine of Double Effect? Contextualizing the Controversy," *Christian Bioethics* 3, no. 2 (1997): 89–114.

3. In the ancient world, some occupations (e.g., soldiering, manual labor, athletic training) were thought to require meat eating. Thus, even the third-century neo-Platonic philosopher Porphyry does not recommend abstinence from animal flesh for all persons, but only those free from the demands of manual labor and who have plenty of leisure time for contemplation. See Veronika Grimm, *From Feasting to Fasting: The Evolution of a Sin* (London: Routledge, 1996), p. 59.

4. This attitude is not limited to patristic asceticism. Caroline Walker Bynum notes that in the Middle Ages, the Carthusian order came to see perpetual abstinence from animal flesh as so crucial to their identity that a violation of this prohibition (even by the sick) meant expulsion from the order. See Caroline Walker Bynum, *Holy Feast and Holy Fast* (Berkeley: University of California Press, 1987), p. 42.

5. Teresa Shaw, *The Burden of the Flesh: Fasting and Sexuality in Early Christianity* (Minneapolis, MN: Fortress Press, 1998), p. 13.

6. St. Benedict, *The Rule of St. Benedict* (Leominster, UK: Gracewing, 1990), rule XXXIX.

7. Grimm, *From Feasting to Fasting*, p. 59.

8. Early Christian asceticism is generally understood to involve acts of physical self-discipline for the purpose of training the bodily appetites to the demands of reason and the law of God. Fasting is a central aspect of early Christian asceticism. While all Christians engaged in asceticism to some degree, there was significant variation among early Christians, and some scholars refer only to those who practiced *askesis* to a high degree to be considered ascetics. See Shaw, *The Burden of the Flesh*, pp. 5–10.

9. I Corinthians 11:20–29.

10. Romans 14:17-23; I Corinthians 8:9–13, 10:14–33.

11. See Andrew McGowan, *Ascetic Eucharist* (Oxford: Oxford University Press, 1998), pp. 221–31.

12. Ibid., pp. 229–30.

13. Bynum, *Holy Feast and Holy Fast*, p. 82.

14. Although fasting in early Christianity is sometimes associated particularly with ascetic individuals, church fathers such as Basil of Caesaria encouraged all Christians, young and old, to fast regularly. See Shaw, *The Burden of the Flesh*, p. 223, n. 7.

15. Ibid., p. 7.

16. Bynum notes that fasting and the Eucharist are the major food practices of medieval Christians, and this seems true of the tradition more generally (Bynum, *Holy Feast and Holy Fast*, p. 5).

17. Aquinas, *Summa Theologiae* (New York: Benziger Bros., 1947), II–II, 147, a. 3.

18. Galen (c. 129–200 CE), physician to emperor Marcus Aurelius, and one of the most eminent physicians of the ancient world, writes extensively on how diet affects one's personality and character. See Shaw, *The Burden of the Flesh*, pp. 53–64.

19. Chrysostom's *Homilies on Matthew*, cited in ibid., p. 133.

20. In addition to numerous patristic authors, this can also be found in medieval authors, e.g., Aquinas, *Summa Theologiae*, II–II, 147, a. 8.

21. Shaw, *The Burden of the Flesh*, pp. 163–219. As an accommodation to human weakness and hardness of heart, Jerome likens the consumption of animal flesh to the Mosaic allowance of divorce (177).

22. See, for example, *The Catechism of the Catholic Church (CCC)*, §376.

23. In Genesis, God gives humans "seed-bearing fruits and plants" to eat (Genesis 1:29 ff.). Considering that the description of the "vegetarian" state of Eden in the Genesis narrative immediately follows the reference to human dominion over the other animals, it would seem that the meaning of human "dominion" over other animals (at least according to Genesis 1) does not include eating them.

24. Hence St. Paul's reference to the situation of the world as "creation in bondage" (Romans 8:21). See also *CCC*, §1046.

25. See Genesis 9:3. The reference to humans being given "garments of skin" (Genesis 3:21) by God after the Fall may be another example, though much of the tradition interprets "garments of skin" as referring to human flesh, as God enfleshing humanity. More generally, the new enmity between humans and animals is only one aspect of the narrative's broader account of alienation. For example, the alienation between God and humans is exemplified by their expulsion from the Garden of Eden (Genesis 3:23); the alienation between men and women is exemplified by Eve's subjugation (Genesis 3:16); the alienation between parents and children is exemplified in the pain of bringing forth children (Genesis 3:16); the alienation between humans is exemplified by the murder of Abel (Genesis 4:8); the alienation between humans and the vegetative creation is exemplified by the fact that humans must till the earth (Genesis 3:17–19).

26. *CCC* §349.

27. A similar picture can be seen in a 1995 encyclical of Pope John Paul II. "Murderous violence profoundly changes man's environment. From being the garden of Eden (Genesis 2:15), a place of plenty, of harmonious interpersonal relationships and of friendship with God, the earth becomes the land of Nod (Genesis 4:16), a place of scarcity, loneliness and separation from God." (Pope John Paul II, *Evangelium vitae*, §9). Henceforth *EV*.

28. See Shaw, *The Burden of the Flesh*, pp. 163, 176, 179. For Maximus of Turin, the faster participates in the redemptive work of Christ. Maximus writes, "What the first man lost by eating, the second Adam recovered by fasting. And he kept in the desert the law of abstinence given in paradise." See Bynum, *Holy Feast and Holy Fast*, p. 35.

29. Shaw, *The Burden of the Flesh*, p. 177.

30. McGowan, *Ascetic Eucharist*, pp. 89–142, 238, esp. 106, 114, 140–142.

31. Shaw, *The Burden of the Flesh*, p. 197.

32. Pope John Paul II, *Crossing the Threshold of Hope* (New York: Alfred Knopf, 1994), pp. 184–85.

33. *EV*, §100.

34. *EV*, §9.

35. "We must celebrate Eternal Life, from which every other life proceeds. From this, in proportion to its capacities, every being which in any way participates in life, receives life." (*EV*, §84).

36. *EV*, §42. To avoid misunderstanding, it must be noted that the primary purpose of *Evangelium vitae* is a vigorous defense of human life, especially those without voices. For a fuller analysis of recent papal reflection on a prophetic witness on behalf of nonhuman animals, see John Berkman, "Prophetically Pro-Life: John Paul II's Gospel of Life and Evangelical Concern for Animals," *Josephinum Journal of Theology* 6, no. 1 (1999): 43–59.

37. *CCC*, § 1046 and *EV*, §§ 38, 80.

17 IS VEGETARIANISM UN-ISLAMIC?

Richard C. Foltz

All your life you have been drinking the blood and eating the flesh of animals without realizing what you have been doing. You love flesh and enjoy murder. If you had any conscience or any sense of justice, if you were born as a true human being, you would think about this. God is looking at me and you. Tomorrow his truth and his justice will inquire into this. You must realize this.

M. R. Bawa Muhaiyadeen,
Come to the Secret Garden: Sufi Tales of Wisdom
(Philadelphia: Fellowship Press, 1985), p. 26.

An estimated twenty percent of the world's population—over one billion people—claims Muslim identity. Though Muslims now inhabit every corner of the globe and live in societies as diverse as those of West Africa, Central Asia, the Philippines, and the United States, one social factor that they all seem to share is the eating of meat. Ethical questions surrounding the use of animals for food are not raised in the legal literature of classical Islam, and even today any serious discourse on the viability of an "Islamic" vegetarianism is difficult to find.

The Islamic scholar Mawil Izzi Dien, in his recent book *The Environmental Dimensions of Islam*, goes so far as to assert the following:

An earlier version of this essay appeared in *Studies in Contemporary Islam* 3, no. 1 (2001): 39–54.

> According to Islamic Law there are no grounds upon which one can argue that animals should not be killed for food. The Islamic legal opinion on this issue is based on clear Qur'anic verses. Muslims are not only prohibited from eating certain food, but also may not choose to prohibit themselves food that is allowed by Islam. Accordingly vegetarianism is not permitted unless on grounds such as unavailability or medical necessity. Vegetarianism is not allowed under the pretext of giving priority to the interest of animals because such decisions are God's prerogative.[1]

In other words, according to Izzi Dien, not only is there no such thing as Islamic vegetarianism, to be a vegetarian is un-Islamic! Such a blanket dismissal of the very possibility of an Islamic vegetarianism, however, is not warranted. Throughout history numerous Muslims have practiced vegetarianism, in many cases for reasons of piety. Since early times many South Asian Sufis, for example, have been vegetarian, including many members of the Chishti order but also the Suhrawardi saint Hamid al-din Nagori and others.[2] Though some have attributed this to Hindu or Buddhist influence, among the Sufis of North Africa and the Ottoman world saints were often believed to take animal form, and vegetarian anecdotes were widely told.[3] An early female Sufi, Zaynab, is said to have been persecuted for her refusal to eat meat.[4]

Today a growing number of Muslims throughout the world are practicing vegetarian lifestyles, not only in the West but in traditional Islamic environments as well. The animal rights organization People for the Ethical Treatment of Animals (PETA) has launched, at the suggestion of its Muslim members, a Web site on Islam and vegetarianism.[5] In Turkey, which has several national vegetarian organizations, an old Istanbul neighborhood known as "Non-meat eater" (Etyemecz) derives its name from the vegetarian practices of a Sufi sect.[6] Iran has at least one registered vegetarian society, the Sana and Shafa Vegetarians' Association, based in Tehran.[7]

AN ANTHROPOCENTRIC TRADITION

Throughout the Qur'an's fourteen-hundred-year history, Muslim commentators on the Islamic Scripture have been both forthright and unapologetic in asserting an anthropocentric worldview. "Verily," the Qur'an states, "we create man in the best conformation" (95:4).[8] Humanity is described in the Qur'an as the "viceregent" (*khalifa*) of God on earth (2:30, 6:165, 35:39), entrusted with the stewardship of maintaining the balance and order of Creation.

The Qur'an has usually been read as allowing the eating of meat, as in verse 5:1, which reads, "O you who have attained to faith! Be true to your convenants! Lawful to you is [the flesh of] every beast that feeds on plants, save what is mentioned to you [hereinafter]: but you are not allowed to hunt while you are in a state of pilgrimage. Behold, God ordains in accordance with his will." A similar permission has been perceived in 6:145: "Say: 'In all that has been revealed unto me, I do not find anything forbidden to eat, if one wants to eat thereof, unless it be carrion, or blood poured forth, or the flesh of swine—for that, behold, is loathsome—or a sinful offering over which any name other than God's has been invoked. But if one is driven by necessity—neither coveting it nor exceeding his immediate need—then [know that], behold, thy Sustainer is much-forgiving, a dispenser of grace."

According to the Qur'an, then, meat eating might seem to be, except under specified conditions, pleasing to God. Since it is incumbent upon Muslims to live in a way that is pleasing to God in every detail, not to eat meat if God wishes us to would constitute an act of infidelity.

Islam's historical tensions with Buddhism (and, in India, with Hinduism), seen as an idol-worshiping religion, provide a further "guilt by association" argument against vegetarianism. The seventh/thirteenth-century legal scholar 'Izz ad-Din b. 'Abd as-Salam, in his *Qawa'id al-Ahkam fi Masalih al-Anam*, observes:

> The unbeliever who prohibits the slaughtering of an animal [for no reason but] to achieve the interest of the animal is incorrect because in so doing he gives preference to a lower, *khasis,* animal over a higher, *nafis,* animal.[9]

An earlier traditional jurist, Ibn Hazm (d. 456/1062), provides an argument against moral consideration being extended to animals, which is later echoed by those heard in nineteenth-century England, when he writes that "the laws of Allah are only applicable to those who possess the ability to speak and can understand them."[10] The faculty of speech has long been proposed as a major criterion of human uniqueness, and some would make this argument even today. But such reasoning can, in light of our improved understanding of animal communication, be turned on its head; it could actually be used in support of making animals morally considerable. Even in the Qur'an one finds a verse that seems to run counter to Ibn Hazm's claim: "And [in this insight] Solomon was [truly] David's heir; and he would say: 'O you people! We have been taught the speech of birds, and have been given [in abundance] of all [good] things: this, behold, is indeed a manifest favor [from God]!" (27:16) Of course, it remains unclear to most humans what laws Allah may have established for other species, and how they may or may not differ from those laid down for humans.

COMPASSION FOR ANIMALS

Within the admitted hierarchy of Creation in which human beings occupy the highest rank, the Qur'an and the *sunna* (the example of the Prophet Muhammad, as attested in reports called *hadith*s) nevertheless strongly enjoin Muslims to treat animals with compassion and not to abuse them. The Qur'an states that all creation praises God, even if this praise is not expressed in human language (17:44). The Qur'an further states that "There is not an animal in the earth, nor a flying creature on two wings, but they are communities like unto you" (6:38). Thus, when in the nature of things (*fitra*), the Muslim must kill in order to survive, Muhammad called for compassion: "If you kill, kill well, and if you slaughter, slaughter well. Let each of you sharpen his blade and let him spare suffering to the animal he slaughters."[11] On another occasion he is reported to have said, "For [charity shown to] each creature which has a wet heart [i.e., is alive], there is a reward." He opposed recreational hunting, saying that "whoever shoots at a living creature for sport is cursed." In another hadith, the Prophet is said to have reprimanded some men who were sitting idly on their camels in the marketplace, saying, "Either ride them or leave them alone." He is also reported to have said, "There is no man who kills [even] a sparrow or anything smaller, without its deserving it, but Allah will question him about it [on the Day of Judgment]," and "Whoever is kind to the creatures of God, is kind to himself."[12]

Classical Islamic law prescribes that domestic animals should not be overburdened or otherwise mistreated or put at risk, that their young should not be killed in their sight, that they should be given adequate shelter and rest, and that males and females should be allowed to be together during mating season. The legal category of water rights extends to animals through the law of "the right of thirst" (*haqq al-shurb*).[13] The *Sahih Bukhari* mentions two contrasting stories with particular relevance to the treatment of animals. In one, a woman is condemned to hell because she has mistreated a cat; in another, a sinner is saved by the grace of Allah after he gives water to a dog dying of thirst. In the observation of G. H. Bousquet, Islam thus "condemns to hell those who mistreat animals, and . . . more importantly, accords extraordinary grace to those who do them good."[14]

Possibly the richest material that Muslim civilization has produced in regard to animal rights is a tenth-century treatise entitled *The Case of the Animals versus Man before the King of the Jinn* by an anonymous group of philosophers who called themselves the Ikhwan al-Safa, or "Pure Brethren." In this unusual work, representatives from the animal kingdom bring a court case against the human race whom they accuse of abusing their position. The animals point out that before the creation of man they roamed the earth in peace and harmony, what might be called in contemporary language "natural balance":

> We were fully occupied in caring for our broods and rearing our young with all the good food and water God had allotted us, secure and unmolested in our own lands. Night and day we praised and sanctified God, and God alone.
>
> Ages passed and God created Adam, father of mankind, and made him his vice-regent on earth. His offspring reproduced, and his seed multiplied. They spread over the earth—land and sea, mountain and plain. Men encroached on our ancestral lands. They captured sheep, cows, horses, mules, and asses from among us and enslaved them, subjecting them to the exhausting toil and drudgery of hauling, being ridden, plowing, drawing water, and turning mills. They forced us to these things under duress, with beatings, bludgeonings, and every kind of torture and chastisement our whole lives long. Some of us fled to deserts, wastelands, or mountaintops, but the Adamites pressed after us, hunting us with every kind of wile and device. Whoever fell into their hands was yoked, haltered, and fettered. They slaughtered and flayed him, ripped open his belly, cut off his limbs and broke his bones, tore out his eyes; plucked his feathers or sheared off his hair or fleece, and put him onto the fire to be cooked, or on the spit to be roasted, or subjected him to even more dire tortures, whose full extent is beyond description. Despite these cruelties, these sons of Adam are not through with us but must claim that this is their inviolable right, that they are our masters and we are their slaves, deeming any of us who escapes a fugitive, rebel, shirker of duty—all with no proof or explanation beyond main force.[15]

The Brethren's view of the natural world is all the more striking for its exceptionality in the context of fourth/tenth-century Muslim society. They were a radical group, as indicated by their choice to remain anonymous, and in subsequent centuries, only the heterodox Sevener-Shi'i or Isma'ili sect, identified today with the Aga Khan, adopted their writings as authoritative. Yet it may be that in regard to animal rights the Pure Brethren were (like St. Francis in Catholicism) simply ahead of their time, and as such may have more to teach us in the twenty-first century than they did to Muslims of their own era.

At least one contemporary Islamic legal scholar has taken issue with the dominant anthropocentric view of animal rights. In the prefaces to his books on the subject, *Islamic Concern for Animals* and *Animals in Islam*, the late Basheer Ahmad Masri (formerly imam of the Shah Jehan mosque in Woking, England) states his opinion that "life on this earth is so intertwined as an homogeneous unit that it cannot be disentangled for the melioration of one species at the expense of the other."[16] Masri understands the superiority of the human species to consist only in its spiritual volition (*taqwa*), that is, its capacity to make moral choices. Without this distinction, Masri believes, the differences between humans and other animal species are superficial.[17]

In fact, Masri notes, animals can even be humanity's teachers; for example 'Ali, the Prophet's nephew and son-in-law, is reported to have said, "Be like a bee; anything he eats is clean, anything he drops is sweet and any branch he sits upon does not break." Despite all this, Masri refrains from discussing the option of vegetarianism. His concern is with eliminating the kinds of unnecessary cruelty and exploitation of animals that he sees as prevalent in modern society, such as laboratory testing.[18] He writes, "To kill animals to satisfy the human thirst for inessentials is a contradiction in terms within the Islamic tradition. Think of the millions of animals killed, in the name of commercial enterprises, in order to supply a complacent public with trinkets and products they do not really need. Any why? Because we are too lazy or too self-indulgent to find substitutes."[19]

Though Masri was himself a vegetarian, he stops short of arguing that meat eating is inconsistent with Islamic compassion for animals. He does raise the question, stating that "Islam is so concerned about compassion for animals that one wonders why it has allowed us to kill them for food and why it did not enjoin us to become vegetarians."[20] He goes on to say that "From the humanitarian point of view, it would be an ideal situation if all the world were to become vegetarian and all the animals were allowed to live their natural lives. Perhaps a time may come, sooner or later, when this would happen. Meanwhile the poor animals will go on having their throats slit."[21] Elsewhere, Masri suggests that "Some may decide that the products of intensive factory farms are not suitable, both from the religious and the health point of view, and seek more naturally produced eggs and meat; or give up eating meat altogether."[22]

The late Sri Lankan Sufi teacher, M. R. Bawa Muhaiyadeen, puts the matter somewhat more strongly. "My children," he writes, "we must be aware of everything we do. All young animals have love and compassion. And if we remember that every creation was young once, we will never kill another life. We will not harm or attack any living creature."[23]

Of course ethical concern for the rights of animals does not necessarily lead to vegetarianism, nor is it the only possible justification for it. Another major motivation is human health. Especially among Sufis, austerities aimed at purifying the body have sometimes entailed abstention from animal flesh. The Indian saint Shaykh Nasir ad-Din Mahmud (d. 757/1356), known as "The Lamp of Delhi," ate plain rice or rice with lentils (a mixture we now know to be protein-complementary!), or else bread and sometimes melons and sweets.[24]

Such practices were not limited to the Indian environment. Even Hellenistically influenced Sufis have sometimes shunned meat eating as nourishing the "animal soul" or *nafs* (also called "the lower self"). Muhyi ad-Din ibn 'Arabi, in his *Risalat al-Anwar*, admonishes the reader to "[b]e careful of your diet. It is better if your food be nourishing but devoid of animal fat."[25] In his commentary on this passage, 'Abd al-Karim ibn Ibrahim al-Jili notes that this is "because animal fat strengthens animality, and its principles will dominate spiritual principles."[26]

Mainstream Islam has never encouraged asceticism in the way many Sufi traditions have. But in light of present-day scientific perspectives on nutritional health, it is clear that Muslims can enjoy physical as well as spiritual benefits from a vegetarian diet. Both aspects would seem to be fully compatible with established Islamic principles of animal rights.

SOCIAL JUSTICE IN ISLAM

The Prophet Muhammad was one of history's great social reformers. He lived at a time of social change and upheaval in western Arabia, when some families were enjoying untold wealth while others suffered in deprivation. Consequently, social justice is one of the major themes of the Qur'an. Muhammad's insistent preaching against the hypocrisy of Mecca's wealthy elite is certainly a major factor accounting for the persecution suffered by the early Muslim community.

In most societies today, meat eating remains by and large a privilege of the wealthy. This is a privilege that comes at a cost not only to the animals who are slaughtered for the tables of the rich, but also in the form of chronic hunger for twenty percent of the world's human population, a disproportionate number of whom are Muslims. Even while so many human beings go permanently malnourished, more than half of all land under cultivation is given over to crops destined for livestock consumption. As contemporary philosopher Peter Singer, guru of the Animal Liberation movement, puts it, "the raising of animals for food by the methods used in the industrial nations does not contribute to the solution of the hunger problem. On the contrary, it aggravates it enormously."[27]

A report from the time of the third Caliph, Umar, seems relevant to the contemporary situation in which the eating of meat by some is tied to the deprivation of sustenance to others:

> Yahya related to me from Malik from Yahya ibn Said that Umar ibn al-Khattab saw Jabir ibn Abdullah carrying some meat. He said, "What is this?" He said, "*Amir al-muminin*. We desired meat and I bought some meat for a dirham." Umar said, "Does any one of you want to fill his belly apart from his neighbor or nephew? How can you overlook this *ayat*? You squandered your good things in this world and sought comfort in them."[28]

It is also worth noting that Middle Eastern countries now import much of their meat from places such as New Zealand, and that factory farming (in which animal remains are typically fed to other animals) presents considerable difficulties in verifying whether meat is *halal*.[29] Even in the 1980s Masri noted that "the general members of the Muslim public who buy their meat from shops in their countries never get a chance to see for themselves the un-Islamic and inhumane scenes within some of their slaughterhouses. If they knew what was happening there, they would either stop eating meat or, at least, start lobbying the powers that be to have the Islamic rules implemented."[30] It must be said that worldwide the situation of factory farming today has made such knowledge and awareness more difficult for Muslims and not less so.

A growing body of contemporary literature asserts that Islam contains strong directives about environmental stewardship, centering on the notion that Allah has appointed humans as vicegerents (*khulafa'*) over creation.[31] This discussion has so far failed, however, to emphasize connections between issues of environmental degradation and meat eating. Among the many other harmful effects of industrial-scale meat production are the clearing of tropical forests for grazing land, the pollution of water supplies by factory farms, and the feeding of hormones and antibiotics to livestock, which then adversely affect human consumers.

While the fact remains that a few small human societies (mainly pastoral groups in arid climates) are still ecologically constrained to diets based on animal products,[32] for the vast majority of Muslims the eating of meat is not only unnecessary but is also directly responsible for causing grave ecological and social harm, as well as being less healthful than a balanced vegetarian regime. Given these considerations, the absence of a serious contemporary Islamic discourse on the benefits of vegetarianism is nothing less than astonishing.

To Kill or Not to Kill?

One issue that many Muslims connect with meat eating is the sacrifice performed once a year on the occasion of 'Eid al-Adha, commemorating Abraham's willingness to sacrifice his son. On this day, Muslims traditionally slaughter an animal they can afford, from a sheep to a camel, and distribute the meat to the poor as an act of charity. However, during the 1990s, King Hassan of Morocco on two occasions banned this slaughter for economic reasons, citing the well-being of his Muslim subjects. In 2001, responding to an outbreak of foot-and-mouth disease in Europe, the Imam of the Paris mosque issued a fatwa to the effect that animal sacrifice on 'Eid al-Adha is not required and that it might be compensated by giving a third of the price of a sheep in cash to the poor.[33]

Ritual slaughter in Islam is merely customary, and not prescribed by law.[34] The Eid celebrations can be seen as a holdover from pre-Islamic blood sacrifice, which the Qur'an specifically qualifies: "It is not their meat, nor their blood, that reaches Allah; it is your piety that reaches Him." (37:22) In a recent essay, Muslim publisher Shahid 'Ali Muttaqi argues against the necessity of performing the traditional sacrifice on the occasion of Eid al-Adha. Contrasting Islam with Judaism and Christianity, he points out that "the notion of 'vicarious atonement for sin' is nowhere to be found in the Qur'an. Neither is the idea of gaining favor by offering the life of another to God. All that is demanded as a sacrifice is one's personal willingness to submit one's ego and individual will to Allah."[35] Muttaqi concludes that the existence of animal sacrifice in Islamic custom derives from the norms and conditions of pre-Islamic Arab society, and not from Islam itself:

> Animals are mentioned in the Qur'an in relation to sacrifice only because in that time, place, and circumstance, animals were the means of survival. In those desert lands, humans were intricately tied up in the natural cycle, and as a part of that, they killed and were killed like every other species of that area. Islam offered conditions to regulate life in that time and place, ensuring the best possible treatment for all under those circumstances, while at the same time broadening people's understanding of life to include a spiritual dimension and a respect for all life as a part of a unified whole. But let us not assume for a minute that we are forever stuck in those circumstances, or that the act of eating meat, or killing an animal is what makes one a Muslim.[36]

Even if one is to accord a cultural (as opposed to strictly religious) value to practices such as the Eid al-Adha sacrifice, it may be noted that a number of religious traditions, including Judaism, Vedism (the predecessor to Hinduism), and others, historically evolved metaphorical substitutions for blood sacrifice; it is therefore not inconceivable that such a development could occur in the future within Islam. Indeed, one Muslim scholar, Sheikh Farid Wagdi, has made just such a suggestion, calling for the substitution of alms-giving for sacrificial meat.[37]

The Qur'an and *sunna* have been shown to enjoin Muslims to treat animals with compassion. This is clearly reflected in the established procedure for *halal* slaughter. It should be obvious, however, that not slaughtering the animal at all would be even more compassionate. As strong as the theme of compassion in Islam is demonstrated to be, the line allowing for "humane" killing seems arbitrarily drawn. As Oliver Goldsmith remarked in regard to certain members of eighteenth-century English society, "They pity, and they eat the objects of their compassion."[38] Peter Singer suggests that "practically and psychologically it is impossible to be consistent in one's concern for nonhuman animals while continuing to dine on them."[39] Since, unlike in early times, most Muslims today are not constrained to eat meat for their survival, 'Ali Muttaqi enjoins Muslims to "cease to do so merely for the satisfaction of ravenous cravings which are produced by nothing more than our *nafs* (lower self)."[40]

It is often remarked, especially by hunters, that since the natural predators of so many animals have been suffering dramatically declining numbers, prey species are in many places proliferating beyond control, and should therefore be hunted by humans. One recent case in India concerned the nilgai, or "blue cow." With the disappearance of tigers, the nilgai population has exploded, but Hindus will not allow the species to be hunted because of its name. In desperation, some Indian Muslims have resorted to the cry, "For God's sake, let's not call it a blue cow. Let's call it a blue bull, and kill it!"[41]

What this sort of argument overlooks, of course, is that population imbalances such as that of the nilgai have been brought on by gross human alterations of habitats, such as those of predators like the tiger. The reasoning, then, is one of punishing the victims. Is that, we may ask, the approach of a conscientious *khalifa*?

A more sympathetic example can be found in a story about the eighth-century female Muslim mystic Rabi'a of Basra. According to the medieval hagiography of Farid al-Din 'Attar:

> Rabi'a had gone up on a mountain. Wild goats and gazelles gathered around, gazing upon her. Suddenly, Hasan Basri [another well-known early Muslim mystic] appeared. All the animals shied away. When Hasan saw that, he was perplexed and said, "Rabi'a, why do they shy away from me when they were so intimate with you?"
> Rabi'a said, "What did you eat today?"
> "Soup."
> "You ate their lard. How would they not shy away from you?"[42]

'Abd al-Karim al-Qushayri (d. 465/1074) tells a similar story about Ibrahim ibn Adham, who, it is said, liked to go hunting. One day, as he was pursuing an antelope, he heard a voice asking him, "O Ibrahim, is it for this that We have created you?" Immediately he got down from his horse, gave his fine clothes to a shepherd in exchange for a wool tunic, and assumed the life of a wandering dervish.[43]

FOOD FOR THOUGHT

Islam has a long tradition of interpreting (*ijtihad*) divine revelation to meet the needs and conditions of the present age. Factory farms did not exist in seventh-century Arabia, nor were large percentages of arable land being used for fodder crops in preference to food for humans while twenty percent of the world's population went chronically malnourished. Traditional Arab pastoralists needed animal products in order to survive, yet their practices did not result in the destruction of entire ecosystems. For the most part, the early community lacked the vast dietary alternatives available to most Muslims today, and, unlike us, they were unaware of the connections between meat eating and heart disease, colon cancer, obesity, and other maladies.

Times have changed. But, for a contemporary Islamic legal scholar to make a case for vegetarianism, the Qur'an-based objections raised by Izzi Dien at the beginning of this essay would have to be addressed. I am not a qualified legal scholar, so the following brief attempt to suggest how this task might be approached is offered only for purposes of initiating discussion. The verse cited above—"The beast of cattle is made lawful unto you [for food]" (5:1)—might be compared with other verses (16:5, 66; 40:79), where the wording is equally general. The theme common to these verses is that of deriving sustenance; in 16:66, milk is explicitly mentioned whereas 40:79 begins, "It is Allah who provided for you all manner of livestock, that you may ride on some of them and from some of them you may derive your food."

The gloss "flesh of" in verse 5:1 is merely inserted into English translations, being absent in the original Arabic. Moreover, the prohibition of hunting while on pilgrimage would seem to indicate that it is an impure act, which might best be refrained from altogether. Likewise, in interpreting the permission in 6:145, which extends even to forbidden meat "if one is driven by necessity," one might choose to generalize the condition of dire need to meat eating in general.

A vegetarian interpretation of these and other Qur'anic verses will not be without problems. In several verses, the eating of meat is mentioned as one of the pleasures of paradise (52:22, 56:21).[44] Nevertheless, it would appear that, in arguments such as Izzi Dien's, we have the perspective of meat eating Muslims seeking the kind of interpretation that will support a carnivorous status quo. Muslims committed to ethical vegetarianism, therefore, might interpret the Qur'an to the opposite end with equal success.

Given all these considerations it is not inconceivable that at some point in the future, Muslim legal scholars will find a basis in the Qur'an and *sunna* for encouraging vegetarianism. Indeed, in cases where abstention from meat does not endanger the welfare of Muslims, perhaps some will even issue *fatwas* ("legal opinions") classifying meat eating as *makruh* (the category of discouraged acts whose commission brings no punishment but abstention from which brings reward). This is an admittedly extreme speculation, yet, in light of the extreme injustices connected with meat eating in the contemporary world, both toward animals and toward human beings, it is perhaps not an entirely outlandish one. That is for the jurists to discuss. In any event, at the very least, one can hope to hear more in the way of Islamic critique of factory farming as being incompatible with the clearly established Islamic principles of compassion toward animals.[45]

It cannot be denied that, since the inception of Islamic civilization fourteen centuries ago, a dietary norm of meat eating has gone largely unquestioned by Muslims, who have interpreted the traditional sources in ways that have affirmed a carnivorous diet. But from the standpoints of human health, social justice, ecological stewardship, and compassion toward nonhuman creation, it can be seen that a vegetarian lifestyle may in fact be preferable for Muslims. Such a lifestyle is not incompatible with the teachings of the Islamic tradition, which can actually be read in ways that fully support vegetarianism.

NOTES

1. Mawil Izzi Dien, *The Environmental Dimensions of Islam* (Cambridge, England: Lutterworth, 2000), p. 146.

2. Annemarie Schimmel, *Mystical Dimensions of Islam* (Chapel Hill: University of North Carolina Press, 1975), pp. 348, 358.

3. Emile Dermenghem, *La culte des saints dans l'Islam Maghrebin* (Paris: Gallimard, 1954), pp. 97–101.

4. Margaret Smith, *The Way of the Mystics* (New York: Oxford University Press, 1978), pp. 154–62.

5. www.IslamicConcern.com.

6. Ibrahim Tütüncüoglu, "The Past and Current Situation of Vegetarianism in Turkey," *European Vegetarian Union News* 4 (1998) and 1 (1999), http://www.ivu.org/evu/english/news/index.html.

7. Baquer Namazi, "Environmental NGOs," *Situational Analysis of NGOs in Iran* (Tehran: United Nations Development Programme, 2000), appendix.

8. Qur'anic citations are given from Muhammad Asad, *The Message of the Qur'an* (Gibraltar: Dar al-Andalus, 1980).

9. 'Izz ad-Din b. 'Abd as-Salam, *Qawa'id al-Ahkam fi Masalih al-Anam* (Damascus: Dar al-Tabba, 1992); cited in Izzi Dien, *The Environmental Dimensions of Islam*, p. 146.

10. Ibn Hazm, *Al-Fisal fi l-Milal wa l-Ahwa' wa n-Nihal*, 5 vols. (Cairo: Yutlab min Muhammad Ali Subayh, 1964), p. 69.

11. *Sahih Muslim*, 2/11, "Slaying," 10:739.

12. Cited in B. A. Masri, *Islamic Concern for Animals* (Petersfield, UK: Athene Trust, 1987), p. 4.

13. James L. Wescoat Jr., "The 'Right of Thirst' for Animals in Islamic Law: A Comparative Approach," *Environment and Planning D: Society and Space* 13, no. 6 (1995), pp. 637–54.

14. G. H. Bousquet, "Des animaux et de leur traitment selon le Judaïsme, le

Christianisme et l'Islam," *Studia Islamica* 9, no. 1 (1958): 41. These *hadiths* are retold in a recent book for Muslim children M. S. Kayani, *Love All Creatures* (Leicester, UK: The Islamic Foundation, 1997 [1981]).

15. Lenn Evan Goodman, trans., *The Case of the Animals versus Man before the King of the Jinn*, (Boston: Twayne, 1978), pp. 5–6.

16. Masri, *Islamic Concern for Animals*, p. vii; Masri, *Animals in Islam* (Petersfield, UK: Athene Trust, 1989), p. vii. The first, shorter work forms chapter one of the second.

17. Masri, *Islamic Concern for Animals*, p. 4.

18. B. A. Masri, "Animal Experimentation: The Muslim Viewpoint," in *Animal Sacrifices: Religious Perspectives on the Use of Animals in Science*, ed. Tom Regan (Philadelphia: Temple University Press, 1986), pp. 171–97.

19. Masri, *Islamic Concern for Animals*, p. 17.

20. Masri, *Animals in Islam*, p. 36.

21. Ibid., p. 36.

22. Ibid., p. 28.

23. M. R. Bawa Muhaiyadeen, *Come to the Secret Garden: Sufi Tales of Wisdom* (Philadelphia: Fellowship Press, 1985), p. 28.

24. Khaliq Ahmad Nizami, *The Life and Times of Shaikh Nasir-u'd-din Chiragh-i-Delh* (Delhi: Idarah-i Adabiyyat, 1991), p. 57, citing Sayyid Muhammad Gisu Daraz, *Jawami' al-Kalim*, p. 162. I am grateful to Emil Ansarov for alerting me to this and the following two references.

25. Muhyi ad-Din ibn 'Arabi, *Risalat al-Anwar*, in *Journey to the Lord of Power*, ed. Rabia Terri Harris (Rochester, VT: Inner Traditions International, 1989 [1981]), p. 31.

26. 'Abd al-Karim ibn Ibrahim al-Jili, *Isfar 'An Risalat al-Anwar*, in Harris, *Journey to the Lord of Power*, p. 81.

27. Peter Singer, *Animal Liberation: A New Ethics for Our Treatment of Animals* (New York: New York Review of Books, 1975), p. 180.

28. Muwatta 49.36. The Qur'anic verse is 46:20.

29. *Halal* refers to food that is ritually pure, thus acceptable for consumption, similar to the notion of kosher in Judaism.

30. Masri, *Animals in Islam*, p. 57.

31. Izzi Dien, see also Akhtaruddin Ahmad, *Islam and the Environmental Crisis* (London: Ta-ha Publishers, 1997); Abou Bakr Ahmed Ba Kader et al., eds., *Islamic Principles for the Conservation of the Natural Environment* (Gland, Switzerland: International Union for the Conservation of the Natural Environment, 1983); S. Hossein Nasr, *Man and Nature: The Spiritual Crisis of Modern Man* (Chicago: Kazi, 2000 [1967]); Iqtidar H. Zaidi, "On the Ethics of Man's Interaction with the Environment: An Islamic Approach" *Environmental Ethics* 3, no. 1 (1981): 35–47; the essays in Harfiya Abdel Haleem, ed., *Islam and the Environment* (London: Ta-ha Publishers, 1998); Fazlun Khalid and Joanne O'Brien, eds., *Islam and Ecology* (New York: Cassell, 1992); and my "Is There an Islamic Environmentalism?" *Environmental Ethics* 22, no. 1 (2000): 63–72.

32. S. Hossein Nasr, plenary address, Islam and Ecology conference, Harvard University, May 8, 1998.

33. "French Shun Sacrifice," *Islamic Voice* 15, no. 4 (April 2001/Muharram 1422): 172.

34. Philip J. Stewart, "Islamic Law as a Factor in Grazing Management: The Pilgrimage Sacrifice," in *Proceedings of the First International Rangeland Congress* (Denver: Society for Range Management, 1978), pp. 119–20.

35. Shahid 'Ali Muttaqi, "The Sacrifice of 'Eid al-Adha': An Islamic Perspective Against Animal Sacrifice" [online], www.islamicconcern.org/sacrifice01.asp [Nov. 19, 2003].

36. Muttaqi, "The Sacrifice of 'Eid al-Adha," p. 5.

37. Masri, *Animals in Islam*, p. 117.

38. Oliver Goldsmith, "The Citizen of the World," in *Collected Works*, ed. A. Friedman, 5 vols. (Oxford: Clarendon Press, 1966), vol. 2, p. 60.

39. Singer, *Animal Liberation*, p. 172.

40. Muttaqi, "The Sacrifice of 'Eid al-Adha," p. 6.

41. Related by Muhammad Aslam Parvaiz at the Islam and Ecology conference, Harvard University, May 8, 1998.

42. Farid ad-Din 'Attar, *Tazkirat al-Awliya*, trans. Paul Losensky and Michael Sells, in Michael Sells, *Early Islamic Mysticism* (Mahwah, NJ: Paulist Press, 1996), p. 160.

43. Qushayri, cited in Dermenghem, *La culte des saints dans l'Islam Maghrebin*, p. 100.

44. I am grateful to an anonymous reviewer for *Studies in Contemporary Islam* for pointing out these verses to me. Of course, likening meat to other heavenly pleasures forbidden on earth could be compatible with some, though not all, arguments for vegetarianism.

45. My anonymous reviewer, citing the Malikite jurist Shatibi's concept of *maslaha* (that is, a ruling for the common good that is compatible with the *shari'a*, even though it is not found in it explicitly), suggests the possibility of an approach whereby "compassion, as one of the overarching principles of Islamic religion, takes precedence over specific legal prescriptions."

18 | EASTERN RELIGIONS AND THE EATING OF MEAT

James Gaffney

n a book called *Mysticism and Morality*, Arthur Danto reviewed a number of moral teachings and practices characteristic of Eastern religions and often admired in the West.[1] He then outlined the reasons and motives typically cited by adherents of these religions as supporting those moral teachings and practices. Finally, he pointed out that Western admirers of the morality very seldom subscribed to the beliefs—mythological, mystical, metaphysical—on which that morality was said to be founded. Thus, readers were left to ponder over just what it meant to embrace, say, Buddhist ethics, while rejecting those Buddhist beliefs on which Buddhists supposed their ethics to depend.

A similar problem arises for anyone who attempts to examine critically, and not simply factually, the normative or customary dietary practices belonging to religions. Not infrequently one finds oneself admiring—or deploring—religious dietary practices for reasons one considers important, but which seem to have had no importance, or only incidental importance, for practitioners of the religion. Thus health experts in the Middle East have suggested that climatic and other environmental conditions in that region, in the absence of refrigeration, make pork a particularly risky food, and have accordingly praised the wisdom of Jewish and Muslim dietary rules for excluding that food. Nevertheless, it can scarcely be supposed that the proscription of pork in these religions derived from enlightened views about dietetics and parasitology. Believers refrained from this food because it was part of their belief that God forbade them to consume it.

Many other foods were likewise considered to be divinely prohibited, and it would be very difficult to find any modern nutritional category that meaningfully included them all.[2] Despite many ingenious conjectures, the origin of distinctions between religiously clean and unclean foods remains mysterious.

Thus, in examining religious traditions of abstinence from meat, one needs to be historically wary. There are many impressive reasons for recommending abstinence from meat, and many thoughtful persons find some or all of them persuasive. It is natural that vegetarians should feel a certain spiritual or ideological affinity with other vegetarians, especially if their abstinence from meat is idealistically or morally motivated. But it should not be casually assumed that all vegetarians share the same ideals and motives, nor, in the case of religious vegetarians, that the motives are persuasive or even fully intelligible outside the religious system of which they are part.

A similar consideration may be made regarding differences of belief not only between adherents of a religion and those who are outsiders, but also between views held within a religious community at different times in its history. It is not rare for a religious practice or regulation to persist even though the reasons once assigned to it have been forgotten or forsaken while new and different reasons have replaced or supplemented them. Thus a historical study of official Roman Catholicism's condemnation of artificial birth control found that, although the prohibition itself persisted over the course of many centuries, the reasons alleged to support it underwent repeated changes. Similarly, modern spokespersons for religions with vegetarian traditions often praise them for reasons that, however persuasive, were unmentioned in the religion's earlier literature, and may have been derived from sources outside the religion. Although there is nothing wrong with this, it can generate anachronisms that misrepresent the history of a religion.

Among living religions, restrictions on the eating of meat have been most prominent among those that originated on the Indian subcontinent, notably in the religions now distinguished as Hinduism, Buddhism, and Jainism. Buddhism especially carried religious vegetarianism with it in its eastward expansion through the Far East. Large Hindu communities in Africa and the Caribbean likewise contributed to its geographic spread. Within India, Islam was at times drawn toward a vegetarianism that, apart from Sufi circles, claimed no Koranic sanction and was not traditional in the Middle East. In very recent times, religious movements of Indian origin have thrived in many parts of Europe and the Americas, gaining Western adherents to their vegetarian practices.

EARLY INDIAN RELIGION

In India as elsewhere, the earliest known human inhabitants were hunters and gatherers, succeeded by farmers who both cultivated crops and domesticated animals, some of them useful only as food.[3] The Aryan hordes who penetrated and eventually dominated the subcontinent were pastoral semi-nomads, who practiced little agriculture and whose religion featured animal sacrifices.[4] It has been remarked that in the *Vedas* cows are occasionally referred to—for whatever reason—as "not to be killed."[5] This may fore-shadow cow protection, so conspicuous in modern Hinduism, which developed gradually from unknown origins, and seems to have taken firm hold before the Christian era. The *Arthashastra* refers to herds of ailing, aged, and sterile cows.[6] A passage in the same work, suggesting a death penalty for cattle slayers, may envisage only cattle in the royal herds.[7] After the cow, the snake was probably the most revered animal in ancient India, but sacredness extended to other animals and to certain plants, mountains, and rivers.[8] Sacredness did not entail immunity from destruction. In the *Rig Veda* the most celebrated animal is the horse, but the most elaborate ritual is the horse sacrifice.[9] There is no general disapproval of slaughter, for food or for ritual, in early Hinduism. And the central, all-important feature of religion is sacrifice.

Later Vedic Hinduism

It was the later Vedic period, marked by many cultural changes, which saw an unprecedented esteem for nonviolence, which had the effect of inhibiting or excluding the use of animals for food. This effect was rein-forced by other developments. One was the monism of the Upanishads, which devalued sharp distinctions among beings, including those sepa-rating humans from other animals.[10] The doctrine of reincarnation, too, saw all living creatures as participating in a cycle of rebirth that included human beings.[11] It was in striving to escape from this dreaded cycle that increased emphasis was placed upon asceticism, and systematic techniques of self-control, known as *yoga*, were developed and widely practiced. Typi-cally, yoga has ethical prerequisites, including abstention from injury, called *ahimsa*, sometimes translated as nonviolence.[12] This development conflicted not only with ritual traditions and dietary habits, but also with the basic division of Hindu society to include a warrior, *Kshatriya*, class, whose moral duty precisely required violent behavior. The famous Hindu narrative, the Bhagavad Gita, is built on the moral conflict between spon-taneous compassionate pacifism and the duties of that social class.[13]

All these factors contributed in different ways to religious inhibitions about killing animals. However, reluctance to kill animals did not necessarily entail an equal reluctance to eat them—so long as they were killed by others less spiritually elevated.[14] This distinction was facilitated by the system of social divisions, wherein *brahmans* might keep their holiness unsullied by animal slaughter, while lowly *shudras* were obliged to assume such defiling tasks. Thus, ascetical nonviolence was not immediately or comprehensively linked to vegetarianism, although it undoubtedly encouraged it. Modern Western vegetarians who are motivated primarily by compassion for animals or by environmental concerns need to be aware that in Indian thought the animal "victim" may be of little importance, while primary concern is the spiritual damage violence does to human beings who indulge in it. This way of thinking has little to do with animal protectionism, and is more comparable to humanitarian criticism of cruelty to animals as making its perpetrators callous and volatile. Such, for example, was Kant's moral objection to cruel treatment of animals, widely shared by Enlightenment thinkers.[15] And it may be recalled that objections to cruelty to animals might lead, not to vegetarianism, but to methods of slaughter that are not regarded as cruel, as, for example, in Kosher practice.[16] Nevertheless, as already suggested, religious practices tend to expand and otherwise alter their rationales over the course of time, and motives of ascetical self-improvement came to be associated with and sometimes overshadowed by motives of altruistic compassion.

Early Buddhism

Major developments in Indian religious history during the sixth century BCE were destined to have profound and lasting effects on the treatment of animals and consequently on the increasing prevalence of vegetarianism. The main sources of these influences were Buddhism and Jainism, both of whose founders rejected sacrifice as futile, thereby abandoning the very center of traditional brahmanic Hinduism. They abandoned the caste system, and with it the notion that certain social classes were obligated to follow violent professions. Buddhism also rejected intense asceticism, thereby distancing itself both from its predecessors and from Jainism. Whether or not the Buddha intended to create a distinct religion, Buddhism came generally to be recognized as one during its first two centuries.

The original essence of Buddhist doctrine appears very early in legendary accounts of the Buddha's conversion and of the first sermon he preached to those who would be his original followers, the "sermon of the Turning of the Wheel of the Law." The following is an early summary of the sermon.

There are two ends not to be served by a wanderer. What are those two? The pursuit of desires and of the pleasure which springs from desires, which is base, common, leading to rebirth, ignoble and unprofitable. The Middle Way of the Tathagata avoids both these ends; it is enlightened, it brings clear vision, it makes for wisdom, and leads to peace, insight, full wisdom, and Nirvana. . . . And this is the Noble Truth of Sorrow. Birth is sorrow, age is sorrow, disease is sorrow, death is sorrow, contact with the unpleasant is sorrow, separation from the pleasant is sorrow, every wish unfulfilled is sorrow. . . . And this is the Noble Truth of the Arising of Sorrow. (It arises from) thirst, which leads to rebirth, which brings delight and passion, and seeks pleasure now here, now there—the thirst for sensual pleasure, the thirst for continued life, the thirst for power. And this is the Noble Truth of the Stopping of Sorrow. It is the complete stopping of that thirst, so that no passion remains. . . . And this is the Noble Truth of the Way which Leads to the Stopping of Sorrow. It is the Noble Eightfold Path—Right Views, Right Resolve, Right Speech, Right Conduct, Right Livelihood, Right Effort, Right Recollection, and Right Meditation.[17]

While interpretation of a number of details remains controversial, the basic message is clear. Sorrow is inherent in ordinary life. It results from individual cravings for satisfaction. It can be stopped only by stopping the craving. And this can be done only by following a course midway between self-indulgence and extreme asceticism and leading a morally well-ordered life. The main aspects of such a life are eight, of which the fourth is called "Right Conduct." It is in the traditional interpretation of right conduct that Buddhism embraces values most pertinent to our topic. "Right conduct" came to be summarized as "Five Precepts," of which the first is "to abstain from taking life." A casuistically refined interpretation of this prohibition is given by Buddhaghosa:

"Taking life" means to murder anything that lives. It refers to the striking and killing of living beings. "Anything that lives"—ordinary people speak here of a "living being," but more philosophically we speak of "anything that has the life-force." "Taking life" is then the will to kill anything that one perceives as having life, to act so as to terminate the life-force in it, in so far as the will finds expression in bodily action or in speech. With regard to animals, it is worse to kill large ones than small, because a more extensive effort is involved. Even where the effort is the same, the difference in substance must be considered. In the case of humans, the killing is the more blameworthy the more virtuous they are. Apart from that, the extent of the offense is proportionate to the intensity of the wish to kill. Five factors are involved: a living being, the perception of a living being, a thought of murder, the action of carrying it out, and death as a result of it. And six are the ways in which the offense may be carried out: with one's own hand, by instigation, by missiles, by slow poisoning, by sorcery, by psychic power.[18]

An interpretative passage of this kind, typical of the development of law, is clearly concerned to remove ambiguities and plug "loopholes" that have revealed themselves in practice. It addresses both internal moral disposition and external behavior, direct and indirect, mediate and immediate. It condemns not only the act but also the intention. But it seems also to attach moral weight to the value of the victim, for not only is the animal's size relevant to the intensity of violence applied to it, there is also an intrinsic "difference in substance." Buddhism's rejection of the caste system obviates any need of reconciling the doctrine with recognized class duties. Evidently, the doctrine is one that would strongly favor vegetarianism. And yet it must be recognized that it is not absolutely incompatible with meat eating. For meat could be provided by others, not sharing the same beliefs, without any "instigation," except insofar as any supply is instigated by demand.

But before considering this more explicitly, it is worth noticing that whereas right conduct is presented as an essential component of Buddhist morality, morality is not here presented as an end in itself, but as a means to the "Stopping of Sorrow" by eliminating passionate craving. In Kantian terms, right conduct is not a categorical imperative but a hypothetical imperative. For one who remains unpersuaded of the first three noble truths there is, strictly speaking, no explicitly Buddhist case for right conduct.

In considering how the Buddhist doctrine of nonviolence was translated from theory into practice, it is well to recall that both warfare and capital punishment continued in Buddhist society, though their intensity was modified by the doctrine.[19] On the other hand, neither hunting nor butchery was considered a legitimate occupation for a Buddhist. When the emperor Ashoka became a follower of Buddhism in the third century BCE, he enjoined mildness on his governors in dealing with their people. He completely forbade animal sacrifice and eliminated it at least from his capital. He restricted animal slaughter, forbidding completely the slaughter of certain species. He replaced royal hunting expeditions with pilgrimages to Buddhist holy places. And he publicly proclaimed his satisfaction that in his palace the consumption of meat had been reduced to negligible proportions.[20] Inscriptions promulgating Ashoka's decrees, his so-called rock edicts, provide an ever-expanding list of animal species that are protected either comprehensively or at certain seasons. There are also restrictions on habitat destruction, castration, and branding, and provisions of medical care for animals as well as humans. It is clear that Ashoka's example and authority played an important part in advancing vegetarianism in India.

Jainism

At around the same time as Buddhism, a rival religion arose in India, whose insistence on *ahimsa* or nonviolence was far more extreme. Unlike

Buddhism, Jainism underwent relatively few historical changes. Jainism did not spread beyond the land of its birth, but it survived in India to a degree that Buddhism did not. Jainism's founder, known by his title as Mahavira, vigorously embraced the asceticism that Gautama Buddha rejected. Despite many religious trappings, often borrowed from Hinduism, Jainism remained doctrinally atheistic, in contrast to the theistic developments that occurred in later Buddhism. And although there are many Jain laity, celibate monasticism is seen as virtually essential for salvation from the cycle of rebirth.

Jain monastic life, lived in great austerity, is governed by five vows. The first of these is to abjure killing, and it is interpreted very strictly, to exclude any violence, even unintentional, to living things.[21] Violence and killing are regarded as the worst source of destructive *karma*, and therefore as the greatest obstacle to salvation. Meat eating is absolutely forbidden. Even agriculture is excluded as an occupation because farming endangers creatures in the soil. Jain monks strain their drinking water and breathe through veils to minimize the destruction of tiny organisms, and carry dusters to brush their path free of creatures that might be trampled. Part of the reason why Jainism did not spread far geographically has been Jain reluctance to travel because travel increases the risk of injuring living creatures.

Although Jain writings about nonviolence are characteristically unsentimental, and focused rather on the mechanical workings of *karma* than on compassion for potential sufferers, a more sympathetic outlook sometimes appears, as in the following:

> A wise man should be neither glad nor angry, for he should know and consider the happiness of all things. . . . For nothing is inaccessible to death, and all beings are fond of themselves; they love pleasure and hate pain; they shun destruction and cling to life. They long to live. To all things life is dear.[22]

Passages of this kind evoke an attitude of animal protectionism and reverence for life, and might even be employed in a modern utilitarian argument for animal rights and vegetarianism. It is important to recognize that such passages are not typical, and such empathetic implications are seldom drawn by Jains. At the same time they remind us that, approached from a somewhat different angle, the Jain doctrine of *ahimsa* could nourish, as it did, the kind of deeply compassionate nonviolence exemplified in modern times by Gandhi.

The Jain view implies that the doer of violence is the real victim of it:

> Injurious activities inspired by self-interest lead to evil and darkness. This is what is called bondage, delusion, death, and hell. To do harm to others

is to do harm to oneself. . . . We corrupt ourselves as soon as we intend to corrupt others. We kill ourselves as soon as we intend to kill others.[23]

Although these words are based on belief in the automatic working of *karma*, they could obviously be adopted in another sense by those who believe that doers of violence are spiritually or morally degraded by their own behavior.

Jains attribute a degree of animation and sensation to virtually every kind of material object. The higher animals, including most vertebrates, share with human beings the power of thinking. Accordingly, there are Jain fables in which animals are not only the objects of *ahimsa* but practitioners of it, as in the story of an elephant whose efforts to avoid stepping on a rabbit led ultimately to the elephant's death—followed by rebirth as a Jain monk.[24]

The more formalistic character of Jain nonviolence toward animals may be illustrated by a modern example. Jain laity have mostly commercial occupations. A Jain pharmaceutical corporation acknowledged its use of domestic rabbits for experimentation under conditions where painlessness was scrupulously maintained. The management also pointed out that, consistently with Jain values, the rabbits were subsequently freed. The fact that these fluffy domestic bunnies were released in open country, where their inefficiency as foragers and their vulnerability to predators virtually guaranteed a swift and bloody fate did not seem to arise as an objection. To be sure, the Jains did not deal violently with the rabbits. Here, once again, we seem to have an ethic of nonviolence, including strict vegetarianism, in which practical concern for the victim appears secondary or even incidental.

Later Buddhism

Buddhism, in contrast to Jainism, underwent many changes, both during its time in India, which ended in the Muslim era, and in the many other parts of the world to which it spread. Fundamental to most of these changes was the emergence of the Great Vehicle, or *Mahayana*, which introduced new doctrines and an openness to further innovations. Whereas original Buddhism was hardly religious in any conventional sense, later developments brought in ritual practices and supernatural beliefs. One major development was the reconception of a *Boddhisattva*, originally one destined to be a Buddha, as a person who postponed his own salvation out of compassionate desire to help others.[25]

As expressed by *Boddhisattvas*, love, as a Buddhist virtue, became intensely altruistic, and made compassion a hallmark of Buddhism. This quality introduced a new warmth that transformed simple nonviolence into a kind of cosmic benevolence that finds vivid expression in the scriptures: "May every living being, weak or strong, large or small, seen or unseen, near or far, born or yet unborn—may every living thing be full of joy. . . . Just as a mother, as long as she lives, cares for her only child, so should a man feel all-embracing love to all living beings. . . . He should feel boundless love for all the world, above, below, and across, unrestrained, without enmity."[26]

Buddhist laity were forbidden to be hunters or butchers. Vegetarianism was strongly encouraged and became widespread, although meat eating might be tolerated when the meat was served by non-Buddhists.[27] Buddhists severely criticized the continuance of animal sacrifices in some Hindu temples. A popular tale told of a goat who protested to the brahman who led him to sacrifice, explaining that the reason he was a goat was because, five hundred rebirths ago, he too had been a brahman, doing just what this brahman was doing to him. The brahman, terrified, released the goat, which was then struck by lightning, reborn as a human, and compassionately interceded to save his erstwhile executioner.[28] As in Jainism, animal tales also illustrated Buddhist altruism, such as that of a monkey who sacrificed himself as a living bridge over the river to aid his fellows' flight from hunters, and a parrot that died trying to extinguish a fire with water drops shaken from its wings.[29] Stories of this kind expressed and popularized a moral culture that found everyday expression, at every social level, in vegetarianism.

In this later Buddhism, we evidently come much closer to the kind of motivation that typically prompts modern conscientious vegetarianism. While the doctrine of *karma* remains as the fundamental requirement for nonviolence, in the spirit of the *Boddhisattva* more immediate demand arises from direct compassion for prospective victims of human violence. Modern terms like "animal protection" and even "animal rights" might be employed here without major qualifications. It may be observed that the new emphasis on self-sacrificing love has prompted many comparisons between *Mahayana* Buddhism and Christianity, and historical conjectures about possible influence on one by the other. Nevertheless, in the mainstream of Christianity, love never assumed the cosmic amplitude it took on in later Buddhism, and vegetarianism has found little religious encouragement in most of the Christian churches. When Christian churches have urged or enjoined abstinence from meat, it has been most often as a penitential practice, carrying no implication that meat eating is objectionable in itself.

CHINESE RELIGIONS

The spread of Buddhism to China brought vegetarianism with it, and Chinese Buddhists seem to have regarded vegetarianism as a measure of Buddhist observance. Thus when the Chinese Buddhist scholar Fa-shien, in the fifth century CE, traveled back to Buddhism's birthplace, he reported with approval that only low-caste persons there ate meat, while vegetarianism prevailed among respectable people.[30] He seems to connect this with his observation of the country's peacefulness and its mild government, and the fact that travelers like him could journey everywhere with perfect safety.

China's dominant religion, Confucianism, had a strongly humanistic orientation that did not encourage vegetarianism on grounds of compassion for animals. Confucius himself is depicted as an angler and archer who behaved in a "sportsmanlike" manner by employing methods that gave a "fair chance" to the fish and game.[31] His commitment to ancient traditions included the approval of animal sacrifices. Although greater sensitivity to animal suffering appears in Confucius's successor, Mencius, its narrow limits are made clear in a dialogue between Mencius and a king who spared an ox from sacrifice because "I cannot bear its frightened appearance, as if it were an innocent person going to the place of death."[32] The king therefore orders the ox to be replaced by a lamb, but on reflection is distressed by his seeming inconsistency. Mencius explains, "Your conduct was an artifice of benevolence. You saw the ox and had not seen the sheep. So is the superior man afflicted toward animals that, having seen them alive, he cannot bear to see them die. Having heard their dying cries he cannot bear to eat their flesh." Despite these words, no inference is drawn that vegetarianism might have moral value for the superior man. On the contrary, in such cases there is a simple remedy for the scruples of the superior man. "Therefore he keeps away from his cookroom." Given Mencius's subtlety as an ethicist, it is hard to suppose that he is here setting menu above morals. Rather he seems to regard the king's qualms as a kind of sentimentality typical of a sensitive aristocrat, but not such as should interfere with normal living.

Vegetarianism has been widespread among Taoists of the Far East, and is congenial to the nonviolent relationship with nature fostered by philosophical Taoism. But it is not in any sense a normative observance. The same may be said of Sufi Islam, where dietary practices are often locally distinctive and vary from place to place.

GANDHI'S MANY-SIDED VEGETARIANISM

Among modern Indian advocates of vegetarianism, perhaps the most influential worldwide was Gandhi. His charismatic leadership and political effectiveness, rooted in a program of nonviolent resistance brought the concept of *ahimsa* to the respectful attention of many who had otherwise no acquaintance with Hindu moral thought. At the same time, it should not be overlooked that Gandhi himself was initially indebted to Western advocates of vegetarianism. Indeed, Gandhi's autobiographical writings give a complex account of his vegetarianism. In Gujarat, where he grew up, meat eating was abhorred by the Jain population and by Hindus of Gandhi's caste. Gandhi was moved to reject this tradition by a naive belief expressed in a current verse: "Behold the mighty Englishman. He rules the Indian small. Because, being a meat eater, he is five cubits tall." Perhaps, thought Gandhi, meat eating must be part of India's preparation to overthrow colonial domination.[33] His first meat meal made him sick and gave him nightmares about the goat whose flesh he had consumed. He persisted but had to hide his new practice from his parents. At last he found the deception unbearable, and gave it up until he left home. On leaving for England, his mother constrained him to take a vow that included abstinence from meat. He kept the vow, solely out of painful filial loyalty. Then one day, he found both a vegetarian restaurant and Salt's book, *Plea for Vegetarianism*. The food and the book made him a zealous vegetarian.[34] His motives were hygienic, economic, and humane. His zeal brought him into vegetarian circles of London society, which often coincided with progressive circles where he found other common values. Gandhi, who had renounced vegetarianism out of hostility to English colonialism, was restored to it by English liberalism.

It is typical of Gandhi's eclecticism that his thoroughly Western vegetarian convictions should later be subsumed under the thoroughly Indian value system represented by *ahimsa*.[35] It is also typical of Gandhi that his commitment to *ahimsa* was not modeled on the scrupulous and legalistic observances of the Jains, but moderated by moral discretion. This has often been discussed in connection with the paradoxical "militancy" of Gandhi's nonviolent political struggle. But it equally affected his treatment of animals.[36] Despite his vegetarianism, he respected the message of a bird hunter in the *Mahabarata* that sometimes life must be preserved by the taking of life. He was criticized for killing a dying calf to end its misery, for driving away monkeys that were destroying peasant gardens, and for approving the destruction of stray dogs that menaced the city's poor. His vegetarianism and animal protectionism were independent though related convictions, and neither of them took the form of an absolute taboo. They were subject, as he said all religion must be subject, to reason and conscience.

Gandhi's vegetarianism may offer the best response to the issue raised at the beginning of this essay. He owed it in part to traditional religious observances linked to indemonstrable beliefs. On that basis he embraced it from extrinsic motives of family loyalty. But it became a personal value for him only as he discovered its moral and social value. He found it to be healthy in very much the same way as many modern Americans do. He was persuaded by agronomic arguments that it was a way to make more food available to more people. He valued it as a means to detach oneself from the infliction of pain on animals. In all of this there is nothing "Eastern" about Gandhi's vegetarianism. But it was confirmed and elevated by convictions about self-control and nonviolence that inhered deeply in later Hindu, Buddhist, and Jain religion that would form the whole basis of Gandhi's extraordinary moral authority. For Gandhi, many arguments led to vegetarianism, some from the West and some from the East. He judged most of them, on grounds of rational morality, to be persuasive. He rejected fanatical excess and shallow formalism. He admitted reasonable exceptions. If one finds nothing in Gandhi's thought to commend vegetarianism, one is unlikely to find it elsewhere.

NOTES

1. Arthur Danto, *Mysticism and Morality: Oriental Thought and Moral Philosophy* (New York: Columbia University Press, 1982).

2. Leviticus 11 and Deuteronomy, 14.

3. A. L. Basham, *The Wonder That Was India: A Survey of the Culture of the Indian Sub-continent before the Coming of the Muslims* (New York: Grove, 1954), p. 10.

4. Mircea Eliade, *A History of Religious Ideas, Volume I, From the Stone Age to the Eleusinian Mysteries* (Chicago: University of Chicago Press, 1978), p. 188.

5. Basham, *The Wonder That Was India*, p. 35.

6. Ibid., p. 195.

7. Ibid.

8. Ibid., p. 319.

9. *The Rig Veda: An Anthology*, trans. Wendy Doniger O'Flaherty (New York: Penguin, 1981), pp. 84–95.

10. R. C. Zaehner, *Hinduism* (Oxford: Oxford University Press, 1966), pp. 53–55.

11. Ibid., pp. 58–62.

12. Ibid., p. 71.

13. *The Bhagavad Gita*, trans. Juan Mascaro. (New York: Penguin, 1963), pp. 48–55.

14. Basham, *The Wonder That Was India*, p. 213.

15. Immanuel Kant, *Lectures on Ethics* (New York: Harper, 1963), pp. 240–41.

16. J. David Bleich, "Judaism and Animal Experimentation," in *Animal Sacrifices*, ed. Tom Regan (Philadelphia: Temple University Press, 1986), pp. 68–76.

17. Basham, *The Wonder That Was India*, p. 269.

18. *Buddhist Scriptures*, trans. Edward Conze (Baltimore: Penguin, 1959), pp. 70–71.

19. Basham, *The Wonder That Was India*, pp. 118–23.

20. Kerry S. Walters and Lisa Postmess, ed., *Religious Vegetarianism: From Hesiod to the Dalai Lama* (Albany: State University of New York Press, 2001), pp. 75–77.

21. Basham, *The Wonder That Was India*, p. 292.

22. Ibid., p. 293.

23. Christopher Chapple, "Noninjury to Animals: Jaina and Buddhist Perspectives," in Tom Regan, *Animal Sacrifices*, p. 216.

24. Ibid., pp. 217–18.

25. *Buddhist Scriptures*, pp. 30–33.

26. Basham, *The Wonder That Was India*, p. 284.

27. Ibid., p. 285.

28. Chapple, "Noninjury to Animals," pp. 221–22.

29. Basham, *The Wonder That Was India*, p. 287.

30. Ibid., pp. 65–66.

31. *The Analects of Confucius*, trans. Arthur Waley (New York: Vintage, 1938), p.128.

32. *Mencius*, trans. D. C. Lau. (Harmondsworth, UK: Penguin, 1970), pp. 54–55.

33. Mohandas K. Gandhi, *An Autobiography: The Story of My Experiments with Truth* (Boston: Beacon, 1957), p. 21.

34. Ibid., pp. 47–48.

35. Ibid., p. 349.

36. Zaehner, *Hinduism*, p. 176.

ASK YOUR BROTHER FOR FORGIVENESS
Animal Respect in Native American Traditions

19

Rod Preece

I

There is a wide variety of Native American nations, each possessing its own independent history and culture. It would accordingly be misleading to write of such diverse peoples as though they enjoyed a common belief system. Nonetheless, just as we can recognize a common European culture while still acknowledging significant differences among, say, Dutch, Swedish, and Italian modes of consciousness and behavior, so too we can recognize significant similarities among the ways of North American Natives while still acknowledging the uniqueness of, say, the Cree, the Hopi, and the Navaho. Indeed, unlike, for example, the Jaina and Brahmins of India, American Native nations are omnivorous. Yet each expresses in its own way the special relationship between the hunter and the hunted.

Today most commentators express the view that Amerindians show great respect for the animals they hunt and kill, and that this respect is predominantly lacking in Western culture. Thus, for example, James P. Sterba remarks:

> It may be that Western social and political ideals are not demanding enough because they have not adequately faced the question of who is to count in ways that other non-Western social and political ideals have done. For example, many, if not all, American Indian tribes regarded ani-

mals, plants, and assorted other natural things as persons in their own right with whom it was possible to enter into complex social intercourse requiring mutual respect.[1]

And Vine Deloria Jr. tells us that we "must carefully accord those other creatures the respect they deserve and the right to live without unnecessary harm. Wanton killings of different animals by some hunters and sportsmen are completely outside the traditional way that Native people have treated other species"[2] Nor is this an especially new commendation of the Amerindian attitude toward animals and nature in contrast with Western attitudes. It can already be found in the sixteenth-century writings of, among others, Bartolomé de las Casas, Peter Martyr, and Michel de Montaigne,[3] and further numerous examples may be found in the subsequent centuries.

It would indeed be churlish to deny the importance for North American Natives of their relationship to animals, and the historical recognition of that relationship. Nonetheless, the type of respect accorded requires a more careful analysis than it is customarily accorded. The following instructions of a Sioux elder to his son are reflective of Native attitudes in general toward hunting:

> Shoot your four-legged brother in the hind area, slowing it down but not killing it. Then, take the four-legged's head in your hands, and look into his eyes. The eyes are where all the suffering is. Look into your brother's eyes and feel his pain. Then, take your knife and cut the four-legged under his chin, here, on his neck, so that he dies quickly. And as you do, ask your brother, the four-legged, for forgiveness for what you do. Offer also a prayer of thanks to your four-legged kin for offering his body to you just now, when you need food to eat and clothing to wear. And promise the four-legged that you will put yourself back into the earth when you die, to become the nourishment of the earth, and for the sister flowers, and for the brother deer. It is appropriate that you should offer the blessing for the four-legged and, in due time, reciprocate in turn with your body in this way, as the four-legged gives life to you for your survival.[4]

Not surprisingly, most observers recognize in such passages a profound respect for the slaughtered animal. The sense of kinship with the prey is apparent, as is the perception of the sentience of the animal, as well as the duty both to kill quickly and to empathize with the quarry in its suffering. Equally, there is an acknowledgment of the debt owed by the hunter to the deer, not only for the sacrifice of his life, but for his willingness to die. In consequence, a reciprocal obligation is owed the animal by the hunter.

A more detailed analysis will, however, reveal a number of factors requiring further consideration. One notices immediately that the prey is killed less quickly than he might have been. The apprentice hunter is instructed to wound and not to kill the animal in the first instance. This teaching will not only increase the animal's pain and suffering, but the hunter must be well aware of the increased harm he is committing. Clearly, intentionally wounding rather than killing the animal must be instrumental to the interests of the hunter and not the hunted. The interest of the prey in the avoidance of suffering is subordinated to the need of the hunter to feel an identity with the prey. Indeed, it is notable that failing to kill with the utmost dispatch is precisely that behavior abominated in Western sport hunting. And if that is a justifiable condemnation, it is difficult to understand how Native behavior should not be subject to a similar reprobation. It is similarly difficult to understand how this action meets Deloria's criterion of Native behavior, which he deems to involve avoiding "unnecessary harm."

While kinship to the animal is emphasized, one is entitled to wonder whether the term "brother" misleads—though certainly no less than in its frequent employment in a similar manner in the Western tradition by, for example, St. Basil, Bishop of Caesarea, St. Francis of Assisi, Johann Wolfgang Goethe, and Samuel Taylor Coleridge, to mention but a few of the more prominent.[5] Certainly, the behavior deemed appropriate to a male child born to one's own mother would not correspond in any manner to what is deemed acceptable to a deer. The kinship, and the corresponding obligation, is a great deal more distant. Moreover, if the deer is a brother in the same sense that a flower is a sister, as the passage of instruction intimates, then we would rightly wonder whether sentience is being given adequate consideration. Of course, using the term "brother" and "sister" in this way, no less than when William Blake says of the worm, "Thou art my mother and my sister,"[6] is a legitimate, and deeply welcome, emphasis on all that animals and humans share in common. Nonetheless, we must be careful not to read a far stronger import into such usage than is intended or felt. After all, one doesn't kill, and then consume, one's sibling for supper. Evocative language may sometimes mask a starker reality than the words suggest. Perhaps, with Louis J. Halle in *The Appreciation of Birds*, we should all acknowledge, just a little less exaggeratedly, but in the same spirit: "So the swallow, if not my brother is at least a cousin, and all life is one."[7]

It is a part of the Native tradition, as expressed in the instructions to the hunter in training, to believe that the prey offers himself willingly to the hunter. One must presume that this belief arises from the earnest desire not to inflict unwelcome harm on the deer. Nonetheless, contrary to the common assumption that, in living close to nature, Natives must have a deep understanding of the realities of the natural realm, such a belief, if genuine, can only reflect a profound lack of awareness that the hunted animal will do everything in his power to avoid the fate the hunter intends for him. To imagine the hunted animal giving himself willingly to the hunter is both to fail to understand the animal's earnest desire to live and to fail to respect the authentic nature of individual and communal animal life. Killing the deer not only deprives the animal of life, but deprives his relatives of their kin. It is a mark of hubris to expect other animals to succumb willingly to human dominance.

There is, in fact, an incongruity between the belief that the targeted animal is giving himself willingly to the hunter and the belief that the hunter has something to atone for—and both those views are represented in the instructions to the novice. If the hunter is to ask the victim for forgiveness, the implication is that the hunter has done something to the animal that is a wrong in itself, something that is unacceptable to the deer, but that may be justified in light of a particular contingency—the necessity of food and apparel for the hunter, which, of course, are accorded a higher priority than the life of the deer. The hunter has committed a crime against the deer, but one that is assuaged by being done in a spirit of respect and regret. Clearly, such a cultural belief contains the logical implication that while respectful killing is preferable to disrespectful killing, it would be better if there were no killing at all, if no harm were inflicted. Yet, of course, no Native nation has ever drawn the practical implications of that conclusion—nor, of course, have any but a few Oriental belief systems, and very occasional Western creeds such as those of the Albigensians, the Bogomils, and the Seventh Day Adventists.

Among some nations, the manner of escape from the guilt of killing a fellow sentient being is through the avenue of the universal soul. While the idea of the universal soul plays an implicit role in many North American Native traditions, it is at its most pronounced among the Netsilik Inuit. When they kill a seal, they sprinkle water on the mouth to satisfy the thirst of the departing soul. We are all, the Inuit believe, as do the Ainu of Hokkaido and many aboriginal cultures, a part of a universal soul, which entails corresponding obligations and rights to each other. The belief was also current in classical Greece and continued at least until recently in popular Judaic culture.[8] To bring about the seal's death does not harm seals provided one reveres and appeases the seal spirit. The seal does not really die. Its soul departs into the universal spirit to be reborn in a new body. The Netsilik place mittens on the carcass of the seal both to please the animal's soul and in the hope and expectation that the seal's spirit will report its favorable treatment and encourage other seals to make themselves available as prey.[9] Thus the killing does not bring about death. Thereby the guilt for the taking of the life of a fellow being is avoided. Of course, this belief does not in any manner deter the Netsilik from doing all in their power to preserve their own individual lives. Nor does it persuade the prey to submit to their fate without a desperate struggle.

As a part of the contract with the animals, the Sioux elder informs his son that he must "promise the four-legged" that he will have himself buried after his own death to provide nutrition for the plants that will in turn be for the benefit of "brother deer." The son is told you should "reciprocate in turn with your body" in exchange for the life of the deer. Yet, it takes only a moment's reflection to realize there is no reciprocity at all. The deer pays with his life. The Sioux gives up nothing of value in life in exchange. This idea of "reciprocity" is at its clearest among the Desana of the Amazon, where the shaman (*payé*) meets with the Animal Master, sometimes in the form of a rare small lizard, to negotiate the sacrifice of a number of game animals for an equivalent number of humans, whose souls will then be reincarnated, not in the preferred manner for the Desana as hummingbirds, but as game animals in replenishment of the slaughtered prey. Again though, the individual animals lose their lives in their prime. The individual Natives reciprocate after their own deaths. They lose nothing from life itself. There is no reciprocity.

The references to the "four-legged" are an intimation of the relative status of different species. As Deloria informs us, "the Plains Indians saw a grand distinction between two-legged and four-legged creatures."[10] But not the Plains Indians alone. It is common to a number of North American aboriginal nations. It is a distinction that functions to elevate the status of humans—and the bear when he is standing upright, for he is the only other land creature classified among the two-legged—above that of all other animals. In this way, preferential rights for humans are ensured. This classification of animals functions in a similar way to that of Western animal taxonomy, when, for example, we acknowledge our similarities to all other species by allotting ourselves the same family grouping with the apes, but distinguish between *homo* and *simia*, as did Linnaeus, or assign the nonhuman apes to "pongid" status, as we do today. Yet, as Linnaeus acknowledged in querying whether there is "a general characteristic . . . by which to distinguish between Man and Ape," he concluded: "I assuredly know of none."[11] And Charles Darwin observed, "If man had not been his own classifier he would never have thought of founding a separate order for his own reception."[12] By classifying themselves alongside the apes, Westerners raise the status of apes, as Native Americans raise the status of the bear, but in both instances the human is raised yet higher. In both instances, it is only humans who, in the words of the Cheyenne, "possess intelligence," or, in the traditional story of "The Coming of Gluscabi" of the Abnaki, it is only man who forms himself out of the dust left over from the deity's creation.

What should be clear is that Native American thought and practice are perhaps not so ideal as they are customarily presented to us, nor so completely different from the Western tradition as so many imagine. Nonetheless, there can be little doubt that, on the basis of the Sioux elder's instructions to his son, in filling the larder the Native hunter's respect for his prey is significantly greater than that of so many Western sport hunters, where lack of consideration for the interest of the animals is often pronounced.

II

The instructions from the Sioux elder to his son are reflective of customary contemporary North American Native expressions of attitudes toward animals. Yet, precisely how consistent such statements are with traditional Native culture is difficult to discern. Much that has been presented as representative is an attempt by Western intellectuals to glorify the Native American tradition in order to criticize their own. The most frequently cited example of aboriginal respect for animals and nature is Chief Seattle of the Duwamish's famed speech of 1853. Yet, detailed research has shown that there is ample evidence to doubt whether the early English language reports of the speech bore very much resemblance to the original, and the constant changes since then in the citations of what he said display significant differences from the earliest accounts, which, anyway, were first reported some thirty-odd years after the speech was delivered.[13] Indeed, the words most frequently quoted today as those of Chief Seattle derive from an entirely fictional 1970 interpretation by a screen writer. Moreover, and this is the crux of the matter, the most purportedly impressive and frequently reported observations of Chief Seattle not only have no counterpart in the earliest printed versions of the speech, but do have direct antecedents in Western tradition instead. Thus, the claim that "the beast, the trees, the man, they all share the same breath" is a repetition of Ecclesiastes 3:19: "They all have one breath; so that a man hath no pre-eminence above a beast." Moreover, "everything in nature is linked together" is not found in early versions of Chief Seattle's statement. But it is found in the section on "Cosmologie" in Jean le Rond d'Alambert's great *Encyclopédie*, published over eighty years before the famous Duwamish speech was delivered.

In like manner, there are grounds for distrusting the almost equally well-known account of the ideas of the Oglala Sioux elder, Black Elk, whose experiences ran from the period of the "Indian wars" through to late industrialism. *Black Elk Speaks* was written by the American poet laureate John Neihardt after lengthy conversations with the Sioux "medicine-man."[14] Yet Alice Beck Kehoe in *The Ghost Dance* has argued compellingly that Neihardt gives us a far more pristine, ecologically utopian Black Elk than he really was, or indeed would have wished to present himself as.[15] Nonetheless, the reality is not entirely hidden. Thus we hear from the mouth of Black Elk that "the buffalo were the gift [to the Oglala Sioux] of the good spirit." Moreover, Black Elk receives a gift from the ancestral spirits whereby "All the nations that have roots or legs or wings shall fear you." Certainly, there is little here that is different from that for which Westerners are normally castigated—the notion that animals and nature are for human use. The ends of animals are subordinated to human ends. Man has dominion over animals.

What should be clear is that we have very good reason to be cautious in accepting the customary interpretations of American Native culture. Wherever possible we should rely on material that has been less subject to ideological mismanagement.

III

Fortunately, Cheyenne myths were collected and recorded verbatim at the Cheyenne Agency in Oklahoma in 1899 by representatives of the American Museum of Natural History. While there remains the perennial problem of expressing the self-identifying ideas of any one culture in the language of another, at least we can be sure the Cheyenne stories have not been altered in the interim to accommodate the experiences of new technology, changed societal norms, further reorientations engendered by the continuing clash of cultures, or the manipulations of advocacy scholarship. This collection of Cheyenne oral traditions provides an excellent vantage point for the understanding of the Native American orientation to the animals they kill for food.

"Great Medicine Makes a Beautiful Country"—the Cheyenne creation myth—provides an illuminating introduction to Cheyenne culture:

> In the beginning the Great Medicine created the earth, and the waters upon the earth, and the sun, moon, and stars. . . .
> In this beautiful country the Great Medicine put animals, birds, insects, and fish of all kinds. Then he created human beings to live with the other creatures. Every animal, big and small, every fish, and every insect could talk to the people and understand them. The people went naked, and fed on honey and wild fruits; they were never hungry. They wandered everywhere among the wild animals, and when night came and they were weary, they lay down on the cold grass and slept. During the days they talked with the other animals, for they were all friends. . . .
> The Great Spirit created three kinds of human beings [the white, the hairy, and the red] . . . the white people with the long beards were in a class with the wolf, for both were the trickiest and most cunning people in that beautiful world . . . the Great Medicine taught [the Cheyenne] to catch and eat fish at a time when none of the other people knew about eating meat . . . the red people clothed themselves because the Great Medicine had told them to.

Later, "the Great Medicine blessed them and gave them some medicine spirit to awaken their dormant minds. From that time on they seemed to possess intelligence . . . they clothe[d] their naked bodies with the skins of panther and deer. . . . They were no longer able to talk to the animals, but this time they controlled all other creatures, and they taught the panther, the bear, and similar beasts to catch game for them. . . . [The Great Medicine] gave them corn to plant and buffalo for meat."[16]

The similarity to Genesis is remarkable. Both are part of universal history of humankind's consciousness rather than distinctive legends of the Cheyenne and the Jews. The order of creation is substantially the same (Genesis 1, passim). Humankind is originally vegetarian (Genesis 1:29 and 2:17), animals are provided for humans as companions and helpers (2:18–19), animals and humans converse (3:1–5), humans become rational beings, recognize their nakedness, and clothe themselves in animal skins (3:5–13). They come to control other animals (1:26), and God permits them to consume flesh for the first time (9:3–4). Both in Genesis and the Cheyenne myth, the acquisition of reason produces a very different kind of human being, and not entirely one for the better. The golden age is left behind, the interests of human and other animals diverge, and the Jews and the Cheyenne become omnivores. Yet, rather than regret the loss of the time of peace and harmony, the Cheyenne pride themselves on being the first to receive the dispensation from the deity to consume flesh.

The story is continued for the Cheyenne in the legend of "How the Buffalo Hunt Began":

> The buffalo formerly ate man. The magpie and the hawk were on the side of the people, for neither ate the other or the people. These two birds flew away from a council between animals and man. They determined that a race would be held, the winners to eat the losers. . . .
>
> All around the mountain the buffalo-cow led the race, but the two birds knew they could win, and merely kept up with her until they neared the finish line. . . . Then both birds whooshed by her and won the race for man. . . .
>
> The buffalo then told their young to hide from the people, who were going out to hunt them, and also told them to take some human flesh with them for the last time. The young buffaloes did this, and stuck that meat in front of their chests, beneath the throat. Therefore, the people did not eat that part of the buffalo, saying it is part human flesh.
>
> From that day onward the Cheyenne began to hunt buffalo. Since all the friendly animals were on the people's side, they are not eaten by the people, but they do wear and use their beautiful feathers for adornments.
>
> Another version adds that when coyote, who was on the side of the buffalo, finished the race, the magpie, who even beat the hawk, said to coyote, "We will not eat you, but only use your skin."[17]

There is no single attitude toward animals. Instead they are divided among friends, foe, and food. The greatest enemy—along with the white man!—is the wolf, as was the wolf traditionally in Europe, too, even if there is an occasional hint of regret, when, for example, Immanuel Kant admires the care animals give to their young and tells us it is difficult for us to be cruel in thought to them—and then adds: "even to a wolf."[18] The coyote, too, finds herself in disfavor—for having sided with the buffalo against the Cheyenne. She will not be eaten, but her pelt alone will be taken. Certainly, this counters the claim customarily made on behalf of Native Americans that they use the entire animal, that no part is wasted. The claim is, of course, equally countered by the use of the coat alone from trapped fur-bearing animals.

Even the friendly birds are not exempt from being put to human use—and not a necessary one, but a decorative one. The Cheyenne use the birds' feathers to adorn themselves. To be sure, in the legend of the "Eagle War Feathers"[19] they claim it is the eagles themselves who have granted permission. Yet, of course, this is subterfuge. The eagles have agreed to no such thing. Indeed, they would far prefer to continue to wear the feathers themselves. It should not escape our attention that, by contrast, many decades ago the use of exotic bird feathers to adorn hats and other raiment was made illegal in many Western nations.

Intriguingly, the buffalo hunt legend tells us that a small part of the buffalo, a human part, must not be eaten. This serves as a reminder that in an ideal world there would once again be no conflict between the buffalo and humans—the same message as Isaiah 11, where the wolf will live with the lamb and the panther lie down with the kid. It serves, too, as a reminder that buffalo and humans are fellow sentient beings, that eating a fellow animal is not too far from cannibalism—hence the human flesh at the buffalo's throat—even though buffalo and human interests have now diverged fundamentally and however much flesh-eating is now considered an entirely justifiable practice. There is a counterpart to this, too, in Genesis. After the Jews have been informed in Genesis 9:3 that they may now consume meat, they are told in the next verse that "you must not eat flesh with life, that is to say, blood in it." Blood was deemed the essence of life that may not be eaten. As with the Cheyenne, the Jews understood thereby that flesh eating was not to be taken lightly, that humans and animals shared the spark of life in common, and that meat consumption was a dispensation granted by the Creator, not a natural human right derived from primordial human nature.[20]

Something that is known to be in and of itself right requires no justification. To provide a justification for meat eating, as the Cheyenne do, is to acknowledge that abstinence would be preferable in an ideal world, and can only be justified through the dispensation of the Great Medicine who changed the original requirements of a plant-based diet. Thus, since it is acknowledged as something that would not be permitted without the dispensation of the deity, the animals, so the myth indicates, should be slaughtered and consumed with respect. And if it is far from a perfect respect in practice, there is evidence that at least some Native Americans who continue to live in traditional aboriginal hunting communities treat the requirement of respect with rather greater seriousness than many in the West.

NOTES

1. James P. Sterba, *Contemporary Social and Political Philosophy* (Belmont, CA: Wadsworth, 1995), p. 101.

2. Foreword to Michael J. Caduto and Joseph Bruchac, *Keepers of the Animals* (Saskatoon, SK: Fifth House Publishers, 1991), p. xii.

3. See Rod Preece, *Animals and Nature: Cultural Myths, Cultural Realities* (Vancouver: University of British Columbia Press, 1999), pp. 12–13.

4. From Karen Warren, "The Power and Promise of Ecological Feminism," *Environmental Ethics* 12, no. 2 (1990): 146.

5. From *The Liturgy of Saint Basil*, quoted in Daniel A. Dombrowski, *The Philosophy of Vegetarianism* (Amherst: University of Massachusetts Press, 1984), p. 142; St. Francis, *The Canticle of the Creatures*, in *Francis and Clare: The Complete Works*, trans. Regis J. Armstrong and Ignatius C. Brady (New York: Paulist Press, 1982), pp. 38–39; Johann Wolfgang Goethe, "Waldhöhle" from *Faust* in *Sämmtliche Werke, nach Epochen seines Schaffens* (Munich: Carl Hanser Verlag, 1986), band 6, 1, 629; "To a Young Ass: Its Mother Being Tethered Near It," in *The Poetical Works of Samuel Taylor Coleridge*, ed. Ernest Hartley Coleridge (London: Henry Frowde, 1912), pp. 74–76.

6. Plate 16 of *For Children: The Gates of Paradise* in *Blake: Complete Writings*, ed. Geoffrey Keynes (London: Oxford University Press, 1966), p. 209.

7. Louis J. Halle, *The Appreciation of Birds* (Baltimore: Johns Hopkins University Press, 1989), p. 6.

8. See, for example, Isaac Bashevis Singer, *Law and Exile: An Autobiographical Trilogy* (New York: Farrar, Strauss and Giroux, 1997), p. 19.

9. See James A. Maxwell, ed., *America's Fascinating Indian Heritage: The First Americans: Their Customs, Art, History and How They Lived* (Pleasantville, NY: Pegasus, 1978), pp. 362, 373, 379. The coffee-table-type title of this book might give the cautious reader cause for concern about its reliability. However, its primary contributor, Stanley A. Freed, was curator of the Department of Anthropology at the American Museum of Natural History. Of the thirteen special consultants, three were museum curators, and ten were professors of anthropology at major American universities, and all were specialists in North American aboriginal traditions.

10. Caduto and Bruchac, *Keepers of the Animals*, p. xii.

11. Letter to J. G. Gmelin, February 14, 1747. Quoted in Carl Sagan and Ann Druyen, *Shadows of Forgotten Ancestors: A Search for Who We Are* (New York: Random House, 1992), p. 274.

12. Charles Darwin, *The Descent of Man, And Selection in Relation to Sex* (New York: A. L. Burt, n.d. [but reprint of second edition of 1874], p. 170.

13. See Rudolf Kaiser, "A Fifth Gospel, Almost: Chief Seattle's Speech(es): American Origins and European Reception," in *Indians and Europe: An Interdiscipli-*

nary Collection of Essays, ed. Christian F. Feest (Aachen, Germany: Ed. Herodot, Rader-Verlag, 1987), pp. 505–26; see also Preece, *Animals and Nature*, pp. 18 ff. For the authentic 1887 version, see Robert Isaak, ed., *American Political Thinking: Readings from the Origins to the 21st Century* (Fort Worth, TX: Harcourt Brace, 1994), pp. 252–54.

14. John Neihardt, *Black Elk Speaks* (New York: Pocket Books, 1975 [1959]).

15. Alice Beck Kehoe, *The Ghost Dance: Ethnohistory and Revitalization* (New York: Holt, Rinehart, Winston, 1989), pp. 51–62.

16. Richard Erdoes and Alfonso Ortiz, eds., *American Indian Myth and Legend* (London: Pimlico, 1997 [1984]), pp. 111–14. The story is based on a rendering by George A. Dorsey in 1905 that is entirely consistent with the reports of the American Museum of Natural History in 1899.

17. Margot Edmonds and Ella Clark, eds., *Voices of the Winds: Native American Legends* (New York: Facts on File, 1989), pp. 184–85. According to the compilers, this version is "only slightly altered" from that recorded in 1899 at the Cheyenne Agency in order "to retain the flavor" of the original.

18. "Duties toward Animals and Spirits," in Immanuel Kant, *Lectures on Ethics*, trans. Louis Infield (New York: Harper and Row, 1963 [1930]), p. 240.

19. See Edmonds and Clark, *Voices of the Winds*, pp. 185–86.

20. In *An Essay on Humanity to Animals* (London: T. Cadell Jun. and W. Davies, 1798 [reprint edition: Lampeter: Mellen Animal Rights Library, 2001, ed. Rod Preece]), chap. 4, Thomas Young argued from a Christian perspective that God has granted humans the right to eat animals, that without such an explicit dispensation, we would possess no such right, and that since God gave us no explicit right to "sport" hunting or "sport" fishing we possess no such right. In his *Principles of Political Philosophy* (1785), William Paley, the originator of the argument from design, follows a similar line of reasoning, although he is not quite so explicit.

Section Five

THE FEMINIST DEBATE OVER THE RELATION BETWEEN THE TREATMENT OF ANIMALS AND OF WOMEN

20 THE SEXUAL POLITICS OF MEAT

Carol J. Adams

I left the British Library and my research on some women of the 1890s whose feminist, working-class newspaper advocated meatless diets, and went through the cafeteria line in a restaurant nearby. Vegetarian food in hand, I descended to the basement. A painting of Henry VIII eating a steak and kidney pie greeted my gaze. On either side of the consuming Henry were portraits of his six wives and other women. However, they were not eating steak and kidney pie, nor anything else made of meat. Catherine of Aragon held an apple in her hands. The Countess of Mar had a turnip, Anne Boleyn—red grapes, Anne of Cleaves—a pear, Jane Seymour—blue grapes, Catherine Howard—a carrot, Catherine Parr—a cabbage.

People with power have always eaten meat. The aristocracy of Europe consumed large courses filled with every kind of meat while the laborer consumed complex carbohydrates. Dietary habits proclaim class distinctions, but they proclaim patriarchal distinctions as well. Women, second-class citizens, are more likely to eat what are considered to be second-class foods in a patriarchal culture: vegetables, fruits, and grains rather than

The material in this essay is reprinted from *The Sexual Politics of Meat: A Feminist-Vegetarian Critical Theory* and is used by permission of the publisher Continuum International and the author, who has updated some of the material, drawing from *The Pornography of Meat* (Continuum, 2003).

meat. The sexism in meat eating recapitulates the class distinctions with an added twist: a mythology permeates all classes that meat is a masculine food and meat eating a male activity.

MALE IDENTIFICATION AND MEAT EATING

Meat-eating societies gain male identification by their choice of food, and meat textbooks heartily endorse this association. *The Meat We Eat* proclaims meat to be "A Virile and Protective Food," thus "A liberal meat supply has always been associated with a happy and virile people."[1] *Meat Technology* informs us that "the virile Australian race is a typical example of heavy meat eaters."[2] Leading gourmands refer "to the virile ordeal of spooning the brains directly out of a barbecued calf's head."[3] *Virile: of or having the characteristics of an adult male*, from *vir* meaning *man*. Meat eating measures individual and societal virility.

Meat is a constant for men, intermittent for women, a pattern painfully observed in famine situations today. Women are starving at a rate disproportionate to men. Lisa Leghorn and Mary Roodkowsky surveyed this phenomenon in their book *Who Really Starves: Women and World Hunger*. Women, they conclude, engage in deliberate self-deprivation, offering men the "best" foods at the expense of their own nutritional needs. For instance, they tell us that "Ethiopian women and girls of all classes are obliged to prepare two meals, one for the males and a second, often containing no meat or other substantial protein, for the females."[4]

In fact, men's protein needs are less than those of pregnant and nursing women, and the disproportionate distribution of the main protein source occurs when women's need for protein is the greatest. Curiously, we are now being told that one should eat meat (or fish, vegetables, chocolate, and salt) at least six weeks before becoming pregnant if one wants a boy. But if a girl is desired, no meat please, rather milk, cheese, nuts, beans, and cereals.[5]

Most food taboos address meat consumption, and they place more restrictions on women than on men. The common foods forbidden to women are chicken, duck, and pork. Forbidding meat to women in nontechnological cultures increases its prestige. Even if the women raise the pigs, as they do in the Solomon Islands, they are rarely allowed to eat the pork. When they do receive some, it is at the dispensation of their husbands.[6] In Indonesia "flesh food is viewed as the property of men. At feasts, the principal time when meat is available, it is distributed to households according to the men in them. . . . The system of distribution thus reinforces the prestige of men in society."[7]

Worldwide this patriarchal custom is found. In Asia, some cultures forbid women from consuming fish, seafood, chicken, duck, and eggs. In equatorial Africa, the prohibition of chicken to women is common.[8] For example, the Mbum Kpau women do not eat chicken, goat, partridge, or other game birds. The Kufa of Ethiopia punished women who ate chicken by making them slaves, while the Walamo, "put to death anyone who violated the restriction of eating fowl."[9]

Correspondingly, vegetables and other nonmeat foods are viewed as women's food. This makes them undesirable to men. The Nuer men think that eating eggs is effeminate. In other groups men require sauces to disguise the fact that they are eating women's foods. "Men expect to have meat sauces to go with their porridge and will sometimes refuse to eat sauces made of greens or other vegetables, which are said to be women's food."[10]

Meat: For the Man Only

In technological societies, cookbooks reflect the presumption that men eat meat. A random survey of cookbooks reveals that the barbecue sections of most cookbooks are addressed to men and feature meat. The foods recommended for a "Mother's Day Tea" do not include meat, but readers are advised that on Father's Day, dinner should include London broil because "a steak dinner has unfailing popularity with fathers."[11] In a chapter on "Feminine Hospitality" we are directed to serve vegetables, salads, and soups. The *New McCall's Cookbook* suggests that a man's favorite dinner is London broil. A "Ladies Luncheon" would consist of cheese dishes and vegetables, but no meat. A section of one cookbook entitled "For Men Only" reinforces the omnipresence of meat in men's lives. What is for men only? London broil, cubed steak, and beef dinner.[12]

What do men want? asked the author of "Love, Sex, and Flank Steak" for the magazine *New Woman*. Her answer?

> Great sex and a great steak and not necessarily in that order. Sure, they want money and power, but only because of what those can win them— sex and steak. Both are closely related, as muscular, full-bodied pleasures of the flesh, and each ignites desire for the other. A hot, juicy, blood-red steak or a succulently thick hamburger induces an overall sense of well- being and a surge of self-assurance that is sure to make him feel good about himself and by association, you. That is especially true in this country [the United States], where beef is the quintessential macho fare.[13]

Twentieth-century cookbooks only serve to confirm the historical pattern found in the nineteenth century, when British working-class families could not afford sufficient meat to feed the entire family. "For the man only" appears continually in many of the menus of these families when referring to meat. In adhering to the mythologies of a culture (men need meat; meat gives bull-like strength) the male "breadwinner" actually received the meat. Social historians continually report that the "lion's share" of meat went to the husband.

What then was for women during the nineteenth century? On Sundays they might have a modest but good dinner. On the other days their food was bread with butter or drippings, weak tea, pudding, and vegetables. "The wife, in very poor families, is probably the worst fed of the household," observed Dr. Edward Smith in the first national food survey of British dietary habits in 1863, which revealed that the major difference in the diet of men and women in the same family was the amount of meat consumed. In one rural county of England, the investigators were told that the women and children "eat the potatoes and look at the meat."[14]

In situations of abundance, sex-role assumptions about meat are not so blatantly expressed. For this reason, the diets of English upper-class women and men are much more similar than the diets of upper-class women and working-class women. Moreover, with the abundance of meat available in the United States as opposed to the restricted amount available in England, there has been enough for all, except when meat supplies were controlled. For instance, while enslaved black men received half a pound of meat per day, enslaved black women often found that they received little more than a quarter pound a day at times.[15] Additionally, during the wars of the twentieth century, the pattern of meat consumption recalled that of English nineteenth-century working-class families with one variation: the "worker" of the country's household, the soldier, got the meat; civilians were urged to learn how to cook without meat.

The Racial Politics of Meat

The hearty meat eating that characterizes the diet of Americans and of the Western world is not only a symbol of male power, it is an index of racism. I do not mean racism in the sense that we are treating one class of animals, those that are not human beings, differently than we treat another, those that are human, as Isaac Bashevis Singer uses the term in *Enemies: A Love Story:* "As often as Herman had witnessed the slaughter of animals and fish, he always had the same thought: in their behavior toward creatures, all men were Nazis. The smugness with which man could do with other species as he pleased exemplified the most extreme racist theories, the principle that might is right."[16] I mean racism as the requirement that power arrangements and customs that favor white people prevail, and that the acculturation of people of color to this standard includes the imposition of white habits of meat eating.

Two parallel beliefs can be traced in the white Western world's enactment of racism when the issue is meat eating. The first is that if the meat supply is limited, white people should get it; but if meat is plentiful all should eat it. This is a variation on the standard theme of the sexual politics of meat. The hierarchy of meat protein reinforces a hierarchy of race, class, and sex.

Nineteenth-century advocates of white superiority endorsed meat as superior food. "Brain-workers" required lean meat as their main meal, but the "savage" and "lower" classes of society could live exclusively on coarser foods according to George Beard, a nineteenth-century medical doctor who specialized in the diseases of middle-class people. He recommended that when white, civilized, middle-class men became susceptible to nervous exhaustion, they should eat more meat. To him, and for many others, cereals and fruits were lower than meat on the scale of evolution, and thus appropriate foods for the other races and white women, who appeared to be lower on the scale of evolution as well. Racism and sexism together upheld meat as white man's food.

Influenced by Darwin's theory of evolution, Beard proposed a corollary for foods: animal protein did to food what our evolution from the lower animals did for humans. Consequently:

> In proportion as man grows sensitive through civilization or through disease, he should diminish the quantity of cereals and fruits, which are far below him on the scale of evolution, and increase the quantity of animal food, which is nearly related to him in the scale of evolution, and therefore more easily assimilated.[17]

In his racist analysis, Beard reconciled the apparent contradiction of this tenet: "Why is it that savages and semi-savages are able to live on forms of food which, according to the theory of evolution, must be far below them in the scale of development?" In other words, how is it that people can survive very well without a great deal of animal protein? Because "savages" are "little removed from the common animal stock from which they are derived. They are much nearer to the forms of life from which they feed than are the highly civilized brain-workers, and can therefore subsist on forms of life which would be most poisonous to us. Secondly, savages who feed on poor food are poor savages, and intellectually far inferior to the beef-eaters of any race."

This explanation—which divided the world into intellectually superior meat eaters and inferior plant eaters—accounted for the conquering of other cultures by the English:

> The rice-eating Hindoo and Chinese and the potato-eating Irish peasant are kept in subjection by the well-fed English. Of the various causes that contributed to the defeat of Napoleon at Waterloo, one of the chief was that for the first time he was brought face to face with the nation of beef-eaters, who stood still until they were killed.

Into the twentieth century the notion was that meat eating contributed to the Western world's preeminence. Publicists for a meat company in the 1940s wrote: "We know meat-eating races have been and are leaders in the progress made by mankind in its upward struggle through the ages."[18] They are referring to the "upward struggle" of the white race. One revealing aspect of this "upward struggle" is the charge of cannibalism, which appeared during the years of colonization.

The word "cannibalism" entered our vocabulary after the "discovery" of the New World. Derived from the Spaniards' mispronunciation of the name of the people of the Caribbean, it linked these people of color with that act. As Europeans explored the continents of North and South America and Africa, the indigenous peoples of those lands became accused of cannibalism—the ultimate savagery. Once labeled as cannibals, their defeat and enslavement at the hands of civilized, Christian whites became justifiable. W. Arens argues that the charge of cannibalism was part and parcel of the European expansion into other continents.[19]

Of the charges of cannibalism against the indigenous peoples, Arens found little independent verification. One well-known source of dubious testimony on cannibalism was then plagiarized by others claiming to be eyewitnesses. The eyewitnesses fail to describe just how they were able to escape the fate of consumption they report witnessing. Nor do they explain how the language barrier was overcome, enabling them to report verbatim conversations with "savages." In addition, their reports fail to maintain internal consistency.

One cause of cannibalism was thought to be lack of animal protein. Yet most Europeans themselves during the centuries of European expansion were not subsisting on animal protein every day. The majority of cultures in the world satisfied their protein needs through vegetables and grains. By charging indigenous peoples with cannibalism (and thus demonstrating their utterly savage ways, for they did to humans what Europeans did only to animals), one justification for colonization was provided.

Racism is perpetuated each time that meat is thought to be the best protein source. The emphasis on the nutritional strengths of animal protein distorts the dietary history of most cultures in which complete protein dishes were made of vegetables and grains. Information about these dishes is overwhelmed by an ongoing cultural and political commitment to meat eating.

Meat Is King

A discussion of nutrition during wartime contained this aside: it was one thing, they acknowledged, to demonstrate that there were many viable alternatives to meat, "but it is another to convince a man who enjoys his beefsteak."[20] The male prerogative to eat meat is an external, observable activity implicitly reflecting a recurring fact: meat is a symbol of male dominance.

The enormous growth of steak houses since the 1990s, the recent success of chains such as Morton's, with waiting lines of two hours on weekend nights in some cities, why not read this phenomenon exactly as a headline in the *Dallas Morning News* did: "Male Call"? The full headline for a review of "Bob's Steak and Chop House" that describes "how masculine" the environment is—a real "no-frills macho" place—declared: "Male Call: Bob's outpost replicates the original's masculine, meaty formula."[21] It is here, in this environment, eating big slabs of meat, that men are confirmed in their sense of identity. Vegetable protein doesn't bleed.

It has traditionally been felt that the working man needs meat for strength. A superstition operates in this belief: in eating the muscle of strong animals, we will become strong. According to the mythology of patriarchal culture, meat promotes strength; the attributes of masculinity are achieved through eating these masculine foods. Visions of meat-eating football players, wrestlers, and boxers lumber in our brains in this equation. Though vegetarian weight lifters and athletes in other fields have demonstrated the equation to be fallacious, the myth remains: men are strong, men need to be strong, thus men need meat. The literal evocation of male power is found in the concept of meat.

Irving Fisher took the notion of "strength" from the definition of meat eating as long ago as 1906. Fisher suggested that strength be measured by its lasting power, rather than by its association with quick results, and compared meat-eating athletes with vegetarian athletes and sedentary vegetarians. Endurance was measured by having the participants perform in three areas: holding their arms horizontally for as long as possible, doing deep knee bends, and performing leg raises while lying down. He concluded that the vegetarians, whether athletes or not, had greater endurance than meat eaters. "Even the *maximum* record of the flesh-eaters was barely more than half the *average* for the flesh-abstainers."[22]

Meat is king: this noun describing meat is a noun denoting male power. Vegetables, a generic term meat eaters use for all foods that are not meat, have become as associated with women as meat is with men, recalling on a subconscious level the days of Woman the Gatherer. Since women have been made subsidiary in a male-dominated, meat-eating world, so has our food. The foods associated with second-class citizens are considered to be second-class protein. Just as it is thought a woman cannot make it on her own, so we think that vegetables cannot make a meal on their own, despite the fact that meat is only second-hand vegetables and vegetables provide, on the average, more than twice the vitamins and minerals of meat. Meat is upheld as a powerful, irreplaceable item of food. The message is clear: the vassal vegetable should content itself with its assigned place and not attempt to dethrone king meat. After all, how can one enthrone women's foods when women cannot be kings?

GENDER INEQUALITY/SPECIES INEQUALITY

What is it about meat that makes it a symbol and celebration of male dominance? In many ways, gender inequality is built into the species inequality that meat eating proclaims, because for most cultures obtaining meat was performed by men. Meat was a valuable economic commodity; those who controlled this commodity achieved power. If men were the hunters, then the control of this economic resource was in their hands. Women's status is inversely related to the importance of meat in nontechnological societies:

> The equation is simple: the more important meat is in their life, the greater relative dominance will the men command. . . . When meat becomes an important element within a more closely organized economic system so that there exist rules for its distribution, then men already begin to swing the levers of power. . . . [W]omen's social standing is roughly equal to men's only when society itself is not formalized around roles for distributing meat.[23]

Peggy Sanday surveyed information on over one hundred nontechnological cultures and found a correlation between plant-based economies and women's power and animal-based economies and male power. "In societies dependent on animals, women are rarely depicted as the ultimate source of creative power."[24] In addition, "When large animals are hunted, fathers are more distant, that is, they are not in frequent or regular proximity to infants."[25]

Characteristics of economies dependent mainly on the processing of animals for food include:

- sexual segregation in work activities, with women doing more work than men, but work that is less valued,
- women responsible for child care,
- the worship of male gods,
- patrilineality.

On the other hand, plant-based economies are more likely to be egalitarian. This is because women are and have been the gatherers of vegetable foods, and these are invaluable resources for a culture that is plant-based. In these cultures, men as well as women were dependent on women's activities. From this, women achieved autonomy and a degree of self-sufficiency. By providing a large proportion of the protein food of a society, women gain an essential economic and social role without abusing it.

"Vegetable": Symbol of Feminine Passivity?

Both the words "men" and "meat" have undergone lexicographical narrowing. Originally generic terms, they are now closely associated with their specific referents. Meat no longer means all foods; the word man, we realize, no longer includes women. Meat represents *the essence or principal part of something* according to the *American Heritage Dictionary*. Thus we have the "meat of the matter," "a meaty question." To "beef up" something is to improve it. Vegetable, on the other hand, represents the least desirable characteristics: *suggesting or like a vegetable, as in passivity or dullness of existence, monotonous, inactive.* Meat is *something one enjoys or excels in,* vegetable becomes representative of someone who does not enjoy anything: a *person who leads a monotonous, passive or merely physical existence.*

A complete reversal has occurred in the definition of the word vegetable. Whereas its original sense was to *be lively, active,* it is now viewed as dull, monotonous, passive. To vegetate is to lead a passive existence; just as to be feminine is to lead a passive existence. Once vegetables are viewed as women's food, then by association they become viewed as "feminine," passive. Examples from the 1988 presidential campaign in which each candidate was belittled through equation with being a vegetable illustrate this patriarchal disdain for vegetables. Michael Dukakis was called "the Vegetable Plate Candidate."[26] Northern Sun Merchandising offered T-shirts that asked: "George Bush: Vegetable or Noxious Weed?" One could opt for a shirt that featured a bottle of ketchup and a picture of Ronald Reagan with this slogan: "*Nutrition Quiz:* Which one is the vegetable?"[27]

The word vegetable acts as a synonym for women's passivity because women are like plants. Hegel makes this clear: "The difference between men and women is like that between animals and plants. Men correspond to animals, while women correspond to plants because their development is more placid."[28] From this viewpoint, both women and plants are seen as less developed and less evolved than men and animals. Consequently, women may eat plants, since each is placid; but active men need animal meat.

Meat Is a Symbol of Patriarchy

In her essay, "Deciphering a Meal," the noted anthropologist Mary Douglas suggests that the order in which we serve foods, and the foods we insist on being present at a meal, reflect a taxonomy of classification that mirrors and reinforces our larger culture. A meal is an amalgam of food dishes,

Billboard in Portland, Oregon, 2002.

each a constituent part of the whole, each with an assigned value. In addition, each dish is introduced in precise order. A meal does not begin with a dessert, nor end with soup. All is seen as leading up to and then coming down from the entrée, which is meat. The pattern is evidence of stability. As Douglas explains, "The ordered system which is a meal represents all the ordered systems associated with it. Hence the strong arousal power of a threat to weaken or confuse that category."[29] To remove meat is to threaten the structure of the larger patriarchal culture.

Marabel Morgan, one expert on how women should accede to every male desire, reported in her *Total Woman Cookbook* that one must be careful about introducing foods that are seen as a threat: "I discovered that Charlie seemed threatened by certain foods. He was suspicious of my casseroles, thinking I had sneaked in some wheat germ or 'good-for-you' vegetables that he wouldn't like."[30]

Mary McCarthy's *Birds of America* provides a fictional illustration of the intimidating aspect to a man of a woman's refusal of meat. Miss Scott, a vegetarian, is invited to a NATO general's house for Thanksgiving. Her refusal of turkey angers the general. Not able to take this rejection seriously—male dominance requiring a continual recollection of itself on everyone's plate— the general loads her plate up with turkey and then ladles gravy over the potatoes as well as the meat, contaminating her vegetable foods as well. McCarthy's description of his actions with the food mirrors the warlike customs associated with military battles. "He had seized the gravy boat like a weapon in hand-to-hand combat. No wonder they had made him a brigadier general—at least that mystery was solved." The general continues to behave in a bellicose fashion and, after dinner, proposes a toast in honor of an eighteen-year-old who has enlisted to fight in Vietnam. During the ensuing argument about war the general defends the bombing of Vietnam with the rhetorical question: "What's so sacred about a civilian?" This upsets the hero, necessitating that the general's wife apologize for her husband's behavior: "Between you and me," she confides to him, "it kind of got under his skin to see that girl refusing to touch her food. I saw that right away."[31]

Male belligerence in this area is not limited to fictional military men. Men who batter their wives have often used the absence of meat as a pretext for violence against women. Women's failure to serve meat is not the cause of the violence against them. Yet, as a pretext for this accepted violence, meat is hardly a trivial item. "Real" men eat meat. Failing to honor the importance of this symbol provides an opportunity for a man to use controlling behavior against his partner. As one battered woman reported, "It would start off with him being angry over trivial little things, a trivial little thing like cheese instead of meat on a sandwich."[32] Another battered wife stated, "A month ago he threw scalding water over me, leaving a scar on my right arm, all because I gave him a pie with potatoes and vegetables for his dinner, instead of fresh meat."[33]

Men who become vegetarians challenge an essential part of the masculine role. They are opting for women's food. How dare they? Refusing meat means a man is effeminate, a "sissy," a "fruit." Indeed, in 1836, the response to the vegetarian regimen of that day, known as Grahamism, charged that "Emasculation is the first fruit of Grahamism."[34]

Choosing not to eat meat means that men repudiate their masculine privileges. The *New York Times* explored this idea in an editorial on the masculine nature of meat eating. Instead of "the John Wayne type," epitome of the masculine meat eater, the new male hero is "vulnerable" like Alan Alda, Mikhail Baryshnikov, and Phil Donahue. According to the *Times*, they might eat fish and chicken, but not red meat. Alda and Donahue, among other men, have not only repudiated the macho role, but also macho food. Writes the editor, "Believe me. The end of macho marks the end of the meat and potatoes man."[35] We won't miss either.

NOTES

1. P. Thomas Ziegler, *The Meat We Eat* (Danville, IL: Interstate Printers and Publishers, 1966), pp. 5, 1.

2. Frank Gerrard, *Meat Technology: A Practical Textbook for Student and Butcher* (London: Northwood Publications, 1945, 1977), p. 348.

3. Waverley Root and Richard de Rochemont, *Eating in America: A History* (New York: William Morrow, 1976), p. 279.

4. Lisa Leghorn and Mary Roodkowsky, *Who Really Starves: Women and World Hunger* (New York: Friendship Press, 1977), p. 21.

5. Lloyd Shearer, "Intelligence Report: Does Diet Determine Sex?" summarizing the conclusions of Dr. Joseph Stolkowski, *Parade*, June 27, 1982, p. 7.

6. Frederick J. Simoons, *Eat Not This Flesh: Food Avoidances in the Old World* (Madison: University of Wisconsin Press, 1961, 1967), p. 110.

7. Leghorn and Roodkowsky, *Who Really Starves*, p. 20.

8. Simoons, *Eat Not This Flesh*, pp. 74, 171 n.93.

9. Ibid., p. 73.

10. Bridget O'Laughlin, "Mediation of Contradiction: Why Mbum Women Do Not Eat Chicken," in *Woman, Culture, and Society*, ed. Michelle Zimbalist Rosaldo and Louise Lamphere (Stanford: Stanford University Press, 1974), p. 303.

11. Sunset Books and Sunset Magazines, *Sunset Menu Cook Book* (Menlo Park, CA: Lane Magazine and Book Co., 1969), pp. 139, 140.

12. *Oriental Cookery* from ChunKing and Mazola Corn Oil.

13. Mimi Sheraton, "Love, Sex, and Flank Steak," *New Woman* (February 1996): 107–10.

14. Edward Smith, MD, *Practical Dietary for Families, Schools, and the Labouring Classes* (London: Walton and Materly, 1864), pp. 199–201.

15. Todd L. Savitt, *Medicine and Slavery: The Diseases and Health Care of Blacks in Antebellum Virginia* (Urbana and Chicago: University of Illinois Press, 1978), p. 91.

16. Isaac Bashevis Singer, *Enemies: A Love Story* (New York: Farrar, Straus and Giroux, 1972), p. 257.

17. George M. Beard, MD, *Sexual Neurasthenia [Nervous Exhaustion]Its Hygiene, Causes, Symptoms, and Treatment with a Chapter on Diet for the Nervous* (New York: E. B. Treat & Co., 1898; New York: Arno Press, 1972). This and succeeding quotations are found on pp. 272–78.

18. Robert B. Hinman and Robert B. Harris, *The Story of Meat* (Chicago: Swift and Co., 1942), p. 1.

19. W. Arens, *The Man-Eating Myth: Anthropology and Anthropophagy* (New York: Oxford University Press, 1979).

20. Helen Hunscher and Margerita Huyck, "Nutrition," in *Consumer Problems in Wartime*, ed. Kenneth Dameron (New York and London: McGraw-Hill, 1944), p. 414.

21. Dotty Griffith, "Male Call: Bob's Outpost Replicates the Original's Masculine, Meaty Formula," *Dallas Morning News Guide*, May 31, 2002, p. 6.

22. Irving Fisher, "The Influence of Flesh Eating on Endurance," *Yale Medical Journal* 13 no. 5 (March 1907): 207.

23. Richard E. Leakey and Roger Lewin, *People of the Lake: Mankind and Its Beginnings* (New York: Doubleday, 1978; New York: Avon Books, 1979), pp. 210–11.

24. Peggy Sanday, *Female Power and Male Dominance: On the Origins of Sexual Inequality* (Cambridge and New York: Cambridge University Press, 1981), p. 65.

25. Ibid., p. 66.

26. Sandy Grady, "The Duke as Boring as Spinach," *Buffalo News*, March 26, 1988.

27. From a catalog from Northern Sun Merchandising, 2916 E. Lake Street, Minneapolis, MN, 55406.

28. From Hegel's *Philosophy of Right*, para. 166, p. 263, quoted in Nancy Tuana, "The Misbegotten Man: Scientific, Religious, and Philosophical Images of Women," unpublished manuscript.

29. Mary Douglas, "Deciphering a Meal," in *Implicit Meanings: Essays in Anthropology* (London: Routledge & Kegan Paul, 1975), p. 273.

30. Marabel Morgan, *The Total Woman Cookbook: Marabel Morgan's Handbook for Kitchen Survival* (Old Tappan, NJ: Fleming H. Revell Co., 1980), p. 13.

31. Mary McCarthy, *Birds of America* (New York: Harcourt Brace Jovanovich, 1965; New York: New American Library, 1972), pp. 167, 180, 183.

32. R. Emerson Dobash and Russell Dobash, *Violence against Wives: A Case against the Patriarchy* (New York: Free Press, 1979), p. 100.

33. Erin Pizzey, *Scream Quietly or the Neighbours Will Hear* (Hammondsworth, England: Penguin Books, 1974), p. 35.

34. James C. Whorton, "'Tempest in a Flesh-Pot': The Formulation of a Physiological Rationale for Vegetarianism," *Journal of the History of Medicine and Allied Sciences* 32 no. 2 (April 1977): 122.

35. *New York Times* editorial, August 17, 1981.

21 | A PARADOX OF ETHICAL VEGETARIANISM
Unfairness to Women and Children

Kathryn Paxton George

Vegetarianism[1] has been promoted by a variety of authorities as both humanitarian and healthful. Not only should people avoid harming animals by eating them, but we can also avoid the harmful effects of high-fat diets by avoiding meat, eggs, and dairy products. The claim that vegetarian diets are healthful is separate from the claim that such diets are morally required, but these ideas do influence one another. I argue here that the apparent safety and benefits of vegetarian diets for adult males between the ages of twenty and fifty has led some philosophers, especially Peter Singer, Tom Regan, and some feminists, to assume—probably unwittingly—that the male body is considered the normal *human* body. Then, assuming facts about this male human norm and using the Principle of Equality, they derive a general moral rule demanding ethical vegetarianism for everyone regardless of age, sex, or environment. I will refer to these arguments as the "Regan-Singer arguments."[2] I will show that their assumption about the male norm is mistaken and their call for ethical vegetarianism results in ageism, sexism, and classism. The Regan-Singer arguments rely on the Principle of Equality, but if all animals are equal, women and children become "less equal" than men. This paradoxical outcome will show that these arguments are incoherent and fail. Finally, the standard against which risk is presumed to be measured is arbitrarily assumed to be the adult male body.[3]

First, let's review the moral claims of the Regan-Singer arguments. The general claim is that we may not kill animals for food. According to Singer, we may not use their products unless we could be sure that these products are obtained under painless conditions. Singer's utilitarian position would permit some people to eat animals or use their products if they have a strong welfare interest (say, for reasons of ill health), but these would be *exceptional cases*. Singer's reasons are similar to those offered by Tom Regan, whose rights position allows certain people to consume meat as an exception based on what he calls the *Liberty Principle*:

> Provided that all those involved are treated with respect, and assuming that no special considerations obtain, any innocent individual has the right to act to avoid being made worse-off even if doing so harms other innocents.[4]

Being made to starve or suffer a significant decline in health and vigor would make a person worse-off, and Regan concedes that if some humans have a strong welfare-interest in consuming meat or animal products, this would excuse them from a duty to be vegetarians. But Regan clearly thinks that most people do not fall into such a category. He briefly discusses protein complementation and then dismisses the argument from nutrition: "Certain amino acids are essential for our health. Meat isn't. We cannot, therefore, defend meat eating on the grounds that we will ruin our health if we don't eat it or even that we will run a very serious risk of doing so if we abstain."[5]

Traditional moral theories used by Regan and Singer assume the moral equality of persons regardless of age, sex, race, and so forth. This assumption is called the *Principle of Equality*. Without the Principle of Equality, Regan and Singer cannot begin to make their arguments for the rights and welfare of animals. Rights-holders deserve equal treatment, and the rules generated by the moral system should be impartial and nondiscriminatory concerning facts about the rights-holders that they cannot change by choice. No particular group of people should bear a very much greater burden than others in attempting to keep the moral rule. That can mean that society should eliminate moral, social, or legal constraints that will cause people to suffer an increased burden in their attempts to function in society, at least as far as possible. For example, the Principle of Equality gives us the underlying reason to provide ramps and elevators for those who cannot use stairs. Because we subscribe to the Principle of Equality, we think it wrong to punish criminal offenders of one race more harshly than those of another. Nondiscrimination is the attempt by fair-minded people to affirm the equal worth of each member of the moral community. No single group can simply assume that its own practices are the only right ones, or even the best ones. If the rule prescribing ethical vegetarian diets is truly impartial, it should not require greater or very much greater burdens for some groups because of facts about themselves that they cannot change by choice and that are thought to be neutral to the interests served by the rule.

Having set out a brief exposition of the foundations for ethical vegetarianism, I will now present a critical examination of this proposed moral rule. My claim is that the rule is partial to adult males and that no one has noticed that the rule systematically imposes greater burdens on women, children, and the elderly. In addition, the rule unfairly penalizes people who live in certain kinds of economic and environmental circumstances. My critique has three parts:

(1) Regan and Singer assume that females, children, and the elderly have no significant differences in nutritional needs from those of adult males. To make their moral arguments, these scholars rely on conclusions drawn from nutritional studies done largely on adult males in industrialized countries. In addition, they do not consider studies citing the limitations of such diets for other age groups and for many women. Instead, the adult male body is assumed to be the norm for all. Women, children, and others are referred to in the scientific literature as "nutritionally vulnerable" with respect to certain vitamins and minerals such as iron, calcium, vitamin D, and zinc. All current arguments for ethical vegetarianism treat such nutritional vulnerability as an *exception* rather than as a norm. But, the very fact that the majority is regarded as a mere exception suggests that the ideal is skewed to favor a group in power.

(2) The requirement of ethical vegetarianism is also inconsistent and classist because it presupposes a society largely structured on wealth generated from unsustainable environmental, agricultural, and industrial practices. But most people in the world live in ethnic, cultural, economic, and environmental circumstances where this supposed ethical ideal poses much more serious health risks than it does for people in the United States, Europe, and other wealthy countries.

(3) Attempts to correct inequities by requiring supplementation for women and children exacerbate rather than resolve the problem of unfairness.

The first criticism will show that the Regan-Singer arguments become incoherent because they cannot consistently apply the Principle of Equality. Neither Singer nor Regan considers the different nutritional needs of adults versus infants and children and men versus women, although these differences are well documented in the medical and nutritional literature.[6] Infants and young children have higher energy, vitamin, and mineral needs than adults do because they are continuously growing and adding new tissue to their bodies. Nationally recognized nutrition authority, Dr. Johanna T. Dwyer, of Tufts University's School of Medicine and Nutrition, writes: "Vegetarianism in children deserves special attention because diets that sustain adults in good health are not necessarily appropriate for infants, young children, or adolescents."[7] Phyllis B. Acosta, of Florida State University's Department of Nutrition and Food Science, states her concerns in stronger terms: "Eating practices that promote health in the adult may have detrimental effects on growth and health status of the infant and young child."[8] Adolescents also need diets that are dense in nutrients per kilocalorie because they undergo the pubertal growth spurt. "Sex differences in nutrient needs become especially pronounced during adolescence."[9] The onset of menstruation in females increases their iron needs, and the need for protein in adolescence increases because the body size is increasing rapidly. Because bone mass is being accumulated, calcium needs remain higher in both sexes until about age twenty-five. The recommended daily allowances (RDAs) are "considerably higher for adolescents than they are for younger children or adults, especially if they are expressed on a nutrients-per-calorie basis."[10] Pregnant adult women have greater protein, calcium, iron, vitamin C, vitamin D, vitamin E, thiamin, riboflavin, niacin, vitamin B_6, folate, vitamin B_{12}, phosphorus, magnesium, zinc, selenium, and iodide needs than adult males, and breast-feeding women have requirements that are higher still for almost all of these nutrients. People over age fifty have different requirements for several nutrients as reflected in the RDAs.

In pregnant women, "certain dietary practices that restrict or prohibit the consumption of an important source of nutrients, such as avoidance of all animal foods or of vitamin D–fortified milk, increase the risk of inadequate nutrient intake."[11] Pregnant vegan women may be at greater nutritional risk for "inadequate weight gain, low protein intake, inadequate iron intake with resulting anemias, low calcium, zinc, and vitamin B_{12} intakes, and in some instances low vitamin D, zinc, and iodide intakes."[12] Because the health of the fetus depends on the health of the individual woman carrying it, these factors may pose a fetal risk as well. In some cases, nutritional deficiency in a woman at the time of conception can seriously impair fetal development or the health of a breast-feeing child (e.g., folic acid deficiency, vitamin B_{12} deficiency).

Women and children are more likely to suffer iron deficiency than adult males even in industrialized societies, but iron deficiency is less severe in countries where food intake is adequate and includes meat. Only a few years ago, marginal iron levels in women were not regarded with much alarm by physicians and nutritionists. Recently, however, scientists have found that iron plays a vital role in childhood development and maintenance of the central nervous system, organ function, and immune function. Researchers usually categorize their test subjects as "normal," "iron deficient," or "iron deficient anemic," where iron deficiency is a state preceding anemia. In a review of forty-five studies on children, Hercberg and Galan note that iron deficiency has

effects on skeletal muscle, cardiac muscle, brain tissue, liver tissue, gastrointestinal tractus [sic], body temperature relation, [and] DNA synthesis
[because] iron participates in a wide variety of biochemical processes. . . .
The key liabilities of tissue iron deficiency, even at a mild degree relate to
decrease in intellectual performance, and in physical capacity during exercise, alteration of temperature regulation, [and] immune function.[13]

Moreover, the effects of diets without adequate available sources of iron in
infancy and young childhood cannot be compensated for by later improvements or later supplementation, and "maternal mortality, prenatal, and
perinatal infant death and prematurety are significantly increased" for iron
deficiency in pregnancy.[14]

Women are particularly sensitive to iron deficiency because of periodic
blood loss at menses and during pregnancy. Because iron carries oxygen to
body cells, anemia causes reduction in capacity to perform work, reduction in
mental acuity, greater vulnerability to other kinds of illnesses, and a variety of
other symptoms. A significant number of women become iron deficient during
pregnancy. "Although pregnant vegan women [in the U.S.] can meet increased
needs for most nutrients during pregnancy by diet alone . . . iron needs rise so
much after the second trimester that supplements are usually needed since
plant sources of iron are less bioavailable than heme iron."[15] Supplements are
commonly available in industrialized environments but are often not available
to women in countries where food supplies are marginal. So both vegans and
vegetarians are at risk for iron deficiency on unsupplemented diets, and women
and children are at significantly greater risk than adult males.

Calcium adequacy is a risk for vegans, and again women, children, and
the elderly are at greater risk on vegan diets than are adult males. Vegans
reject dairy products, significantly reducing their dietary sources of calcium.
Most concern about calcium centers on bone health. Continued inade-
quacy of calcium, especially in childhood and adolescence, is a major contributing factor to osteoporosis. Milk is regarded as the best source of calcium because of its bioavailability. Osteoporosis is a major concern for
postmenopausal women because it causes bone loss and fractures, particularly of the hip, forearm, and vertebrae. Women are at much greater risk for
this disease than are men, although males are affected in later old age. The
generally denser skeletons and testosterone levels in males prevent its
occurrence until quite late in life.

The time to prevent osteoporosis appears to be in childhood and adolescence. Peak bone mass is built at that age, and the better bone is built
the more there will be. When bone loss begins, the time to reach a stage of
severe depletion is longer. Young women have already built almost all of
their bone by age seventeen, with some new bone formation perhaps continuing into the twenties. By age thirty, many women begin to lose bone.

In women, "over the first several years after menopause, the skeleton undergoes a period of accelerated mineral loss in the process of adapting to declining concentrations of estrogen. After this period of adjustment, the rate of bone loss declines and remains fairly constant."[16]

The nutritional evidence suggests that the best candidates for vegetarianism and veganism are young, adult, healthy males living in industrialized cultures. Males have generally larger skeletons, maintain bone health due to higher levels of testosterone, and so have a lower risk of osteoporosis in late middle and old age. Adult males have higher iron levels than females and are at much less risk of anemia in adolescence and adulthood because they do not have periodic blood loss with menstruation and childbirth. They do not have protein, vitamin, or mineral stresses from feeding a rapidly growing fetus or a nursing infant, nor are they unduly stressed by their own growth requirements, as most of their growth is accomplished.

Do these facts mean that women and children in the United States cannot be healthy vegetarians? No, they do not. All risks for vegans in the United States can be overcome with a well-planned and well-supplemented diet. What does "well-planned" mean? Here is Johanna Dwyer's answer:

> For those who wish to progress to a vegan diet that includes no animal foods whatsoever, additional care in dietary planning is needed. In addition to iron and zinc, unplanned vegan diets are often low in kilocalories, calcium, and are always low in vitamin B_{12} and vitamin D unless supplementary sources of these vitamins are provided, since plant foods contain no known sources of these vitamins. The assistance of a registered dietitian is helpful, since a good deal of skill in planning and familiarity with unconventional food sources is needed by omnivores who wish to alter their dietary intakes in this way. *Certainly, if the individual in question is an infant, child, pregnant or lactating woman, over 65 years of age, recovering from an illness, or a chronic sufferer of a disease, dietetic consultation is highly advisable in order to incorporate these additional considerations into dietary planning and to avoid or circumvent adverse nutritional consequences.* Several good articles are available to guide counseling efforts for vulnerable groups.[17]

Moralists like Regan and Singer claim that anyone can be an ethical vegetarian with no extra special burden, but as shown above, that is not true. If the risk of harm can be overcome only by imposing significantly greater burdens on the groups highlighted above, while adult males gain health benefits, then the standard against which the risk is measured must surely be unfair.

Those defending vegetarianism with Regan-Singer arguments and feminist moral theories would say that anyone who needs to eat eggs, meat, or milk should not be required to abstain.[18] But they assume or argue that these people will be *exceptional cases* falling outside of the norm. This assumption is false.

Here is the core of my objection: Who are these others that tradition-alists like Regan and Singer think may be excused? They are the vast majority of the *world's* population. And, if women, infants, children, ado-lescents, the elderly, and people who live almost everywhere else besides Western societies are *routinely* excused for doing what would normally be considered wrong, this relegates them to a *moral underclass* of beings who, because of their natures or cultures, are not capable of being fully moral. They are *physiologically* barred from doing the right thing because they are not the right *kind* of thing. The structure of this ethical thinking degrades the reality and human worth of these groups of people who do not fit.

Second, the Regan-Singer arguments assume a social standard struc-tured largely on wealth generated from unsustainable environmental, agri-cultural, and industrial practices. These arguments also require women, children, and people who live in poorer cultures and environments to con-form their ethical behavior as if they have the same kind of bodies as adult males living in wealthy cultures or be granted an exception.

From the perspective of a white middle-class college professor, Amer-ican or Western society may appear quite homogeneous. The education level is high, food is plentiful, fortified, and available in great variety; the unemployed have food stamps; supplements seem readily available. These are conditions of great wealth by world standards, and they make vegetari-anism reasonably safe. But, even in the United States, many people in poor economic circumstances do not have access to adequate food or to nutri-tional information. For example, many inner-city residents cannot buy veg-etables—there is no supermarket nearby. Shall we simply excuse them then? But there really is something quite arrogant about excusing all of these people from attaining the ideal; it supposes the richer are better. They are not. They are just luckier.

Now I wish to discuss and reply to two possible counterarguments to my critique of ethical vegetarianism: (1) if these vulnerable groups use supple-ments, concerns about inequity vanish; and (2) improved medical care, edu-cation, and sanitation will make ethical vegetarianism globally equitable.

The first claim is that if women, children, and other nutritionally vul-nerable groups use dietary supplements, then their risk is minimized. Therefore, these people should take supplements. This counterargument is flawed for two reasons. First, even if risks for vegetarians were equalized, burdens would not be. Western adult male vegetarians have many fewer burdens to bear, while women and child vegetarians must work harder to be "equal" simply because of their age or sex. Adult males rarely suffer anemia; they do not lose iron through periodic menstruation; they do not carry fetuses in their bodies or nurse infants; their growth is completed, and they almost always have larger skeletons than females and so have a much lower incidence of osteoporosis. Supplements are expensive; some are best prescribed by a physician to avoid overdose; they are usually not covered by insurance; and they may increase a vegetarian woman's personal and psychological worries. Second, the arbitrary adult male norm remains. Even if it is not too risky for a middle-class infant, child, adolescent, pregnant, lactating, perimenopausal, postmenopausal female, or elderly person to be an ethical vegetarian, that judgment will surely be made from a biased perspective—one that assesses the risk from the standpoint of the supposed male norm. Women, children, and seniors are being told to fix, mend, or correct their imperfect bodies as necessary (by supplementation, fortified foods, or eating in special ways) to meet a vegetarian ideal that is much less burdensome for adult males.

Now for the second counterargument: many nutritionists point out that people in "developing" countries are vegans not by choice but by circumstance of having no meat or dairy products available. Such people have a poor health status attributable to "environmental factors (such as lack of medical care, vaccination, education, and sanitation) rather than solely to diet."[19] Morally, we should improve these background conditions to a level similar to that of the United States. Then, supplemented vegan diets would constitute little risk in those places, too. We might conclude that the risks would then be equalized (although burdens would not be equalized) among the sexes and ages, at least in theory. Not only would the fundamental problem of bias remain, but such a program would come at a cost to humans and to animals. Vegan and vegetarian diets are lower in risk in Western nations when individuals have access to education, medical care, and sufficient resources to buy proper foods and supplements. Most importantly, these diets pose less risk in our culture largely because much of our food is fortified. We tend to think of our food as "naturally" protecting us. And it does! A diet consisting of the worst junk food is unlikely to result in pellagra or beriberi in the United States because virtually all flours are vitamin B fortified. Vitamin D is added to milk and is perhaps the single most important factor in the near eradication of rickets in children and osteomalacia in women and adolescents.

In many other parts of the world, beriberi, pellagra, rickets, scurvy, kwashikor, megaloblastic anemia, and iron deficient anemia are still endemic, although the incidence has declined in the twentieth century and the severity of the affected is usually less marked. Our food system protects us against these diseases, but that protection depends on an industrialized and unsustainable network of mono-cropping, food preservation, transportation, fortification, variety, and plenty—a system that is often inconsistent with environmental goals. In our culture, fortification and food processing require a complex industrialized food system with research biochemistry laboratories, food processing plants, mines to produce supplements, quality control bureaucracies, food-preservation techniques including spraying and refrigeration, trucking and other petro-leum-consuming industries, and perhaps even chemical-dependent agri-culture. A sophisticated scientific research and industrial complex with vitamin and mineral factories able to synthesize supplements without using animal products would be needed. For that, research biochemistry and chemistry labs are necessary, mines for extraction of raw materials, a network of universities to train scientists, and so forth. All of these aspects of our food systems have environmental consequences, many or most of which are at odds with environmental goals such as the preservation of habitat and reduction of pollution. Exporting safe vegan or vegetarian diets to the rest of the developing world would export these food systems and their environmental consequences, too. A strict moral censure of meat eating will be hard-pressed to escape the exploitation of the earth, of non-industrialized cultures, and of the animals it seeks to spare. Such censures are more likely to preserve class distinctions and discrimination than to dissipate them.

While we should, of course, encourage the worldwide availability of health care and good nutrition, the concomitant requirement of ethical vegetarianism may defeat environmental sustainability and would sustain a false norm in nutrition. The best course seems to be a middle ground such as semivegetarianism with moderate continued food fortification and preservation. Individuals should choose whether or not they wish to be vegetarians for reasons of health or personal taste. But I argue no one has a *moral* requirement to adopt this diet, even though we do have duties not to overconsume. People commonly eat together in families and among friends. We influence each other profoundly about diet and the accept-ability of certain foods. Thus, each of us must consider his or her individual context and balance common-sense duties to animals and humans. Should we admire the strict moral vegetarian as going "above and beyond the call of duty"?[20] While this is a tempting tack to take, I must answer, "no." Semi-vegetarianism provides balanced diets and can be tolerated by almost everyone, and so the practice is good. But because there is no duty of strict ethical vegetarianism, we have no basis to admire the vegetarian on moral grounds. And, such admiration may even be pernicious to equality and human rights due to the inherent bias that lies within the assumption of the adult male norm.

NOTES

1. Lacto-ovo vegetarians include plant foods, milk, eggs, and dairy products in their diets, but they exclude all meat, fish, and poultry. Semivegetarian diets include plant foods, milk and dairy products, eggs, and some fish and poultry.

Vegans omit all meat, fish, and animal products. When I use the term "vegetarians," I will generally be referring to lacto-ovo vegetarians, whereas the term "strict vegetarians" refers to vegans.

2. Singer's arguments are developed in his *Animal Liberation*, 2d ed. (New York: Random House, 1990); Regan's in his *The Case for Animal Rights* (Berkeley: University of California Press, 1983). These arguments and the feminist arguments are discussed in detail in my book, *Animal, Vegetable or Woman? A Feminist Critique of Ethical Vegetarianism* (Albany: State University of New York Press, 2000).

3. "Adult male body" shall always refer, in this essay, to men aged twenty to fifty living in industrialized societies.

4. Regan, *The Case for Animal Rights*, p. 333.

5. Ibid., p. 337.

6. For recent examples, in addition to the studies quoted in this essay, see: A. W. Root, "Bone Strength and the Adolescent," *Adolescent Medicine* 13, no. 1 (2002): 53–72; M. K. Javaid and C. Cooper, "Prenatal and Childhood Influences of Osteoporosis," *Best Practice and Research, Clinical Endocrinology and Metabolism* 16, no. 2 (2002): 349–67; E. Seeman, "Pathogenesis of Bone Fragility in Women and Men," *Lancet* 359, no. 9320 (2002): 1841–50; North American Menopause Society, "The Role of Calcium in Peri- and Postmenopausal Women," *Consensus Opinion of the North American Menopause Society* 8, no. 2 (2001): 84–95; E. M. Lau and J. Woo, "Nutrition and Osteoporosis," *Current Opinion in Rheumatology* 10, no. 4 (1998): 368–72; and A. Hackett, I. Nathan, and I. Burgess, "Is a Vegetarian Diet Adequate for Children?" *Nutrition and Health* 12, no. 3 (1998): 189–95.

7. Johanna T. Dwyer, "Vegetarianism in Children," in *Handbook of Pediatric Nutrition*, ed. Patricia M. Queen and Carol E. Lang (Gaithersburg, MD: Aspen Publishers, 1993), p. 171.

8. Phyllis B. Acosta, "Availability of Essential Amino Acids and Nitrogen in Vegan Diets," *American Journal of Clinical Nutrition* 48 (1988): 872.

9. Johanna T. Dwyer, "Nutrition and the Adolescent," in *Textbook of Pediatric Nutrition*, 2nd ed., ed. Robert M. Suskind and Leslie Lewinter-Suskind (New York: Raven Press, 1993), p. 258.

10. Ibid., p. 257.

11. Institute of Medicine, Subcommittee on Nutritional Status and Weight Gain during Pregnancy, Subcommittee on Dietary Intakes and Nutrient Supplements during Pregnancy, Committee on Nutritional Status during Pregnancy and Lactation, Food and Nutrition Board, National Academy of Sciences, "Nutrition during Pregnancy" (Washington, DC: National Academy Press, 1990), p.18.

12. Johanna T. Dwyer, "Nutritional Consequences of Vegetarianism," *Annual Reviews in Nutrition* 11 (1991): 75–76.

13. Serge Hercberg and Pilar Galan, "Biochemical Effects of Iron Deprivation," *Acta Paediatrica Scandinavica* 361 (1989 supplement): 63–70.

14. Nevin S. Scrimshaw, "Iron Deficiency," *Scientific American* (October 1991): 50.

15. Johanna T. Dwyer and Franklin M. Loew, "Nutritional Risks of Vegan Diets to Women and Children: Are They Preventable?" *Journal of Agricultural and Environmental Ethics* 7, no. 1 (1994): 91. (An abridged version of this essay is included in this anthology.)

16. Bess Dawson-Hughes, "Calcium Supplementation and Bone Loss: A Review of Controlled Clinical Trials," *American Journal of Clinical Nutrition* 54 (1991 supplement): 274S–80S.

17. Dwyer, "Nutritional Consequences of Vegetarianism," pp. 82–83 (emphasis added).

18. Singer's view is less strict than Regan's since Singer is a utilitarian. If it could be shown that more aggregate harm would result from universal vegan diets, then he could admit some use of animal products and even some meat eating. But his view still fails on the same assumptions as Regan's, as I will show.

19. Dwyer and Loew, "Nutritional Risks of Vegan Diets to Women and Children," p. 88.

20. My thanks to Andrea Veltman of the University of Wisconsin–Madison for this possible resolution.

22 | CONTEXTUAL MORAL VEGETARIANISM
Deane Curtin

1

I f we claim to live moral lives, we must be willing to subject our most closely held principles to rigorous scrutiny. "Common sense" once told us that men are morally superior to women, and that white skin deserves moral preference over black skin. Today, "common sense" tells us that the human species is morally superior to other beings, that "animals" were made to be consumed and used by humans. Like other forms of moral prejudice, I do not think that this contemporary claim to moral privilege can be defended.

Any simple attempt to classify approaches to the question of vegetarianism and, more generally, the moral treatment of animals is likely to be contentious, but it helps my thinking to view the various approaches under three possible headings:

1. **Conservative**: This approach says that our traditional ways of thinking about the moral standing of animals in Western thought are still acceptable. Following much of medieval Christianity and the Enlightenment philosophy of Kant, "animals" are not considered to be moral ends in themselves. They can, therefore, be put to human use, either for labor or

for food. This does not permit abuse of animals, however, since, as Kant argued, animal abuse may lead to the abuse of persons who are moral ends in themselves.

2. **Liberal**: This approach agrees with the conservative approach that ethics properly focuses on the moral rights of individuals. However, it typically argues that conservatism does not go far enough. It needs to be revised to include all candidates for moral standing, not just human beings. Peter Singer and Tom Regan represent very different approaches to liberalism. Singer, a utilitarian, argues that if the ability to experience pleasure and pain can serve as a criterion of moral standing for humans, it must serve, equally, as a criterion for any being that can experience pleasure and pain. Regan, a frequent critic of Singer's utilitarianism, argues for a much more Kantian approach to the question of moral standing: any being that is a "subject of a life" has moral standing.

3. **Radical**: By a radical approach I mean any of a number of rather heterogeneous views that agree that liberalism cannot achieve a genuinely new, unbigoted, moral relationship to nonhuman beings. As an extension of conservatism, it bears the legacy of a Western, masculine-centered view of moral standing. That is, the approaches that were specifically designed to single out the moral uniqueness of men remain male-centered in morally important ways even when they are extended to nonhuman beings. By "radical," therefore, I mean literally a view that says, "We must begin again."

The view I develop here, contextual moral vegetarianism, is radical in this sense. It is an ecological feminist approach to vegetarianism, which takes *relationships* among beings as central, rather than the "rights" of isolated individuals. Although the moral standing of individuals is important for me, as it is for Singer and Regan, I am also interested in seeing "animals" in a larger ecological context, in their relations to each other and to nonanimal "others" in nature. Furthermore, I do not see the commitment to vegetarianism as a decontextualized, purely rational duty, but as a situated, feminist response to the contemporary moral landscape. The approach I propose is contextual, though not relativistic. That is, it sees vegetarianism as one situated response to a complex set of neocolonial, ecological, and feminist issues. Although it is contextualist, it is not relativist since it resolutely opposes neocolonialism, naturism, speciesism, and sexism. Finally, it is moral in the sense that, while its situatedness may include health issues, for example, it is to be understood primarily as a moral response, a way of *being* ethically in the contemporary world.

2

Contextual moral vegetarianism represents one approach to ecological feminism. Ecofeminism is the position that "there are important connections—historical, experiential, symbolic, theoretical—between the domination of women and the domination of nature."[1] It argues that the patriarchal conceptual framework that has maintained, perpetuated, and justified the oppression of women in Western culture has also, and in similar ways, maintained, perpetuated, and justified the oppression of nonhuman animals and the environment

Karen Warren has raised the issue of how to express ecofeminist moral insights in beginning to develop "ecofeminism as a feminist and environmental ethic."[2] She notes that a feminist ethic is pluralist and it may use rights language "in certain contexts and for certain purposes," but she says, and I agree, that ecofeminism "involves a shift *from* a conception of ethics as primarily a matter of rights, rules, or principles predetermined and applied in specific cases to entities viewed as competitors in the contest of moral standing" *to* an ethic that "makes a central place for values of care, love, friendship, trust, and appropriate reciprocity-values that presuppose that our relationships to others are central to our understanding of who we are."[3]

Although some ecofeminists, such as Carol J. Adams and Marti Kheel, are committed to animal rights, I am not clear from reading their works precisely what they think the connection is between ecofeminism and a rights perspective. In *The Sexual Politics of Meat: A Feminist-Vegetarian Critical Theory*, Adams says, "Not only is animal rights the theory and vegetarianism the practice, but feminism is the theory and vegetarianism is part of the practice."[4] Kheel is founder of Feminists for Animal Rights, but it is difficult to see how her approach is best characterized as a rights-based ethic. In "The Liberation of Nature: A Circular Affair," for example, Kheel criticizes Regan. Her criticisms are distinctively feminist for reasons I shall elucidate below. The question arises, then, whether the feminist insights she brings to ecological ethics are best expressed as issues of animal rights.

The classic definition of rights is in terms of a contract between independent and autonomous agents who are in a position to make claims against each other. As Joel Feinberg has said, "To have a right is to have a claim to something against someone."[5] Such rights to something also incur correlative obligations. One cannot expect to exercise the right to freedom of speech, for example, unless one respects another's right to speak freely.

The requirement of the correlativity of rights and obligations has been regarded as sufficient to deny rights to nonhumans. Other animals to whom we extend the treatment of a life without unnecessary pain may be singularly disinclined to extend the same consideration to us. Animals, on this view, are to be used according to the self-interest of human beings. If there are any moral strictures on the treatment of animals, they are based on whether certain practices offend the sensibilities of those who possess rights.

Responding, in part, to the problems of extending rights to nonhumans based on exchange value, Tom Regan, James Rachels, and others have argued that nonhuman sentient beings can have rights based on the claim to inherent value. Rachels's procedure depends on selecting clear cases in which humans can be said to have rights. He then asks whether there are relevant differences between humans and other animals that would justify refusing to ascribe the human right to the nonhuman. If there is no difference, the right is said to be possessed by all similar animals, not just humans.

In some cases, Rachels finds that there are relevant differences. A right to exercise freedom of religion cannot be extended to other animals. The right to liberty can be. With John Locke's definition of rights in mind, he asserts, "The central sense of Freedom is that in which a being is free when he or she is able to do as he or she pleases without being subject to external constraints on his or her actions."[6] The Enlightenment definition of liberty based on doing whatever one wishes, without external constraints, applies across species. The caged tiger in the zoo is not free; the tiger in the wild is.

In a similar vein, Tom Regan has argued that "Inherent value . . . belongs equally to those who are the experiencing subjects of a life."[7] He emphasizes that this is a theory about the inherent value of "individuals," and that "reason   not sentiment, not emotion—reason compels us to recognize the equal inherent value of these animals and, with this, their equal right to be treated with respect."[8]

Judged from the perspective of much in the feminist literature, this "inherent value" approach to animal ethics makes a number of assumptions that have been widely challenged:

a) It assumes, most clearly in the cases of Regan and Singer (recalling the very important differences between the two), that the project of morality is a project of reason to the exclusion of sentiment or emotion. A recurring theme in feminist epistemology has been the tendency in the Western philosophical tradition to connect reason with the mind, culture, the universal, the public domain, and the male; emotion has been associated with the body, nature, the particular, the private domain, and the female.[9] The assumption that only the appeal to the rational can be compelling replicates an ideology that has tended to oppress women.

b) As is implied in the previous point, the assumptions on which the rights project is based include a dualistic conception of personhood. This, too, has been criticized. More than one attempt has been made to offer an alternative understanding of the self based on the idea of a "unified sensibility" that integrates the rational and the emotional,[10] or that critiques the liberal idea of an autonomous self in favor of a relational understanding of self.[11]

c) It is also arguable that the rights approach is anthropocentric in that, in principle, it allows us to recognize only those rights-making characteristics that nonhuman animals have in virtue of being like humans. James Rachels has recognized, for example, that by his procedure of establishing animal rights on the basis of whether they are like humans, we are theoretically unable to recognize rights that other animals may possess uniquely.[12]

d) The rights approach is committed to the idea that equality is the central concept of morality, where "equality" is defined as "treatment neutral with respect to context." Yet this focus on equality apart from context allows for the idea that reverse discrimination is on a par with discrimination. It treats moral claims apart from the dialectic of oppressor and oppressed.

e) At a more intuitive level, my concern about liberalism is that it is simply too inflexible to act as a public vegetarian ethic. What would liberalism say, for example, about the question of whether the Arctic Ihalmiut people are morally compelled to practice a vegetarian diet? Farming is difficult in the Arctic. Furthermore, if we believe that eating locally makes sense in a globalized food economy, eating locally seems to conflict in this case with the obligation to be a vegetarian.

f) There is also a well-known connection between vegetarianism and certain health disorders in women. One of the first signs of anorexia nervosa, for example, is a shift to a vegetarian diet. I cannot, in good conscience, recommend a vegetarian diet to all women without knowing a good deal about their psychological and social well-being.

All this suggests, then, that liberalism, as applied to the treatment of animals, is not very promising for many feminists. If one accepts that there is a deep ideological connection between the oppression of nature and the oppression of women in Western culture, one must look to an entirely different alternative than the one offered by philosophers of animal rights.

Considerations such as these lead me to look beyond liberalism to a new, radical approach to our treatment of other animals. A source for much of the feminist literature on women's psychological and moral development is Carol Gilligan's *In a Different Voice*.[13] Her work, in turn, was developed partly in response to Lawrence Kohlberg's cognitive model of moral development, which stresses that a sense of personal autonomy, in which the self is clearly differentiated from others, is the basis of moral development. Kohlberg's autonomy requirement is consistent with classical rights-based moral theory.

Kohlberg's Kantian conception of ethics has been presented by philosophers and psychologists as morality per se. But Gilligan's research strongly suggests that it accurately depicts only the typical goal of a (Western) man's moral development. In ordering the development into moral personhood as the movement from interdependence to independence, this model prioritizes men's typical development over women's.

A simple illustration of the difference can be seen in a conflict that arises during a baseball game. Boys, according to Gilligan's model, would tend to resolve the conflict by appeal to a formalistic hierarchy of impersonal rules. Rules would be used to resolve conflict impersonally in such a way that the game can go on, and each player's autonomy is maintained. Girls, faced with the same conflict, would tend to resolve it contextually and interpersonally, referring not to rules, but to relationships. Having no appeal to an impersonal decision procedure, girls would often prefer to quit the game than risk rupture in a relationship.

Gilligan argues, then, that male and female conceptions of personhood and morality differ. Whereas the male model is one of autonomy and rights, the female model is one of interdependence, personal relationships, and caring. She says, "The morality of rights differs from the morality of responsibility in its emphasis on separation rather than connection, in its consideration of the individual rather than the relationship as primary."[14]

Gilligan's research provides evidence that there is a coherent alternative to the rights model of ethics. However, without further development into a political dimension, I believe Gilligan's research may be turned against feminist objectives. In contrast to the rights model, which seeks to cordon off "my" territory over which I have control, the caring for model may often suggest that the interests of others should sometimes come before one's own, that knowing what to do in a particular situation requires empathetic projection into another's life. Putting the other in front of oneself can easily be abused. The wife who selflessly cares for her husband, who cares only about himself, is only too well-known.

The injunction to care must be understood as part of a radical political agenda that allows for development of contexts in which caring for can be nonabusive. It should claim that the relational sense of self, the willingness to empathetically enter into the world of others and care for them, can be expanded and developed as a matter of character so that it may include those outside the "normal" circle of caring for.

If one danger of Gilligan's research is that it can be privatized, a second concern is that it can be localized. Caring for resists the claim that the moral project depends on a criterion of abstract, purely rational universalizability, and insists that it depends on special, contextual relationships. This might be, and has been, taken to mean that we should care for the homeless only if our daughter or son happens to be homeless. Or, it might mean that persons in dominant countries should feel no need to care for persons in dominated countries. Or, it might mean that we should care for only those of the same species.

Ecofeminism is in a position to encourage the development of caring for to relationships with nature, or, better, to point out that there is no categorical way of distinguishing caring for persons from caring for nature. To take only a single example among many, one of the sources of the oppression of women in "developing" countries is that deforestation has a disproportionate effect on women whose responsibilities include food preparation. A common sight in these countries is village women walking farther every year in search of safe water and fuel for food. In such contexts, the destruction of the environment is a source of women's oppression.

Ecofeminism seeks not only to understand the condition of women, but also to use that understanding to liberate women and nature from the structures of oppression. In achieving a new sense of relatedness of the kind that ecofeminism can provide, one enters into caring for relationships that were not available earlier. One may come to see, for example, that the white, middle-class American woman's typical situation is connected with—though not identical to—the condition of women in oppressed countries. Moreover, the caring for model does not require that those we care for are "equal" to us. Neither does it assume they are not equal. It is based on the capacity to care, not the criterion of equality.

3

On the face of it, the introduction of this expanded conception of caring for to the topic of how nonhuman animals ought to be treated seems quite intuitive. Humans do care very deeply for certain animals: humans may grieve the loss of a pet in ways that are very much like grieving for the loss of a human companion. One may care for a dog by providing it with safe water, healthful food, and treatment of its wounds, and one may miss it when it disappears for several days.

These relationships are often quite selfless. We may get something in return, as with any relationship, but that is not the reason we enter into them. They are not intended to be reciprocal; we often tend to give more than we get. Such relationships of caring for can be expanded through coming to see the contemporary world through feminist eyes.

More than the intuitive plausibility of the approach, it seems to me there are some clear advantages that the caring for model has over the rights model as an approach to the problem of the treatment of animals.

a) In stressing the claim to the autonomy of reason made for the rights model, advocates of the model stress precisely what distinguishes some humans from other animals. By contrast, in stressing our deep sense of embodiment and the interplay between emotion and cognitive skills, the caring for approach stresses our relatedness to (though not identity with) other animals. It gives a convincing account of why we should care for other animals grounded in our own "nature" that is lacking in the picture presented in the rights model.

b) The formalistic approach of the animal rights or animal liberation theorist, which tries to extend rights to nonhumans on the grounds that other animals are sufficiently similar to us, depends on the claim that "all animals are equal." For example, Peter Singer has said, "Ethics takes a universal point of view. . . . Ethics requires us to go beyond 'I' and 'you' to the universal law, the universalizable judgment."[15]

The caring for approach does not require abstract equality; in fact, it is based on relationships that need not be equal, or even reciprocal. The compassion that a mother feels for her injured child in no way rests on a judgment of equality. It rests on a simple act of compassion for the suffering of a loved one. Caring for does not require that we treat nonhuman animals in the same way as we treat humans; it does not even require that we treat all human beings in the same way. For example, it may be that a dog with a severely broken leg may be mercifully killed, whereas one would not, one hopes, suggest that for a human being. The relevant difference may simply be that a dog cannot go through rehabilitation in the way that a human being can.

The conceptual core of the caring for approach to animals does not rest on any universalized prescriptions. It grows out of the context of caring for beings that suffer, particularly for beings that suffer needlessly. Most of our treatment of animals—and it has been an enduring contribution of the animal rights movement to have forcefully pointed this out—is senselessly brutal and entirely avoidable. No one can tour a modern stockyard with senses open to the experience without suffering pangs of moral doubt. It is beyond question, for example, that hogs suffer terribly before they are killed. No one can really know much about the "modern" genetically engineered hog or cow without beginning to question whether one wants to continue to be a consumer of these "products." Again, the core intuition is not that a cow is equal—or unequal—to us; it is that our practices are in gruesome conflict with compassion for beings that suffer needlessly.

Since contextual moral vegetarianism is distinct from liberal approaches because of its ecological (relational) commitments, critics often question whether we should be as concerned about killing plants for food as we are about killing animals. My answer is that we should be concerned morally about killing plants, just so we recognize that the context is different. One of the special moral concerns about killing animals for food is that it causes avoidable pain and suffering. It is possible to suggest that plants experience "pain" when they are harvested, but I think this stretches any real meaning of the word "pain" to the breaking point. Recognition of diversity should bar traditional liberal, extensionist arguments of this sort: we ought to grant plant rights because they are like already recognized animal rights.

If plants are different from animals, however, there may still be persuasive reasons to care for plants, as well as the ecosystems that sustain them.

Although I will not get into these arguments here, I believe we should eat locally, and organically, if possible. Because I care about healthy ecosystems, I oppose industrial farming.

Finally, the contextual approach offers a clear answer to the problem of predation. We are often asked, "Why should human beings commit to a less violent, vegetarian life when other animals would kill us for food?" There are important differences between a wolf and a human being. Wolves are carnivores; they cannot survive without meat. (We should note that their diet almost never includes human beings.) Humans, by contrast, are omnivores; we can survive, and thrive, without eating meat. If we have a choice of diet, without endangering our health, then we have an obligation to defend our choices. Vegetarianism is a moral issue for humans in a way that it cannot be for carnivores.

Another difference between the wolf and the human is that, as far as we know, wolves are not moral agents, whereas human beings are. The context of being an adult human involves the ability to anticipate, and to be held responsible for, our actions. This is not true of adult wolves. Although contextual moral vegetarianism holds that both wolves and humans are *morally considerable*, only human beings are *moral agents*. We must consider wolves morally, even if they cannot reciprocate. The same is true of the ways competent human adults must treat other human beings if they are not able to govern their own moral lives.

4

Contextual moral vegetarianism is a measured response to the injunction to care in the contemporary world. Granted, living sometimes unavoidably inflicts pain on others. But in the case of killing animals for human consumption, this practice inflicts pain that is almost always completely unnecessary and avoidable. The injunction to care for, considered as an issue of moral and political development, should be understood to include the injunction to eliminate needless suffering wherever possible. Caring for urges us to move in the *direction* of less violence, even if perfect nonviolence may not be achievable.

We should take seriously the old saying, "we are what we eat." A unified sensibility, which regards our mental and physical aspects as equally "ourselves," cannot simply dismiss what happens to our bodies as accidental to our selves. It is an old point in moral theory that an action performed does not simply have its effect on the recipient alone. When I tell a lie to harm someone, I may succeed in harming that person, but I also harm my character by becoming the sort of person who would tell a lie. I harm myself just as much as, and quite possibly more than, the other.

We have been taught by our cultural dualism not to think about the effect of what we eat on our concept of personhood. But is it too strong to say that, in eating animals when it is completely avoidable, we—our bodies—quite literally become graveyards for animal flesh? Again, I think there are other perfectly legitimate responses to taking seriously the idea that we are what we eat. But to simply neglect the maxim, as we are encouraged to do by our cultural dualism, is to risk one's health, one's person.

Thus far, my remarks in favor of an embodied, contextual, feminist vegetarianism have paralleled the concerns of liberal vegetarians in the sense that they encourage moral concern of sentient others. However, as I said in initially describing contextual moral vegetarianism, the view I am proposing goes beyond care for individuals. It is, at its core, an ecological vegetarianism. As I have contended elsewhere,[16] a contemporary understanding of the reality of food consumption and production reveals that these ecological issues are also feminist and neocolonial issues. The process of globalization is, at its very heart, about transformation of sustainable, local relationships to food into a global system of industrialized food production. Since women are mainly responsible for sustainable, local land relationships, it is women who most directly suffer from the globalization of food.

The green revolution, which began in the 1950s, was a system through which agriculture was industrialized in order to plant genetically engineered "miracle crops" of wheat, rice, and other important foods. Enormous amounts of fertilizer were required to gain increased crop yields from these new seeds. In turn, fertilizer required constant access to ample water supplies and irrigation. In most parts of the world, regular access to water required mega-dam projects. In short, the infrastructure of the green revolution favored wealthy farmers who were willing to engage in plant monoculture to provide the cheapest export crops. Women and their families were displaced from traditional relationships to land. In a system that favored men for wage-labor jobs, women and children were literally left behind, cut off from the land, when men migrated to cities to find work. In the contemporary world, food production is an ecofeminist issue.

My point is that the issue of moral vegetarianism cannot be separated from other feminist ecological issues. The question I raise, therefore, is how to respond to the reality of contemporary food production from the context of a first-world ecological feminist. That is, when people have been displaced and are malnourished, it is morally repugnant to insist that they practice vegetarian diets, just as it is morally repugnant to insist that the Ihalmiut become farmers. The question of vegetarianism as a moral choice in the contemporary world becomes urgent for those of us who have the power to choose. It is incumbent upon those of us in the first world, who have been the beneficiaries of centuries of economic colonialism, to respond in a mindful, caring way to our positions of privilege. Given that we are the products of systemic violence,[17] it is especially incumbent upon us to deliberately reduce violence in our lives, most particularly unnecessary violence.

Contextual moral vegetarianism, I suggest, is one response to the context many of us find ourselves in, a neocolonial world in which the rich are getting richer and the poor poorer. Let me conclude with one concrete example, which shows the complexity of our present moral situation. Most of us are familiar with some aspects of the crisis in the Amazon River basin: deforestation, massive environmental destruction due to oil spills, cattle production on land that is poorly suited to intensive livestock operations, displacement of indigenous peoples. We know that most of the cattle farms produce beef for first-world fast food restaurants, and cheap beef at supermarkets that advertise low prices. One of the reasons for committing to contextual moral vegetarianism is that it removes one from the cycle of violence in the Amazon. Knowing what is happening in the Amazon should also encourage us to shop mindfully from local farmers. As a contextual moral vegetarian, however, I do not focus simply on the beef production in the Amazon, apart from its context. For example, a relatively new problem is the massive shift to industrial agriculture in the Amazon to produce soybeans for animal feed. As with any system of food monoculture, Amazonian soybeans are sprayed with chemicals, in this case Roundup-Ready pesticides made by Monsanto. In context, it is just as important to express moral concern for soybean production as it is to boycott Amazon beef.

Contextual moral vegetarianism is in a position to insist that the oppression of women, the oppression of the environment, and the oppressive treatment of nonhuman animals are deeply linked. It is also in a position to offer a contextual ethic that promises liberation from these connected forms of oppression.

NOTES

1. Karen Warren, "The Power and Promise of Ecological Feminism," *Journal of Environmental Ethics* 12 (Summer 1990): 126.

2. Ibid., p. 138.

3. Ibid., pp. 141 and 143.

4. Carol J. Adams, *The Sexual Politics of Meat: A Feminist-Vegetarian Critical Theory* (New York: Continuum, 1989), p. 167.

5. Joel Feinberg, "The Rights of Animals and Unborn Generations," in *Responsibilities to Other Generations*, ed. Ernest Partridge (Amherst, NY: Prometheus Books, 1980), p. 139.

6. James Rachels, "Why Animals Have a Right to Liberty," in *Animal Rights and Human Obligations*, ed. Tom Regan and Peter Singer (Englewood Cliffs, NJ: Prentice Hall, 1989), p. 125.

7. Ibid., p. 112.

8. Ibid., p. 113.

9. See Allison M. Jaggar, "Love and Knowledge: Emotion in Feminist Epistemology," in *Gender/Body/Knowledge: Feminist Reconstructions of Being and Knowing*, ed. Alison M. Jaggar and Susan R. Bordo (New Brunswick, NJ: Rutgers University Press, 1989).

10. Marti Kheel, "The Liberation of Nature: A Circular Affair," *Environmental Ethics* 7 (1985): 141–49.

11. Maria Lugones, "Playfulness, 'World'-Traveling, and Loving Perception," *Hypatia* 2, no. 2 (1987): 14–17.

12. Rachels, "Why Animals Have a Right to Liberty," p. 124.

13. Carol Gilligan, *In a Different Voice: Psychological Theory and Women's Development* (Cambridge, MA: Harvard University Press, 1982).

14. Ibid., p. 19.

15. Peter Singer, *Practical Ethics* (Cambridge: Cambridge University Press, 1979), p. 11.

16. See Deane Curtin, *Chinnagounder's Challenge: The Question of Ecological Citizenship* (Bloomington: Indiana University Press, 1999).

17. Ibid., p. 29.

EMPATHY AND VEGETARIAN COMMITMENTS

23 | **Lori Gruen**

I

Feminist activists and theorists have varied and complicated responses to the moral demand for vegetarianism. For some feminists, the very idea that there should be another restriction on what women do raises hackles. Since vegetarianism is viewed as a restriction on eating, in cultures like our own—in which beauty norms, a glorification of slimness, and eating disorders have significant negative impacts on women, particularly young women—moral arguments against the consumption of meat are met with suspicion, at best. Still other feminists are concerned about the way that universal arguments for vegetarianism fail to adequately take into account traditional values in cultures other than those from which demands for vegetarianism are made. The worries here are that moral requirements that insist that people refrain from eating meat represent a form of value imperialism or cultural chauvinism.[1] At least one feminist has suggested that arguments for ethical vegetarianism are based on a white male health norm and relegate women to a moral underclass. Women may be excused from moral requirements to refrain from meat consumption because our bodies are supposedly weaker, but being excused in this way puts women in a position of moral inferiority.[2] Some feminists who adhere to what has been called "an ethics of care" have argued that because non-human animals are not able to enter into reciprocal relations with us, we have no moral obligation to become vegetarians.[3] And some feminists working for environmental and economic justice see the demand for vegetarianism as elitist, classist, and racist and argue that such a demand represents a potential hindrance to building meaningful alliances across class and race lines.[4]

A number of feminists have attempted to address these important concerns while nonetheless maintaining a commitment to vegetarianism.[5] These feminists have argued, among other things, that there are important conceptual and material links among racism, classism, sexism, and speciesism; that cultural traditions often provide the institutional structures for male domination and thus are the appropriate targets of criticism; and that meat eating itself is a form of patriarchal domination and by consuming animal bodies, women are implicitly supporting their own domination. For these feminists, vegetarianism is one part of a larger project to dismantle the structures of oppression. Feminists should, these scholars and activists maintain, be vegetarians.

Despite how compelling feminist arguments for vegetarianism are in the abstract, many feminists have not been convinced that vegetarianism, even contextual vegetarianism,[6] is an important feminist philosophical and practical commitment. In this essay I want to explore this reluctance to commit to vegetarianism. I will start by speculating about what may be a cause of this reluctance—namely the alienating nature of the demand for vegetarianism. Arguments for vegetarianism have tended to appear as external constraints on behavior. The ethical requirement works from the outside-in. Despite allowing for the context in which the agent may find herself, for example that she may have nutritional needs that make a vegetarian diet potentially harmful to her health or that in her culture and climate a vegetarian diet is close to impossible to adopt, the demand does not arise from the agent herself. This distance may be an implicit source of resistance to vegetarianism.[7] I will then offer an alternative argument in favor of contextual vegetarianism that minimizes this alienation by locating the force and authority of the ethical demand within the agent. Here I will build on feminist vegetarian arguments in a largely Humean vein, drawing on the experiences of sympathy, empathy, and compassion.[8]

II

The standard arguments for vegetarianism, arguments that are most commonly associated with Tom Regan and Peter Singer, maintain that there is no morally relevant distinction between human and nonhuman animals that can justify humans raising and slaughtering nonhumans for food. Regan argues that we should not focus on the differences between humans and nonhumans but the similarities. Because both humans and nonhumans are individually experiencing subjects-of-a-life who have an individual welfare that matters to them regardless of what others might think, there is no morally important difference between them. Regan argues that subjects-of-a-life "want and prefer things, believe and feel things, recall and expect things. And all these dimensions of our life, including our pleasure and pain, our enjoyment and suffering, our satisfaction and frustration, our continued existence or our untimely death—all make a difference to the quality of our life as lived, as experienced, by us as individuals. As the same is true of . . . animals . . . they too must be viewed as the experiencing subjects-of-a-life, with inherent value of their own."[9] For Singer, because animals used for food are beings that can suffer and who have an interest in not suffering, we are no more justified in violating their interests than we are in violating the like interests of any being who has such interests. To confine, control, manipulate, transport, and ultimately slaughter animals for food in contexts in which there are other foods available is to disregard their morally important interests in ways that cannot be justified.[10] By carefully reasoning about the capacities that matter morally—being a subject-of-a-life, in Regan's case, or being an individual who has interests and can suffer, in Singer's case—and by carefully documenting the ways that modern, first-world food production disrespects animals and violates their rights or interests, both philosophers conclude that vegetarianism is the only morally justified option. Both also maintain that it is through reason, not appeals to emotion, by which they come to this conclusion.

Many have suggested that this focus on reason continues a tradition that problematically separates reason from emotion, thought from feeling. Philosophical and psychological investigations into the nature of emotion suggest that a moral psychology that attempts to uphold the dichotomy between reason, and the cognitive capacities with which it is associated, and emotion, which is assumed to be noncognitive, is mistaken.[11] Feminists have gone further and suggested that this dichotomy represents a value dualism, where appeals to reason are thought to be more important or more legitimate than those based on emotion or feeling. This value dualism is one of the central political tools by which women, who are supposedly less rational and more emotional than men, are thought to be less important and less legitimate and thus inferior to men. In addition, some feminists have argued that women, people of color, nonheterosexuals, and others who are associated with passion and emotion are linked to animals, a linkage that further undermines all the inferior others' attempts to have their interests considered equally, to be valued appropriately, or to be seen as worthy of respect. This value dualism is part of what has been called a "logic

of domination" that operates to reinforce sexism and other forms of prejudicial oppression and supports the exploitation of nonhuman animals.

Interestingly, both the standard arguments that underlie a moral commitment to vegetarianism and the feminist arguments that are meant as
responses to these arguments have features in common, which, I believe,
may contribute to the resistance to vegetarianism that some feminists
express. Both types of arguments focus on similarity or sameness. Singer
and Regan are interested in identifying those features that nonhumans
share with humans. Pigs are highly sensitive and intelligent animals and
these capacities are not valued when pigs are confined in sowing pens,
denied access to fresh air, water, and contact with their offspring, and eventually slaughtered. Chickens have elaborate social systems that are con-
founded when they are forced to live in confined spaces with thousands of
other birds. And, of course, the billions of animals who are slaughtered for
food each year in the United States are creatures that can and do suffer. We
share these capacities and probably others with them, and since we value
our intelligence, our relative freedom, our ability to navigate complex
social terrain, and our desires to live free from suffering, we should also
value these things in nonhuman animals. The feminist arguments also
highlight similarities, but usually the similarities are between attitudes
toward and treatment of groups, rather than individuals. Women, people
of color, nonheterosexuals, and nonhuman animals are all thought to be
lower in the hierarchy than white, heterosexual, able-bodied human men.
The conceptual tools and institutional structures that maintain the status of
these men are employed against women and animals. Oppression of any of
these groups is thus linked, and if one is opposed to sexism, racism, heterosexism, etc., she should also oppose speciesism. The best way to oppose
speciesism is to become vegetarian, so feminists should be vegetarian.

Yet this focus on similarity tends to obscure the important differences
between individuals and between groups. Comparisons cut in both direc-
tions. From one perspective making connections between the oppression
of women or African Americans and the treatment of animals, or between
the Nazi holocaust and factory farming, or between mentally disabled
humans ("marginal cases") and animals can be understood as a way of
undervaluing the former in order to elevate the latter. In addition to being
conceptually problematic, such comparisons can have chilling political
consequences as potential alliances are often undermined.[12] By focusing
on similarities among individuals, groups, or events one often obscures
morally salient differences. Consider the widespread use of the term "rape"
to describe environmental destruction. In describing clear-cutting as the
rape of a forest, the very real trauma that women who are raped must live
with when they survive the experience is ignored. This trauma and the
anger, fear, doubt, and other emotions that rape survivors have to deal with

are not—indeed, cannot be—experienced by trees. When rape is used to describe anything violent and horrible, the particular violence and horror of a man raping a woman is obscured.[13] Feminist activism and scholarship has warned of the dangers lurking in categorical generalizations—the term "woman" although generally meant to include all females, often represents the particular perspective of some females, those who are white, hetero-sexual, middle-class, able-bodied, and otherwise relatively privileged. In making claims about "women" and "animals" or in focusing on similari-ties between otherwise quite different individuals, one runs the risk of engaging in problematic overgeneralizations. This sort of generalizing appears to exclude some individuals who don't recognize themselves in the description. If a moral or political commitment is spelled out in terms of similarities that miss differences, then many will find such commitments alienating. One of the important lessons that feminists have learned from the criticisms raised of these generalizations is how to think harder about understanding "difference" while maintaining the ability to make mean-ingful normative claims that do not reduce to a collection of particular atti-tudes and experiences.

One of the most important capacities for understanding and respecting difference is the capacity to empathize. Empathy is an ability that a person with a distinct self concept has to reflectively engage with the situation of another. It is important that an empathetic person has a distinct self so when she is imaginatively engaging with the other, she doesn't believe her-self to be in the other's situation. Only certain beings have this ability, those who are able to make a distinction between self and other. While individuals without distinctive self concepts often behave as if they are empathizing—they may, for example, respond to the pain or fear or joy that they see others experiencing—this reaction is different than what I am calling empathy. Rather it involves what has been called "emotional conta-gion" and it involves the unreflective perception of another's emotional or mental state, and a spontaneous reaction to it. Empathy, on the other hand, requires reflection.

Empathy is different from the related phenomena called sympathy. Sympathy involves maintaining one's own attitudes and preferences and adding to them a concern for another. Sympathy for another is felt from the outside, the third-person perspective. I can feel sympathy for another's plight, even pity, but remain rather removed from that plight. Sympathy as I am understanding it, more than empathy, has the potential for being con-descending, or paternalistic. Because one maintains one's own attitudes, beliefs, even prejudices, one can sympathize with another when sympathy isn't called for. Sympathy, understood in this way, also can be viewed as another form of distance. Empathy, on the other hand, requires some engagement with and understanding of the circumstances of the other.

Empathy is thus more suited to situations in which there are significant differences between the empathizer and those with whom she is empathizing. And empathy has more grip than sympathy; it packs a greater motivational punch. Here are some examples of what I think of as empathetic responses:

> The production-line maintenance of animals . . . is without a doubt one of the darkest and most shameful chapters in human culture. If you have ever stood before a stable where animals are being fattened and have heard hundreds of calves bleating, if you can understand the calf's cry for help, then you will have had enough of those people who derive profit from it.[14]

Or consider these remarks from a nineteen-year-old woman working on a farm as part of a college course:

> The first time I went into the slaughter room I had just haltered and pulled a steer into the waiting line. I could tell that the steer sensed what was going to happen to him. He was doing anything to get away. Then when I walked to the slaughter room I was amazed at the amount of blood. It was an awful feeling to look at that steer with its eyes open and his feet pointing up, so I had to look at the ceiling. Mr. ——— told me to cut off the head with a saw. I couldn't do it so I left. I guess slaughtering affects me more than the usual person because I raised calves for 4-H at home and became quite attached to them—but I don't butcher them.[15]

These reactions suggest that experiencing empathy for different others requires attentiveness to their experiences as well as reflection on the particular features of the situation, for example, that people profit from the animals' suffering, that having an attachment to some animal can provide a connection to another animal to whom one is not similarly attached. However, many of us are not in situations in which we bear witness to the pain of animals. We are usually at some distance from the immediate pain, distress, fear, confusion, and suffering of others. Few of us look into animals' eyes as we slit their throats. So how, from our comfortable distance, do we develop empathy for these animals that will motivate a commitment to contextual vegetarianism? One way for this to happen is to start from our particular experiences in particular contexts with nonhuman others, as the young woman did with the 4-H calves. Chris Cuomo and I have identified interspecies relationships and friendships as particularly rich sites of information for bridging distance across difference.[16] The bonds we develop with the nonhumans in our lives require us to hone our empathetic awareness. We simply cannot know what a nonhuman needs or wants, what he may be nervous about, when he is annoyed or content, without such an awareness. Because nonhumans cannot explicitly tell us what is in their interests, we must develop skills to understand them across our differences. These particular experiences are important opportunities for developing empathy that can help us in navigating other contexts in which our moral responses are required. Once we empathize with the non-humans with whom we have developed friendships, it becomes easier to empathize with others.

Empathetic engagement with different others is a form of moral attention that not only brings into focus the claims that nonhumans make on us but also helps to shift our moral attention. Features of a particular situation that may be obscured if we were simply to reason abstractly about our duties to animals or their rights come to the fore. When we begin to identify non-human animals as worthy of our moral attention because they are beings with whom we can empathize, they can no longer be seen merely as food. They are creatures with whom we share a way of being in the world. Seen from this perspective, the demand for moral vegetarianism comes from within us. It is not some abstract requirement deduced through careful argumentation. If we desire to see the world better, to understand our reactions to particular situations, and to reflect on the meaning of those reactions, then we cannot help but accept contextual vegetarianism.

III

These musings on a possible source of resistance to vegetarianism and my view of the importance of empathetic engagement with creatures different from ourselves are not meant to detract from the power of feminist vegetarian arguments or, for that matter, the standard arguments for vegetarianism where either is compatible with the recognition of the importance of empathetic engagement with nonhuman animals. When billions of animals are still being born to be slaughtered, when the environment is being destroyed by agribusiness, when maldistribution of food leads to the starvation of thousands of children around the world, when the activities of the rich and powerful cause untold suffering to marginalized peoples and animals, one may sensibly be pragmatic. There are many reasons to think hard about what one is contributing to when purchasing the products of modern factory farming and many reasons to stop eating animals.

NOTES

1. The earliest discussion of the topic of cultural imperialism and vegetarianism I am aware of is Jane Meyerding's "Feminist Criticism and Cultural Imperialism," in *The Animals' Agenda* (November/December 1982). Chris Cuomo and I

touch on the topic in "On Puppies and Pussies: Animals, Intimacy, and Moral Distance" in *Daring to Be Good: Essays in Feminist Ethico-Politics*, ed. Bat-Ami Bar On et al. (New York: Routledge, 1998), p. 140.

2. This line of thinking has been developed by Kathryn George. There are a number of deep problems with her attempt to reject vegetarianism from a feminist perspective. First, she misrepresents what I call the standard arguments for vegetarianism developed by Tom Regan and Peter Singer. While both Regan and Singer make arguments for vegetarianism, George's claim that these arguments relegate women to a moral underclass by granting women exemptions from moral rules is based on objections to views that Regan, and particularly Singer, simply do not hold. Importantly, the utilitarian argument that addresses animal suffering in meat production is not, strictly speaking, an argument for vegetarianism. If an animal lived a happy life and was painlessly killed and then eaten by people who would otherwise suffer hunger or malnutrition by not eating the animal, then painlessly killing and eating the animal would be the morally justified thing to do. It would not be an exception to the rule; it would be precisely what the theory dictates. In many parts of the world where economic, cultural, or climatic conditions make it virtually impossible for people to sustain themselves on plant-based diets, killing and eating animals that previously led relatively unconstrained lives and are painlessly killed, would not be morally objectionable. The same would hold for individuals who, for dietary reasons, would be risking their own suffering if they did not eat animals. Singer's utilitarian position can thus avoid both the charges of cultural chauvinism and moralism and George's attempt to paint this aspect of it with an antifeminist brush. Second, there are interesting questions about whether in fact women, as a group, have a greater dietary need to eat animals. In the May 1994 issue of the *American Journal of Clinical Nutrition* there is a symposium reporting the numerous health benefits of a vegetarian diet for women, children, and men of various ethnic and racial backgrounds, data that directly contradict George's claims. George wants to point out that nutritional research that equates women's bodies with men's bodies is mistaken. This is an important insight, and nutritionists and others in the medical community have become increasingly aware of this. However, one woman's body and nutritional needs are often different than another's. To lump all women together as if they had the same body "ideal" and suggest that women should not be vegetarian based on this is to be engaged in the same problematic reasoning that George accuses others of. Third, George consistently has ignored the richness and complexity of feminist arguments for vegetarianism. For a look at an early set of debates between George and Carol Adams, Josephine Donovan, Greta Gaard, and me, see *Signs* 21, no. 1 (Autumn 1995): 221–61.

3. This is the view of Nel Noddings, *Caring: A Feminine Approach to Ethics and Moral Education* (Berkeley: University of California Press, 1984). For an alternative ethic of care that does include nonhumans, see Deane Curtin, "Toward an Ecological Ethics of Care," *Hypatia* 6, no. 1 (1991).

4. See, for example, Noel Sturgeon, *Ecofeminist Natures: Race, Gender, Feminist Theory, and Political Action* (New York: Routledge, 1997).

5. See the work of Carol Adams, Lynda Birke, Deane Curtin, Josephine Donovan, Greta Gaard, Ronnie Zoe Hawkins, Marti Kheel, Biran Luke, Deborah

Slicer, and myself, for example. For a comprehensive review, see Greta Gaard, "Vegetarian Ecofeminism: A Review Essay," *Frontiers: A Journal of Women Studies* 23, no. 3 (2002): 117–46.

6. This is a term originally developed by Deane Curtin, "Toward an Ecological Ethics of Care." Greta Gaard and I develop the idea in "Ecofeminism: Toward Global Justice and Planetary Health," *Society and Nature* 2, no. 1 (1993).

7. This is not meant to be an empirical claim, but a philosophical one.

8. For an excellent example of this sort of work, see Josephine Donovan, "Attention to Suffering: Sympathy as a Basis for Ethical Treatment of Animals," in *Beyond Animal Rights: A Feminist Caring Ethics for the Treatment of Animals*, ed. Josephine Donovan and Carol Adams (New York: Continuum, 1996). See also the other essays in that volume.

9. Tom Regan, "The Case for Animal Rights," in *In Defense of Animals*, ed. Peter Singer (Oxford: Basil Blackwell, 1985).

10. Peter Singer, *Animal Liberation*, 2nd ed. (New York: New York Review of Books, 1990).

11. Feminist theorists as well as not explicitly feminist philosophers, neuroscientists, psychologists, and others have made convincing arguments in support of this view of emotion.

12. In my "Dismantling Oppression: An Analysis of the Connection between Women and Animals," in *Ecofeminism: Women, Animals, Nature*, ed. Greta Gaard (Philadelphia: Temple University Press, 1993), I discuss an experience I had with a group of radical feminists opposed to pornography. They were displaying a picture of a woman in a meat grinder, and I approached them to discuss the parallels between the oppression of women and the treatment of animals in factory farming; they were appalled at the comparison.

13. I discuss this topic in "Thought on Exclusion and Difference: A response to "On Women, Animals, and Nature," in *American Philosophical Association Newsletter on Feminism and Philosophy* 91, no. 1 (Spring 1992): 78–81.

14. Konrad Lorenz, *On Life and Living* (New York: St. Martin's, 1988), p. 113, cited in Brian Luke, "Justice, Caring, and Animal Liberation," in *Beyond Animal Rights*, ed. Donovan and Adams, p. 83. Though Luke uses the term "sympathy" to describe these forms of "direct responsiveness," I think they are more appropriately instances of empathy, as I am using the term.

15. Cited in Luke, ibid., p. 82.

16. Cuomo and Gruen, "On Puppies and Pussies."

Section Six

THE ENVIRONMENTAL DEBATE OVER RESPECTING PREDATORY NATURE AND PROTECTING ANIMALS

24 | BAMBI LOVERS VERSUS TREE HUGGERS
Ned Hettinger

This essay extends Holmes Rolston's environmental ethics without undermining his acceptance of certain types of meat eating and hunting.[1] As the quintessential natural process, carnivorous predation is rightfully valued and respected by environmentalists such as Rolston. By condemning human participation in predation, animal activists risk hating nature. The challenge for animal activists is to show that one can properly appreciate natural predation while consistently and plausibly objecting to human participation in it.

A UNIQUE GOAL OF MEAT EATING AND HUNTING

Do meat eaters and hunters have legitimate goals that are not achievable through vegetarianism or wildlife photography? Holmes Rolston believes that there can be positive values in the lives of hunters and meat eaters that are lacking in the lives of vegetarians and nonhunters. "Meat eaters," Rolston has suggested, "know their ecology and natural history in a way that vegetarians do not. . . . I'm not sure a vegetarian even understands the way

This essay is a shortened version of "Valuing Predation in Rolston's Environmental Ethics: Bambi Lovers versus Tree Huggers," *Environmental Ethics* 16, no. 1 (Spring 1994): 3–20.

the world is built."[2] Eating meat involves "participating in the logic and biology of one's ecosystem."[3] Predation is a fundamental feature of the natural world manifest in the lives of meat eaters and hunters.

An advocate of vegetarianism might wonder why we cannot equally well participate in "the logic of ecology" by mimicking herbivores? After all, herbivores are also predators: they exploit other life to nourish their own. Is there special value in mimicking predation on animal life? Is it better to be like a falcon, a shark, or a bear than like a goose, an anchovy, or a gorilla? Are the stealth and cunning of some carnivores "greater ecological achievements" than the alertness of some herbivores? If we assume that predators at higher trophic levels are of greater intrinsic value, then mimicking carnivores rather than herbivores is to participate in the logic of ecology at an elevated and more sophisticated level. Additionally, since humans have evolved as omnivores (i.e., we have the capacity to be nourished by both plants and animals), meat eating and hunting are truer to our *own* ecological history than is a vegetarian abstinence from killing and consuming animal life.

Furthermore, Rolston thinks that we would not have evolved into human beings without the evolution of the human mind and hand to hunt; if our ancestors had remained herbivores, he suggests, there would have been no human culture.[4] Thus by hunting and eating meat, one can embrace human nature by participating in a process that made us what we are. To reject our predatory history and still try to value the human being isolates a product from its essential historical genesis. One can imagine beings very much like us who came into existence without a predatory past. But if we assume that the basic features of a species' evolutionary history are essential to what that species is, then these beings would not be human. Viewed as responses to openings in ecological resource relationships ("niche fillers"), species (including *Homo sapiens*) are essentially tied to their evolutionary history.

Rolston repeatedly insists that the products and processes of natural history are interrelated in such a way that it is inappropriate to value the products without valuing their essential generative processes. For Rolston, valuing species really involves valuing the generative process of speciation. One reason to value ecosystems is that they are the creative context that produces the products we value (species and individuals). Individuals and species are what they are only in their ecosystems (a lion in a cage is hardly the same creature). When a process that produces a product is essential to *understanding* what that product is, one cannot consistently affirm the value of the product while denying the value of the process that created it.[5] One might as well try to value the culture of Native American plains tribes while rejecting their tradition of killing buffalo for food, clothing, and shelter.

The behavior of meat eaters and hunters can affirm dimensions of value in nature that it is difficult for animal activists to appreciate. If carnivorous predation in nature is *good*—and not merely an unpleasant fact we must learn to live with—then human carnivorous predation can be seen as an affirmation of this valuable natural process. Respecting nature means respecting the ways nature trades values, and this includes painful killings for the purpose of life support.

The hunter does not show greater respect for the deer's life than does the photographer, for the former, but not the latter, destroys that life. But the hunter can show greater respect for natural processes by affirming through participation the violent sacrifice of sentient life for the sustenance of other sentient life. The once meat-eating hunter-turned-vegetarian photographer embraces an ethic of respect for *individual* sentient life and a hedonistic utilitarian concern to minimize suffering. But this caring and loving approach to wild animals is in serious tension with a healthy respect for the sometimes violent, painful, and life-sacrificing *processes* of nature.

Thus, there are goals that meat eaters and hunters can have that are not satisfied by the animal activists' proposed alternatives. The goal of nourishing oneself by taking part in the painful sacrifice of sentient life for the sustenance of other life cannot be achieved by vegetarianism or wildlife photography. If one's goal is to participate in this fundamental feature of the natural world (that is, carnivorous predation), there are no less value-destructive ways to do it. There may even be a spiritual value to hunting, according to Rolston: "In this sense, hunting is not *sport*; it is a *sacrament* of the fundamental, mandatory seeking and taking possession of value that characterizes an ecosystem and from which no culture ever escapes."[6]

Of course, the vast majority of meat eaters and hunters have no such goals in mind. Most meat eaters would rather not even think about the fact that they are consuming the flesh of another sentient being who has painfully died in order that they may live. The way meat is advertised, packaged, and consumed in our culture helps hide this fact from them. Similarly, numerous hunting practices suggest that many hunters are not trying to nourish themselves by participating in the painful, value-trading ways of the natural world. Thus this argument suggests only that it is *possible* to hunt and eat meat in ways that reflect legitimate goals unavailable to vegetarian antihunters. It does not justify these activities as they are typically practiced in our culture.

WHY VALUE PREDATION?

From the perspective of an animal activist, the goal to participate in carnivorous predation is likely to appear mysterious and illegitimate. Why would any morally enlightened person want to cause sentient animals to suffer and die? Why participate in such a nasty and unpleasant business?

Environmentalists and animal activists will disagree over how to conceptualize and value predation. By arguing that humans should not join the other predators and must not kill animals to nourish themselves, animal activists risk being committed to the view that all carnivorous predation is intrinsically evil. Although people often claim that predation in nature is a neutral fact without positive or negative value, I do not think this view can be accepted either by an environmentalist who values nature or by an animal activist who values sentient life and disvalues suffering. That animal predation is not morally right or wrong (because animals cannot be held morally accountable for what they do) is consistent with insisting that environmentalists and animal activists must assess it as good and bad, respectively. Thus, I am claiming that consistent animal activists should believe that a world without predation (involving sentient animals as prey) would be a better world, other things being equal. Such a view is something that no true lover of the wild can support.

Animal activists frequently do embrace this position. For example, Gary Comstock has suggested that in a Christian heaven, though there will be wild animals, there will be no predation, for "the wolf shall live with the sheep" and "the lion shall eat straw like cattle."[7] Because a predatory lifestyle is essential to the natures of such animals as wolves and lions—a wolf would not be a wolf, certainly not a *wild* wolf, if it peaceably coexisted with sheep—Comstock is essentially arguing that in an ideal world there would be no wolves or lions. Peter Singer has hinted that he, too, thinks a world without predation would be a better world:

> Nonhuman animals are not capable of considering the alternatives, or of reflecting morally on the rights and wrongs of killing for food; they just do it. We may *regret* that this is the way the world is, but it makes no sense to hold nonhuman animals morally responsible.[8]

Steve Sapontzis has argued that "we are morally obligated to prevent predation whenever we can do so without occasioning as much or more unjustified suffering than the predation would create."[9] In practice, animal activists frequently are strong critics of predator reintroduction programs. These views are anathema to environmentalists whose major policy goals include the reintroduction of predators.

Rolston's attitude toward predation stands in stark contrast:

> Nature is bloody, the top trophic rungs are always raptors, cats, wolves, hunters, and I'm one of those, and unashamed of it. Eating meat continues that sacrificial nature, feeding even the life of culture in which we make much exodus otherwise from nature.[10]

Rolston's metaphysic of nature underlies and supports this attitude.[11] The biological world—on Rolston's interpretation—is "sacrificial" or "cruciform": It involves struggling and suffering in the achievement of something higher. The evolutionary advancements Rolston sees as the trend of natural history—from matter to microbes to plants to animals, from reflex to instinct to learning, and from nature to culture—have been earned at the price of extinction, death, and suffering. To attain the marvelous life forms we find in nature today, millions of species and billions upon billions of individuals have been sacrificed. "Adaptation," he says, "is imperfect, but if it were perfect evolution would cease. . . . It is the imperfection that drives the world toward perfection, and in that sense it is a necessary evil."[12] Rolston argues that suffering and death are *necessary* for advancing life:

> We do not really have available to us any coherent alternative models by which, in a painless world, there might have come to pass anything like these dramas of nature and history that have happened, events that in their central thrusts we greatly treasure. . . . There are sorts of creation that cannot occur without death, and these include the highest created goods.[13]

Predation has the same dialectical character as does natural history: Death and pain of one individual turned into life and pleasure of another, all the while advancing the system. Evolutionary history is (as Rolston says of animal suffering) "a sad good,"[14] and predation, perhaps especially carnivorous predation, mirrors it and drives it. Dissected and viewed myopically from the perspective of the prey who loses, predation does appear evil. But predation should be understood holistically as the process of advancement and flourishing of life that it is. For Rolston, the most important goal of an environmental ethic is to defend the creative, fertile, and sacrificial process of natural history itself. So Rolston must value predation; it is simply natural history writ small.

Thus when animal activists oppose predation, they are opposing nature. Albert Schweitzer, the sensitive and thoughtful advocate of revering life and minimizing killing, takes an attitude toward nature I think many animal activists must share.

> The world is indeed the grisly drama of will-to-live at variance with itself. One existence survives at the expense of another of which it yet knows nothing. . . . I have been cast by my reverence for life into a state of unrest foreign to the world. . . . I choose as my activity the removal of the self-contradiction of the will-to-live, as far as the influence of my own existence extends.[15]

Schweitzer is tormented by the natural fact of predation. He feels "foreign" to the world and desires to transcend nature's ways. In a very real sense,

Schweitzer opposes and rejects nature. By rejecting the legitimacy of the desire to participate in carnivorous predation and by lamenting the existence of carnivores, animal activists are doing the same thing. Although what they oppose is a more particular instantiation of nature's "grisly drama," namely, carnivorous predation involving sentient prey, they are rejecting the extension of nature's fundamental pattern into the realm of sentient creatures.

In contrast, environmentalists such as Rolston value and celebrate predation, including this quintessential development of it. They accept nature's ways and desire to participate in them. Hunting and meat eating can be such an attempt to embrace the natural world and to participate in it.

Can Animal Activists Value Predation?

To avoid the charge of rejecting nature, animal activists might consider embracing wild carnivorous predation as good, while continuing to condemn human predation on animals as immoral. Is this a consistent position, and if so, is it plausible? Rolston thinks not: "Human predation on nature, more or less within the natural pattern, cannot be condemned simply because humans are moral agents, not if nonhuman predation has been accepted as a good in the system."[16] But why not? The question is not about the consistency of claiming that animal predation is *morally neutral* and that human predation is *morally wrong*—that clearly is a consistent position. Rather, we are questioning the consistency of condemning human predation as immoral (disvaluable in a moral sense) while claiming that animal predation is positively good (valuable in a nonmoral sense).

There are important differences between the two sorts of predation. Human predators are moral agents and they have alternative means of nourishment, whereas no animal predators are moral agents and many have no alternative means of nourishment. Thus one might hold that there is moral evil in the painful taking of sentient life by a being who is aware of the awfulness of pain and the value of life (and who has alternative less costly means of nourishment), but good in the painful taking of sentient life by a being who has no such awareness or alternatives.

Although I do not think this position is strictly inconsistent, I do think that animal activists who accept animal predation as good and condemn human predation as immoral have a great deal of explaining to do. The usual tactic of simply pointing out that animals are not moral agents is certainly not a sufficient explanation.

Animal activists who are consequentialists will especially have trouble defending this position. Consequentialists hold that it is the (nonmoral) value of the consequences of an act that determine the morality of the act. But for both kinds of predation, the results are much the same: animal pain and death transformed into pleasure and life for another. So if what results from animal predation is judged to be good, then the results of human predation on animals must also be judged as good (in a nonmoral sense). And if the results of human predation are good, how could a consequentialist claim that the act that brings them about is nonetheless immoral?

Animal activists who are deontologists will not have this same problem. Since deontologists divorce the morality of an act from the nonmoral value of its results, accepting that the results of both animal and human predation are good does not suggest (as it does for consequentialists) that one must accept human predation as morally legitimate. Still, deontologists will have to explain why human predation is immoral, and it is not clear that any such account will fit plausibly with the view that animal predation is good.

For example, the most prominent animal activist who condemns meat eating and hunting on deontological grounds is Tom Regan. He claims that such behavior is wrong because it violates animals' rights.[17] Regan argues that since animals are not moral agents, they do not violate rights when they kill and eat each other. Thus, he claims, we have no obligation to protect prey from predators, though we must stop preying on animals ourselves.[18] This makes it look as if Regan could value animal predation while condemning human predation, since only the latter violates rights. But Regan cannot successfully limit duties of assistance to cases where the threats are caused by moral agents violating rights, otherwise we would have no obligation to warn someone that a boulder was about to fall on her head.[19] And in fact Regan does claim that we ought to "nullify the threat posed by" rabid foxes who are biting children, even though the rabid foxes are not moral agents violating rights.[20] Why then are we not obliged to nullify the threat posed to prey by their animal predators?[21] The best-known defender of animal rights appears to be committed to human obligations to protect animals from the harmful behavior of other animals. Such a position is not compatible with accepting predation in nature as good.

I conclude that when hunting and meat eating are based on a desire to participate in carnivorous predation, they are legitimate, nature-respecting activities whose goals cannot be achieved in other ways. Animal activists who oppose these activities are left with the following options: Either consider animal predation as evil (and explain why this does not involve hating nature) or show that there is some way to value animal predation as good while consistently and plausibly condemning human predation.

NOTES

1. The original version of this essay contains a number of qualifications (mainly in the footnotes) that temper somewhat the conclusions arrived at here. I thank Steve Sapontzis for encouragement and assistance in reworking that paper for this volume. I thank Gary Comstock, Dale Jamieson, Eric Katz, Holmes Rolston, and Bill Throop for stimulating comments and criticisms that helped shape the original paper.

2. Rolston made these remarks on a draft of the original paper.

3. Holmes Rolston III, *Environmental Ethics: Duties to and Values in the Natural World* (Philadelphia: Temple University Press, 1988), p. 60.

4. There is debate about whether hunting or scavenging played a larger role in human evolution. See Robert Blumenschine and John Cavallo, "Scavenging and Human Evolution," *Scientific American* 267, no. 4 (October 1992): 90–96.

5. Jennifer Everett has some forceful counterexamples to this claim in her essay in this volume. I am not sure how to reconstruct the argument to handle them.

6. Rolston, *Environmental Ethics*, p. 91.

7. Gary Comstock, "Must Mennonites Be Vegetarians?" *Mennonite* 107 (June 23, 1992): 273. The quotes are from Isaiah 11:5–9.

8. Peter Singer, *Animal Liberation* (New York: Avon Books, 1975), p. 237 (emphasis added).

9. Steve Sapontzis, *Morals, Reason, and Animals* (Philadelphia: Temple University Press, 1987), p. 247.

10. These comments come from Rolston's remarks on a draft of the original paper.

11. Although these ideas can be found in *Environmental Ethics*, Rolston develops them in depth in his *Science and Religion: A Critical Survey* (Philadelphia: Temple University Press, 1987). See chapter 3 on the biological sciences, especially pp. 133–46, where he interprets "the way of nature as the way of the Cross." Also see pp. 286–93, where he explicitly deals with the problem of suffering.

12. Ibid., p. 143.

13. Ibid., p. 289.

14. Rolston, *Environmental Ethics*, p. 60.

15. Albert Schweitzer, "The Ethic of Reverence for Life," in *Animal Rights and Human Obligations*, 2nd ed., ed. Tom Regan and Peter Singer (Englewood Cliffs, NJ: Prentice Hall, 1989), p. 35.

16. Rolston, *Environmental Ethics*, p. 59.

17. Tom Regan, *The Case for Animal Rights* (Berkeley: University of California Press, 1983).

18. Ibid., p. 285.

19. For this argument, see Dale Jamieson, "Rights, Justice, and Duties to Provide Assistance: A Critique of Regan's Theory of Rights," *Ethics* 100 (1990): 349–62.

20. Regan, *The Case for Animal Rights*, p. 353.

21. For this criticism of Regan, see J. Baird Callicott, "The Search for an Environmental Ethic," in *Matters of Life and Death*, 2nd ed., ed. Tom Regan (New York: Random House, 1986), pp. 398–99.

25 VEGETARIANISM, PREDATION, AND RESPECT FOR NATURE
Jennifer Everett

Consider the natural process of carnivorous predation. Cheetahs, bears, wolves, sharks, and other predators rip and tear into their struggling and terrified victims with bloody regularity, day in and day out, as they have for millennia. Gruesome as it is for their prey, there is clearly nothing wrong with what these predators are doing; they are carrying out the essential drama by which the play of evolution unfolds.

Consider next the evolutionary history of our own species. The fact that our prehistoric ancestors hunted and ate other animals no doubt helped them to survive and reproduce. The challenges of the hunt probably presented selective pressures that favored the development of ever-higher reasoning abilities as well as physical skills. Had these prehistoric hominids not hunted, contemporary humans would likely be very different than we now are; our species might not even exist.

Confronted with the argument that those of us who *need* not consume animals *should* not, meat eaters regularly trot out these details in response, as if we benighted vegetarians are either ignorant of or loathe to confront the cold, hard facts of life. The most common (but, as I will show, least plausible) arguments claim that these facts in themselves prove that meat eating must be morally permissible. More intriguing, sophisticated, and troubling arguments appealing to the same facts, however, have been put forth by certain environmental philosophers, who advance the surprising position that meat eating is not merely permissible, but morally admirable from an environmental point of view. Insofar as it is based on considerations of animal rights or welfare, they claim, vegetarianism is ecologically unenlightened, and vegetarians are inadequate environmentalists.[1]

In what follows I will consider a set of such arguments drawn mainly, albeit loosely, from Ned Hettinger's defense of a related position.[2] I begin by rehearsing the failures of popular predation-related defenses of meat eating, as it is these failures that Hettinger's more challenging arguments seek, but in the end fail, to overcome. Once we examine the argument that vegetarians don't really belong in the environmental camp, I think it will be apparent that this claim can be maintained only by combining an oversimplified version of vegetarian commitment with a narrow, purist, and peculiar conception of environmentalism. Indeed, I will ultimately argue that vegetarian attitudes toward predation may evince an attitude more respectful of nature than the meat-eating environmentalist's glorification of the kill.

DOOMED DEFENSES OF MEAT EATING

How can we be required to abstain from meat eating, it is sometimes asked, if it's alright for nonhuman predators to kill and eat other animals? They eat each other; given the chance, some even try to eat us. Why should we be any different?[3] Many meat eaters seem to find it unfair that we have obligations to nonhuman animals while those beneficiaries are entirely free from such constraints. But the reasons for this asymmetry are as plain as they are compelling. One is that wild predators, unlike most of us, need to consume meat in order to survive. In those few contemporary cases where people do depend on meat for subsistence, vegetarians typically agree that it's permissible to eat it. But since the majority of us could live affordably, easily, healthily, and pleasurably without meat, comparisons to wild predators are spurious. A second, more fundamental difference between ourselves and other animals is that we are, while they are not, moral agents, capable of and accountable for conforming our actions to a conception of what is right or wrong. Just as we have obligations toward babies while babies have no obligations of any kind, we have obligations toward nonhuman animals while they have none. Neither asymmetry is unfair; both reflect the commonsense understanding that moral rules apply to all and only those who are capable of understanding and abiding by them.

A second popular defense of meat eating claims no parity of moral demands between humans and nonhumans, but rather insists that human nature itself limits our moral obligations to other animals. We are predators too, it is said; meat eating is instinctive, deeply ingrained in who we are. Often certain physiological facts are assembled, such as that we have pointy "canine" teeth that must have evolved for tearing meat. We are reminded that our earliest ancestors were hunters as well as gatherers, and that the evolution of our species' distinctive capacities depended on the challenges of hunting. From these observations many conclude that humans are naturally omnivorous, which in turn is thought to entail that meat eating must be morally permissible.

But this argument is specious as well. There are, first of all, good reasons to doubt that meat eating *is* natural in any morally relevant sense. What little plausibility naturalness has as an ethical justification rests on combining the sensible idea that we must be permitted to do what we cannot help doing with the faulty presumption that any behavior with a biological basis presents us with an irresistible bodily imperative. But the desire for meat, like that for French fries, whether biologically derived or not, is far from the irresistible "instinct" that many meat eaters present it to be. Besides, since meat eating is not culturally universal, we may well suspect that our current practice—however deeply rooted it seems to us—is at least as much determined by nurture as by nature. Most fundamentally, the inference from the naturalness to the permissibility of meat eating is subject to decisive counterexamples. Even if omnivory *is* "natural" in some evolutionary or genetic sense, this goes absolutely no distance toward providing a *moral* defense of meat eating, for clearly, not everything "deeply ingrained in human nature" is morally permissible. Some biologists have argued that male aggressiveness, dominance, promiscuity, and even a propensity toward rape are products of natural selection.[4] But surely the immorality of violence, subordination of women, infidelity, absentee fatherhood, and rape do not depend on such evolutionary explanations turning out to be false. Put simply, the knowledge that some behavior is natural, has a biological basis, played a role in our evolution, or what have you, tells us absolutely nothing about whether our engaging in it is morally defensible.

Thus, contrary to popular opinion, vegetarians have not been in the dark about or unwilling to face the cold, hard facts set out above. The naïveté belongs instead to those who believe that the permissibility of meat eating follows directly from such facts. Shortly we will consider a set of arguments that appeal to the same basic facts, but that take a subtler approach, arguing that the attitudes environmentalists must take toward them are unavailable to vegetarians. Since these arguments reach the startling conclusion that, contrary to first appearances, vegetarians cannot consistently be environmentalists, we should first give a fair hearing to the view these arguments are intended to uproot—that vegetarianism and environmentalism are mutually supporting commitments.

First Appearances: The Seeming Alliance between Vegetarianism and Environmentalism

The charge that vegetarianism is inconsistent with environmentalism is, at first glance, a bewildering one. For vegetarians, like environmentalists, seek a new moral relationship between humans and the extra-human animals. In place of the exploitation, cruelty, and indifference toward other species that have prevailed for so long in Western culture, we envision a future in which humanity recognizes and honors the inherent worth of all creatures and constructs societies in harmony with rather than in domination over the rest of nature. The prevailing practices that vegetarians condemn— treating other species as our resources, our tools, our tasty nuggets; subjecting billions of animals each year to a living hell for the sake of cheap cheeseburgers—stem from the same arrogant anthropocentrism that regards wild places as worthless unless they hold oil reserves, forests as just so many board feet of timber, and open fields as mere empty space to be "improved" with strip malls. The vegetarian refusal to treat other animals as lunch meat is thus of a piece with and flows naturally out of a broader environmental conviction that human dominance over the rest of nature is not only imprudent but also morally wrong.

Nor is the egregious anthropocentrism behind factory farming the strongest environmental argument for vegetarianism, for there is also the simple fact that contemporary meat production practices are ecologically reprehensible. Here we may briefly mention the tremendous waste of land, water, and energy required to convert plant protein into animal protein; the clearing of rain forests, degradation of prairie ecosystems, loss of topsoil, and destruction of stream habitat due to cattle grazing; and the monstrous quantities of animal waste produced by industrial cattle, pig, and chicken operations.[5] As many environmentalists recognize, the commitment to preserving a world in which all creatures can thrive advises a move away from consumption of commercially produced meat no less than a move away from SUVs, long commutes, and toxic household products. Eating lower on the food chain is generally the more ecological choice.

Despite the dismal environmental record of commercial animal agriculture, however, some environmental philosophers have remained skeptical of vegetarianism. Their doubts stem from a longstanding tension between holistic environmental ethics and the animal-centered ethics— such as Peter Singer's animal liberation[6] or Tom Regan's theory of animal rights[7]—often endorsed by vegetarians. In what have come to be standard criticisms, J. Baird Callicott argued[8] both that animal-centered ethics would have disastrous environmental consequences if applied to wild nature—for example, we would have obligations to intervene in natural predation—and that the domestic animals that are the focus of those theories are not the objects of concern of a genuinely environmental ethic. He advocates instead the holistic land ethic of Aldo Leopold,[9] and the reigning voices of holism have joined in rejection of animal-centered theories in the field of environmental ethics ever since.

Challenges to this received view notwithstanding,[10] many advocates of animal-centered ethics have been content to concede to the holists that not *all* of our duties regarding the natural world are duties to sentient animals. Vegetarians may thus agree, for example, that additional ethical tools, including more holistic environmental values, account for our duties with respect to nature when the avoidance of needless suffering conflicts with other environmental priorities or does not arise. Moreover, although vegetarians certainly differ as to which circumstances count as legitimate exceptions to the prima facie wrongness of meat eating, few in the mainstream would deny that such exceptions exist. For instance, in Native communities of rural Alaska, subsistence hunting is arguably both ecologically and culturally more appropriate than a vegetarian diet, since a nutritionally adequate supply of plant-based foods cannot be produced locally and would be ecologically wasteful as well as culturally disruptive to import. Indeed, subsistence hunting could be defended on animal welfare grounds alone if shipping food over great distances would cause greater aggregate harms to individual animals than do Native subsistence hunters. Such concessions maintain the compatibility between vegetarianism and environmentalism without jeopardizing the core conviction that our prima facie duty to avoid causing needless suffering prohibits eating meat unless there is an overriding justification for doing so. Thus most vegetarians would agree, first, that we should reject meat from factory farms in most circumstances, and, second, that we should not hunt other animals when this is not necessary for some weighty reason—certainly not merely for the sake of our own enjoyment.

Yet for some environmental ethicists, the moderate position just described is still unacceptable. Their argument isn't just that vegetarians don't have a *sufficiently* environmental ethic—a shortcoming that is presumably overcome by including holistic ecological values in an overall ethical theory. Rather, the argument is that the vegetarian attitude toward animal suffering is intrinsically and thus unavoidably inconsistent with a properly environmental attitude toward predation. The only way to attain this attitude is to abandon the core vegetarian commitment outlined above.

The Alleged Incompatibility

According to Ned Hettinger, vegetarians who would be environmentalists are in a sticky position. They typically oppose factory farming and recreational hunting at least in part on the grounds that each causes unnecessary animal suffering. But consistency requires that they regard such suffering as a bad thing wherever it occurs. If suffering is so bad when humans cause it (which is at least in part why it is *wrong* for us to cause it), then it must also be bad when other animals cause it (even though, since they aren't moral agents, it is not wrong for them to cause it). Given that vegetarians must find such suffering regrettable, it is difficult to see how they can regard wild predation as a good thing. And they certainly cannot admire people who make a purely optional choice to participate in this essentially painful process through hunting; indeed, their core principles entail that it is obligatory not to hunt or to eat meat except in cases of necessity.

Environmentalists, Hettinger suggests, do and should take a very different attitude, although it is not entirely clear how strict this requirement is meant to be. At times we encounter the relatively mild stipulation that *good* environmentalists—those worthy of particular esteem—model their behavior on wild carnivorous predators, expressing their respect for nature by hunting and/or eating meat. If this is what it takes to be a good environmentalist, then vegetarians' disapproval of recreational hunting and meat eating would merely (albeit inevitably) consign them to an inferior form of environmental commitment, like conservationism or "shallow ecology"—views that fall short of the "greener" doctrines of preservationism or deep ecology. At other times, however, Hettinger seems to endorse the stronger claim that in order to be an environmentalist at all, one must consider predation, at least by nonhuman animals and perhaps by human hunters, a good thing—something that adds value to the world. If vegetarians are prohibited by their principles from adopting the requisite attitudes, then their fundamental convictions are, like it or not, anti-environmental.

These conditions on prospective environmentalists are drawn from the facts discussed at the outset of this essay—the *omnivorous ancestors* thesis, which asserts that predation played an essential role in the evolution of our species; and the *natural processes* thesis, which emphasizes that the killing and eating of some animals by others is the key engine by which evolution is advanced in the wild. But in each case Hettinger's argument is more subtle than those rehearsed above.

On Hettinger's version of the omnivorous ancestors argument, it is not the naturalness of omnivory per se that justifies our eating meat; rather, it's that a properly environmental commitment to respect nature on its own terms requires a holistic sort of appreciation of our species' history and may even commend contemporary efforts to relive it. Thus, Hettinger invokes Holmes Rolston's argument[11] that approving of human hunting is essential to respecting the natural processes that formed us:

> To reject our predatory history and still try to value the human being isolates a product from its essential historical genesis . . . . [W]hen the process that produces a product is essential to the understanding of what that product is, one cannot consistently affirm the value of the product while denying the value of the process that created it. One might as well try to value the culture of Native American plains tribes while rejecting their tradition of killing buffalo for food, clothing, and shelter.[12]

Since predation was a necessary part of human evolution, the suggestion goes, predation is a constitutive aspect of what humans now are. So in order to take an appropriately environmental attitude toward our own history and nature, we need to value the process of predation (as opposed to merely tolerating it with distaste), a sort of affirmation that vegetarians arguably are not in a position to offer.

Hettinger's version of the natural processes argument, on the other hand, draws on the role of predation in the nonhuman world to support pro-predation moral positions that are apparently off-limits to vegetarians. Life flourishes at the expense of life. If environmentalism is about anything, it is about understanding and appreciating nature as it is in itself, without imposing the norms appropriate to human culture on a realm that proceeds according to nonhuman standards. If we cannot regard the killing of rodents by raptors as a good thing, a contribution to rather than a detraction from the glory of nature, then we have not achieved environmental consciousness. Vegetarians' refusal to engage in meat eating looks suspiciously to Hettinger like an inability to value wild creatures and natural processes in the ways an environmentalist must.

Indeed, the most venerable environmentalists seem to Hettinger to be those who make a point of displaying their respect for nature by mimicking wild carnivores' visceral involvement in natural processes. Hunters, he argues, "can show greater respect for natural process by affirming through participation the violent sacrifice of sentient life for the sustenance of other sentient life"[13] than vegetarians can by renouncing such participation. To be an environmentalist at all, Hettinger maintains, one must regard the activities of wild predators as good. To be an admirable environmentalist, he seems to suggest, one should seek to share with nature's most magnificent creatures as well as our own evolutionary ancestors a participation in the quintessentially natural process of carnivorous predation.

A Preliminary Response

Before addressing the substance of these arguments, it is important to be clear about what would (and would not) be established if they succeed. So far Hettinger has argued that hunting and meat eating are environmentally admirable just *insofar as they are carried out as a means of affirming the value of nature through participation in the process of predation*. Since, as he acknowledges, the vast majority of hunters and meat eaters have no such goals in mind, his argument "does not justify these activities as they are typically practiced in our culture."[14] Indeed, many recreational hunters would reject Hettinger's ecocentric environmentalism and defend their own practice on grounds of an open-access, anthropocentric conservation ethic that he would clearly oppose.

More importantly, the presence of these esoteric motivations is not sufficient to render all meat eating environmentally admirable. Despite Hettinger's repeated lumping together of "meat eating and hunting," the argument above provides *no* support to the only sort of meat consumption in
which most Americans engage—grocery store and restaurant purchases of
meat from factory-farmed animals. This is not merely because such meat is
not consumed with the requisite aim of participating in "nature's painful
ways of trading value," although that is also true. (As Hettinger points out,
most meat eaters—far from *affirming* their participation in animal suffering—
would rather *not* acknowledge that the meat they consume comes from sentient beings who lived horrible lives and/or died gruesome deaths.) Rather,
the fundamental reason that all nonhunted meat consumption remains
unsupported by his argument is that one cannot even symbolically "participate in predation" by consuming the processed and packaged flesh of domesticated (especially factory-farmed) animals. Wild predators do not domesti-
cate their prey; so we do not mimic predators by consuming Big Macs. And
the domestication of other animals occurred too recently in human history to
be responsible for the evolution of our species' distinctive characteristics; so
eating Chicken McNuggets can hardly be said to be an affirmation of the
"essential historical genesis" of our species. Indeed, since the domestication
of animals for agricultural use marks a transition toward increasing cultural
complexity and ecological manipulation, and since the character of contemporary meat production is more a reflection of *industrial* than even agricultural forms of human society, it is precisely the sort of practice that Hettin-
gerian environmentalists should be expected to rue rather than celebrate.[15] In
any event, one does not emulate a wolf, a lion, an aboriginal hunter-gatherer,
or even a high-tech "weekend warrior" by consuming the meat of animals
who are essentially captives raised for slaughter rather than prey.

Thus, even if Hettinger's argument succeeded, he would apparently be
committed to the view that most contemporary Westerners have no justification for their meat eating ways—a significant concession in the direction
of de facto vegetarianism. Whether a more rigorous vegetarianism can
retain its environmental credentials then turns on whether Hettinger correctly portrays the attitudes that vegetarians do and environmentalists must
take toward predation by wild animals or our evolutionary ancestors.

THE MORAL SIGNIFICANCE OF OMNIVOROUS ANCESTORS

As we have seen, Hettinger goes out of his way to avoid the fallacies committed by more naive appeals to human nature or evolutionary biology as
justifications for meat eating. Nevertheless, it's difficult to see why counterexamples to the naïve, what's-natural-is-permissible argument don't serve

equally well against the intermediate stipulations of environmentally man-dated attitudes in his argument. A tendency among males to engage in rape may, after all, have conferred adaptive advantage on our early ancestors that contributed to the evolution of our species. Humans as we know them might not exist (although similar creatures might) had our early ancestors not engaged in rape. But this is no better reason to think that *environmen-talists* must regard rape as a good thing, much less want to participate in rape as a fundamental, natural process, than it is grounds for inferring the moral permissibility of rape directly. Should contemporary men congratu-late themselves for their respect for nature if they invest minimally in their children and engage in promiscuous infidelity, provided they do so in order to emulate an evolutionarily advantageous strategy without which our species would have evolved quite differently?

Surely no plausible form of environmentalism would have such impli-cations. What examples like these show is that we should not regard as per-missible, value as good, or want to emulate today every behavior, activity, or trait that happened to play a formative role in our species' genesis, even if we agree on the importance of a robust respect for nature. In turn, this means that environmentalists' appreciation of nature and our species' nat-ural history should not be indiscriminate in the way Hettinger suggests.

Perhaps we could, however, accept a qualified version of his principle: If something, x, is an essential part of the process by which something else, y, comes to be what it is, then in order to value y, we need to value x *insofar as it contributes to y's being what it is*. But this does not mean that we need to value x in every respect. So for instance, loving a child whose conception was the result of a rape may require being grateful *in a qualified way* that the rape occurred, but would by no means require an unqualified endorsement of even that particular rape, much less an affirmation of rape in general. Similarly, valuing humanity in a properly environmental way might require having a certain ecological respect for the fact that we wouldn't exist if not for the past predominance of behaviors we now repudiate (such as hunting or aggression or sexual dominance). But it certainly would not require an unqualified affir-mation of those behaviors, or a desire to emulate them in the present.

Drawing such distinctions is not extraordinary, confused, illegitimate, or antienvironmental. Indeed, it is both essential to clear thinking and per-fectly familiar to common sense. To fret that it's somehow illegitimate to "isolate" a product from its "essential historical genesis" merely obfuscates these perfectly obvious and sensible distinctions. Vegetarians thus *can* value our predatory past in the sense of respecting the magnificence of the amoral processes that made us what we are. Admiration for atavistic attempts to relive this past, however, is surely not a precondition for any reasonable form of environmentalism.

THE MORAL SIGNIFICANCE OF NATURAL PROCESSES

No true lover of the wild, Hettinger argues, can believe that nature would be better if wild carnivores were not carnivorous. Can we be admirable environmentalists if we do not seek to participate in these processes, to emulate the wild animals we profess to respect? Can we be environmentalists at all if we cannot embrace the quintessentially natural but unavoidably painful process of one creature feeding on another?

The response here is by now a familiar one. Yes, respect for nature does require an admiration for natural processes. It requires that we respond with wonder, admiration, and humility about the significance of human concerns in the face of a world that is much greater and far older than us. If we are to respect nature on its own terms rather than in excessively sentimental anthropomorphic terms, we must recognize that predation is one of the vital processes through which creatures thrive and evolution proceeds, and we must celebrate the values that predation promotes—for example, flourishing of predators, promotion of beneficial traits in both predator and prey species, ecosystem health, etc. All of this is available to the vegetarian. It is neither charitable nor credible to assume that vegetarians' opposition to animal suffering blinds us to the values that any biologically informed and environmentally concerned observer could be reasonably expected to appreciate.

Nor is it credible or reasonable to insist that truly admirable forms of environmentalism prohibit the type of sensitivity to the suffering of prey to which vegetarians are committed. Virtuous environmentalists, Hettinger seems to suggest, must identify exclusively with the predator, must emulate the predator's obliviousness to the prey's suffering by refusing to acknowledge the badness of suffering. He seems to think that one can't find predation—and thus nature—*good* if one cannot manage to be indifferent to the suffering it causes. But why in the world should we accept that?[16] There is certainly very little by way of argument for it. (The closest thing to a defense of our mimicry of wild predators' indifference to their prey's suffering appears in Hettinger's argument that it's better for environmentalists to mimic wild carnivorous predators like wolves and bears than wild herbivores like gorillas. This is because, since predators are "higher in the trophic pyramid" than herbivores, mimicking them allows us to participate in natural processes "at an elevated and more sophisticated level."[17] But since a thing's level in the trophic pyramid *just is* a function of what it eats, carnivores are higher in the trophic pyramid than herbivores *by definition*, and the supposed premise that things higher in the trophic pyramid are more valuable than things lower in it is in fact just a masked assertion of the conclusion that carnivory is better than herbivory. This argument begs the question.)

At the end of the day, I rather doubt that Hettinger's natural processes argument rings true to those not already convinced that vegetarians are inferior to hunters as environmentalists. To insist that one falls short of environmental consciousness to the extent one identifies with herbivores or finds suffering bad is to paint environmentalism into a narrow, peculiar, and indefensible corner. Indeed, this call for one-sided celebration of the predator's perspective seems hardly in the spirit of the clear-headed, realistic, biologically informed attitude of respect that environmentalists rightly advocate. It's as if we dare not acknowledge that anything in nature could be rightly regarded by moral agents as bad, ugly, or unfortunate, for fear that we won't be able to love it anymore.

Such an attitude, I submit, is more akin to *infatuation* than mature love or respect.[18] To be infatuated with someone is to see only her merits, to cast her character and actions always in a radiant light, and to be (perhaps willfully) oblivious to or excessively indulgent of her faults. It is a fragile sort of admiration, however, which cannot endure an honest evaluation of morning breath, bad moods, and stomach flu. We may be able to be infatuated with someone whose faults we deliberately overlook or pretend to find charismatic, but we could not genuinely know her, much less love or respect her. Hettinger is willing to acknowledge the *facts* of pain, terror, and suffering in predation, but seems unwilling to see these aspects of nature ungilded by his determination to find her attractive in all aspects and all ways. We need not hold, as Callicott once did and Hettinger seems to still, that "if nature as a whole is good, then pain and death are also good,"[19] for genuine love and respect do not require embracing a beloved's defects as if they were virtues. Vegetarians' respect for nature endures the assessment that suffering is bad and should not be needlessly inflicted. In the world as we know it, suffering is, regrettably, a necessary effect of processes that perpetuate pleasure, happiness, and the flourishing of life. Vegetarians can respect nature by facing those facts squarely, and loving it nonetheless.

CONCLUSION

The argument we have been considering is indeed an extreme one. Hettinger argued that, because our species would not now exist had our ancestors not hunted, and because predation by wild carnivores is a vital natural process, there is insufficient appreciation of predation, and thus a repudiation of nature, in vegetarian dismay over animal suffering and refusal to endorse recreational hunting. I have argued, to the contrary, that vegetarians can value the role of predation in evolution and in producing other values even while deploring the suffering it causes and, in addition, that to require more than this is to demand infatuation with rather than respect for nature from would-be environmentalists.

But if, contrary to my arguments above, the rejection of any trait, behavior, or characteristic that was essential to the evolution of our species constituted a rejection of nature, if admirable environmentalists must emulate behaviors that turn the crank of evolution, then those who dismiss the vegetarians' sympathies for suffering creatures must swallow the tail of their own critique. There is, after all, every reason to think that a sympathetic affective response to the suffering of others, no less than predatory skill, was essential to our evolutionary history, that we would be a vastly different species without it, and that such responses enable nonhuman creatures to survive and thrive in the wild. The capacities to comprehend and lament another's terror and agony thus do not set us apart from natural processes— and certainly not above them. To acknowledge this, rather than dismissing it as a product of hypercultural sentimentality, is to be fully connected with the kind of beings we are, and to share something in common with many of nature's other inhabitants. The environmentalist who interprets the vegetarian's sensitivity to suffering as a desire to "transcend nature" seems to presuppose that such sensitivity is not part of the natural order. Vegetarians reject this untenable assumption, insisting that our moral capacities are as much a part of nature's bounty as the wolf's distinctive howl.[20]

NOTES

1. Of course, many people are vegetarians for reasons quite independent of the rights or welfare of individual animals—e.g., strictly for health, environmental, or humanitarian reasons. For ease of reference, the term "vegetarian" is used throughout this essay to refer only to those whose rejection of meat eating is *at least in part* based on concerns about animal suffering.

2. Ned Hettinger, "Valuing Predation in Rolston's Environmental Ethics: Bambi Lovers versus Tree Huggers," *Environmental Ethics* 16 (1994): 3–20. (An abbreviated, updated version of this article is contained in this volume.)

3. Peter Alward attempts a philosophically robust defense of this argument in "The Naïve Argument against Moral Vegetarianism," *Environmental Values* 9 (2000): 81–89. See also David Benatar's response, "Why the Naïve Argument against Moral Vegetarianism Really is Naïve," *Environmental Values* 10 (2000): 103–12.

4. See Randy Thornhill and Craig T. Palmer, *A Natural History of Rape: Biological Bases of Sexual Coercion* (Cambridge: MIT Press, 2000). The scientific adequacy of this thesis is challenged in Cheryl Brown Travis, ed., *Evolution, Gender, and Rape* (Cambridge: MIT Press, 2003).

5. See Michael Allen Fox, *Deep Vegetarianism* (Philadelphia: Temple University Press, 1999); Frances Moore Lappé, *Diet for a Small Planet* (New York: Ballantine, 1992), and John Robbins, *Diet for a New America* (Walpole, NH: Stillpoint, 1987).

6. Peter Singer, *Animal Liberation* (New York: New York Review, 1975).

7. Tom Regan, *The Case for Animal Rights* (Berkeley: University of California Press, 1983).

8. J. Baird Callicott, "Animal Liberation: A Triangular Affair," *Environmental Ethics* 2 (1980): 318–24. It should be noted that Callicott has significantly tempered his critique. See his "Animal Liberation and Environmental Ethics: Back Together Again," *Between the Species* 4 (1988): 163–67 and "'Back Together Again' Again," *Environmental Values* 7 (1988): 461–75.

9. See "The Land Ethic," in Aldo Leopold, *A Sand County Almanac* (Oxford: Oxford University Press, 1949).

10. See, e.g., Jennifer Everett, "Environmental Ethics, Animal Welfarism, and the Problem of Predation: A Bambi-Lover's Respect for Nature," *Ethics and the Environment* 6 (2001): 42–67; Dale Jamieson, "Animal Liberation Is an Environmental Ethic," *Environmental Values* 7 (1998): 41–57; Edward Johnson, "Animal Liberation versus the Land Ethic," *Environmental Ethics* 3 (1981): 265–73; Paul Veatch Moriarty and Mark Woods, "Hunting ≠ Predation: An Instance of the Compatibility of Animal Welfare and Environmental Ethics," *Environmental Ethics* 19 (1997): 391–404; Gary Varner, "Can Animal Rights Activists Be Environmentalists?" in *Environmental Philosophy and Environmental Activism*, ed. Don E. Marietta Jr. and Lester Embree (Lanham, MD: Rowman & Littlefield, 1995), pp. 169–201.

11. Holmes Rolston III, *Environmental Ethics: Duties to and Values in the Natural World* (Philadelphia: Temple University Press, 1988).

12. Hettinger, "Valuing Predation in Rolston's Environmental Ethics," p. 14.

13. Ibid.

14. Ibid., p. 15.

15. This is indeed the main complaint against factory farming in Callicott, "Animal Liberation: A Triangular Affair."

16. Although I focus on other problems in the text, this claim is worrisome in its unwitting congeniality to a rather macho preoccupation with violence. For feminist critiques of common Western hunters' ideals of masculinity, see e.g., Marti Kheel, "License to Kill: An Ecofeminist Critique of Hunters' Discourse," in *Animals and Women: Feminist Theoretical Explorations*, ed. Carol Adams and Josephine Donovan (Durham, NC: Duke University Press, 1995), pp. 85–125, and Brian Luke, "Violent Love: Hunting, Heterosexuality, and the Erotics of Men's Predation," *Feminist Studies* 24 (1998): 627–55.

17. Hettinger, "Valuing Predation in Rolston's Environmental Ethics," p. 13, n. 25.

18. Stephen Nathanson draws the same distinction in the context of patriotism in his *Patriotism, Morality, and Peace* (Lanham, MD: Rowman & Littlefield, 1993).

19. Callicott, "Animal Liberation: A Triangular Affair," p. 333.

20. For an extended development of these arguments, see Everett, "Environmental Ethics, Animal Welfarism, and the Problem of Predation." I would like to thank Richard Cameron, Jennifer Ritter, and Steve Sapontzis for generous feedback on earlier drafts.

26 | MODERATION, MORALS, AND MEAT

Frederick Ferré

I

An ecological ethic, one that I have elsewhere detailed as "personalistic organicism,"[1] will affirm from the start that life as we know it is an intense consumer of energy. The role of living organisms, as Alfred North Whitehead points out,[2] is not merely to survive (the rocks win the competition for longevity) but to manifest complex structure and dynamic variety. This is accomplished by a constant feeding upon energy found in the environment.

Except for the green plants, with their wondrous capacity to synthesize their own complex chemical structures from less complex elements by means of energy drawn from the light of the sun, all life on earth feeds on other life for its very existence. From the broadest biotic perspective, life is cannibalistic upon itself. An ecological ethic must begin with the affirmation of this nutrient cycle.

Since all animal life depends for its energy on consuming vegetable life, any nonbiophobic ethic must affirm the use at least of vegetables and

An earlier version of this essay appeared in *Inquiry* 29 (1986): 391–406. The Web site for *Inquiry* is www.tandf.no/inquiry.

vegetable products for food. This seems an obvious ethical point, but even this would seem to run foul of sensitivities explicit or implicit in some forms of ethics. If certain botanical entities are of a sort to have rights asserted on their behalf,[3] then it is not a long step to affirming that human beings have the duty to refrain from eating them, since that would seem to treat them as a "means only" in our dietary practices. And if trees can enjoy legal and moral considerability, it seems manifestly unjust not to extend the same status to shrubs; but if shrubs, why not to grasses, and so on to the whole botanical kingdom? If this step is taken, then one must conclude with Kenneth E. Goodpaster: "I continue to believe that 'being alive' is the only plausible and nonarbitrary criterion of moral considerability."[4]

The ethical consequence of taking such steps toward including the whole biosphere in the domain of moral considerability need not be advocacy of animal extinction through self-starvation. On the contrary, I support expanding moral considerability to all living things and yet maintain that such considerability per se does not rule out the killing and eating of plants.

The burden lies upon the plant eater, of course, to show how this may be ethically justified if we agree that plants have interests (e.g., in being watered, in growing to maturity, in scattering seed, etc.) but yet are to be deliberately killed and consumed, thus treated as a means for our metabolic satisfaction or even, as with a vase of cut flowers, for our aesthetic pleasure. I shall return to this burden in the next section, but the answer would seem to lie in a moderate interpretation of the Kantian dictum that we should not treat morally considerable entities as "means only."[5] Perhaps acknowledging a genuine degree of moral considerability for an entity may not rule out the use of that entity under some morally appropriate circumstances as a means to our ends. Perhaps those appropriate circumstances sometimes may include the eating even of entities with interests of their own and status in the moral universe.

II

Some might prefer to escape the ethical burden of justifying the eating of plants by attacking the argument that leads in the first place to the acknowledgment of their moral considerability. It is hard, however, to take this route in connection with eating animals. First, animal interests are even more difficult to deny than plant interests; second, the fact of animal pain is far less speculative, especially among the species with more fully developed nervous systems, than is the possibility of plant perception; and, third, in the case of human beings, who are by nature omnivores, it is arguable that there is no biological necessity to eat animal flesh, though there is a necessity to gain energy from plant life, directly or indirectly.

Peter Singer places the primary weight of his argument for vegetarianism on the duty to refrain from causing pain to beings that can feel pain. I shall return to this concern, which I fully share, in a later section in connection with the moral meat eater's obligations and limitations. But first it is necessary to deal with another, logically primary, argument that Singer employs, an argument that is even more general than the objection from animal pain. This more comprehensive argument, to which I alluded in the foregoing in connection with eating plants, points out that even if animal husbandry and slaughter were entirely painless (as is, presumably, the harvesting of grains or the picking of berries), the *attitude* toward animals reflected in these practices is morally wrong since "so long as we think that a nonhuman may be killed simply so that a human can satisfy his taste for meat, we are still thinking of nonhumans as means rather than as ends in themselves."[6]

My response, already suggested in connection with plant eating, is that the morality of ends and means is not so simple as this argument assumes. Surely, at one extreme, it would be morally intolerable to treat the persons around one as nothing but utensils. This is exactly the moral pathology that Kant was warning against. On the other hand, it would be impossible to go through life without accepting the services of others, who in that respect become means for us. My postman, whom I greet and recognize as a fellow end in himself, is also a useful means to my ends. Even more obvious is our need to accept the anonymous services of other human beings, ends in themselves for themselves, of course, but known to us only vaguely for what they accomplish in the freight yards or the telephone exchanges of the world for our general benefit. Real human life depends constantly on the fully licit acceptance of others as means for us as well as ends for themselves.

Finally, I know that I am an end in myself for myself; but I have no moral objection to being also a means to the economic support of my wife or to the educational ambitions of my students. Becoming a means is not necessarily being "used" in the objectionable sense of the term. On the contrary, part of the fulfillment one has in life is the sense of contributing to the legitimate ends of others. If others were morally required always to treat me *only* as an end in myself to the exclusion of accepting what I offer them as means to their proper ends, my life as a social being would be stunted.

A still more radical challenge to the moral possibility, in principle, of eating animals comes from Tom Regan, who adds to Singer's objection to "using" animals the further claim that animals have an absolute right to being treated with the respect due to persons.

> The *basic* wrong is that animals raised for commercial profit are viewed
> and treated in ways that fail to show respect for their moral right to

respectful treatment. *They* are not (though of course they may be treated as if they are) "commodities," "economic units," "investments," "a renewable resource," etc. They are, like us, persons and so, like us, are owed treatment that accords with their right to be treated with respect, a respect we fail to show when we end their life before doing so can be defended on the grounds of mercy. Since animals are routinely killed on grounds other than mercy in the course of commercial animal agriculture, that human enterprise violates the rights of animals.[7]

This is indeed, as Regan acknowledges, a radical ethical approach. The key attribution of personhood for animals in turn rests on a five-part doctrine of individual value:[8]

1. The inherent value of an individual who has such value is not the same as, is not reducible to, and is incommensurate with the intrinsic value of that individual's, or of any combination of individual's, mental states, including pleasures, pains, and other happy or unhappy experiences.
2. All individuals who have inherent value have it equally. Inherent value, that is, does not come in degrees; some who have it do not have it more or less than others.
3. The possession of inherent value by individuals does not depend on their utility relative to the interests of others.
4. Individuals cannot acquire or lose such value by anything they do.
5. The inherent value of individuals does not depend on what or how others feel about them.

Assertions 3 and 5 are not controversial, since they reflect the very definition of inherence. Usefulness to others and the opinions of others are paradigms of what "extrinsic" means.

The other three assertions, however, are by no means equally secure. Assertion 1 seeks to seal off the concept of inherent value from the mental states of individuals, but when Regan himself comes to discuss "line drawing" as to which animals should be included as persons with inherent value, he argues from behavioral and physiological similarities and on evolutionary grounds to the probability of a *mental life* worthy of respect. "What we must ask," he writes, "is where in the animal kingdom we find individuals who are *most like* paradigmatic persons—that is, most like us, both behaviorally and physiologically. The greater the similarity in these respects, the stronger the case for believing that these animals have a *mental life similar to our own* (including memory and emotion, for example), a case that is strengthened given the major thrust of evolutionary theory."[9] As a result, Regan includes adult mammalian animals within the pale. No other differentiating characteristic than mentality is adduced, and no other group of animals is explicitly included among persons.

This seems quite in keeping with the view shared by such divergent philosophers as Sartre and Whitehead that what constitutes the inherent value of anything is its value *for itself*.[10] If an entity has no value for itself, that is, cannot participate in any sense in its own valuation, in what could inherent value be located? To be valued by another is extrinsic, whether the other's valuing is on utilitarian or purely disinterested grounds. Even if God were to value a wholly mindless entity, assuming (with Sartre but not with Whitehead) that some genuine individual entities can have no mentality at all, such a divine valuation might provide a basis on which everyone else should also respect and value the thing, but it would not provide the entity with inherent value—unless, with some forms of pantheism, God is taken not to be external to the entity. Even then (or especially then) the value of the entity would be derivative from God's capacity for self-valuation and not inherent in the thing itself.

If we take, with Regan, the value of an individual *for itself* to be the basis of inherent value, then assertion 2, that all inherent value is equal among entities with any inherent value at all, seems most implausible. Regan's own adducing of the evolutionary argument for mental analogies to personhood reminds us of the infinite gradations among species with respect to apparent mental quality: namely, capacity to learn and remember, to feel and express emotion, to respond flexibly and creatively to changing circumstances, and the like. If physiological similarities can count as relevant for this topic, so then can physiological differences, as among nervous systems. If, that is, higher mammalian adults can be seen as having much in common with human persons, so the grasses, the bacteria, the earthworms, the insects, the fish, and the birds can be seen has having much to differentiate them from human persons as well as from each other. There is no reason to suppose that the quality and intensity of the mental life—and with it its value for itself—of an oyster is on a par with that of a pheasant; but there is likewise no reason to suppose that the quality and intensity of the mental life of the pheasant is on a par with that of a human person.

Finally, it seems hard to accept, with assertion 4, that individuals cannot acquire or lose inherent value. The capacity to be of value for oneself can be enhanced by significant growth in mental powers. This is the claim of every proponent of liberal education: mental growth affects not only the value of what one can *do* but what one can *be* for oneself. Unfortunately, the reverse is also true: that one's value for oneself can be diminished by drugs, accident, or disease and can be made negligible in case of severe brain damage and irreversible comatose condition. There are of course good extrinsic moral reasons to provide civil protections to even such individuals, but the appropriateness of designating them "persons" is cast in doubt if the ground of personhood is meeting the threshold of mental capacity that allows us a significant value for ourselves.

These reflections on Tom Regan's assertions lead to finer moral distinctions than the either/or's that "rights" language suggest. He does well to recast his own argument in terms of inherent value, on which animal rights are in the end held to rest. That animals—at least many animals—have inherent value for themselves can be accepted without becoming involved in the fearful tangle of rights and counter-rights that arises when one considers not only human-nonhuman relations but what might be called the "intra-nonhuman" rights situation. For example, the carnivore must be acknowledged to have the "right" to catch and kill its prey as a minimum due its (and its species') need for survival, but also the prey must possess the "right" to be respected in its peaceful pursuit of grasses to graze, as well as the "right" to escape from the carnivore.[11] The whole language of "rights" seems infelicitous in this connection, especially when only nonhumans are interacting. Regan wisely does not attribute to his animal "persons" the capacity for free moral deliberation and responsible action, but where there can be no moral obligations and no rights can be claimed, it seems better to look for another, more suitable formulation of the moral situation. Indeed, as H. J. McCloskey concludes, "It is not simply that there can be no priority rules, nor that the weighing up of the conflicting rights is extremely difficult, but that there is a logical incompatibility in the claims made by the rights."[12]

The better formulation is in terms of a *principle of moral obligation of an appropriate sort toward all entities with inherent value.* The situation does not depend on reciprocity. Humans are beings that can be morally obligated, and so far as we have yet discovered, they are the only ones so obligated. If there are other "persons" among the species on this planet (and the language of personalism has its own difficulties),[13] they are (so far as we can tell) not *morally responsible* persons. In this situation, in which human beings must both declare "rights" on behalf of nonhumans and also must recognize the obligation to respect such "rights," it seems conceptually preferable to apply Ockham's razor to "rights" talk. It would be far cleaner simply to demand *due respect for inherent value wherever it may be found.*

But as we have seen, inherent value—the capacity to be of value for oneself—is not, despite Regan, a categorical either/or. The intuitive gradations of inherency are reflected, indeed, in many vegetarians' practice of refraining from mammal meat while allowing themselves fish or eggs. It is reflected in Regan's own discussion of where to "draw the line" regarding the personhood of animals. I submit that there is no "line." Following Whitehead, I believe that all living things have some degree of inherent value (even vegetable species without nervous systems qualify, though to a significantly lesser degree), but different organisms call for different expressions of respect. The proper form of respect for vegetable species is not necessarily violated by harvesting and eating them, though even toward botanical organisms, morally objectionable human behavior is quite possible. Again, perhaps "due respect" for a freshly laid egg is not violated by its being eaten. May this extend to oysters? We need some principles to go on, but at this point absolutist prohibitions on principle have been set aside for a more case-by-case examination of the moral circumstances under which human beings might, or might not, eat other entities, even those with more significant degrees of inherent value.

III

The problem for ethical theory, then, is to weigh the net goods over evils that follow from various choices regarding the eating of meat.

The status quo involves far too much brutality toward sentient creatures to be a viable choice for those who both accept the principle that inherent value obligates due respect and also accept as fact that most of the animals we raise for food can feel frustration and pain.

Is the protest best waged by vegetarianism, then? The argument may be made, assuming that one should always calculate one's behavior so as to bring about the greatest balance of well-being over pain in the world of sentient creatures, as follows:

1. Animals are capable of feeling pleasure and pain.
2. Animal farming causes animals to feel pain.
3. If enough people stop eating meat, animal farming will cease.
4. Therefore if I stop eating meat, I will be bringing about a lesser net quantity of pain in the world of sentient creatures.

The argument, however, does not show that vegetarianism is the uniquely moral policy, even for one who acknowledges that the status quo in the meat production industry is clearly objectionable. Much less does it prove that vegetarianism would be morally required under more traditional, pastoral farming conditions.

To take the latter first, it seems on grounds of pains and pleasures that *if* conditions for farm animals are good, so that the net balance of the life experience of the typical animal being raised is positive, then it is morally right to support such practices, even if they lead to the "premature" deaths of the animals in question. Having respect for inherent value means, among other things, taking a favorable attitude toward bringing into existence as many bearers of inherent value as is reasonably compatible with the total sum of well-being. If people did not eat meat, many fewer bearers of inherent value would be brought into the world. Therefore under ideal husbandry conditions, the eating of meat makes possible a larger net good than its opposite.

That leaves the problem of slaughter, which may be approached in two steps. First, one must remember that much of the evil in the "premature" death of a human person rises from fear and frustration in anticipating the loss of life. Thus, while we may agree with point 1, above, that animals are capable of feeling pains and pleasures, we should not attribute to all animals the same *sorts of* pains and pleasures, and surely not the pains and pleasures that presume sophisticated conceptual powers. Specifically, the anxiety for the distant future that so colors human feeling about death should not be attributed to animals. It is true that animals in the abattoir may become frightened by the cries of other animals and the smells of slaughter. Our ethical obligation, then, is to insulate animals from such sounds and smells.

Indeed, if we cared (and paid) enough, slaughter itself could be accomplished under total anesthesia. That this may appear ludicrously extreme shows how far toward the other extreme current consciousness tilts. But even short of such "coddling," decent attention to animal well-being will raise costs for meat. Since competitive economic pressures will prevent businesses from responding to this ethical need without social coercion, and since evasion of these responsibilities should not be allowed across state or national lines, what ethics requires is laws and treaties mandating higher standards in the slaughterhouses of the world.

If there is any clear ethical obligation in the matter of meat eating, it is to effective action on the political level, where major reforms need to be enacted by the society at large for the humane and respectful treatment of the animals we raise. The moderate eating of meat per se is no matter for moral shame, but indifference to misery in the lives of creatures brought into existence by humans and dependent upon humans for their protections, is culpable.

IV

Two problems remain.

First, in view of the inevitable increase in the cost of meat and meat products that would be entailed by the far-reaching reforms needed in agricultural practices, it seems inevitable, though unfair, that the poor will carry the heaviest burden. Social conscience has its costs. If needed reforms were to be implemented, they would end the age of the cheap hamburger meal. But it must be kept in mind, as well, that the problem of justice to the poor (and, in general, to the marginalized, see Adams in this volume) is not at all confined to the issue of the fair distribution of meat. When some new (and socially mandated) antipollution device adds to the cost of some product, for example, it is the poorest who first feel the pain. When gasoline made its multifold price jump at the time of the oil embargo in 1973, it was again the poor who were hurt the most at the gasoline pumps. The requirement of justice for those least advantaged in a society that too often depends primarily upon the marketplace for distributing goods and status is a general one. If it is to receive its proper solution, it requires a general answer, probably in terms of a modified economic system in which basic needs are met by social policy shaped outside the marketplace, while the free institutions of the market are retained for distribution of other discretionary goods in order to maximize efficiency and freedom from coercion.[14] At any rate, the issue of higher meat prices resulting from treating our animal dependents with ethical concern should not become an excuse for abandoning efforts at reform. It should, rather, become a spur to the widening of efforts to include the plight of disadvantaged humans, and blemishes in our social system, high on the moral agenda as well.

Second, regarding the charge of "speciesism," does my suggestion entail favoring unduly one species (our own) at the expense of others without justifying warrant? Is it mere speciesism that makes us consider the moderate eating of animal flesh, under proper constraints, a legitimate practice, while forbidding the eating of human meat?

The grounds for the prohibition of the eating of human meat are immensely strong, and seem to be reinforced by an emotional revulsion that goes deep in human consciousness. The fact that there have been cannibalistic societies shows that rejection of the practice is not "instinctive" (very little human behavior is merely that), but the horror in which cannibalism is generally held shows that it is no light moral question.

Psychological grounds aside, the strongest ethical ground for the avoidance of eating human flesh is, once again, the principle of due respect for inherent value. Human beings are capable of the most complex and free-ranging mental activities we know of. It would be gross disrespect for such qualitative excellence—the capacity for intense awareness of being oneself—to look at such an entity and see only meat. Since humans can and do worry about the future, it is ethically right, as well, that they should be spared the worry about being thus hungrily eyed by their neighbors. To break the taboo on cannibalism would be consequentially unsettling in the extreme, since it would put everyone at risk of being reduced to pot roast.

Still, there are moral circumstances under which the eating of human flesh by other humans is not wrong. In extreme conditions, such as were experienced by the survivors of the famous air crash in the Andes,[15] cannibalism of dead human bodies may be in keeping with the principle of due respect—respect for the surviving human lives themselves. These situations are as rare as they are extreme, but make in any case no real exception to the rule of due respect. The door is not opened for killing humans for food. Beyond the threshold of personhood there is no relevant moral difference sufficient to make it just that one human's mentality should be so reduced in inherent value as to render that person's body food for another's metabolism.

The principle of due respect for inherent value, however, extends beyond our species alone. It is the principle on which needed reforms in animal husbandry should be built and on which consideration should be extended to all organisms, in ways appropriate to the intensity of each creature's ability to be of value for itself. Thus the respect due to a flea is not identical to the respect due to the dog on which the flea feeds. Biologically and psychologically, this is not an egalitarian universe. Appropriate respect for human beings requires that humans can count on almost complete exemption from the prospect of being eaten by other human beings. Appropriate respect for the higher mammals requires from us sustained and costly consideration for their mental as well as their physical well-being, and calls for severe controls on methods of administering death without causing fear or pain, even if we choose to kill and eat them. Appropriate respect for birds requires the avoidance by their human caretakers at least of practices that would severely frustrate instinctual needs. Appropriate respect for fish mandates that we inflict no avoidable damage in catching and handling them. Appropriate respect for crawling things, concerning which even Peter Singer acknowledges that "it may be that in our present state of knowledge we must be agnostic about whether they are capable of suffering,"[16] means that humans should live and let live, adopting only proportioned measures of self-defense, but swatting without guilt when necessary.

There are, then, discriminations between the species that are warranted on this position. The question, however, is whether they are *unjust* discriminations. They are just to the extent they are based on real, morally relevant differences. The differences are real enough, as shown by evolutionary evidence, by behavioral studies, and by physiological fact. And these differences—in capacity to have interests, to feel pain, and to experience one's own value—are morally relevant to the highest degree: fundamental good is finally defined by the possibility of experiencing satisfaction or frustration, and degree of inherent worth is defined by the quality of self-valuation.

These discriminations, so understood, are not speciesist. They would apply to the moral situation faced by another species, if one should appear from outer space with yet higher mentality and inherent quality of self-valuation than is possible for humankind. On the principle of due respect for inherent value, the alien species would have exactly the same ethical reasons not to eat human beings that human beings have to refrain from cannibalism. Only the prohibition, applicable to humans even in extreme circumstances, to refrain from killing humans for the sake of survival would be lifted, since *ex hypothesi*, this more intellectually developed species would be respecting higher inherent value in so acting as a last resort. Still, it is possible (who are we to read their alien minds?) that they would opt on moral ground for suicide rather than destroy, for mere metabolic energy, beings who have reached the delicacy of mental potential that is represented in the human species. Some pet lovers would rather starve than eat their companion dogs or cats. So much the more might highly personal alien visitors love and respect their human companions.

We have traveled far into speculation in these latter thoughts on cannibalism and extraterrestrial visitations. Following the argument begun at the dining table leads to distant vistas in ethics and metaphysics. What is close at hand, however, is the need to lead the examined life in all domains of our behavior, including our dietary choices. My conclusion is that we may, if we desire, eat meat from humanely raised and slaughtered animals in moderation and with appreciation. But whether we eat meat or refrain from it, we are in duty bound to concern ourselves with the well-being of the animals who supply it. This discovery is both food for thought and a call to political action.

NOTES

1. Frederick Ferré, *Living and Value: Toward a Constructive Postmodern Ethics* (Albany: State University of New York Press, 2001), esp. chap. 8; see also Frederick Ferré, *Shaping the Future: Resources for the Post-Modern World* (New York: Harper & Row, 1976), esp. chaps. 5–9.

2. Alfred North Whitehead, *The Function of Reason* (Boston: Beacon Press, 1929), chap. 1, p. 4.

3. Christopher D. Stone, *Should Trees Have Standing?* (New York: Avon Books, 1975).

4. Kenneth E. Goodpaster, "On Stopping at Everything: A Reply to W. M. Hunt," *Environmental Ethics* 2, no. 3 (Fall 1980): 284. See also Goodpaster's initial statement, "On Being Morally Considerable," *Journal of Philosophy* 75 (1978): 308–25.

5. Immanuel Kant, *Critique of Practical Reason and Other Works on the Theory of Ethics*, 6th ed., trans. T. K. Abbott (London: Longman's Green & Co.). See esp. "Fundamental Principles of the Metaphysics of Morals," p. 56.

6. Peter Singer, "Animal Liberation," originally published in *New York Review of Books*, April 5, 1973, reprinted in *Moral Problems: A Collection of Philosophical Essays*, 3rd ed., ed. James Rachels (New York: Harper & Row, 1979), p. 98.

7. Tom Regan, "Ethical Vegetarianism and Commercial Animal Farming," originally published in the *Proceedings of the University of Florida's Conference on Agriculture, Change and Human Values*. It is reprinted in *Today's Moral Problems*, 3rd ed., ed. Richard A. Wasserstrom (New York: Macmillan, 1985), p. 472.

8. Regan, "Ethical Vegetarianism and Commercial Animal Farming," p. 469.

9. Ibid., p. 471.

10. Jean-Paul Sartre, *Being and Nothingness*, trans. Hazel E. Barnes (New York:

Philosophical Library, 1956); Alfred North Whitehead, *Process and Reality* (New York: Humanities Press, 1929); *Science and the Modern World* (New York: Free Press, 1925), esp. pp. 93–94.

11. Mary Midgley, *Animals and Why They Matter* (Athens: University of Georgia Press, 1984).

12. H. J. McCloskey, "Moral Rights and Animals," in Wasserstrom, *Today's Moral Problems*, pp. 479–505.

13. Frederick Ferré, "Personalism and the Dignity of Nature," *Personalist Forum* 2, no. 1 (Spring 1986): 1–28.

14. Frederick Ferré, *Living and Value*, pp. 318–20.

15. Piers Paul Read, *Alive: The Story of the Andes Survivors* (Philadelphia: Lippencott, 1974), and Richard Cunningham, *The Place Where the World Ends: A Modern Story of Cannibalism and Human Courage* (New York: Sheed & Ward, 1973).

16. Singer, "Animal Liberation," p. 89.

VEGETARIANISM[1] AND ECOFEMINISM
Toppling Patriarchy with a Fork

Marti Kheel

27

F or centuries, advocates for vegetarianism have sought to reform meat eaters through rational arguments. Behind this attempt lies a faith in the ability of reason to enforce a moral obligation to be vegetarian. However, the arguments for why someone should be vegetarian may have little to do with the actual factors that influence people to adopt vegetarianism. In this essay, I offer an alternative approach to the debate over meat eating. Rather than trying to develop a rational foundation in support of vegetarianism, I draw on ecofeminist theory to subject the dominant norm, meat eating, to closer scrutiny. I examine the sociocultural substructure that supports the practice of meat eating and, in particular, its foundation in patriarchal modes of thought. I focus on the Western world, since that is the area where meat eating predominates and where the connection between meat dominance and male dominance is most apparent. It is also the area where the most widespread abuse of nonhuman animals occurs, that is, on factory farms. I do not attempt to "defend" vegetarianism as a universal norm to be imposed on all people as a moral imperative; rather, I ask, what are the factors that support meat eating as a dietary norm? Moreover, what factors might invite vegetarianism as a response? By developing this invitational approach to vegetarianism, I seek to move away from the construction of universal norms and abstract principles to the deconstruction of a dominant dietary norm, namely, meat eating.

ECOFEMINIST PHILOSOPHY

Feminism and vegetarianism have been intimately intertwined both as movements and as philosophies for many years. Feminists typically have condemned forms of domination and have expressed compassion for the downtrodden. Nonhuman animals, including the animals living on farms, have often been on the receiving end of this compassion. In spite of the support for vegetarianism among many feminists, there has also been a countervailing trend. Feminism was an outgrowth of the European Enlightenment, which subscribed to the idea of a dualism between humans and the rest of nature. In the Enlightenment worldview, human beings alone are made in the image of God and endowed with reason, setting them apart from the rest of the natural world. Progress, thus, is predicated upon severing one's ties to the nonhuman world. The demand not to be treated like animals was a common rallying cry among early feminists. Underlying this idea is the notion that the exploitation of rational beings (namely humans) is morally wrong whereas the exploitation of nonhuman animals is not.

Ecofeminist philosophers have a different vision of human beings' relation to the natural world. Rather than seeking to sever human ties to the natural world, ecofeminists critique the worldview that devalues both women and nature. Ecofeminism is a loosely knit philosophical school of thought that draws connections between the domination of nature and the domination of women.[2] Despite variations in viewpoints, most ecofeminists are united in their critique of the dualistic worldview of patriarchal society. Ecofeminists argue that Western patriarchal society operates by means of a series of gendered dualisms. The male half of the dualism is associated with "culture," "good," the "rational," and the "spiritual," while the female half is associated with "nature," "evil," the "nonrational," and the "profane." Ecofeminists are also critical of the atomistic worldview of patriarchal society, which overvalues autonomy and the role of reason, and devalues relationships of care. In place of this atomistic worldview, ecofeminists view nature as an interconnected web of life, no part of which may be said to be superior to the other.

By and large, ecofeminists have been content to speak generally about their vision of a holistic web of life. There has been little discussion among ecofeminists about what particular practices constitute care; nor has there been much discussion about the practice of vegetarianism.[3] Like feminists more generally, ecofeminists have become increasingly wary of abstract norms and universal rules that purport to apply to all people without regard to gender, race, class, and culture. Since vegetarianism typically is viewed as endorsing a universal dietary norm, some ecofeminists have explicitly argued against it. But although ecofeminist philosophy may not support the case for vegetarianism as a universal norm, it may, nonetheless, help to dislodge the conceptual substructures that support the practice of meat eating. In so doing, it can clear a space in which to plant the seeds that invite the vegetarian ideal.

COMPULSORY MEAT EATING

Meat eating has been the dominant norm for centuries in the Western world. It is the nature of dominant norms to be accepted without question. Thus, when people become vegetarians they are typically asked to explain their dietary choice. But no one thinks to ask meat eaters why they became meat eaters. An analogy with the institution of heterosexuality helps to shed light on this phenomenon. In a well-known article the feminist author Adrienne Rich argues that in patriarchal society, heterosexuality is not simply a choice or preference, but rather a compulsory institutional norm, which is "imposed, managed, organized, propagandized, and maintained by force."[4] The purpose of this enforcement is to maintain "male right of physical, economic and emotional access" to women.

A similar attitude may be argued to exist in relation to meat eating in Western culture. Meat eating, like heterosexuality, is viewed as a compulsory institutional norm that is "imposed, managed, organized, propagandized, and maintained by force" for the purpose of ensuring male-dominated society's rightful access to nonhuman animals and to their flesh.

Individuals who defy the mandatory norm of meat eating encounter similar obstacles to those faced by people who challenge the norm of heterosexuality. Just as a woman is considered incomplete without a man, so, too, vegetarian foods are viewed as incomplete without the addition of flesh.[5] And just as people often wonder how a lesbian can possibly find sexual fulfillment without a man, many people wonder how vegetarians can possibly find dietary fulfillment without meat. People ask vegetarians, "What do you eat?" with the same combination of incomprehension and bewilderment that they ask lesbians, "What do you do?" In each case, people imagine the person to be deprived or incomplete, lacking a full sexual or dietary identity. A number of vegetarians report that they had more difficulty "coming out" as vegetarians than coming out as gay.[6]

MEAT EATING, MANHOOD, AND THE CULTURE OF VIOLENCE

Meat eating is a biological activity, but it is also a practice that is steeped in culture and encoded with symbolic meanings.[7] Meat eating forms the crucible of a network of relationships. Obtaining meat, eating meat, and sharing meat are modes of establishing particular kinds of relationships. Relationships are formed with family and friends and severed with those who are excluded from the circle of sharing (and of course with the animal who is killed). Historically, relationships with those outside the circle of sharing have been based on hierarchical divisions, particularly those based on gender, class, and status.

Meat is widely recognized as a food that is eaten predominantly by those who have greater prestige. In most countries, people with higher incomes eat proportionately greater amounts of flesh foods. Similarly, hunting reserves traditionally have belonged to the royalty who are accorded privileged access to the meat obtained from the hunt. Conferring meat on others is often seen as a status symbol, signifying one's wealth and class. Meat is also typically associated with virility, strength, aggression, as well as with sexual potency. Men are typically given a disproportionate share of meat, and men who do not eat meat are often viewed as effeminate. During warfare, it is considered especially important for men to eat meat.

An opposing phenomenon exists in the realm of spirituality. Whereas consuming flesh typically is thought to signify higher status and virility in the secular realm, abstaining from flesh has typically been thought to signify higher status in the spiritual realm.[8] Throughout human history eating the flesh of animals has been thought to arouse the animal passions and to therefore be unsuitable for those in holy orders. Holiness or purity, therefore, is typically established by denying oneself flesh foods. Rather than battling external nature, spiritual devotees direct their conquest against internal nature, that is, the "animal passions." The ancient Greek philosopher Pythagoras, best known for his mathematical theories, is an example of this spiritual orientation. Pythagoras viewed meat eating as an impediment to the soul's ascent to its divine origins. While Pythagoras combined concern for moral purity with concern for the suffering of nonhuman animals, many spiritually oriented vegetarians viewed vegetarianism only as a means of rising above the realm of carnal desires. Many of the early church fathers exemplify this view, believing that spiritual life required renouncing both sex and flesh foods; vegetarianism was considered praiseworthy only if it was practiced with the correct intention, namely, as a spiritual discipline by which one conquered the carnal desires. The association of meat with privilege and prestige made it additionally unsuitable for those in holy orders.

The association between meat eating and class, status, and gender can be clearly seen in the oldest forms of meat eating, namely hunting and animal sacrifice. Hunting, although not an exclusively male activity, has a long history of association with masculine self-identity.[9] Many cultures require a young boy to hunt and kill an animal as a symbolic rite of passage into manhood. The initiation is designed to help the boy to detach from natural ties of affection, enabling him to transfer his allegiance to an external standard of manliness based on self-control and control over others.[10] Significantly, the young boy initiate is frequently sequestered from the world of women as well and sexual relations with women are often prohibited before and after the hunt. Hunting has also frequently been viewed as "combat training" or a sort of "war game." Aristotle argued that hunting was good preparation for war and that killing wild animals constituted a "just war."

Hunting has also often been viewed as an erotic activity, which is one of the reasons why it has historically been forbidden to those in holy orders. The ingestion of the flesh is similarly viewed as part of the erotic experience. The anthropologist Paul Shepard writes, "whereas the ecstatic consummation of love is killing, the formal consummation is eating."[11] Hunting in this conception has a narrative structure whose denouement requires the eating of flesh. To remove the consumption of the flesh from the hunting experience renders the narrative meaningless.

Like hunting, animal sacrifice is an activity that is intimately tied to meat eating and masculine self-identity. Sacrifice and meat eating were widely practiced in the ancient world, and inextricably intertwined. The ancient temples were more akin to abattoirs and butcher shops than our modern conception of holy places. In ancient Greece sacrifice was part of the state religion, and the flesh of the sacrificed animal was eaten at all public festivals. Animal sacrifice was performed for a variety of reasons, but the underlying theme entailed the idea that the sacrifice of the animal helped to mediate between the material and transcendent realms. In this conception, the consumption of the animal's flesh cements the bond between the two spheres. The mediating role of flesh can be seen in the Hebrew tradition, where the priest consumed part of the sacrificed animal, reserving the rest for God. In partaking of the same flesh that is eaten by God, the sacrificers engaged in a kind of metaphorical "intercourse" with God. The Hebrew God's anger at those who sacrificed to other gods (or idols) was an expression of anger over a metaphorical infidelity of the flesh. The idea of a metaphorical intercourse with God can still be found in the Christian religion where the congregation symbolically eats the body and "blood of Christ."

According to the anthropologist Nancy Jay, men perform sacrifice in an effort to achieve the sense of continuity across the generations that women are endowed with by nature.[12] The logic of the sacrificers, who are ordinarily male, is governed by the urge to replicate the birthing process on a purportedly more spiritual plane. The sacrificers perform a role analogous to mothers, initiating the participants into a transcendent male order that connects men with one another across the generations. Birth from a woman condemns one to death, but "rebirth" through sacrifice integrates men into a transcendent order that transcends mortality and death.

WOMEN, NONHUMAN ANIMALS, AND THE "OTHER"

Women have also been viewed as symbols that mediate a relationship with a transcendent order. According to Simone de Beauvoir, due to the contingencies of women's biology, that is, pregnancy, menstruation, and childbirth, women have historically been viewed as mired in the realm of nature.[13] Men, by contrast, are perceived as free to transcend the natural world. Historically, she argues, men have achieved this transcendence by means of the subordination of women and the natural world. In the process of pursuing transcendence, men establish their identities as distinct and opposed to nature. Women, thus, become the "other" against which masculine self-identity is established. Significantly, she argues that the prototypical acts of transcendence over the natural world are hunting, fishing, and warfare.

The idea that masculine self-identity entails separation from women and the natural world can also be found in the psychological school of object relations theory.[14] According to this theory, both boys and girls begin life with a sense of oneness with the mother figure. Unlike girls, however, boys go through a two-staged process of maturation. They must not only disengage from the mother figure, but they must deny all that is female within themselves as well as their ties to the female world. The mother thus becomes an object in relation to which the boy must develop his identity as "not female."

The conception of women and animals as objects or the "other" can also be found in the Western religious and philosophical tradition.[15] As previously mentioned, ecofeminist philosophers point out that in the Western tradition, women and nature are associated with a series of dualisms. They are viewed as "evil," "nonrational," and as "matter," in contrast to that which is "good," "rational," and "divine." Both Aristotelian and Platonic philosophy contributed to the conception of nature as mindless matter. Perhaps, most harmful in its effects, however, has been the Aristotelian and Stoic legacy, which postulates that the nonrational functioned for the benefit of the rational. Thus according to Aristotle, plants functioned to give subsistence to animals and animals to give subsistence to "Man." Although nonhuman animals have their own individual telos or ends, the final result of this world ordering functions to free "Man" for the highest good, namely rational contemplation. Significantly, women, slaves, and foreigners are viewed as part of the inferior, nonrational world that exists to serve "rational" Man.

Judaism and Christianity have given further support to the idea that women and nature exist to serve men's needs. Since Adam was God's first creation and God is typically imaged as male, it is men in particular who have been associated with the divine. The Genesis accounts of creation underline the view of the subservient status of women and animals. In the priestly account of Creation, "Man," is assigned "dominion" over the rest of creation (Genesis 1:26). And in the Yahwist account, nonhumans are created to be helpers or companions for Adam, and when they were seen as unfit, Eve was created to fulfill this role (Genesis 2:22). Once again, women and nonhuman animals function to serve the needs of others.

ANIMAL HUSBANDRY

The association between meat eating and masculine self-identity can readily be seen in the examples of hunting and animal sacrifice. But it can also be discerned in the practice of "animal husbandry." The term "animal husbandry" suggests the association between ownership of women and nonhuman animals. Just as a husband is assumed to possess a wife, so, too, the producers of animal flesh are thought to own the animals on their farms. And just as a marriage ceremony symbolically obliterates the identity of a woman by uniting "man" and "wife" as "one in flesh," (namely, the man's), so, too, the consumption of animal flesh entails the literal obliteration of animals.

The view of women and animals as flesh is accompanied by their image as property or "chattel," a word that significantly derives from the same root word as "cattle." Women are owned by male husbands, just as cattle are owned by men who perform "animal husbandry." Animals are kept on "farms," just as women are kept in "families." Significantly, the word "family" derives from the Roman word "famulus," meaning "slave," and refers to a husband's legal ownership of his wife and children.

Animal husbandry is based upon the control of the reproductive process of nonhuman animals. Factory farms require the continued reproduction of animals, as well as the "products" of female animals' reproductive cycles, such as milk and eggs. The animals that do not conform to the design of this institutional complex are literally discarded as trash or sent off to slaughter. Thus, male baby chicks that are born to egg-laying chickens are regularly gassed or thrown in trash cans to die slow, agonizing deaths because they serve no function in the egg industry. Artificial insemination, which maximizes male control of female reproduction, has become the norm on most factory farms. As soon as the reproductive capacity of factory-farm animals begins to wane, they are sent off to be slaughtered, since they are no longer of use.

Women, like nonhuman animals, are also exploited for their reproductive capacity. A woman's ability to bear children is considered one of the major assets that she brings to a marriage, and women who are infertile are made to feel inadequate, which often leads them to jeopardize their own health in an effort to overcome their infertility. Women's fertility is also increasingly being exploited by the male-dominated medical establishment, which now routinely "harvests" women's eggs. The underlying idea behind both operations is the same—women's bodies and animals' bodies belong first and foremost to men.

Along with the notion of ownership of women and animals, the modern production of flesh promotes the notion of women and animals as objects to be consumed. Men consume women's bodies in sex shows, houses of prostitution, and pornographic magazines. Their sexual "appetites" are aroused by women's bodies in the same way that their taste buds are aroused by animal flesh. Although women are not literally consumed, many women describe their experience of sexual objectification as one in which they are treated like a piece of meat. Women's body parts are also fetishized in our culture, as are animal body parts. Women's identities are also consumed by men. Symbolically, the woman is transferred in the wedding ceremony, like a commodity, from the property of the father to that of the husband. The loss of a woman's self-identity is reinforced by the loss of her name. Marriage is also thought to be consummated by the husband's sexual access to his wife's flesh.

CULTURAL AND ECOLOGICAL CRITIQUES

The above analysis does not make the case directly for why someone should become a vegetarian. Yet, it invites vegetarianism as a response. If people are opposed to the domination of women, they may be more inclined to empathize with the plight of nonhuman animals once they understand the connections between the domination of women and of nonhuman animals. It is empathy, not abstract norms, that provides the motivation for vegetarianism in this invitational approach. Vegetarianism thus becomes part of a larger resistance to violence and domination. Renouncing meat becomes an affirmation of one's connection to nonhuman animals and to the earth.

A number of ecofeminist and other philosophers have charged vegetarians in the West with trying to impose a white, middle-class norm on other cultures where people eat meat out of necessity or due to their own cultural norms. They advocate a "contextual" approach to vegetarianism in recognition of the particular situation that exists within each cultural context.[16] Inviting vegetarianism as an ethical ideal, however, is not the same as seeking to impose one's beliefs on other people and other cultures. The invitational approach to vegetarianism recognizes that the subject of meat eating differs across the boundaries of culture, race, gender, and class. It acknowledges that there may be limiting factors, such as geography and climate, which preclude the possibility of eating a vegetarian diet for some people. Vegetarianism, conceived as an ideal, however, may be viewed as an invitation; and invitations cannot always be honored and may be declined. Recognition of cultural context should also not preclude a critical examination of the practice of meat eating and the factors that prevent vegetarianism as a choice. The sensitivity to racial and cultural differences that has emerged among feminists and other theorists in recent years is extremely valuable, but it should not be used to try to suppress the expression of the vegetarian ideal, which in and of itself is not oppressive.

It is interesting to note that "contextual" approaches to meat eating often fail to examine the cultural associations that exist between meat eating and gender, status, and class. Typically, the contextual approach focuses on the importance of understanding and respecting meat eating within the overall context of particular cultures, without examining the subcultural contexts that exist within the larger culture. While it is important to try to understand, and where appropriate, respect the practices of other cultures, this should not preclude a deeper analysis of the cultural associations that may underlie those practices, and in particular the cultural associations between masculine self-identity and meat eating. Understanding the meanings that attach to behaviors of other cultures is fraught with difficulties. But this should not preclude the attempt to understand them.

The charge of cultural insensitivity and cultural imperialism tends to be made selectively against Western advocates for vegetarianism. The example of indigenous cultures is typically used to advance the argument that vegetarianism is disrespectful of those cultures where meat is obtained in respectful ways, as evidenced by the prayers of forgiveness that are said before the killing of an animal.[17] Little if any mention is made of the vegetarian traditions in Eastern cultures, where vegetarianism is sometimes the norm. Jains and some Buddhists make strong statements in favor of vegetarianism, and yet they are not charged with cultural insensitivity. Thich Nat Hanh, for example, has endorsed vegetarianism as an embodiment of the ideal of nonviolence, but no one to my knowledge argues that he is guilty of cultural imperialism.[18] Vegetarianism is not simply a lifestyle of white, middle-class people, but a cherished ideal of many cultures throughout the world, which a growing number of people in the Western world embrace.

Vegetarians are also often charged with having an anti-ecological awareness. By trying to extend moral consideration to nonhuman animals, Val Plumwood, for example, argues that vegetarians inadvertently establish a neo-Cartesian view, which extends moral consideration to human and nonhuman animals, thereby excluding plants.[19] But Plumwood presumes that the avoidance of flesh foods is based on an abstract philosophical viewpoint. While some advocates for vegetarianism may invoke abstract philosophical arguments in support of their vegetarianism, many people are motivated by a visceral repugnance to the idea of the suffering and death of nonhuman animals, hardly a disembodied Cartesian response. Often, it is the ability to put oneself into the bodies of other animals, rather than abstract philosophical thought, that motivates people to become vegetarian. The ability to feel empathy for the suffering of other animals is no more anti-ecological than is our repugnance for other forms of violence, including the killing of human beings.[20]

It is also often argued that vegetarians fail to accept that predation is a natural part of the life cycle and that eating flesh is an affirmation of human participation in the web of life.[21] But predators represent only 20 percent of the animals in the natural world; and apart from animals slaughtered by humans, only 5 percent of all animals are killed by other animals.[22] In addition, the capture and domestication of other animals in order to breed them for their flesh and the products that they produce is without parallel in the natural world.

ECOFEMINISM AND AN ETHIC OF CARE

The philosophical underpinnings of the modern animal advocacy movement typically draw on the philosophy of justice and rights. To the extent that nonhuman animals share morally significant qualities in common with humans, it is argued, they must be accorded rights. The idea of rights is conceived as an impartial ethic that transcends feelings of care.[23] A growing number of feminists, however, have sought to move away from an emphasis on universal norms and abstract rules to a focus on the importance of care in ethical decision making.[24] Feminists argue that the emphasis on the superiority of the universal norms of justice and rights over an ethic of care is a masculinist orientation, which overvalues the role of reason and autonomy in ethical decision making and undervalues the importance of interdependence and care. The notion of moral conduct as an activity that is performed by an isolated and autonomous decision maker fails to take into account the contingencies, both external and internal, which limit our choices; they also overvalue the role of conscious choice in moral decision making.

The emphasis on the importance of an ethic of care is a welcome insight; nonetheless, much of the discussion of an ethic of care has often sought to use the same conceptual tools used by traditional moral theories.

The point has been to show that the traditionally female imaged ethic of care can, in fact, break out of its traditional role in the domestic sphere and "make it" in the public realm of justice and rights. But what if we refrain from the urge to make an ethic of care emulate the purported rigor of a theory of justice and rights? What if we ask the more important questions: What is it that nourishes care and connection and what causes it to fail? And how are caring relationships forged? Since traditional moral theories have tended to presume the predisposition toward aggressive conduct, they have overlooked the underlying reasons why such tendencies may exist. As Alison Jaggar has argued, "Because we expect humans to be aggressive, we find the idea of cooperation puzzling. If, instead of focusing on antagonistic interactions, we focused on cooperative interaction, we would find the idea of competition puzzling."[25]

An ethic of care, while useful, has particular limitations with respect to the nonhuman world. Caring for and about nonhuman animals must be distinguished from caretaking or stewardship. The tradition of stewardship has been interpreted as a human obligation to manage the rest of nature. The stewardship model of caretaking has been an underlying idea behind both animal farming as well as the conservation movement. This form of caretaking focuses on the functioning of the whole of nature, not the well-being of individual beings, who may be "sacrificed" for the whole.

A number of feminist philosophers have focused on the act of attention as an alternative to the emphasis on abstract rules and universal norms. Iris Murdoch has argued that when one devotes a "patient, loving regard" upon a "person, a thing, a situation," the will is presented not as "unimpeded movement" but as "something very much more like obedience."[26] In this alternative vision of ethics, empathy and imagination are more critically important than conscious reasoning and choice. With respect to nonhuman animals, the question that can then be posed is why has this patient, loving regard been so singularly absent in human treatment of nonhuman animals, including the ones whom people eat?

The act of attention functions not only to forge bonds of relationships; it also functions to maintain oppressive structures. Sarah Hoagland argues that values flow from the choices that we make and the things that we choose to focus upon.[27] Using the Wittgensteinian notion of an axis that is held in place by what surrounds it, Hoagland shows the ways in which patriarchal thought is held in place by a system of dominance and subordination. Justice under this system is designed to sort out competing claims within an axis of domination and subordination. Hoagland does not attempt to disprove patriarchal values, but rather to transform perceptions "so that existing values cease to make sense."[28] Her strategy is to make existing perceptions inconceivable. In the new paradigm that she calls for, "rape, pogroms, slavery, lynching, and colonialism" are inconceivable.[29]

Similarly, one can ask the question, what are the factors that support meat eating, and what would it take to create a world in which the human consumption of other animals was inconceivable?

CONCLUSION

In the foregoing analysis, I have sought to offer an invitational approach to vegetarianism. I have suggested that the focus on developing compelling arguments for why it is morally correct to become vegetarian may be missing the mark. The more important question, I suggest, is: what are the factors that support the practice of meat eating and that give meat eating its compelling force? A major factor that buttresses meat eating in the Western world, I have argued, is its intimate ties to masculine self-identity. Meat eating is both an expression of a patriarchal worldview as well as one of its central supports. It is a symbol of dominance over the natural world that has been intimately tied to the domination of women.

Ecofeminist philosophy provides an important lens through which to examine the practice of meat eating. By bringing meat eating into critical scrutiny, and examining the nature of the relationships that surround meat eating, ecofeminism can help to challenge the conceptual force that holds meat eating in place. Ecofeminist philosophy can thus open up a space in which to plant the seeds of a new relationship to food. In this new dietary paradigm, meat eating is not renounced due to the compelling force of an abstract norm; nor is it renounced as an expression of asceticism. Instead, people are drawn to vegetarian food by its positive allure. The appeal of vegetarian foods flows at once from an urge to resist patriarchal forms of dominance and control, and from positive feelings of empathy and care for the other animals with whom we share the earth. It is an invitation that many cannot refuse.

NOTES

1. Although I use the more familiar word "vegetarian" throughout this essay, it would often be more accurate to use the word "vegan," since I use "vegetarian" to signify a diet that excludes animal products as well as animal flesh.

2. On ecofeminist philosophy, see, for example, Greta Gaard, ed., *Ecofeminism, Women, Animals, Nature* (Philadelphia: Temple University Press 1993), and Karen J. Warren, *Ecofeminist Philosophy: A Western Perspective on What It Is and Why It Matters* (Lanham, MD: Rowman and Littlefield, 2000).

3. Two notable ecofeminist anthologies that do focus on the importance of nonhuman animals and vegetarianism are Gaard, *Ecofeminism, Women, Animal,*

Nature, and Josephine Donovan and Carol J. Adams, eds., *Animals and Women: Theoretical Explorations* (Durham, NC: Duke University Press, 1995).

4. Adrienne Rich, "Compulsory Heterosexuality and Lesbian Existence," *Signs* 5, no. 4 (1979): 631–90.

5. This analogy is drawn by Carol Adams in *The Sexual Politics of Meat* (New York: Continuum, 1990), pp. 33–34.

6. For example, a college student recently told me that some of his classmates, although vegan, had not yet "come out of the pantry." Private communication, Francisco Rodriguez, January 22, 2003.

7. On the symbolic role of meat eating in culture, see Nick Fiddes, *Meat: A Natural Symbol* (New York: Routledge, 1991), and Adams, *The Sexual Politics of Meat.*

8. On vegetarianism in religious traditions, see, for example, Rynn Berry, *Food for the Gods: Vegetarianism and the World's Religions: Essays and Conversations* (New York: Pythagorean, 1998), and Steve Rosen, *Diet for Transcendence: Vegetarianism and the World Religions* (Badger, CA.: Torchlight Publishing, 1997).

9. On the connection between hunting and masculine self-identity, see, for example, David Gilmore, *Manhood in the Making: Cultural Concepts of Masculinity* (New Haven: Yale University Press, 1990), and Matt Cartmill, *A View to a Death in the Morning: Hunting and Nature Through History* (Cambridge: Harvard University Press, 1993).

10. See Marilyn French, *Beyond Power: On Women, Men, and Morals* (New York: Summit Books, 1985).

11. Paul Shepard, *The Tender Carnivore and the Sacred Game* (New York: Scribner's, 1973), p. 173.

12. Nancy Jay, *Throughout Your Generations Forever: Sacrifice, Religion, and Paternity* (Chicago: University of Chicago Press, 1992).

13. See Simone de Beauvoir, *The Second Sex,* trans. H. M. Parshley (New York: Vintage Books, 1974).

14. Object relations theory has been criticized by a number of feminists on a number of accounts, including the charge that it contains universal, monocausal claims about men's and women's essential identities. While some of these claims are well founded, I find the central insight of object relations theory into the oppositional nature of the construction of masculine self-identity to be, nevertheless, instructive. On object relations theory, see, for example, Nancy Chodorow, *The Reproduction of Mothering: Psychoanalysis and the Sociology of Gender* (Berkeley: University of California Press, 1978), and Dorothy Dinnerstein, *The Mermaid and the Minotaur: Sexual Arrangement and Human Malaise* (New York: Harper and Row, 1976).

15. The following analysis of the images of women and nonhuman animals in the Western philosophical and religious traditions focuses on the predominant historical view and is not intended to overlook minority traditions in the West that have recognized the idea of kinship with nonhuman animals, as well as compassion.

16. See, for example, Val Plumwood, "Integrating Ethical Frameworks for Animals, Humans, and Nature: A Critical Feminist Eco-Socialist Analysis," *Ethics and the Environment* 5, no. 2 (2000): 285–322, and Deanne Curtin, "Toward an Ecolog-

ical Ethic of Care," in *Ecological Feminist Philosophies*, ed. Karen J. Warren (Bloomington: Indiana University Press, 1966), pp. 66–81.

17. The significance of the prayers and rituals that are directed toward non-human animals among indigenous people is the subject of controversy. While many people view them as evidence of respect, other commentators have suggested that they are based on fears about retribution from the animals, or pragmatic concerns about ensuring a continued supply of animals for future hunts. Indigenous cultures are often treated as a monolithic block, overlooking the differences that exist among particular tribes. For challenges to the romantic contention that all indigenous cultures treated animals with reverence and respect, see, for example, Calvin Martin, *Keepers of the Game: Indian-Animal Relations and the Fur Trade* (Berkeley: University of California Press, 1978); Clifford D. Presnall, "Wildlife Conservation as Affected by American Indian and Caucasian Concepts," *Journal of Mammalogy* 24, no. 4 (1943): 458–64; Shepard Krech, *The Ecological Indian: Myth and History* (New York: W.W. Norton, 1999); and Tom Regan, "Environmental Ethics and the Ambiguity of the Native American's Relationship with Nature," in *All That Dwell Therein: Essays on Animal Rights and Environmental Ethics* (Berkeley: University of California Press, 1982), pp. 206–39.

18. Thich Nat Hahn, "Cultivating Compassion, Responding to Violence" (lecture presented at the Berkeley Community Theater, Berkeley, CA, September 13, 2001). Audio and videotape copies are available from the Deer Park Monastery, attn: AV Team, Escondido, CA, or via e-mail, dpavideo@earthlink.net, or fax: 760-291-1010.

19. Plumwood, "Integrating Ethical Frameworks."

20. Plumwood recognizes this visceral response in the natural repugnance that humans have for eating other humans. As she states, "Many animals do not eat their own kind for what appear to be ethical bonding and species life reasons. . . ." (ibid., p. 319). She fails to appreciate that this visceral response to eating one's kind need not be restricted to only humankind; it is equally repugnant for some people to eat other (nonhuman) animals. The aversion to eating the flesh of other animals does not exclude a consideration for the well-being of plants. Many vegetarians find comfort in the fact that far fewer plants need to be killed in order to sustain a vegetarian diet.

21. See, for example, Holmes Rolston III, *Environmental Ethics: Duties to and Values in the Natural World* (Philadelphia: Temple University Press, 1998).

22. Stephan Lackner, *An Optimistic View of Life on Earth* (San Francisco: Harper and Row, 1984), p. 12.

23. For a feminist critique of the idea of rights with respect to nonhuman animals, see the essays in Josephine Donovan and Carol Adams, eds., *Beyond Animal Rights: A Feminist Caring Ethic for the Treatment of Animals* (New York: Continuum, 1996). For Tom Regan's response to feminist critics, see "The Case for Animal Rights: A Decade's Passing," in *Defending Animal Rights* (Chicago: University of Illinois Press, 2001).

24. There is a large body of feminist literature on an ethic of care. See, for example, Carol Gilligan, *In a Different Voice: Psychological Theory and Women's Development* (Cambridge: Harvard University Press, 1993), and Victoria Ward and Jill

McLean Taylor, with Betty Bardige, eds., *Mapping the Moral Domain* (Cambridge: Harvard University Press, 1993).

25. Alison Jaggar, *Feminist Politics and Human Nature* (Totowa, NJ: Rowman & Allanheld, 1983), p. 41.

26. Iris Murdoch, *The Sovereignty of Good* (Boston: Routledge and Kegan Paul, 1970), p. 40.

27. Sarah Lucia Hoagland, *Lesbian Ethics: Toward New Value* (Palo Alto, CA: Institute of Lesbian Studies, 1989).

28. Ibid., p. 234.

29. Ibid., p. 73.

Section Seven

WHICH IS MORE IMPORTANT, RESPECTING CULTURAL DIVERSITY OR PROTECTING ANIMALS?

ANIMALS AND ECOLOGY
Toward a
Better Integration
Val Plumwood

28

Agriculture has become agribusiness after all. So the creatures that have been under our "stewardship" the longest, that have been codified by habit for our use, that have always suffered a special place in our regard—the farm animals—have never been as cruelly kept or confined or slaughtered in such numbers in all of human history.... The factory farm today is a crowded stinking bedlam, filled with suffering animals that are quite literally insane, sprayed with pesticides and fattened on a diet of growth stimulants, antibiotics, and drugs. Two hundred and fifty thousand laying hens are confined within a single building. (The high mortality rate caused by overcrowding is economically acceptable; nothing is more worthless than an individual chicken).[1]

1: ECOLOGICAL ANIMALISM VERSUS ONTOLOGICAL VEGANISM

Many thinking people have come to believe that there is something profoundly wrong in commodity culture's relationship to living things. That something is expressed perhaps most obviously in the factory farms that profit from distorting and instrumentalizing animal lives. In numerous books and articles I have argued that these abuses are enabled and justified by a dominant human-centered ideology of mastery over an inferior sphere of animals and nature.[2] It is this ideology that is expressed in economies that treat commodity animals reductively as less than they are, as a mere human resource, little more than living meat or egg production units.

People aiming to clarify and deepen their experience of contemporary abuse of animals and nature face an important set of choices in philosophical theory. In particular, they have to choose whether to opt for theories of animal ethics and ontology that emphasize discontinuity and set human life apart from animals and ecology, or theories that emphasize human continuity with other life forms and situate both human and animal life within an ethically and ecologically conceived universe. I represent this choice in this essay by comparing two theories that challenge—in quite different ways—the dominant ideology of mastery. Ontological veganism is a theory that advocates universal abstention from all use of animals as the only real alternative to mastery and the leading means of defending animals against its wrongs. But, I shall argue, another theory that also supports animal defense, which I shall call ecological animalism, more thoroughly disrupts the ideology of mastery and is significantly better than ontological veganism for environmental awareness, for human liberation, and for animal activism itself.

Ecological animalism supports and celebrates animals and encourages a dialogical ethics of sharing and negotiation or partnership between humans and animals, while undertaking a reevaluation of human identity that affirms inclusion in animal and ecological spheres. The theory I shall develop is a context-sensitive semivegetarian position, which advocates great reductions in first-world meat eating and opposes reductive and disrespectful conceptions and treatments of animals, especially in factory farming. The dominant human mastery position that is deeply entrenched in Western culture has constructed a great gulf or dualism between humans and nature, which I call human/nature dualism. Human/nature dualism conceives humans as inside culture but "outside nature" and conceives nonhumans as outside ethics and culture. The theory I advocate aims to disrupt this deep historical dualism by resituating humans in ecological terms at the same time as it resituates nonhumans in ethical and cultural terms. It affirms an ecological universe of mutual use, and sees humans and animals as mutually available for respectful use in conditions of equality. Ecological animalism uses the philosophical method of contextualizing to allow us to express our care for both animals and ecology, and to acknowledge at the same time different cultures in different ecological contexts, differing nutritional situations and needs, and multiple forms of oppression.

The theory I shall recommend rejecting, ontological veganism, has numerous problems for both theory and activism on animal equality and ecology. It ties strategy, philosophy, and personal commitment tightly to personal veganism, that is, abstention from eating and using animals as a form of individual action. Ontological veganism insists that neither humans nor animals should ever be conceived as edible or even as usable, confirming the treatment of humans as "outside nature" that is part of human/nature dualism, and blocking any reconception of animals and humans in fully ecological terms. Because it is indiscriminate in proscribing all forms of animal use as having the same moral status, it fails to provide philosophical guidance for animal activism that would prioritize action on factory farming over less abusive forms of farming. Its universalism makes it highly ethnocentric, universalizing a privileged "consumer" perspective, ignoring contexts other than contemporary Western urban ones, or aiming to treat them as minor, deviant "exceptions" to what it takes to be the ideal or norm. Although it claims to oppose the dominant mastery position, it remains subtly human-centered because it does not fully challenge human/nature dualism, but rather attempts to extend human status and privilege to a bigger class of "semihumans" who, like humans themselves, are conceived as above the nonconscious sphere and "outside nature," beyond ecology and beyond use, especially use in the food chain. In doing so it stays within the system of human/nature dualism and denial that prevents the dominant culture from recognizing its ecological embeddedness and places it increasingly at ecological risk.

Human/nature dualism is a Western-based cultural formation going back thousands of years that sees the essentially human as part of a radically separate order of reason, mind, or consciousness, set apart from the lower order that comprises the body, the animal, and the prehuman. Inferior orders of humanity, such as women, slaves, and ethnic others ("barbarians"), partake of this lower sphere to a greater degree, through their supposedly lesser participation in reason and greater participation in lower "animal" elements such as embodiment and emotionality. Human/nature dualism conceives the human as not only superior to but as different in kind from the nonhuman, which as a lower sphere exists as a mere resource for the higher human one. This ideology has been functional for Western culture in enabling it to exploit nature with less constraint, but it also creates dangerous illusions in denying embeddedness in and dependency on nature, which we see in our denial of human inclusion in the food web and in our response to the ecological crisis.

Human/nature dualism is a double-sided affair, destroying the bridge between the human and the nonhuman from both ends, as it were, for just as the essentially human is disembodied, disembedded, and discontinuous from the rest of nature, so nature and animals are mindless bodies excluded from the realms of ethics and culture. Reenvisaging ourselves as ecologically embodied beings akin to rather than superior to other animals is a major challenge for Western culture, as is recognizing the elements of mind and culture present in animals and the nonhuman world. The double-sided character of human/nature dualism gives rise to two tasks that must be integrated. These are the tasks of situating human life in ecological terms and situating nonhuman life in ethical terms. Ecological animalism takes up both of these tasks, whereas ontological veganism addresses only the second.

Conventional animalist and conventional ecological theories as they have evolved in the last four decades have each challenged only one side of this double dualist dynamic, and they have each challenged different sides, with the result that they have developed in highly conflictual and incompatible ways. Although each project has a kind of egalitarianism between the human and nonhuman in mind, their partial analyses place them on a collision course. *The ecology movement has been situating humans as animals, embodied inside ecological systems of mutual use, of food and energy exchange, just as the animal defense movement has been trying to expand an extension to animals of the (dualistic) human privilege of being conceived as outside these systems.* Many animal defense activists seem to believe that ecology can be ignored and that talk of the food web is an invention of hamburger companies, while the ecological side often retains the human-centered resource view of animals and scientistic resistance to seeing animals as individuals with life stories of attachment, struggle, and tragedy not unlike our own, refusing to apply ethical thinking to the nonhuman sphere. As I will show, a more double-sided understanding of and challenge to human/nature dualism can help us move on toward a synthesis, a more integrated and less conflictual theory of animals and ecology, if not yet a unified one.

2: NONUSE OR RESPECTFUL USE?

Human/nature dualism constructs a polarized set of alternatives in which the idea that humans are above embodiment and thus any form of bodily use is complemented at the opposite extreme by the idea that nonhumans are only bodies and are totally instrumentalizable, forming a contrast based on radical exclusion. Human/animal discontinuity is constructed in part by denying overlap and continuity between humans and animals, especially in relation to food: nonhuman animals can be our food, but we can never be their food. Factory-farmed animals are conceived as reducible to food, whereas humans are beyond this and can never be food. Domination emerges in the pattern of usage in which humans are users who can never themselves be used, and which constructs commodity animals in highly reductionist terms.

Although, by definition, all ecologically embodied beings exist as food for some other beings, the human supremacist culture of the West makes a strong effort to deny human ecological embodiment by denying that we humans can be positioned in the food chain in the same way as other animals. Predators of humans have been execrated and largely eliminated. This denial that we ourselves are food for others is reflected in many aspects of our death and burial practices—the strong coffin, conventionally buried well below the level of soil fauna activity, and the slab over the grave, to prevent anything digging us up, keep the Western human body (at least sufficiently affluent ones) from becoming food for other species. Sanctity is interpreted as guarding ourselves jealously and keeping ourselves apart, refusing even to conceptualize ourselves as edible, and resisting giving something back, even to the worms and the land that nurtured us. Horror movies and stories reflect this deep-seated dread of becoming food for other forms of life: horror is the wormy corpse, vampires sucking blood, and sci-fi monsters trying to eat humans. Horror and outrage usually greet stories of other species eating live or dead humans, as various levels of hysteria greet our being nibbled by leeches, sand flies, and mosquitoes.

Upon death, the human essence is seen as departing for a disembodied, nonearthly realm, rather than nurturing those earth others who have nurtured us. This concept of human identity positions humans outside and above the food web, not as part of the feast in a chain of reciprocity but as external manipulators and masters separate from it. Death becomes a site for apartness, domination, and individual salvation, rather than for sharing and for nurturing a community of life. Being food for other animals shakes our image of human mastery. As eaters of others who can neither be eaten in turn by them nor even conceive ourselves in edible terms, we take, but do not give, justifying this one-way arrangement by the traditional Western view of human rights to use earth others as validated by an order of rational meritocracy in which humans emerge on top. Humans are not even to be conceptualized as edible, not only by other humans, but by other species.

But humans *are* food, food for sharks, lions, tigers, bears, and crocodiles, food for crows, snakes, vultures, pigs, rats, and goannas, and for a huge variety of smaller creatures and microorganisms. An ecological animalism would acknowledge this and affirm principles emphasizing human-animal mutuality, equality, and reciprocity in the food web; all living creatures are food, and also much more than food. *In a good human life we must gain our food in such a way as to acknowledge our kinship with those whom we make our food, which does not forget the more than food that every one of us is, and which position us reciprocally as food for others.* This kind of account does not need to erect a moral dualism or rigid hierarchy to decide which beings are beneath moral consideration and are thus available to be ontologized as edible, and does not need to treat nonanimal life as lesser.

Its stance of respect and gratitude provides a strong basis for opposing factory farming and for minimizing the use of sensitive beings for food.

A more egalitarian vision of ecological embodiment as involving not apartness but mutual and respectful use has been articulated by many ecological thinkers and indigenous philosophies. Thus Francis Cook, elaborating the ecological philosophy of Hua-Yen Buddhism, writes:

> I depend upon [other] things in a number of ways, one of which is to use them for my own benefit. For I could not exist for a day if I could not use them. Therefore, in a world in which I must destroy and consume in order to continue to exist, I must use what is necessary with gratitude and respect. . . . I must be prepared to accept that I am made for the use of the other no less than it is made for my use . . . that this is the tiger's world as well as mine, and I am for the use of hungry tigers as much as carrots are for my use.[3]

A corollary of accepting that one is for the use of the other is willingness to share one's region with predators of humans and to support the restoration to their original range of the many endangered species of large animals human dominance is eliminating from the face of the earth.

Ontological veganism's treatment of use and instrumentalism could hardly be a greater contrast: it extends vegetarianism, prohibiting animal use as food, to veganism, prohibiting any kind of use. For ontological vegans all the problems of animal reduction, of denial of animal communicativity, individuality, and basic needs in factory farming stem from a simple cause: ontologizing them as edible. It is a curious and paradoxical feature of ontological veganism that it basically shares the taboo on envisaging the human in edible terms, and that its strategy for greater equality is the extensionist one of attempting to extend this taboo to a wider class of beings. The paradox is that it was precisely in order to give expression to such a radical separation between humans and other animals that the taboo on conceiving humans as edible was developed in the first place.

Carol Adams, in various books and articles,[4] provides a very useful and thorough account of the commodity concept of meat as a reductionist form and of associated food concepts and practices as sites of domination.[5] However, Adams goes on to present the reductions and degradations of animals she describes so convincingly as the outcome of ontologizing them as edible.[6] But saying that seeing earth others as edible is responsible for their degraded treatment as "meat" is much like saying that ontologizing human others as sexual beings is responsible for rape or sexual abuse. Ontologizing others as sexual beings is not correctly identified as the salient condition for rape or sexual abuse; rather, it is the identification of sexuality with domination. Similarly, it is the identification of food practices with human domination and mastery that underlies the abusive use of food animals. The complete exclusion of use denies ecological embodiment and the important alternative of respectful use.

Thus, Carol Adams argues that any use of animals (for food or anything else) involves instrumentalizing them,[7] stating that "the ontologizing of animals as edible bodies creates them as instruments of human beings."[8] Instrumentalism is widely recognized (though often unclearly conceptualized) as a feature of oppressive conceptual frameworks, but instrumentalism is misdefined by Adams as involving making any use of the other, rather than reductive treatment of the other as *no more than* something of use, a means to an end.[9] This definition of instrumentalism as the same as use is not a viable way to define instrumentalism even in the human case, since there are many cases where we can make use of one another for a variety of purposes without incurring any damaging charge of instrumentalism.[10] The circus performers who stand on one another's shoulders to reach the trapeze are not involved in any oppressively instrumental practices. Neither is someone who collects animal droppings to improve a vegetable garden. In both cases the other is used, but is also seen as more than something to be used, and hence not treated instrumentally. Rather, instrumentalism has to be understood as involving a reductionist conception in which the other is subject to disrespectful or totalizing forms of use and defined as no more than a means to some set of ends.

3: DISCONTINUITY, CULTURE, AND NATURE: DEMONIZING AND EXCEPTIONALIZING PREDATION

By affirming that we ourselves are subject to use and that all uses of others must involve respect for individual and species life, an ecological animalism can affirm continuity of life-forms, including humans. An ontological veganism that occludes the possibility of respectful use and treats food as degraded, must assume that only things that are not morally considerable can be eaten. It is then tied to an exclusionary imperative, requiring a cutoff point to delineate a class beneath ethical consideration, on pain of having nothing left to eat. Such a position retains the radical discontinuity of Cartesian dualism, repositioning the boundary of ethical consideration at a different point (higher animals possessing "consciousness"), but still insisting on an outsider class of sensitive living creatures virtually reduced to machine status and conceived as "beyond ethics." It is a paradox that, although it claims to increase our sensitivity and ethical responsiveness to the extended class of almost-humans, such a position also serves to reduce our sensitivity to the vast majority of living organisms that remain in the excluded class beyond consideration.

Ontological veganism's subtle endorsement of human/nature dualism and discontinuity also emerges in its treatment of predation and its account of the nature/culture relationship. Predation is often demonized as bringing unnecessary pain and suffering to an otherwise peaceful vegan world of female gathering, and in the human case is seen as an instrumental male practice of domination directed at animals and women. But if instrumentalism is not the same as simply making use of something, predation is not necessarily an instrumental practice, especially if it finds effective ways to recognize that the other is more than "meat." Ecologically, predation is presented as an unfortunate exception and animals, like women, as always victims: fewer than 20 percent of animals, Adams tells us, are predators[11]—a claim that again draws on a strong discontinuity between plants and animals. In this way it is suggested that predation is unnatural and fundamentally eliminable. But percentage tallies of carnivorous species are no guide to the importance of predation in an ecosystem or its potential eliminability.

An ecological animalist could say that it is not predation as such that is the problem but what certain social systems make of predation. Thus I would agree that hunting is a harmful, unnecessary, and highly gendered practice within some social contexts but reject any general demonization of hunting or predation, which would raise serious problems about indigenous cultures and about flow-on from humans to animals. Any attempt to condemn predation in general, ontological terms will inevitably rub off onto predatory animals (including both carnivorous and omnivorous animals), and any attempt to separate predation completely from human identity will also serve to reinforce once again the Western tradition's hyperseparation of our nature from that of animals, and its treatment of indigenous cultures as animal-like. This is another paradox, since it is one of the aims of the vegan theory to affirm our kinship and solidarity with animals, but here its demonization of predation has the opposite effect of implying that the world would be a better place without predatory animals. Ontological vegans hope to avoid this paradox, but their attempts to do so, I shall argue, are unsuccessful and reveal clearly that their worldview rests on a dualistic account of human identity.

The main move ontological vegans make to minimize the significance of predation and block the problematic transfer of their antipredation stance from humans to animals is to argue that human predation is situated in culture while animal predation is situated in nature.[12] Human participation in predation therefore cannot be justified as participation in an integral natural process, as philosophers like Holmes Rolston[13] have justified it. Against simple naturalism, Moriarty and Woods argue that "meat eating and hunting are cultural activities, not natural activities."[14] They claim that our distinctively human evolutionary achievement—culture—has strongly separated us from nonhuman nature. We have found freedom from ecosystems . . . [and] are no longer a part of ecosystems.[15]

Because meat eating is influenced by culture, it can be considered to "involve no participation in the logic and biology of natural ecosystems."[16] For ontological vegans, human hunting and meat eating has an entirely different status from the "instinctual" predatory activity of nonhuman animals—so much so that they treat the term "predation" as inadmissible for the case of human hunting.

There are several further problems and paradoxes here. One paradox is that animal activists who have stressed our continuity with and similarity with animals in order to ground our obligation to extend ethics to them now stress their complete dissimilarity and membership of a separate order, as inhabitants of nature not culture, in order to avoid a flow-on to animals of demonizing predation. Embracing the claim that humans "don't live in nature"—in order to block the disquieting and problem-creating parallel between human hunting and animal predation—introduces a cure that is worse than the disease and that is basically incompatible with any form of ecological consciousness. The claim that humans are not a part of natural ecosystems is on a collision course with most fundamental points of ecological understanding because it denies the fundamental ecological insight that human culture is embedded in ecological systems and dependent on nature. It also denies an important insight many students of animals have rightly stressed—that culture, learning, and choice are not unique to the human and that nonhuman animals also have culture. In fact, Moriarty and Woods's solution rests on a thoroughly dualistic and hyperseparated understanding of human identity and of the terms "nature" and "culture." In order to attain the desired human-animal separation, nature must be "pure" nature, "strictly biological," and culture conceived as "pure" culture, no longer in or of nature: an activity is no longer natural if it shows any cultural influence, and culture is completely disembedded from nature, "held aloft on a cloud in the air."

Of course, ontological vegans are right to object to any simple naturalization of human hunting and meat eating. On the kind of account I have given, both the claim that meat eating is in nature rather than culture and the counterclaim that it is in culture and therefore not in nature are wrong and are the product of indefensible hyperseparated ways of conceptualizing both these categories that are characteristic of human/nature dualism. It is only if we employ these hyperseparated senses that the distinction between nature and culture can be used to block the flow-on problem that demonizing human predation also demonizes animal predation. On the sort of account I have given above, any form of human eating (and many forms of nonhuman eating) is situated in both nature and culture—in nature as a biologically necessary determin*able* and in a specific culture as a determin*ate* form subject to individual and social choice and practice. Eating food, like most other human (and many nonhuman) activities, is a thoroughly mixed activity, not one somehow throwing together bits of two separate realms, but one expressing through the logic of the determinate-determinable relationship one aspect of the "intricate texture" of the embedment of culture in nature. Both naturalizing and culturalizing conceptual schemes are inadequate to deal with the problem; both sides of this debate deny the way our lives weave together and crisscross narratives of culture and nature, and the way our food choices are shaped and constrained both by our social and by our ecological context.

4: UNIVERSALISM AND ETHNOCENTRISM

Ontological veganism assumes a universalism that is ethnocentric and fails to allow adequately for cultural diversity and for alternatives to consumer culture. Carol Adams's work, for example, follows a methodology that universalizes a U.S. consumer perspective and hopes to deal with other cultures as exceptions to the "general" rule. Universalism is supplemented by an exceptionalist methodology that dispenses excuses for those too frail to follow its absolute abstentionist prescriptions. Deviations from the norm or ideal "may occur at rare times," when justified by necessity.[17] A methodology that deals with universal human activities such as eating in terms of U.S.-centered cultural assumptions, applicable at most to the privileged 20 percent, treating the bulk of the world's people as "deviations" or exceptions, is plainly highly ethnocentric.

In addition, Adams strives to assimilate all possible animal food practices to those of commodity culture in what seems to be an effort to deny that any cultural difference involving noninstrumental forms of eating animals can exist. Thus her discussion of the cultural context of the "relational hunt" (a crude attempt to model noninstrumental, indigenous food practices) criticizes those who refuse to absolutize the vegan imperative, declaring that "there is, in general, no need to be eating animals."[18] She goes on to suggest that eating an animal after a successful hunt, like cannibalism in emergency situations, is sometimes necessary, but like cannibalism it is morally repugnant and should properly be marked by disgust. Clearly indigenous foraging cultures are among those that would fall far short of such an ideal.

Ontological veganism is based around a mythical gender anthropology that valorizes Western women's alleged "gathering" roles in contrast to demonic "male" hunting. A cultural hegemony that falsifies the lives of indigenous men and women underlies the strong opposition it assumes between "male hunting" and "female gathering," the sweeping assumption that "women" do not hunt and that female-led "gathering" societies were vegetarian or plant-based.[19] The assumption is that active, aggressive men hunt large animals in what is envisaged as a precursor of warfare, while passive, peaceful women gather or nurture plants in a precursor of agriculture. This imaginary schema reads contemporary Western meanings of gender and hunting back in a universal way into other cultures, times, and places, assuming a gendered dualism of foraging activities in which the mixed forms encountered in many indigenous societies are denied and disappeared. Thus Adams urges us to base our alternative ideals not on hunting societies but on "gatherer societies that demonstrate humans can live well without depending on animals' bodies as food."[20] But no such purely vegan "gatherer" societies have ever been recorded! Adams denies the undeniable evidence from contemporary indigenous women's foraging practices that they often include far more than collecting plants. Australian Aboriginal women's gathering contributes as much as 80 percent of tribal food, but women's "gathering" has always involved killing a large variety of small to medium animals. This is not a matter of speculation about the past, but of well-confirmed present-day observation and indigenous experience.

In assuming that alternatives to animal food are always or "generally" available, Adams universalizes a context of consumer choice and availability of alternatives to animal food that ignores the construction of the lifeways of well-adapted indigenous cultures around the ecological constraints of their country, which do not therefore represent inessential features of ethnic cultures in the way she assumes.[21] The successful human occupation of many places and ecological situations in the world has required the use of at least some of their animals for food and other purposes: the most obvious examples here are places like the high Arctic regions, where for much of the year few vegetable resources are available, but other indigenous "hunter-gatherer" cultures are similarly placed—for example Australian Aboriginal cultures, whose survival in harsh environments relies on the finely detailed knowledge and skillful exploitation of a very wide variety of seasonally available foods of all kinds, essential among which may be many highly valued animal foods gathered by women and children.

This gives rise to another paradox: the superficially sensitive ontological vegan can implicitly assume an insensitive and ecologically destructive economic context. From the perspective of the "biosphere person" who draws on the whole planet for nutritional needs defined in the context of consumer choices in the global market, it is relatively easy to be a vegan, and animal food is an unnecessary evil. But the lifestyle of the biosphere person is, in the main, destructive and ecologically unaccountable. From the perspective of the more ecologically accountable "ecosystem person" who must provide for nutritional needs from within a small, localized group of ecosystems, however, it is very difficult or impossible to be vegan: in the highly constrained choice context of the ecosystem person, some animal-based foods are indispensable to survival. Vegan approaches to food that rely implicitly upon the global marketplace are thus in conflict with ecological approaches that stress the importance of ecological accountability and of local adaptation.

A similarly ethnocentric and inadequately contextualized methodology is applied by ontological vegans to the issue of the ecological consequences of animal food.[22] The cultural hegemony and universalism openly espoused by leading vegan theorists assimilates all planetary meat-eating practices to those of North American grain feeding and its alternatives, and is insensitive to the culturally variable ecological consequences involved in the use of other animals as food. Animal defense theorists stress the ecological and health benefits of eating lower down the food chain.[23] These principles may be a useful general guide, but they are subject to many local contextual variations that are not recognized by ontological vegans. In some contexts, for instance that of the West Australian wheat belt, the ecological costs of land degradation (including costs to nonhuman animals) associated with grain production are so high that eating free-living, low-impact grazing animals like kangaroos must at least sometimes carry much lower animal and ecological costs than eating vegetarian grains. A vegan diet derived from this context could be in conflict with obligations to eat in the least harmful and ecologically costly way.

Veganism does not necessarily minimize ecological costs and can be in conflict in some contexts with ecological eating. Yet vegan universalists employ a set of simplistic arguments that are designed to show that the vegan way must always and everywhere coincide with the way that is least costly ecologically. David Waller quotes as decisive and universally applicable statistics drawn from the North American context comparing the ecological costs of meat and grain eating. This comparison is supposed to show that grain is ecologically better and to dispose of the problem of conflict between animal rights and ecological ethics. But these universalist comparisons assume that grain production for human use is always virtually free of ecological costs or costs to animal life (whereas it is in many arid land contexts highly damaging to the land and to biodiversity). They ignore the fact that in much of the world animals used for food are not grain-fed and that the rangeland over which they graze is often not suitable for crop tillage agriculture.

5: SUITABILITY FOR ACTIVISM

The appeal of ontological veganism largely depends on the false contrast it draws between veganism and commodity culture traditions of animal reduction and human/nature dualism, that is between no use at all and ruthless use based on domination and denial. But this is in effect a choice between alienation and domination. Adams's ethnocentric ontological veganism succeeds in this false contrast because its conceptual framework obscures the distinction between meat and animal food: meat is a determinate cultural construction in terms of domination, while animal food is a cultural determinable. Meat is the result of an instrumentalist-reductionist framework, but the concept of animal food allows us the means to resist the reductions and denials of meat by honoring the edible life form as much more than food, and certainly much more than meat. If we must all, including humans, be ontologized ecologically as edible, as participating in the food web as a condition of our embodiment, that does not mean we must all be ontologized reductively as meat. Food, unlike the reductive category of meat that does not recognize that we are all always more than food, is not a hyperseparated category and does not have to be a disrespectful category.

This distinction enables ecological animalism to stand with ontological veganism in affirming that no being, human or nonhuman, should be ontologized reductively as meat, and hence in opposing reductive commoditization of animals. But unlike ontological veganism, it can combine the rejection of commoditization with the framework of ecology and cultural diversity by maintaining that all embodied beings are food and more than food (i.e., with an ecological ontology). A careful contextualization of food practices provides much better guidance for activism than a culturally hegemonic universalism. Ecological animalism can provide a strong basis for opposing the "rationalized" commodity farming practices that reduce animals to living meat and are responsible for the great bulk and intensity of domestic animal misery in the modern West. It is of necessity more flexible, less dogmatic and universalist, but it can still vindicate the major activist concerns of the animal defense movement. It would require us to avoid complicity in contemporary food practices that abuse animals, especially factory farming, and can agree there are plenty of good reasons for being a vegetarian in modern urban contexts where food sources are untraceable or treatment of animals known to be cruel or reductive. But for ecological animalism, vegetarianism would not represent any disgust at "corpses" or ontological revulsion against our mutual condition as food, but rather protest at the unacceptable conditions of animal life and death in particular societies that reduce animals and commodify their flesh as "meat," in terms that minimize their claims on us and on the earth.

By insisting on highly polarized alternatives ("either one eats animals or one does not"), ontological veganism obscures useful intermediate positions other than total abstention, such as semivegetarian positions which boycott those forms of production that do not respect animal lives or species being. The spaces of ecological ontology and respectful use this polarization obscures are precisely the ones that could be occupied by an ecological worldview which sees the food chain in terms of mutuality and reciprocity rather than domination or alienation, for example, as a sacrament of sharing and exchange of life in which all species ultimately participate as food for others, and the "moreness" of all beings is recognized. Ecological animalism thus makes a better range of activist strategies, philosophies, and spiritualities available.

NOTES

1. Joy Williams, "The Inhumanity of the Animal People," *Harper's* (August 1997): 60–66.

2. See especially Val Plumwood, *Feminism and the Mastery of Nature* (London: Routledge, 1993); Plumwood, "Integrating Ethical Frameworks for Animals, Humans, and Nature: A Critical Feminist Eco-Socialist Analysis," *Ethics and the Environment* 5, no. 3 (2000): 1–38; Plumwood, *Environmental Culture: The Ecological Crisis of Reason* (London: Routledge, 2002); and Plumwood, "Being Prey," *Terra Nova* 1, no. 3 (1996): 32–44, reprinted in *The New Earth Reader*, ed. David Rothenberg and Marta Ulvaeus (Cambridge, MA: MIT Press, 1999), pp. 76–92.

3. Francis Cook, *Hua-Yen Buddhism: The Jewel Net of Indra* (College Park: Pennsylvania State University Press, 1977).

4. See especially Carol Adams, *The Sexual Politics of Mea: A Feminist-Vegetarian Critical Theory* (New York: Continuum, 1990); Adams, "The Feminist Traffic in Animals," in *Ecofeminism: Women, Animals, and Nature*, ed. Greta Gaard (Philadelphia: Temple University Press, 1993), pp. 195–218; and Adams, *Neither Man nor Beast: Feminism and the Defense of Animals* (New York: Continuum, 1994).

5. For useful contributions on reductive treatments and vocabularies, see also Mary Midgley, *Animals and Why They Matter* (Athens: University of Georgia Press, 1984); Barbara Noske, *Humans and Other Animals* (London: Pluto Press, 1989); Marti Kheel, "From Heroic to Holistic Ethics," in Gaard, *Ecofeminism: Women, Animals, and Nature*, pp. 243–71; and "License to Kill: An Ecofeminist Critique of Hunters' Discourse," in *Animals and Women*, ed. Carol J. Adams and Josephine Donovan (Durham, NC: Duke University Press, 1995), pp. 85–125; Gaard, *Ecofeminism*; Plumwood, *Feminism and the Mastery of Nature* and *Environmental Culture*; Adams and Donovan, *Animals and Women*; and Karen Warren, "The Power and Promise of Ecological Feminism," *Environmental Ethics* 12, no. 2 (1990): 121–46; and Warren, *Ecofeminist Philosophy: A Western Perspective on What It Is and Why It Matters* (Lanham MD: Rowman and Littlefield, 2000).

6. Adams, "The Feminist Traffic in Animals," p. 103.

7. Ibid., p. 200.

8. Adams, *Neither Man nor Beast*, p. 103.

9. Ibid.

10. On Kant's basically confused treatment of this problem, see my discussion in *Feminism and the Mastery of Nature*, chap. 6.

11. Adams, "The Feminist Traffic in Animals," p. 200.

12. Ibid., p. 206, and Paul Veatch Moriarty and Mark Woods, "Hunting/Predation: An Instance of the Compatibility of Animal Welfare and Environmental Ethics," *Environmental Ethics* 18, no. 4 (Winter 1997): 391–404.

13. Holmes Rolston III, *Environmental Ethics: Duties to and Values in the Natural World* (Philadelphia: Temple University Press, 1988).

14. Moriarty and Woods,"Hunting/Pedation," p. 399.

15. Ibid., p. 401.

16. Ibid.

17. Adams, *Neither Man nor Beast*, p. 103.

18. Ibid.

19. See Andrew Collard, with Joyce Contrucci, *Rape of the Wild: Man's Violence against Animals and the Earth* (Bloomington: Indiana University Press, 1989); Marti Kheel, "From Heroic to Holistic Ethics" and "License to Kill"; and Adams, *Neither Man nor Beast*, pp. 105 and 107.

20. Adams, *Neither Man nor Beast*, p. 105.

21. On the construction of Australian indigenous cultures around their ecological contexts, see Deborah Bird Rose, *Nourishing Terrain: Australian Aboriginal Views of Landscape and Wilderness* (Canberra: Australian Heritage Commission, 1996).

22. Adams, *Neither Man nor Beast*, pp. 92 ff.

23. John Robbins, *Diet for a New America* (Walpole, NH: Stillpoint, 1987), and David Waller, "A Vegetarian Critique of Deep and Social Ecology," *Ethics and the Environment* 2, no. 2 (1997): 187–98.

29 | SUBSISTENCE HUNTING
Gary L. Comstock

For many centuries indigenous people along the United States' north-west coastline hunted gray whales for food and fiber. Enveloped in reli-gious mythology and using handheld harpoons, the Makah braved choppy waters in slim boats to bring whale meat to shore. By the 1970s commercial whaling had decimated whale populations and, with all eight great whale species listed as endangered, the International Whaling Com-mission (IWC) issued a moratorium. The Makah ceased whaling.

Within three decades, however, whale numbers had recovered suffi-ciently to support a modest kill rate. In 1995, five Makah men petitioned the IWC to allow them to revive their tradition. Asking permission to use rifles to shoot five animals per year, the Makah expressly connected their request to a desire to restore an ancient tribal custom.[1] They argued it was necessary to reinstitute the hunt for their group to survive as a distinctly Makah people.[2]

Many cultures have engaged, and still engage, in subsistence hunting; suppose someone pondering subsistence whaling were to read the words of the former chair of the U.S. Marine Mammal Commission:

> Whales are different. They live in families, they play in the moonlight, they talk to one another, and they care for one another in distress. They are awesome and mysterious. They deserve to be saved.[3]

Convinced that whales should not be killed—except, perhaps, in situations where human life depends on it—the animal defender decides to try to intervene to stop the Makah. Could such intervention be justified by arguments analogous to those used to justify interventions to stop slavery, apartheid, or female circumcision? Or would any such intervention inevitably be yet another misguided case of cultural imperialism, the defender failing to respect cultural diversity while trying to force foreign values on autonomous peoples?

Our answer will turn on our views about the relative strength of the duty to defend innocent animal life compared to the duty to respect other cultures. Before we examine those two values, however, let us bring the act itself into sharper focus.

A. Definitions

There are many forms of hunting. *Trophy* hunters hunt for the sheer pleasure of the pursuit and kill, with no intent to use the carcass except perhaps to display the preserved head. Trophy hunting is not necessary for subsistence. Like trophy hunters, *sport* hunters hunt for the pleasure of the act; hunting is not necessary for them to survive. Unlike trophy hunters, however, sport hunters consume the meat. Unlike trophy and sport hunters who hunt habitually, *emergency* hunters kill animals only under the extremely rare condition that the hunters must do so to preserve their life in the short term; they do not hunt as a way of life. *Therapeutic* hunters hunt to preserve the health or integrity of an ecosystem, killing individual animals as a way, as Gary Varner writes, "to secure the aggregate welfare of the target species, the integrity of its ecosystem, or both."[4]

Subsistence hunters, unlike any of the previous hunters, must habitually kill animals for one of two reasons: either to survive or to preserve intact their traditional way of life. Subsistence hunting is the traditional practice, often imbued with religious significance, of habitually killing animals at a sustainable rate to feed one's self and family when no other adequate sources of protein are available.

B. Four Cases

Should we condone such hunting? To begin to unpack the myriad morally relevant considerations, allow me to direct attention away from the facts of the Makah case toward the imagined features of several fictional cases. I will return eventually to the Makah proposal and in conclusion make some remarks about other real-life cases.

Case 1: *The Relaxed Cannibals*

> The Relaxed Cannibals (RCs) command a vast expanse of rich, arable land. Rather than peacefully raising crops, they hunt, kill, and eat humans of a different ethnic origin residing within RC territory. The cannibals call their prey Meat Men (MM). RCs eat only a fraction of the carcasses of the MM they kill. Ruling males oppose all efforts to foreswear cannibalism in favor of farming because they think farming an effeminate way of life unbecoming of them as warriors. There is no critical discussion about the hunting.

There are at least three good reasons to justify intervention in the lives of the RCs, reasons centering on the importance of the interests of the hunted group; the relatively minor consequences to the RCs of ceasing hunting; and environmental benefits.

1. Interests of the hunted: Like the cannibals, the people being hunted have serious interests they wish to pursue, including a basic interest in continuing to live. Like the cannibals, the people being hunted should be free to pursue their interests. If the RCs were acting in self-defense, if the MM were also hunting them, the RCs might be able to justify the RC actions. But the RC reason for hunting—to continue a way of life—is an interest the satisfaction of which is not necessary for the satisfaction of other important RC interests. The interest of the MM in living is necessary for the satisfaction of other important MM interests. The interests of the hunted are more basic than, and therefore trump, the interests of the cannibals.

2. Consequences to the group: A decision about whether to intervene will also depend upon an assessment of the beneficial and harmful consequences of the act. Since the RCs have plenty of land available for productive agriculture, giving up cannibalism would not deprive them of the ability to feed themselves. At worst, ceasing hunting would take away one of the RCs' recreational activities, an activity presumably that could be replaced by other forms of entertainment. And there are benefits. Abandoning the hunting of MM will not only improve the RCs' view of MM and similar groups; it is also likely to improve the RCs' view of one another.

3. Environmental benefits: Humans constantly on the run and fearful of being killed are likely to have little regard for conservation of natural resources. Hunters who have no regard or use for the lives or carcasses of those they kill are unlikely to be concerned with the health of their ecosystems. If RCs give up hunting MM, both groups will have more energy, resources, and time to devote to conserving a diverse environment.

These three considerations establish a presumption in favor of intervention. But one might raise either of two objections: that intervention will restrict RC autonomy, or that the RCs possess no reasons to change their behavior. Let us consider each in turn.

Successful intervention certainly will curtail the RCs' autonomy, especially harming those whose livelihood depends on hunting and who celebrate it in art, dance, and legend. Autonomy, the ability to make one's own choices and pursue one's own interests, is a valuable good. All other things being equal, the burden of proof is on outsiders proposing to curtail the range of a group's freedoms.

We protect freedom because it is a necessary condition for the development of other traits of human excellence, intellect, and character. Humans are not only the sorts of creatures who enjoy pleasure, contentment, and the satisfaction of a comfortable existence. We are also capable of making meaningful plans, deliberating about and settling upon a vision of the good life, and giving our existence significance by ordering our priorities and foregoing trivial satisfactions to pursue more significant ones. Moral reflection profitably begins with a presumption in favor of respecting others' capacity to set their own goals for growth and development simply because of the kind of beings we are: beings capable of forming ground projects, overall plans for how we wish to conduct our lives.[5] The first argument against intervention seeks to protect the RCs' consciously chosen way of life.

The second argument against intervention concerns motives for changing behavior. When there are no reasons internal to one's culture to change, change inevitably appears as an imposition from the outside and, as such, a serious impediment to one's moral development. Given what we have been told about the RCs, we have no reason to believe that there are resources in their traditions to explain or motivate a more peaceful way of life.

How should we weigh these two arguments against intervention? Let us begin by distinguishing several kinds of interests.

Categorical interests are overarching interests or ground projects by which we shape our lives. Categorical interests are long-term projects that give our life meaning when we devote ourselves to them: raising children well, composing string quartets uniquely, playing cello in accordance with appropriate standards of excellence, designing quilts creatively, fulfilling one's institutional duties better than expected. While categorical interests are consciously chosen, one can live to an old age without having pursued them. However, as we are beings capable of pursuing categorical interests, it is not possible to live well without having pursued some such interest or other.

Basic interests are biological interests that must be satisfied if one is to satisfy any other interest whatsoever. These include interests in having access to clean drinking water, an adequate amount of nutritional food, and an intact, efficiently operating physiological system. Unlike categorical interests, basic interests must be satisfied if we are to continue to exist.

Serious interests are goals at which we consciously aim but which are neither basic nor categorical, such as being able on a regular basis to exercise, play a musical instrument, or read recreationally. The satisfaction of serious interests is more important to our welfare than the satisfaction of *trivial* interests, which are mere wishes or whims, such as a desire to have the opportunity to buy light green rather than dark green napkins.

Now, the RCs might claim, their interest in cannibalism is a necessary part of their way of life, a part of the ground project that gives their lives meaning. Granting this claim, we have a conflict between a *categorical* interest of the RCs and a *basic* interest of the MM. When the satisfaction of one human's categorical interest (call this human #1) requires the sacrifice of another human's basic interest (call this human #2), we ought always to act to satisfy the interest of human #2. Here is the argument for this principle.

The two humans in question each have basic and categorical interests, for a total of four interests. All other things being equal, the best world is one in which all four interests are satisfied. If a situation arises in which one interest must be sacrificed, however, it is better to choose a course that will satisfy more rather than fewer interests.[6] To allow human #1 to satisfy a categorical interest that entails depriving human #2 of the ability to satisfy basic interests deprives human #2 both of the ability to satisfy basic interests *and* categorical interests, since by definition satisfying basic interests is necessary to the satisfaction of any other interest whatsoever. Should human #1 be allowed to kill human #2, only two interests are satisfiable: human #1's basic and categorical interests. On the other hand, to deny human #1 the ability to satisfy his categorical interest while allowing #2 to satisfy both basic and categorical interests produces an overall rise in utility. In this case, both humans remain alive to satisfy their basic interests, and #2 can also satisfy categorical interests, for a total of three interests being satisfied.

We have agreed to grant (although I have my doubts about the validity of) the RCs' claim that hunting MM is an essential component of their vision of the good life. Even so, we may deny the RCs of the opportunity to hunt MM without preventing them from satisfying their basic interests. One may plausibly add, given the plasticity of categorical interests, that depriving RCs of the ability to pursue a particular categorical interest need not deprive them of the ability to pursue any categorical interest. The RCs, no doubt, can imagine many ground projects not involving cannibalism.

True, intervening with the RCs restricts their liberty. But this cost does not outweigh the virtue of preserving the ability of the MM to satisfy their basic and categorical interests, since freedom is not always good, not good in itself, especially when it is used to compromise the freedoms of others. The argument that we should not intervene with the RCs because they should be free to pursue their traditional way of life is a nonstarter for anyone interested in protecting the lives of the so-called MM.

Case 2: The Hunters of the Misfortunates

Many generations pass and the RCs continue their cannibalism. Due to years of inbreeding, however, the identity of the prey changes. MMs suffer a debilitating narrowing of their gene pool; all children are now born with serious genetic abnormalities. All are able to feed themselves, associate with others, flee the RCs, reproduce, and care for their young. However, none has the mental sophistication to form plans that reach more than thirty or forty minutes into the future. Consequently, none is capable of subordinating simple current interests in favor of more complex longer-term interests. Today's relaxed cannibals hunt and kill these pitiable people, the Misfortunates, for sport, just as their ancestors once hunted MMs. In so doing, however, they are not depriving the Misfortunates of the opportunity to pursue categorical desires since the Misfortunates have no categorical desires.

Are there morally relevant differences between cases 1 and 2? An obvious difference is in the mental capacities of the hunted. Whereas the MM were the intellectual equals of the cannibals in every way, the Misfortunates do not have similar sophisticated mental capacities. Like fortunate humans, Misfortunates have basic interests. But they lack the cognitive agility and higher-order thoughts required to form categorical interests.

Misfortunates have serious interests and they include avoiding capture, finding places of safety, experiencing the companionship of others, and feeding one's offspring. They can take conscious pleasure in enjoying the warmth of the sun on a pleasant afternoon. They can experience contentment in knowing—and the reverie that potentially accompanies such knowing—that predators are satiated and not on the hunt. Misfortunates have a serious interest in being able to enjoy such experiences.

Is the killing of a Misfortunate any less a harm than the killing of an MM? It would seem so, for if death harms some individuals more than others, then death is, all else being equal, worse for an ordinary human than it is for a Misfortunate. Death for a Misfortunate, therefore, constitutes less harm for the Misfortunate than does death for an ordinary human being.

There are reasons to believe death is a variable harm if death is worse for a healthy twenty-three-year-old pregnant woman than for either a twenty-three-day-old fetus or a 103-year-old woman. One reason is that each individual is variably related to her future. The strength of the pregnant woman's psychological internal relatedness to her future self is different, because more intense and complex, than the elderly woman's relatedness to her future self.

A pregnant woman has strong ties to the person she will be in a year, or two, or twenty when, for example, her baby will be maturing into a young woman. Envisioning the role that she will play in her child's future life, the mother has powerful reasons to take an urgent interest in her own future. For these and other reasons, death during pregnancy is one of the worst tragedies imaginable. To kill a pregnant woman is to inflict grave harm upon her.

On the other hand, a very old woman has by comparison much weaker internal psychological relatedness to the person she will be in twenty years, or even in two years. Perhaps she has little interest in the person she will be even two months into the future. While the very old may well take an interest in continuing to live, this interest cannot reasonably be as long-term, complex, or intense as the interest taken by the young pregnant woman. Therefore, while death surely harms the very old, it is not as great a harm as it is to those in the prime of their lives.

Arguably, a three-week-old fetus has at most a biological tie to the person it will be in the future. It cannot have any conscious psychological ties to its future person because it is not (yet) conscious. Therefore, death is less of a harm to the fetus than to either the pregnant or elderly.

In the same way, death is less of a harm to a Misfortunate than it is to an ordinary human being. Lacking categorical interests, the strength of the Misfortunate's psychological relatedness to its future self is far weaker than that of the humans in the prime of their lives. But it is important here to remain clear about the question we are addressing. If we had to decide whether to kill an MM or a Misfortunate, we would do less harm, all other things being equal, by killing the Misfortunate because the MM is capable of pursuing ground projects whereas the Misfortunate is not.

But that is not the question on the table. We are rather concerned to discover whether the killing of a Misfortunate is justified by the categorical interest of the RCs in hunting them. I know of no good reasons to think such killing justified, and many good reasons for thinking it unjustified. The hunters of Misfortunates need not hunt them to survive, and they have alternative ways of life open to them to supply them with food. They, like their ancestors, are cruel, unjust, and unfeeling. Defenders of Misfortunates would be well justified in intervening.

Case 3: The Bonobo Hunters

> Bonobo Hunters (BHs) hunt, kill, and eat bonobos, highly intelligent apes, for reasons similar to those that motivate RCs. BHs eat only a fraction of the meat they kill; they are killing their prey at such a rate they may eventually reduce the target population below a sustainable level; and whereas there is much land available to them for agriculture, the males who rule the BHs are opposed to farming. There is no discussion among the BHs about their hunting traditions; questioning voices are ruthlessly repressed.

There are at least four good reasons to justify intervention.

1. Moral standing of animals: The defender of bonobos has good reasons to think that the harm of death to a bonobo is similar to the harm of death

to a Misfortunate. Bonobos possess complex brains and sophisticated neuro-logical systems, and they exhibit pain-avoiding and pleasure-seeking behav-iors. Such evidence strongly suggests the capacity of bonobos to take a serious interest in enjoying companionship and sex, forming familial bonds, and rearing offspring. If Misfortunates should not be killed for the kinds of reasons that the hunters of Misfortunates provide, then it is equally true that bonobos should not be killed for the kinds of reasons that the BHs provide.

2. Consequences to the group: To insist that the BHs give up hunting and develop alternative sources of food production would entail, at worst, the BHs losing this one particular activity from their tradition. The signifi-cance of this loss could be minimized by the group developing other ways of celebrating its past, passing on its legends, and entertaining itself. Arable land is available to develop other sources of protein, and abandoning the killing of bonobos would almost certainly stimulate new traditions, stories, and rituals, and, to be sure, a more peaceful way of life.

3. Consequences to the environment: The BHs are currently taking bonobos at rates that apparently cannot be sustained. Ceasing hunting bonobos will lead to a more stable ecosystem and diverse environment and promote the conservation of resources.

4. Autonomy of humans: The BHs have not arrived at their practice of subsistence hunting through a reflective democratic procedure of consid-ering their options and autonomously selecting a path. Societies should provide all citizens with an opportunity to learn about and influence policy. Minority voices should be respected, not silenced.

Not many animals have the mental sophistication of pygmy chimpanzees. To finish sharpening our concepts, therefore, consider one last fictional case.

Case 4: The Confined Clammers

> The Confined Clammers (CCs) are coastal people who gather and eat clams and other animals lacking consciousness. CCs will kill and eat only animals without brains. Indeed, traditional lore expressly forbids killing bears, seals, elk, and octopuses. The CCs regularly engage in public con-versations about their practices and have on occasion considered the pos-sibility of growing beans as an alternative source of protein. However, such a plan is not open to them since they are physically hemmed in by groups that have reacted menacingly in the past whenever the CCs have expressed a desire to purchase arable areas. CCs cannot cease clamming; they must habitually hunt the animals they hunt.

There are four good reasons to believe that an animal defender would not be justified in intervening to change the CC's way of life.

1. Moral standing of animals: We have good reasons to believe the CC's

target species are animals without serious, much less categorical, interests. Clams do not have brains that are, for all we know, necessary to support even as low a mental state as reverie or contentment. Neither do they possess neurological systems sufficiently sophisticated to bring the kind of information out of which a brain, were it present, could form concepts, beliefs, and desires—the stuff of which serious interests are made. While clams have welfare or biological interests—interests in being covered in water rich in nutrients, for example—such interests do not by themselves suffice to establish moral standing. And, like early fetuses, clams have only biological relatedness—no internal psychological relatedness—to the clams they will be in the future. While whales and bonobos apparently have the physiological hardwiring necessary to support internal psychological relatedness between their selves in the present and their selves, say, twenty minutes from now, clams lack the sort of hardwiring necessary for any mental states at all. As such, whales and bonobos, but not clams, are in the same position as Misfortunates. Death is a serious harm for whales and bonobos because they have serious interests. Death is not a serious harm for clams because they do not have serious interests.

2. Consequences for the group: To insist that the CCs quit clamming and develop alternative sources of food production would not only require the CCs to give up their way of life; it would also require that they leave the place that provides them with coherence, self-sufficiency, and the memories and wisdom of ancestors. To be required to pack up and move, to quit clamming, would entail that the CCs lose irrevocably their vision of the good life in this place. Loss of place—and loss of a sense of one's place—is a tragic, because categorical, loss.

3. Consequences for the environment: There are no reasons to think that giving up clamming will lead to a more diverse environment. The CCs take clams at a sustainable rate so it is plausible to wonder whether they do not in fact stimulate biodiversity in their coastal basins. The CCs may, as far as we know, be engaged in a form of therapeutic hunting, keeping a target population from overshooting its range.

4. Autonomy of humans: CCs have not been coerced in developing their practice of subsistence hunting, and they do not hunt this way unreflectively. They regularly follow transparent, democratic procedures to discuss their behavior, inviting all interested parties to contribute opinions. Clamming is consistent with respect for the autonomy of individuals and minorities.

C. The Makah

Finally, let us return to the Makah, who have petitioned for permission to shoot five animals per year. Those speaking for the group claim the rifle hunt is not only consistent with tribal values but required for the survival of the Makah *as* the Makah. Is this convincing?

Unlike thought experiments, real cases are messy, complex, and not designed for tidy analysis. At the risk of putting on full display my general ignorance about the facts of the Makah case, let me attempt to make some concluding remarks about the kinds of questions we would at least want to have answered before making anything like a final judgment about the Makah. For the sake of argument, I will also hazard my own tentative conclusions.

1. Moral Standing of Humans

How did the Makah arrive at their decision? Did those petitioning for permission to kill whales actively solicit widespread input, carefully weighing contrary opinions? Or did they act as lone rangers, circumventing an open process of inviting all parties to contribute their opinions? When the Makah suggest that they wish to reinstitute the hunt because their identity as a people is at stake, what are the grounds of this claim? If the Makah will literally cease to exist if whaling is not resumed, why have they not ceased to exist in the two decades when they have not been whaling? Is shooting a whale with a rifle from a motorboat consistent with the ancient practice of spearing it with a harpoon from a paddled craft? Perhaps these questions can all be satisfactorily answered in terms favorable to the Makah's petition. In that case, whaling might be a genuine categorical interest of the group.

If, on the other hand, the answers to these questions suggest that whale shooting is a serious rather than a categorical interest of the Makah, then these considerations would be less weighty in favor of allowing the hunt. If whaling is a historic, enjoyable practice that will, among other things, teach children important social lessons about the group's history and environment, then we can ask whether there are not nonlethal ways of achieving the same goals.

Lacking information about whether the petitioners genuinely speak for the entire group or whether the practice proposed is consistent with the past, let us presume positive answers to both questions and, giving the Makah the benefit of the doubt, presume they have a consensus about the desire to reinstitute whaling.

2. Moral Standing of Animals

The Makah hunt whales. Whales are more like bonobos than clams. Like all mammals, whales have the physiological equipment—brains, sensory receptors, neural transmitting and processing systems, etc.—to support arguments from analogy that they are sentient. They also engage in behaviors suggesting they are capable of having a set of serious interests analogous to those of bonobos or Misfortunates. The way seems prepared, therefore, to argue for a presumption against killing them except for reasons that would justify killing Misfortunates. The reasons offered by the Makah for killing whales would not justify the Makah in killing Misfortunates. For reasons presented above, the whales should be considered the moral equivalents of misfortunate humans. The Makah must explain why this claim is not true if they want to overcome this hurdle.

3. Consequences for the Group

To insist that the Makah give up whaling and develop alternative sources of food production would entail, at best, that the group might lose a measure of self-sufficiency and become dependent on trading with other cultures if we assume there is no arable land available to them within their own borders. At worst, abandoning whaling could lead to the group's demise, a catastrophic consequence from the group's perspective. On balance, therefore, and assuming that whale shooting counts as traditional whale hunting and that Makah have a consensus about their interest in reinstituting the practice, the group consequences would argue for allowing the Makah to resume whaling.

4. Consequences for the Environment

If the gray whale has recently been delisted from the endangered species list, then killing five whales would not seem to be an environmental cost. On the other hand, it appears that while the gray whale is not endangered, neither has it recovered the robust numbers it once had. Killing additional whales will at best retard the rate at which the stocks recover. Not killing additional whales will speed up that rate. Killing whales is not necessary to keep the species from overshooting its range, nor will killing lead to a more diverse environment or better conservation of resources. Not killing whales may eventually lead to those outcomes. On balance, the environmental arguments seem to lean against whaling resumption.

5. Motivating Reasons

During the decades when whaling was not allowed, the Makah must have developed explanations for how their identity could survive decades of nonwhaling. These explanations might not suffice to explain how their identity can survive a permanent cessation of whaling, but they at least provide a resource for dealing with a further extension of the period of nonwhaling. The consensus of Makah opinion to begin whaling, coupled with the successful ability to have withstood together an extended period of nonwhaling, would presumably be useful in assisting the culture to endure a few more years of continued frustration in its desire to resume hunting. While a nonwhaling policy decision would be an unwelcome imposition from the outside, it would not be utterly unintelligible, nor would it seem a decision impossible for the Makah to honor as a single people. Therefore, there appear to be resources within the culture that will allow the Makah to continue as the Makah without whale shooting.

Our tentative answers to the Makah case mirror our answers to the cases in which Misfortunates and bonobos are hunted, except that the consequences to the Makah group might be worse than in either of those cases, assuming the Makah are of a common mind about the importance of whaling. Even granting that assumption, however, the balance of arguments inclines toward deciding the Makah case in the way we decided the Misfortunates and bonobos cases.

Are we justified in intervening in cultures that practice subsistence hunting? It will depend on the particular facts of each case and on the nature of the specific human and animal interests in conflict. Subsistence hunting of animals without serious interests will be the easiest to justify. Subsistence hunting of animals with serious interests is most likely to be justifiable if necessary to serve basic human interests. It may be justified if necessary to serve a categorical interest that cannot be satisfied in any other way. It is unlikely to be justifiable if it serves serious human interests for which the group could substitute alternative, equally serious interests.

NOTES

1. D. J. Orth, "Marine Mammal Protection and Management: A Case Study," *Ag Bioethics Forum* 9 (November 1997): 2.

2. Cetacean Society International, "Makah Whaling Stopped, For Now," *Whales Alive!* 12 (January 2003), http://csiwhalesalive.org/csi03109.html.

3. Orth, "Marine Mammal Protection and Management," p. 2. Orth does not provide the name of the commission chair.

4. Gary Varner, *In Nature's Interests? Interests, Animal Rights, and Environmental Ethics* (New York: Oxford University Press, 1998), p. 100.

5. See Bernard Williams, *Moral Luck* (Cambridge: Cambridge University Press, 1981), pp. 12–13; Tom Regan, *The Case for Animal Rights* (Berkeley: University of California Press, 1983); Varner, *In Nature's Interests?* pp. 88–93.

6. See Varner, *In Nature's Interests?* "Perry's Principle of Inclusiveness," pp. 80–88. Varner cites Ralph Barton Perry, *General Theory of Value* (New York: Longman's, Green, and Co., 1926).

FURTHER READING

Adams, Carol J. *The Sexual Politics of Meat*. New York: Continuum, 1990.

———. *Neither Man nor Beast: Feminism and the Defense of Animals*. New York: Continuum, 1994.

———. *The Pornography of Meat*. New York: Continuum, 2003.

Arens, W. *The Man-Eating Myth: Anthropology and Anthropophagy*. New York: Oxford University Press, 1979.

Armstrong, Susan, and Richard Botzler, eds. *The Animal Ethics Reader*. New York: Routledge, 2003.

Barad, Judith. *Aquinas on the Nature and Treatment of Animals*. Lanham, MD: Rowman and Littlefield, 2001.

Bergman, Charles. *Orion's Legacy: A Cultural History of Man as Hunter*. New York: Dutton, 1997.

Berman, Louis. *Vegetarianism and the Jewish Tradition*. New York: Ktav, 1982.

Bratman, Steven. *Health Food Junkies: Overcoming the Obession with Healthful Eating*. New York: Bantam Doubleday Dell, 2000.

Bynum, Caroline Walker. *Holy Feast and Holy Fast*. Berkeley: University of California Press, 1987.

Caduto, Michael J., and Joseph Brucnac. *Keeper of the Animals*. Saskatoon, Canada: Fifth House, 1991.

Carruthers, Peter. *The Animals Issue*. Cambridge: Cambridge University Press, 1992.

Clark, Stephen R. L. *The Moral Status of Animals*. Oxford: Clarendon, 1977.

———. *Animals and Their Moral Standing*. London: Routledge, 1997.

Coetzee, J. M., et al. *The Lives of Animals*. Princeton: Princeton University Press, 1999.

Cohen, Carl, and Tom Regan. *The Animal Rights Debate.* Lanham: Rowman and Littlefield, 2001.

Collard, Andrew, with Joyce Contrucci. *Rape of the Wild: Man's Violence against Animals and the Earth.* Bloomington: Indiana University Press, 1989.

Cooper, John. *Eat and Be Satisfied: A Social History of Jewish Food.* Northvale, NJ: Jason Aronson, 1993.

DeGrazia, David. *Animal Rights: A Very Short Introduction.* New York: Oxford University Press.

Dien, Mawil Izzi. *The Environmental Dimensions of Islam.* Cambridge, England: Lutterworth, 2000.

Dombrowski, Daniel. *The Philosophy of Vegetarianism.* Amherst: University of Massachusetts Press, 1984.

Donovan, Josephine, and Carol J. Adams, eds. *Animals and Women: Theoretical Explorations.* Durham, NC: Duke University Press, 1995.

———. *Beyond Animal Rights: A Feminist Caring Ethic for the Treatment of Animals.* New York: Continuum, 1996.

Dresner, Samuel. *The Jewish Dietary Laws: Their Meaning for Our Time.* New York: Rabbinical Assembly of America, 1982.

Eisnitz, Gail. *Slaughterhouse.* Amherst, NY: Prometheus Books, 1997, pp. 17–108.

Fiddes, Nick. *Meat: A Natural Symbol.* New York: Routledge, 1991.

Fox, Michael Allen. *Deep Vegetarianism.* Philadelphia: Temple University Press, 1999.

Frey, R. G. *Interests and Rights.* Oxford: Clarendon, 1980.

———. *Rights, Killing, and Suffering: Moral Vegetarianism and Applied Ethics.* Oxford: Blackwell, 1983.

Gaard, Greta, ed. *Ecofeminism, Women, Animal, Nature.* Philadelphia: Temple University Press, 1993.

Grimm, Veronika. *From Feasting to Fasting: The Evolution of a Sin.* London: Routledge, 1996.

Gruzalski, Bart. *On Gandhi.* Belmont, CA: Wadsworth, 2002.

Harris, Marvin. *Good to Eat.* New York: Simon and Schuster, 1985.

Harris, Marvin, and Eric B. Ross, eds. *Food and Evolution.* Philadelphia: Temple University Press, 1987.

Harrison, Ruth. *Animal Machines.* London: Vincent Stuart, 1967.

Hursthouse, Rosalind. *Ethics, Humans, and Other Animals: An Introduction with Readings.* London: Routledge, 2000.

Kalechofsky, Roberta. *Vegetarian Judaism: A Guide for Everyone.* Marblehead, MA: Micah Publications, 1998.

———, ed. *Rabbis and Vegetarianism: An Evolving Tradition.* Marblehead, MA: Micah Publications, 1995.

Kapleau, Philip. *To Cherish All Life: A Buddhist Case for Becoming Vegetarian,* 2nd ed. Rochester, NY: Rochester Zen Center, 1986.

Kass, Leon. *The Hungry Soul: Eating and the Perfection of Our Nature.* Chicago: University of Chicago Press, 1999.

Lappé, Francis Moore. *Diet for a Small Planet,* 20th anniversary ed. New York: Ballantine, 1991.

Leahy, Michael. *Against Liberation.* London: Routledge, 1991.

Leghorn, Lisa, and Mary Roodkowsky. *Who Really Starves: Women and World Hunger.* New York: Friendship Press, 1977.

Linzey, Andrew. *Animal Rights: A Christian Assessment of Man's Treatment of Animals.* London: SCM Press, 1976.

———. *Christianity and the Rights of Animals.* New York: Crossroads, 1989.

———. *Animal Theology.* Champaign: University of Illinois Press, 1995.

Linzey, Andrew, and Tom Regan, eds. *Animals and Christianity: A Book of Readings.* New York: Crossroads, 1988.

Lovenheim, Peter. *Portrait of a Burger as a Young Calf: The Story of One Man, Two Cows, and the Feeding of a Nation.* New York: Harmony Books, 2002.

Machan, Tibor. *Putting Humans First: Why We Are Nature's Favorite.* Lanham, MD: Rowman and Littlefield, 2004.

Marks, Jonathan. *What It Means to Be 98% Chimpanzee: Apes, People, and their Genes.* Berkeley: University of California Press, 2002.

Mason, Jim, and Peter Singer. *Animal Factories.* New York: Crown, 1980.

Masri, B. A. *Islamic Concern for Animals.* Petersfield, England: Athene Trust, 1987.

———. *Animals in Islam.* Petersfield, England: Athene Trust, 1989.

Masson, Jeffrey. *The Pig Who Sang to the Moon: The Emotional World of Farm Animals.* New York: Ballantine, 2003.

Maurer, Donna. *Vegetarianism: Movement or Moment?* Philadelphia: Temple University Press, 2002.

McGowan, Andrew. *Ascetic Eucharist.* Oxford: Oxford University Press, 1998.

Midgley, Mary. *Animals and Why They Matter.* Athens: University of Georgia Press, 1984.

Miller, Harlan B., and William H. Williams, eds. *Ethics and Animals.* Clifton, NJ: Humana Press, 1983.

Noske, Barbara. *Humans and Other Animals.* London: Pluto Press, 1989.

Pence, Gregory, ed. *The Ethics of Food: A Reader for the Twenty-first Century.* Lanham, MD: Rowman and Littlefield, 2000.

Pluhar, Evelyn. *Beyond Prejudice: The Moral Significance of Human and Nonhuman Animals.* Durham, NC: Duke University Press, 1995.

Plumwood, Val. *Environmental Culture: The Ecological Crisis of Reason.* London: Routledge, 2002.

Rachels, James. *Created from Animals: The Moral Implications of Darwinism.* Oxford: Oxford University Press, 1990.

Regan, Tom. *All That Dwell Therein: Essays on Animal Rights and Environmental Ethics.* Berkeley: University of California Press, 1982.

———. *The Case for Animal Rights.* Berkeley: University of California Press, 1983.

———. ed. *Animal Sacrifices.* Philadelphia: Temple University Press, 1986.

———. *Animal Rights and Human Wrongs: An Introduction to Moral Philosophy.* Lanham, MD: Rowman and Littlefield, 2003.

———. *Empty Cages: Facing the Challenge of Animal Rights.* Lanham, MD: Rowman and Littlefield, 2004.

Regan, Tom, and Peter Singer, eds. *Animal Rights and Human Obligations,* 2nd ed. Englewood Cliffs, NJ: Prentice-Hall, 1989.

Reichmann, James. *Evolution, Animal "Rights," and the Environment.* Washington, DC: Catholic University of America Press, 2000.

Robbins, John. *Diet for a New America.* Walpole, NH: Stillpoint, 1987.

———. *Diet for a New World.* New York: Avon Books, 1993.

———. *The Food Revolution: How Your Diet Can Help Save Your Life and the World.* Berkeley, CA: Conari Press, 2001.

Rollin, Bernard. *The Unheeded Cry: Animal Consciousness, Animal Pain, and Science.* Oxford: Oxford University Press, 1989.

Rolston, Holmes, III. *Environmental Ethics: Duties to and Values in the Natural World.* Philadelphia: Temple University Press, 1988.

Root, Waverley, and Richard de Rochemont. *Eating in America: A History.* New York: William Morrow, 1976.

Rosen, Steven. *Food for the Spirit.* New York: Bala Books, 1987.

Rowlands, Mark. *Animals Like Us.* London: Verso, 2002.

Sabaté, Joan. *Vegetarian Nutrition.* New York: CRC Press, 2001.

Sapontzis, Steve. *Morals, Reason, and Animals.* Philadelphia: Temple University Press, 1987.

Schimmel, Annemarie. *Mystical Dimensions of Islam.* Chapel Hill: University of North Carolina Press, 1975.

Scruton, Roger. *Animal Rights and Wrongs,* 3rd ed. London: Metro Books and Demos, 2000.

Scully, Matthew. *Dominion: The Power of Man, the Suffering of Animals, and the Call to Mercy.* New York: St. Martin's, 2002.

Shaw, Teresa. *The Burden of the Flesh: Fasting and Sexuality in Early Christianity.* Minneapolis, MN: Fortress Press, 1998.

Singer, Peter. *Practical Ethics.* Cambridge: Cambridge University Press, 1979.

———. *Animal Liberation,* 3rd ed. New York: Ecco, 2001.

Singer, Peter, and Paola Cavalieri. *The Great Ape Project: Equality and Beyond.* London: Fourth Estate, 1993.

Smith, Margaret. *The Way of the Mystics.* New York: Oxford University Press, 1978.

Sorabji, Richard. *Animal Minds and Human Morals.* Ithaca, NY: Cornell University Press, 1993.

Taylor, Angus. *Animals and Ethics: An Overview of the Philosophical Debate.* Peterborough, ON: Broadview Press, 2003.

Taylor, Paul. *Respect for Nature.* Princeton: Princeton University Press, 1986.

Townend, Christine. *Pulling the Wool: A New Look at the Australian Wool Industry.* London: Hale and Iremonger, 1985.

Varner, Gary. *In Nature's Interests? Interests, Animals Rights, and Environmental Ethics.* New York: Oxford University Press, 1998.

Walters, Kerry S., and Lisa Portmess, eds. *Ethical Vegetarianism from Pythagoras to Peter Singer.* Albany: State University of New York Press, 1999.

———. *Religious Vegetarianism.* Albany: State University of New York Press, 2001.

Wynne-Tyson, Jon. *Food for a Future.* London: Davis-Poynter Ltd., 1975.

The editor wishes to thank Nathan Nobis for his help in compiling this list.

LIST OF CONTRIBUTORS

Carol J. Adams is the author of *The Sexual Politics of Meat: A Feminist-Vegetarian Critical Theory*; *Living Among Meat Eaters: The Vegetarian's Survival Handbook*; *The Pornography of Meat*; *Neither Man nor Beast: Feminism and the Defense of Animals*; and a series on *The Inner Art of Vegetarianism*. She is also the author of a guide for parents of vegetarians and vegans, *Help! My Child Has Stopped Eating Meat! An A–Z Guide to Surviving a Conflict in Diets*, the editor of several anthologies on animals and feminism, ecofeminism, and violence against women. She also arranged for the nineteenth-century classic of vegetarian history, *The Ethics of Diet: A Catena of Authorities Deprecatory of Meat-Eating* to be republished. Web site: www.caroljadams.com.

Neal Barnard, M.D., is a nutrition researcher, an author, and the founder of the Physicians Committee for Responsible Medicine (PCRM), a nationwide organization of physicians and laypersons that promotes preventive medicine, especially good nutrition, and addresses controversies in modern medicine, including ethical issues in research. Web site: www.pcrm.org.

John Berkman teaches moral theology at The Catholic University of America, where he is the academic area director for moral theology/ethics. His articles on questions related to vegetarianism include "Is the Consistent Ethic of Life Consistent without a Concern for Animals?" in Andrew Linzey and Dorothy Yamamoto, eds., *Animals on the Agenda* (1998); "Prophetically Pro-Life: John Paul II's Gospel of Life and Evangelical Concern for Animals,"

Josephinum Journal of Theology 6, no. 1 (Winter/Spring 1999); and "A Trinitarian Theology of the 'Chief End' of 'All Flesh'" (with Stanley Hauerwas) in Charles Pinches and Jay B. McDaniel, eds., *Good News for Animals?* (1993).

Stephen R. L. Clark is Professor of Philosophy at the University of Liverpool. His books include *The Moral Status of Animals* (1977); *The Nature of the Beast* (1982); *From Athens to Jerusalem* (1984); *Civil Peace and Sacred Order* (1989); *How to Think about the Earth: Models of Environmental Theology* (1993); *Animals and Their Moral Standing* (1997); and *Biology and Christian Ethics* (2000). He has been a vegetarian for thirty years. A full CV and publications are available at http://www.liv.ac.uk/~srlclark/srlc.html. E-mail: srlclark@liv.ac.uk.

Carl Cohen has been a member of the philosophy faculty at the University of Michigan since 1955, where he has served as chairman of the faculty senate, and was one of the founding members of that university's Residential College. His books and essays have been mainly in the sphere of political and moral philosophy and logic. Defending the use of animals in biomedical research, he published a point/counterpoint volume (with Tom Regan): *The Animal Rights Debate* (Rowman and Littlefield, 2001). A point/counterpoint volume with James Sterba, *Affirmative Action and Racial Preference*, was published in 2003 by Oxford University Press. He serves as a labor arbitrator for the American Arbitration Association and served for years as a member of the National Board of the American Civil Liberties Union. E-mail: ccohen@umich.edu.

Randall Collura is a molecular biologist who is currently a Ph.D. candidate in the anthropology department at Harvard University. He is a lifelong vegetarian who has raised two vegan children and has been involved in the vegetarian movement for more than twenty-five years.

Gary L. Comstock is Professor of Philosophy and director of the Ethics Program at North Carolina State University. Perhaps best known as the founder of the Bioethics Institutes, a faculty development workshop that has helped hundreds of life scientists from around the world integrate discussions of ethics into their courses, Comstock has published more than fifty articles and book chapters in ethics. He wrote *Vexing Nature? On the Ethical Case against Agricultural Biotechnology* (Boston: Kluwer, 2000) in which he explains how, after writing essays against genetic engineering, he changed his mind to become a "cautious proponent" of genetically modified foods. Comstock has edited three books: *Life Science Ethics* (Iowa State Press, 2002); *Religious Autobiographies* (Wadsworth, 1995); and *Is There a Moral Obligation to Save the Family Farm?* (ISU Press, 1987). A member of the Center of Theological Inquiry at Princeton, Comstock served as president of the Society for Agriculture and Human Values. He is a popular speaker who has lectured internationally across Europe and Canada, and in Belize, New Zealand, Israel, and South Korea. His work has been translated into Spanish, Russian, Portuguese, and Bulgarian. In 1998 he won his college's Award for Excellence in Outreach. E-mail: gcomstock@ncsu.edu.

Deane Curtin is Professor of Philosophy at Gustavus Adolphus College. He is the author of *Chinnagounder's Challenge: The Question of Ecological Citizenship* (Indiana University Press, 1999) and *Greystoke's Legacy: People and Place in a World of Bare Necessity* (forthcoming, Rowman and Littlefield). His major interest is in the ethical dimensions of cross-cultural conflicts over the relationships of people and place, especially conflicts caused by globalization. Currently, he is writing on the debates over ethics and population growth since Malthus.

Daniel Dombrowski is Professor of Philosophy at Seattle University. He is the author of thirteen books and over a hundred articles in scholarly journals in philosophy, theology, classics, and literature. His main areas of intellectual interest are history of philosophy, philosophy of religion (from a neoclassical or process perspective), and ethics.

Johanna T. Dwyer, D.Sc., R.D., is the director of the Frances Stern Nutrition Center at New England Medical Center, Professor of Medicine (Nutrition) and Community Health at the Tufts University Medical School, and Professor of Nutrition at Tufts University School of Nutrition. She is also Senior Scientist at the Jean Mayer/USDA Human Nutrition Research Center on Aging at Tufts University. She is the author or coauthor of more than 150 research articles and 280 review articles published in scientific journals on topics including preventing diet-related disease in children and adolescents; maximizing quality of life and health in the elderly; and vegetarian and other alternative lifestyles. She recently finished an appointment in Washington, DC, as the Assistant Administrator for Human Nutrition, Agricultural Research Service, U.S. Department of Agriculture. She currently serves as senior scientist, Office of Dietary Supplements, National Institutes of Health. She is the past President of the American Institute of Nutrition, past Secretary of the American Society for Clinical Nutrition, and past President and current Fellow of the Society for Nutrition Education. She served on the Program Development Board of the American Public Health Association from 1989 to 1992 and is a member of the Food and Nutrition Board of the National Academy of Sciences, the Technical Advisory Committee of the Nutrition Screening Initiative, the Board of Advisors for the American Institute of Wine and Food, and the Executive Committee for

Nutrition, Harvard Medical School. She is a Fellow of the American Society of Nutritional Sciences and a member of the Institute of Medicine, National Academy of Sciences. She has published approximately four hundred articles in the peer-reviewed literature.

Jennifer Everett is Assistant Professor of Philosophy at the University of Alaska Anchorage. She teaches courses in ethics, environmental ethics, and feminist philosophy. Her research focuses on animal welfare ethics, environmental justice, and the ethics of consumption.

Frederick Ferré is Professor Emeritus of Philosophy at the University of Georgia, where he also founded the Environmental Ethics Certificate Program and the interdisciplinary graduate Faculty of Environmental Ethics. His principal early books include *Language, Logic and God* (Harper, 1961); *Basic Modern Philosophy of Religion* (Scribner, 1967); *Shaping the Future* (Harper, 1976); *Philosophy of Technology* (Prentice Hall, 1988); and *Hellfire and Lightning Rods* (Orbis, 1993). More recently, his career-crowning trilogy is *Being and Value* (SUNY Press, 1996), *Knowing and Value* (SUNY Press, 1998), and *Living and Value* (SUNY Press, 2001). He is past president of the American Theological Society, the Society for Philosophy of Religion, and the Metaphysical Society of America. E-mail: fpferre@bellsouth.net.

Richard C. Foltz is Associate Professor of Religion, History, Natural Resources, and Asian Studies at the University of Florida. He is editor of *Islam and Ecology* (Harvard, 2003) and *Worldviews, Religion, and the Environment* (Wadsworth, 2002), and author of several books on the history of Central Asia.

R. G. Frey is Professor of Philosophy at Bowling Green State University and a Senior Research Fellow of the Social Philosophy and Policy Center there. He was educated at the College of William and Mary, the University of Virginia, and Oxford University, from which he received his D. Phil. degree. He has written numerous articles and books in moral and political philosophy, eighteenth-century British moral philosophy, and applied ethics, including animal ethics. His most recent books are a jointly authored work with Gerald Dworkin and Sissela Bok entitled *Euthanasia and Physician-Assisted Suicide*, published by Cambridge University Press (1998) and, with Christopher Wellman, *The Companion to Applied Ethics*, published by Basil Blackwell (2003). E-mail: rfrey@bgnet.bgsu.edu.

James Gaffney was born in New York City, received his doctorate from the Gregorian University in Rome, and master's degrees from Fordham (psychology), and Texas Southern (African studies). Currently Professor Emeritus of Ethics at Loyola University in New Orleans, he has held visiting professorships in Europe, Africa, and Latin America, as well as at several U.S. universities. He is the author of *Moral Questions* (1973); *Focus on Doctrine* (1974); *Newness of Life* (1978); *Sin Reconsidered* (1983); *Biblical Notes on the Lectionary* (1978); *Matters of Faith and Morals* (1987); *Augustine Baker's Inner Light* (1989); editor of *Essays on Morality and Ethics, Conscience, Consensus and Development* (1992); *J. H. Newman's Roman Catholic Writings on Development* (1997), a contributor of chapters in several collective volumes, and the author of articles in many journals. His current research is on the historical development of the concept of just war as reflected in international law. A frequent participant in environmental and wildlife protection programs, he recently returned from a clean-water restoration project in Nicaragua.

Kathryn Paxton George is Professor of Philosophy at the University of Idaho in Moscow. She received her interdisciplinary PhD in genetics and philosophy from Washington State University in 1985. She has lectured widely, published many articles, and taught a variety of courses on ethics in science and technology. In addition to her appointment in philosophy, she is a member of the faculty of environmental sciences and the faculty of women's studies. She currently teaches ethics and reasoning in scientific research, bioethics, philosophy of science, and philosophy of biology. She is the author of *Animal, Vegetable, or Woman? A Feminist Critique of Ethical Vegetarianism* (Ithaca, NY: State University of New York Press, 2000).

Lori Gruen teaches philosophy at Wesleyan University, in Connecticut, where she currently lives with two canine companions and a very old cat (none of whom are vegetarians). Wesleyan just became the first U.S. campus to ban battery eggs. She is coauthor, with Peter Singer, of *Animal Liberation: A Graphic Guide*, has published on numerous topics in practical ethics, is engaged in activism and scholarship on human relations with nonhumans, environmental justice, feminism, and is currently working on a manuscript that attempts to develop a nonalienating ethical theory. E-mail: lgruen@wesleyan.edu.

Bart Gruzalski left a tenured associate professorship at Northeastern University in Boston to help found the Pacific Center for Sustainable Living in Redway, California. His two recent books are *On the Buddha* (2000) and *On Gandhi* (2001). Since September 11, 2001, he has been lecturing at universities around the country on nonviolence. His e-mail address is: pcslgruz@humboldt.net.

Ned Hettinger teaches at the College of Charleston in South Carolina where he is Professor of Philosophy and Coordinator of the Minor in Environmental Studies. He has written on a variety of topics in animal and environmental ethics, including articles on animal experimentation, exotic species, biotechnology and the ownership of life, law-breaking for environmental goals, the value of wildness, eco-spirituality, and the idea of owning nature. Web site: http://www.cofc.edu/~philo/dept.htg/hettinger.htm.

Roberta Kalechofsky is the author of seven works of fiction, a monograph on George Orwell, poetry, and two collections of essays. Several of her stories, and two novellas, *La Hoya* and *Stephen's Passion*, have been translated into Italian and published in Italy. She was the recipient of Literary Fellowships from the National Endowment for the Arts and the Massachusetts Council on the Arts. She began Micah Publications in 1975 and has received publishing grants from the National Endowment for the Arts and the Massachusetts Council on the Arts, in addition to her literary fellowships. She began the organization Jews for Animal Rights in 1985, and she coordinates publishing projects with this organization. She graduated from Brooklyn College and received a doctorate in English literature in 1970 from New York University. A critical essay on her work can be found in the *Dictionary of Literary Biographies*, Volume 28: *Jewish Fiction Writers*. A list of her published work and/or extended resumé is available upon request. E-mail: micah@micahbooks.com; Web site: www.micahbooks.com.

Marti Kheel is a writer and activist in the movements for animal liberation, ecofeminism, and vegetarianism. Her articles have been translated into several languages and have appeared in numerous journals and anthologies, including *Healing the Wounds: The Promise of Ecofeminism; Reweaving the World: The Emergence of Ecofeminism; Ecofeminism: Women, Animals and Nature; Animals and Women: Feminist Theoretical Explorations*, and *Environmental Ethics*. She cofounded Feminists for Animal Rights in 1982 and holds a doctorate from the Graduate Theological Union.

Kristine Kieswer is staff writer with Physicians' Committee for Responsible Medicine and editor of *Good Medicine* magazine, a quarterly publication for the organization's members. E-mail: kkieswer@pcrm.org.

Andrew Linzey is an Anglican priest, a writer, a theologian, and is internationally known as an authority on Christianity and animals. He is a member of the Faculty of Theology in the University of Oxford, and he holds the world's first post in theology and animal welfare—the Bede Jarrett Senior Research Fellowship at Blackfriars Hall, University of Oxford. He is also Honorary Professor of Theology at the University of Birmingham, England, and Special Professor at St. Xavier University, Chicago. He has written or edited twenty books including pioneering works on animals:

Animal Theology (London: SCM Press, and Chicago: University of Illinois Press, 1994); *Animals on the Agenda* (edited with Dorothy Yamamoto) (London: SCM Press, and Chicago: University of Illinois Press, 1998); *Animal Gospel: Christian Faith as if Animals Mattered* (London: Hodder and Stoughton, and Louisville, Kentucky: Westminster/John Knox Press, 1999); and *Animal Rites: Liturgies of Animal Care* (London: SCM Press, and Cleveland, Ohio: The Pilgrim Press, 1999). In 2001, he was awarded a Doctor of Divinity by the Archbishop of Canterbury in recognition of his "unique and massive pioneering work" on the "rights and welfare of God's sentient creatures." E-mail: andrewlinzey@aol.com.

Franklin M. Loew passed away in April 2003. He served as dean of the School of Veterinary Medicine at Tufts University and was an outstanding scholar and accomplished educator.

Evelyn B. Pluhar is Professor of Philosophy at Pennsylvania State University, Fayette Campus, where she has been the winner of three teaching awards and three scholarship awards. Professor Pluhar has authored numerous articles and one book on moral theory and the treatment of nonhuman animals. She lives happily with four feline companions in Uniontown, Pennsylvania. Her family will soon be augmented by a husband, stepson, and step-puppy. For further information, see www.personal.psu.edu/exp5.

Val Plumwood is a longtime forest activist, forest dweller, and forest traveler. She is a pioneer of environmental theory and philosophy who, in numerous papers from 1975 onward, helped develop the critique of anthropocentrism and instrumentalism. Plumwood has published more than one hundred papers and four books in environmental theory, including the ecofeminist classic *Feminism and the Mastery of Nature* (1993), and has lectured in the United States, Germany, Finland, Spain, Canada, Indonesia, and the United Kingdom. In 1985 she survived a crocodile attack in Kakadu National Park in northern Australia. Her latest book is *Environmental Culture: The Ecological Crisis of Reason* (Routledge, 2002), and coming soon, *The Eye of the Crocodile: Nature in the Active Voice*. She is currently Australian Research Council Fellow at the Australian National University.

Rod Preece is Professor of Political Philosophy in the Department of Political Science at Wilfrid Laurier University in Waterloo, Ontario. Among his thirteen authored and edited books are *Animals and Nature: Cultural Myths, Cultural Realities* (1999), which received a Choice Outstanding Academic Book Award and was short-listed for the Raymond Klibansky Prize, and *Awe for the Tiger, Love for the Lamb: A Chronicle of Sensibility to Animals* (2002.)

James Rachels taught philosophy at the University of Alabama at Birmingham for twenty-five years. His writings include *Created from Animals: The Moral Implications of Darwinism* (1991), *Can Ethics Provide Answers?* (1997), and *The Elements of Moral Philosophy* (4th edition, 2002). Professor Rachels passed away in September 2003.

Tom Regan is Emeritus Professor of Philosophy at North Carolina State University. Among his many books are *The Case for Animal Rights* and, most recently, two companion volumes: *Animal Rights, Human Wrongs: An Introduction to Moral Philosophy* and *Empty Cages: Facing the Challenge of Animal Rights*. Further information is available at www.lib.ncsu.edu/archives/exhibits/regan/.

Steve F. Sapontzis is Professor of Philosophy Emeritus at the Hayward campus of the California State University. He is the author of *Morals, Reason, and Animals* (Temple University Press, 1987) and of many articles on animal liberation, moral relativism, and other philosophical topics. He was cofounder and co-editor of *Between the Species: A Journal of Ethics* and has long been active in the animal rights movement, particularly as cofounder and president of Hayward Friends of Animals Humane Society. E-mail: ssapontzis@earthlink.net.

Roger Scruton was until 1990 Professor of Aesthetics at Birkbeck College, London, and subsequently Professor of Philosophy and University Professor at Boston University, Massachusetts. He now lives with his wife and two small children in rural Wiltshire, where he and his wife run a small post-modern farm and public affairs consultancy. He has published more than twenty books, including works of philosophy, literature, and fiction, and his writings have been translated into most major languages. His recent books include *The West and the Rest* (Continuum, [UK] and ISI [United States], 2002); *England: An Elegy* (Chatto & Windus, 2000); *Animal Rights and Wrongs* (Demos, 1996, 1998, 3rd ed. Metro Publishing, now distributed by Claridge Press, 2000); *On Hunting* (Yellow Jersey Press, 1998). He is currently writing a study of Wagner's *Tristan und Isolde*.

Peter Singer has been actively involved with the animal movement since he became a vegetarian while a graduate student at the University of Oxford in 1971. He is now Ira W. DeCamp Professor of Bioethics at Princeton University. His books include *Animal Liberation, Practical Ethics, How Are We to Live?, Writings on an Ethical Life*, and *One World*.